MICROSOFT® EXCEL®
FUNCTIONS
AND
FORMULAS

FIFTH EDITION

MICROSOFT® EXCEL®
FUNCTIONS
AND
FORMULAS

With Excel 2019 / Office 365

FIFTH EDITION

BERND HELD
BRIAN MORIARTY
THEODOR RICHARDSON

MERCURY LEARNING AND INFORMATION
DULLES, VIRGINIA
Boston, Massachusetts
New Delhi

Publisher: David Pallai
MERCURY LEARNING AND INFORMATION
22841 Quicksilver Drive
Dulles, VA 20166
info@merclearning.com
www.merclearning.com
(800) 232-0223

B. Held, B. Moriarty, and T. Richardson. *Microsoft® Excel® Functions and Formulas, Fifth Edition.*
ISBN: 978-1-68392-373-2

Microsoft, Excel, Visual Basic, and Windows are registered trademarks of Microsoft Corporation in the U.S. and other countries.

The publisher recognizes and respects all marks used by companies, manufacturers, and developers as a means to distinguish their products. All brand names and product names mentioned in this book are trademarks or service marks of their respective companies. Any omission or misuse (of any kind) of service marks or trademarks, etc. is not an attempt to infringe on the property of others.

Library of Congress Control Number: 2019931784

192021321   This book is printed on acid-free paper in the United States of America.

Our titles are available for adoption, license, or bulk purchase by institutions, corporations, etc. *Digital versions of this title are available at www.academiccourseware.com and most digital vendors. Companion disc files are available for downloading by contacting info@ merclearning.com.* For additional information, please contact the Customer Service Dept. at (800) 232-0223 (toll free).

The sole obligation of MERCURY LEARNING AND INFORMATION to the purchaser is to replace the disc, based on defective materials or faulty workmanship, but not based on the operation or functionality of the product.

CONTENTS

Chapter 3 : Text Functions   69

ACKNOWLEDGMENTS

I appreciate the patience and understanding my wonderful wife and adorable daughter inured while I diverted time from them to express my knowledge of Excel to you.

I would also like to thank the dedicated individuals at Mercury Learning and Information who labored in producing this book for their indefatigable work and generous commitment to quality, informational books.

INTRODUCTION

Microsoft Excel is the well-known standard spreadsheet application that allows you to easily perform calculations and recalculations of data by using numerous built-in functions and formulas. Although you may be familiar with simple functions such as SUM, this is just one of the many Excel functions and formulas that can help you simplify the process of entering calculations. Because there are so many other useful and versatile functions and formulas inside Excel that most users have yet to discover, this book was written to help readers uncover and use its wide range of tools.

For each function or formula, we started with a simple task that can be solved with Excel in an efficient way. We added tips and tricks and additional features as well to provide deeper knowledge and orientation. After you have stepped through all the lessons, you will have a great toolbox to assist you with your projects and make many everyday workbook tasks much easier. The most notable changes from Excel 2016 to 2019 are more robust features rather than the formulas. In this edition, we will include some features such as Stock and Geography data types along with formulas that have been around since 2016 and are widely used such as IFERROR, COUNTIFS, CHOOSE, and COLUMN. Features explained in the last chapter include inserting icons, drawing, Smart Lookup, sharing files, flash fill, and the Quick Analysis Tool. Some functions that are not available in 2019 but are available with an Office 365 subscription are demonstrated in the last chapter.

The content of the book is as follows:

Chapter 1 describes practical tasks that can be solved by using formulas.

In Chapter 2 you learn the usage of logical functions that are often used in combination with other functions.

Chapter 3 shows how text functions are used. You will often need these functions when working with text in tables or if the text needs to be changed or adapted, especially when it is imported into Excel from other applications.

In Chapter 4 you learn about the date and time functions in Excel. Times and dates are automatically converted inside Excel to the number format, which makes it easier to perform calculations.

With Chapter 5 you delve into the secrets of working with statistics in Excel.

Chapter 6 describes the most commonly used functions for mathematics and trigonometry, along with easy-to-follow tasks. The most common function here is the SUM function, with which you may already be familiar. However, you may be surprised about the additional possibilities shown.

If you want to learn more about functions for financial mathematics, study Chapter 7. Here you will find examples of how to calculate depreciation of an asset and how long it takes to pay back a loan using different interest rates.

With Chapter 8 you get into the secrets of database functions. There are a variety of functions explained that can be used for evaluation of data, especially when using different criteria.

Chapter 9 is about lookup and reference functions inside Excel. With these functions, you can address data in various ranges and look up values in a reference.

Chapter 10 goes into the depth of conditional formatting. Even though this feature has been available since Excel 97, there are new features that allow you to express information without programming.

Chapter 11 introduces array formulas. With these you learn how to perform multiple calculations and then return either a single result or multiple results. This special feature is similar to other formulas, except you press Ctrl+Shift+Enter after entering the formula.

Chapter 12 shows special solutions with formulas, such as creating a function to color all cells containing formulas inside an Excel spreadsheet.

Chapter 13 goes even deeper into user-defined functions with examples that use Visual Basic for Applications inside Excel. This chapter will show you how to solve problems even when Excel cannot calculate an answer.

With Chapter 14 we present some examples of tasks that combine several functions shown in the previous chapters. Use these to get more experience. Read the description of the task first and try to determine the functions that are needed to get the desired result. Compare your solution to the one shown beneath the task.

Chapter 15 details a few features that will enhance how you develop, test and present the Excel products you create for efficiency.

Appendix A provides an overview of the current versions of Excel. This includes Excel 2019 for Windows, the primary version used for the images and examples in the text. The interface for Macintosh is also covered; the appearance of this version is different, but it can perform the same calculations. The Excel Web App available as part of the Microsoft OneDrive and Office 365 is also demonstrated in this appendix; it has limited functionality compared to the complete installations, but it still has a significant capacity for performing calculations.

Have fun reading the book and in the continuous usage of the functions and formulas you will discover here.

Formulas in Excel

1

Calculate production per hour

Data for some employees is recorded in a worksheet. They work a varied number of hours each day to produce clocks. By calculating the number of pieces each employee produces per hour, it can be determined who is the most productive employee.

▶ To see who is the most productive employee:

1. In a worksheet, enter your own data or the data shown in Figure 1–1.

2. Select cells D2:D7.

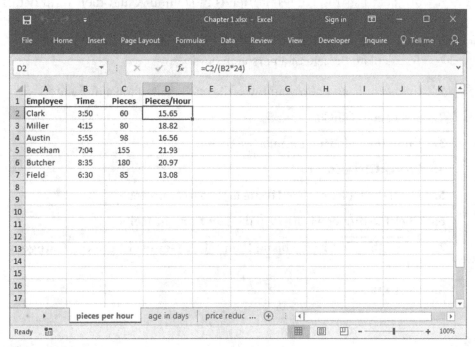

Figure 1–1

3. Enter the following formula: **=C2/(B2*24)**.

4. Press **<Ctrl+Enter>** to fill the selected cell range with the current entry:

5. From the toolbar select **Home** and go to **Number**.

6. Click the dropdown arrow and select **Format Cells**.

7. Select the **Number** tab and then select **Number** from the Category list.

8. Set **Decimal places** to **2**.

9. Click **OK**.

Beckham is the most productive. He produces an average of just below 22 clocks per hour.

Calculate the age of a person in days

A worksheet lists the names of friends in column A and their birth dates in column B. To calculate the number of days each person has been alive, enter the current date in cell B1 and perform the following steps:

▶ To calculate the age of a person in days:

1. In a worksheet, enter your own data or the data shown in Figure 1–2.

2. Select cells C5:C9.

3. Enter the following formula: **=$B$1-B5**.

4. Press **<Ctrl+Enter>**.

5. From the toolbar select **Home** and go to **Number**.

6. Click the dropdown arrow and select **Format Cells**.

7. Select the **Number** tab and then select **General** from the **Category** list.

8. Click **OK**.

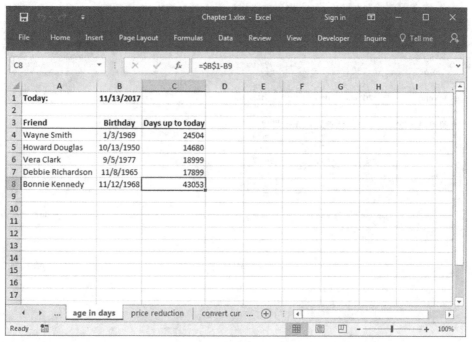

Figure 1–2

NOTE: The formula must have an absolute reference to cell B1, which is available by going to the formula bar, highlighting the cell reference, and pressing F4 until the appropriate reference appears or you can enter a "$" before the "B" and the "1." This tells excel not to change either the "B" or the "1" when copying the formula to another cell.

Calculate a price reduction

All prices in a price list need to be reduced by a certain percentage. The amount of the price reduction is 15%; this is entered in cell C1.

▶ To reduce all prices by a certain percentage:

1. In a worksheet, enter your own data or the data shown in Figure 1–3.

2. Select cell C1 and type **–15%**.

3. Select cells C4:C8.

4. Enter the following formula: **=B4+(B4*$C$1)**.

5. Press **<Ctrl+Enter>**.

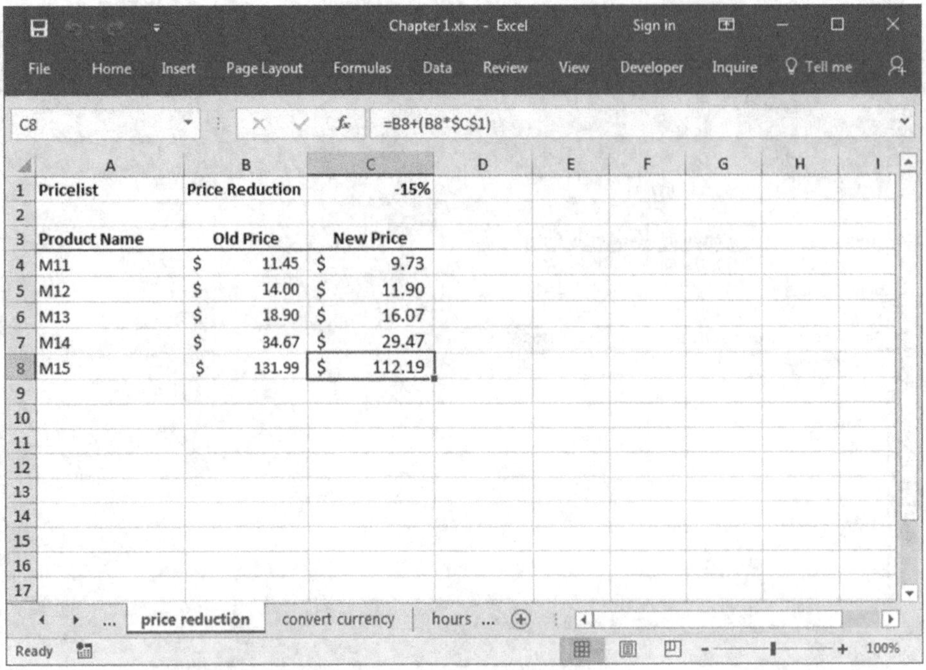

Figure 1–3

NOTE: Please note that the formula must have an absolute reference to cell C1. Also, columns B and C are formatted with the Currency style, which is available by clicking on the $ button in the Home ribbon toolbar.

Convert currency

In a worksheet, currency need to be converted from dollars (column B) to euros (column C). The rate of exchange from dollars to euros is placed in cell C1; here we use 0.747.

▶ To convert currency:

1. In a worksheet, enter your own data or the data shown in Figure 1–4.

2. Select cells C4:C8.

3. Enter the following formula: **=B4*$C$1**.

4. Press **<Ctrl+Enter>**.

5. Press **<Ctrl+1>** to show the dialog **Format Cells**.

6. Select the **Number** tab and then select **Currency** from the **Category** list.

7. Choose the required € Euro format.

8. Click **OK**.

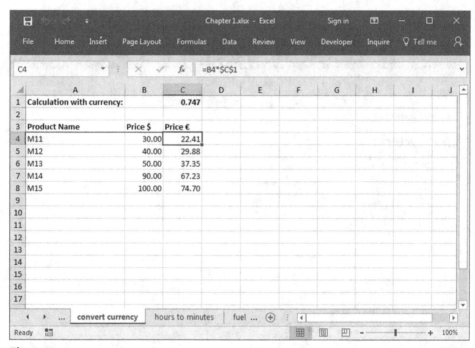

Figure 1–4

NOTE: To convert euros back to dollars, use the following formula: **=C4/$C$1**.

Convert from hours to minutes

As a task, time in a timesheet needs to be converted from hours to minutes.

▶ To convert time to minutes:

1. In a worksheet, enter your own data or the data shown in Figure 1–5.

2. Select cells B4:B8.

3. Enter the following formula: **=A4*24*60**.

4. Press **<Ctrl+Enter>**.

5. Format cells B4:B8 as general by pressing **<Ctrl+1>** and then selecting the **Number** tab and then **General** from the **Category** list.

6. Click **OK**.

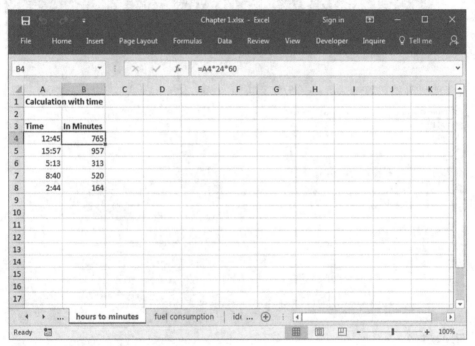

Figure 1–5

NOTE: To convert a minutes format to an hours-and-minutes format, use the formula **=B4/24/60.** Remember to format the cells with a time format, as shown in cell C4 in Figure 1–5.

Determine fuel consumption

In a worksheet, fuel consumption data is recorded. Each time you refill your gas tank, record the following data: date, miles traveled, and gallons purchased. Then reset the mileage counter. To calculate the fuel consumption of your vehicle, perform the following steps:

▶ To determine fuel consumption:

1. In a worksheet, enter your own data or the data shown in Figure 1–6.

2. Select cells D5:D10.

3. Enter the following formula: **=B5/C5**.

4. Press **<Ctrl+Enter>**.

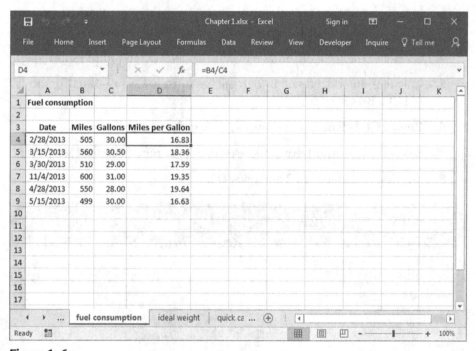

Figure 1–6

Calculate your ideal and recommended weights

Formulas for calculating ideal body weight first came into existence in 1871, when a French surgeon, Dr. P. P. Broca, created this formula (known as Broca's index):

> Weight (in kg) should equal height (in cm) – 100,
>
> plus or minus 15% for women or 10% for men

In recent years, the body mass index (BMI) has become the standard for calculating ideal weight.

▶ To determine ideal and recommended weights:

1. In a worksheet, enter your own data or the data shown in Figure 1–7.

2. Select cell B5 and type the following formula to determine your ideal weight (BMI = body mass index): **=(B3-100)*0.9**.

3. Select cell B7 and type the following formula to calculate your recommended weight: **=B4-100**.

4. Calculate the total difference in cells D6 and D7 by simple subtraction.

5. Calculate the difference in percentage in cells E6 **(=1-B4/B5)** and E7 **(=1-B4/B6)**.

6. Press **<Ctrl+Enter>** to show the dialog Format Cells.

7. Select the **Number** tab and then select **Percentage** from the Category list.

8. Set Decimal places to **2** and click **OK**.

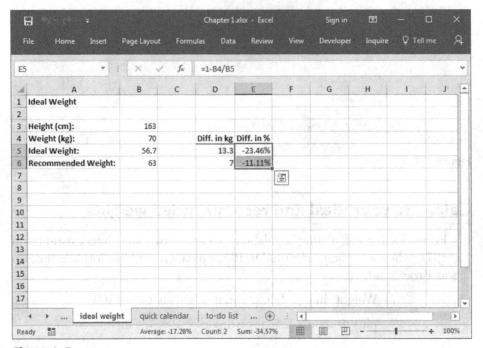

Figure 1–7

The quick calendar

To create a simple calendar, use the Fill command in combination with a formula.

▶ To create a quick calendar:

1. Select cell A1 and type the following formula: **=TODAY()**.

2. Select cell A2 and type the following formula: **=A1+1**.

3. Select cells B1:G1.

4. From the **Edit** menu, select **Fill** and **Right**.

5. In cell A2, type **=A1**.

6. Drag the bottom-right corner of cell A2 with the mouse cursor right-ward through cell F2.

7. Press **<Ctrl+1>** to show the dialog **Format Cells**.

8. Select **Custom** under Category.

9. Enter the custom format **ddd** and press **OK**.

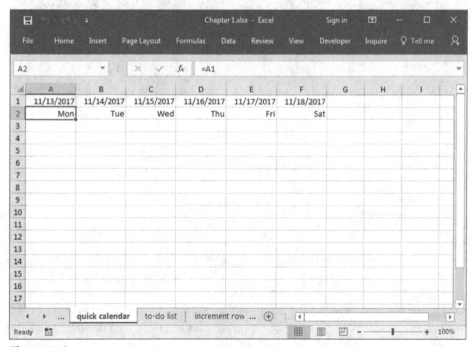

Figure 1–8

Design your own to-do list

Generate your own to-do list by entering the hours of the day in column A and making space for your daily tasks in column B.

▶ To generate your own to-do list:

1. Select cell B1 and type **=TODAY()**.

2. Select cell A3 and type **7:00 a.m**.

3. Select cell A4 and type the following formula in the Formula Bar: **=A3+(1/24)**.

4. Select cells A4:A13.

5. Go to the **Editing** group and choose the boxed downward arrow.

6. Click on **Down**.

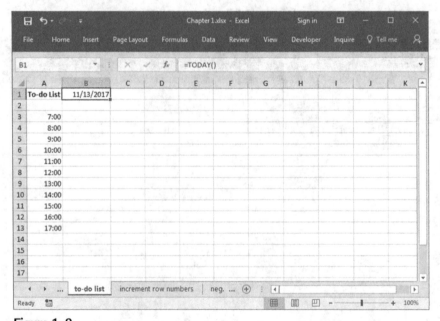

Figure 1–9

NOTE: To get increments of half an hour, use the formula **=A3+(1/48)**. To display the time in column A as shown in Figure 1–9, select **Cells** from the **Home** tab, click the **Number** group, select **Time** from the **Category** list, select **1:30 p.m.**, and click OK.

Increment row numbers

Standard row numbering in Excel is often used, but you can also create your own numbering system in a table, such as incrementing by 10 as described below.

▶ To increment row numbers by 10:

1. Select cell A2 and type **0**.

2. Select cell A3 and type the following formula: **=A2+10**.

3. Select cells A3:A12.

4. Select **Editing** from the ribbon, choose the downward button, and select **Down**.

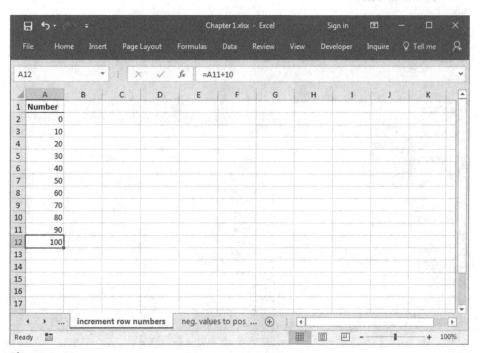

Figure 1–10

NOTE: If the value of cell A2 is changed, the values in all the other cells change, too.

Convert negative values to positive

A worksheet contains negative values. To convert all the negative values to positive values, perform the following steps.

▶ To convert negative values to positive values:

1. Enter a series of negative values in cells B1:B10.

2. Select cell C1 and type **-1**.

3. Copy this cell.

4. Select cells B1:B10.

5. In the **Home** tab, in the **Clipboard** group, click **Paste**, and then click **Paste Special**.

6. In the **Paste Special** dialog box, under **Paste**, select **Multiply**.

7. Click **OK**.

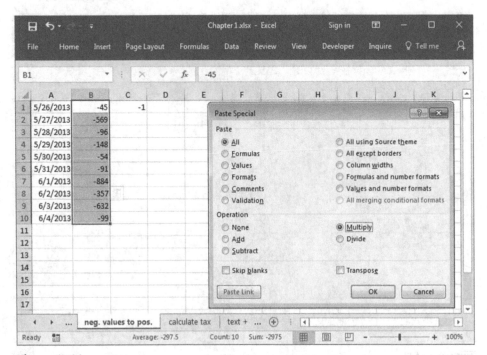

Figure 1–11

NOTE: After this, C1 can be cleared.

Calculate sales taxes

In this exercise, tax on an item needs to be calculated. We can also find the original price, given the tax rate and the final price.

▶ To calculate the price with tax:

1. Select cell A2 and type 8%.

2. Select cell B2 and type **120**.

3. Select cell C2 and type the following formula: **=B2+(B2*A2)**.

▶ To calculate the original price:

1. Select cell A4 and type **8%**.

2. Select cell C4 and type **129.60**.

3. Select cell B4 and type the following formula: **=C4/(1+A4)**.

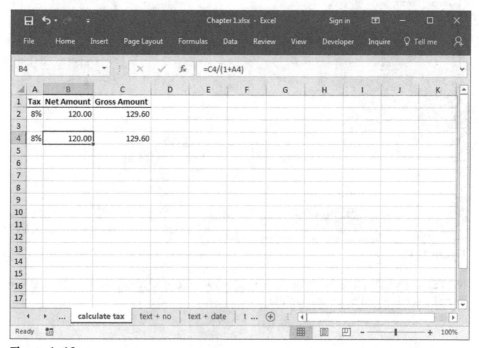

Figure 1–12

Combine text and numbers

In this example, we want to combine text and numbers. Use the & operator to accomplish this.

▶ To combine cells containing text and numbers:

1. Select cell B1 and type **computers**.

2. Select cell B2 and type **5**.

3. Select cell B4 and type the following formula in the Formula Bar: **="You ordered " & B2 & " " & B1 & " today!"**.

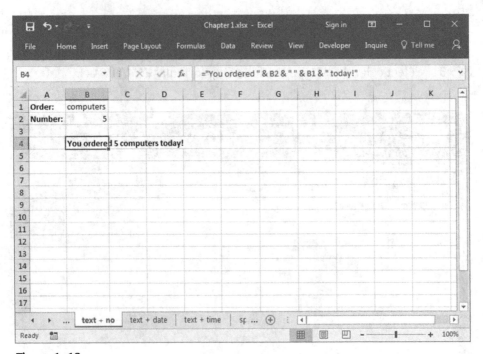

Figure 1–13

NOTE: Each cell reference must be placed between **&** operators, and additional text must be surrounded by quotation marks.

Combine text and date

Excel has a problem combining cells that contain text and dates. This results in the date's showing up as a number value, because Excel has lost the format. To get the desired result, use the following work-around.

▶ To combine text and date:

1. Select cell A1 and type **actual status**.

2. Select cell D1 and type the following formula: **=TODAY()**.

3. Select cell A3 and type the following formula:
   =A1& " " &TEXT(D1,"MM/DD/YYYY").

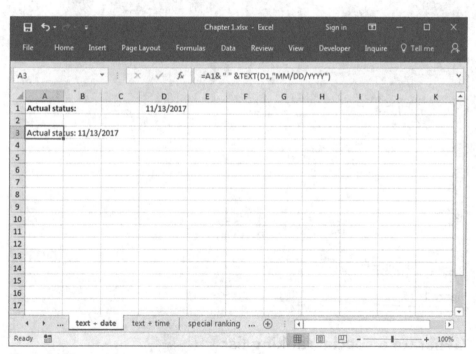

Figure 1–14

Combine text and time

This example shows how to combine text and time successfully.

▶ To combine text and time:

1. Select cell A1 and type **Shutdown**.

2. Select cell D1 and press **<Ctrl+Shift+:>** to insert the current time.

3. Select cell A3 and type the following formula:
   =" Today " & A1 & " at " & TEXT(D1,"hh:mm").

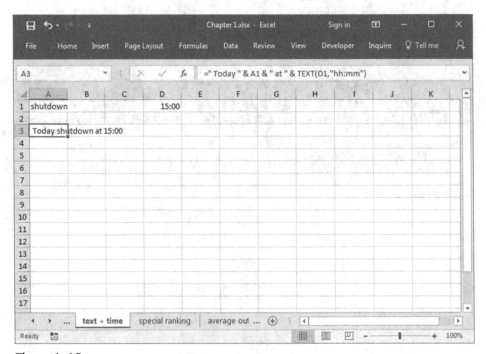

Figure 1–15

Generate a special ranking list

You can use Excel to generate a special ranking list. Let's say a worksheet contains a few values, some of which are repeated. To rank the list in a particular order, follow these instructions.

▶ To rank a list in a particular order:

1. Select cell A1 and type **Value**.

2. In cells A2:A12 enter a selection of values from 10 to 20.

3. Select cell A2.

4. In the **Home** tab, click on the **AZ** icon in the **Editing** group.

5. Select **Sort Smallest to Largest**.

6. Select cell B1 and type **Rank**.

7. Select cell B2 and type **1**.

8. Select cells B3:B12 and type the following formula: **=B2+(A2<A3)**.

9. Press **<Ctrl+Enter>**.

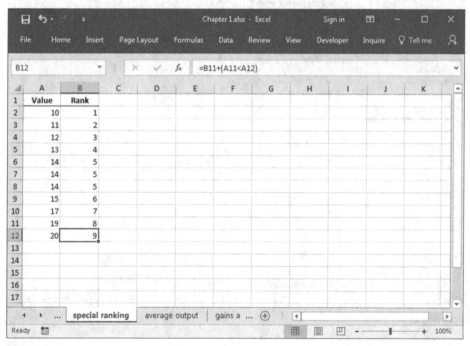

Figure 1–16

Determine average output

In a worksheet, the start and end production dates of a machine's operation are given, as well as its output during this period. How do you calculate the average daily production?

▶ To calculate the average daily production:

1. Select cell B1 and type **10/18/2004**.

2. Select cell B2 and type **11/13/2002**.

3. Type **55900** in cell B3.

4. Select cell B5 and type the following formula: **=B3/(B1-B2)**.

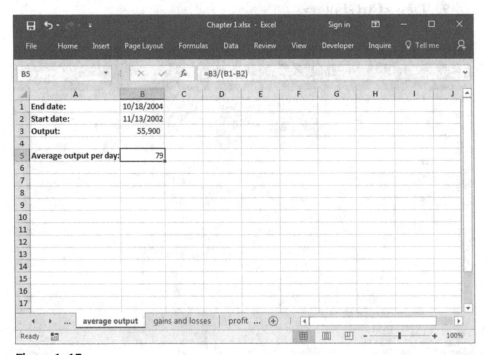

Figure 1–17

Determine stock gains and losses

Imagine your stocks have fallen 11.5% in value in one day. What is the percentage of gain that will be needed the next day to compensate for the loss?

▶ To determine the gain/loss of a stock:

1. Select cell C2 and type **1000**.

2. Select cell B3 and type **11.50%**.

3. Select cell C3 and type the following formula: **=C2-(C2*$B$3)**.

4. Select cell B4 and type the following formula: **=B3/(1-B3)**.

5. Select cell C4 and type the following formula: **=C3+(C3*$B$4)**.

6. Be sure to format column C as **Currency**.

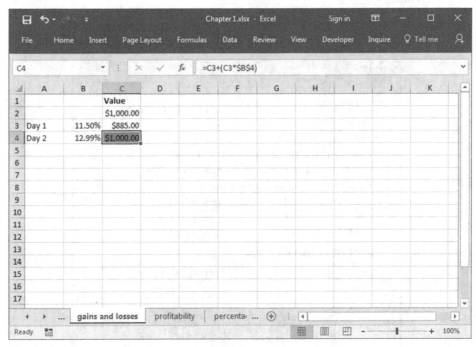

Figure 1–18

Evaluate profitability

You have some products for sale and you want to know which one is the most profitable. Use conditional formatting for this purpose.

▶   To determine the most profitable product:

1. In a new worksheet, type the cost of each product in column B and the corresponding price in column C.

2. Select cells D2:D6 and type the following formula: **=1-(B2/C2)**.

3. Press **<Ctrl+Enter>**.

4. In the **Home** tab, in the **Styles** group, click the arrow next to **Conditional Formatting**.

5. Select **New Rule** and select the options shown to highlight the top 1 value.

6. Click **Format**, select the **Fill** tab, choose a color, and click **OK**.

Figure 1–19

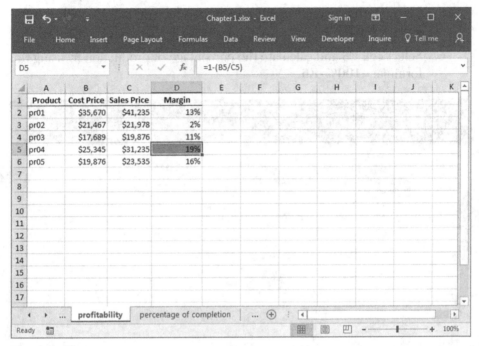

Figure 1–20

NOTE: Product pr04 has the greatest profit margin as calculated in column D. The conditional formatting highlights the cell automatically.

Determine percentage of completion

To manage a project it is necessary to determine the percentage of completion. This can be accomplished with the following calculation.

▶ To calculate percentage of completion:

1. In a worksheet, enter data in columns A, B, and D as shown in Figure 1–20.

2. Select cell E2 and type **=B2+B3**.

3. Select cell E3 and enter the target value of **200**.

4. In cell E5, type the formula **=E3-E2** to get the difference between the target and the number already produced.

5. Calculate the percentage of missing products in cell E6 with this formula: **=1-E2/E3**.

6. Select cell E8 and calculate the percentage of production by using this formula: **=100%-E6**.

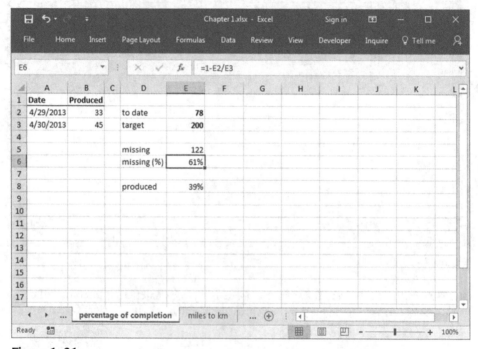

Figure 1–21

Convert miles per hour to kilometers per hour

A worksheet contains speed in miles per hour. To convert the data to kilometers per hour, use the following calculation.

▶ To convert miles per hour to kilometers per hour:

1. In a worksheet, enter the data shown or use data of your own creation in Figure 1–21.

2. Select cell D1 and enter the conversion value **0.621371**.

3. Select cells B2:B8 and type the following formula: **=A2/$D$1**.

4. Press **<Ctrl+Enter>**.

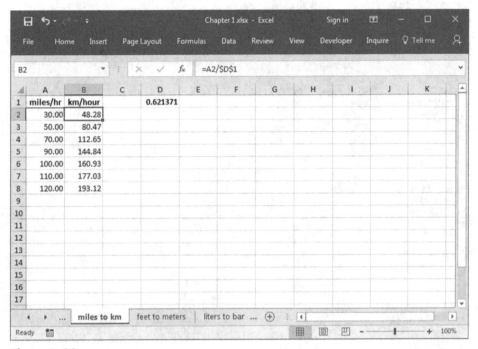

Figure 1–22

NOTE: To convert the other way around, from kilometers per hour to miles per hour, use the formula **=B2*$D$1.**

Convert feet per minute to meters per second

A worksheet contains speed data. To convert feet per minute to meters per second, use the calculation described as follows.

▶ To convert feet per minute to meters per second:

1. In a worksheet, enter the data shown in Figure 1–22, or use your own data.

2. Select cell D1 and enter the conversion value **196.858144.**

3. Select cells B2:B10 and type the following formula: **=A2/$D$1.**

4. Press **<Ctrl+Enter>.**

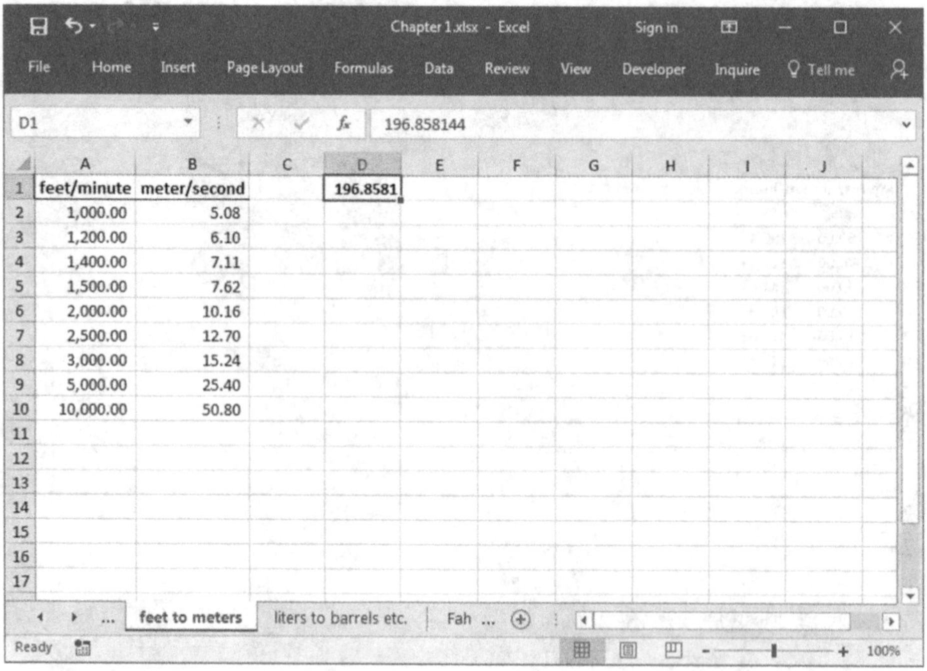

Figure 1–23

NOTE: To convert the other way around, from meters per second to feet per minute, use the formula =B2*$D$1.

Convert liters to barrels, gallons, quarts, and pints

In a worksheet, data is input as liters. To convert the value to different scales, use the following formulas.

▶ To convert liters to barrels, gallons, quarts, and pints:

1. Select cell B1 and enter **150**.

2. Select cell B3 and type the formula **=$B$1/158.98722** to convert to barrels.

3. Select cell B4 and type the formula **=$B$1/3.78541** to convert to gallons.

4. Select cell B5 and type the formula **=$B$1/1.101241** to convert to quarts.

5. Select cell B6 and type the formula **=$B$1/0.5506** to convert to pints.

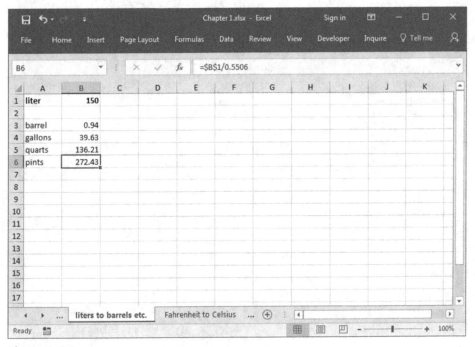

Figure 1–24

Convert from Fahrenheit to Celsius

To convert temperatures from Fahrenheit to Celsius, you can use the formula =**(Fahrenheit–32)*5/9**, or you can use the calculation described here.

▶ To convert from Fahrenheit to Celsius:

1. In a worksheet, enter some temperatures in Fahrenheit in column A.

2. Select cells B2:B13 and type the following formula: =**(A2-32)*(5/9)**.

3. Press **<Ctrl+Enter>**.

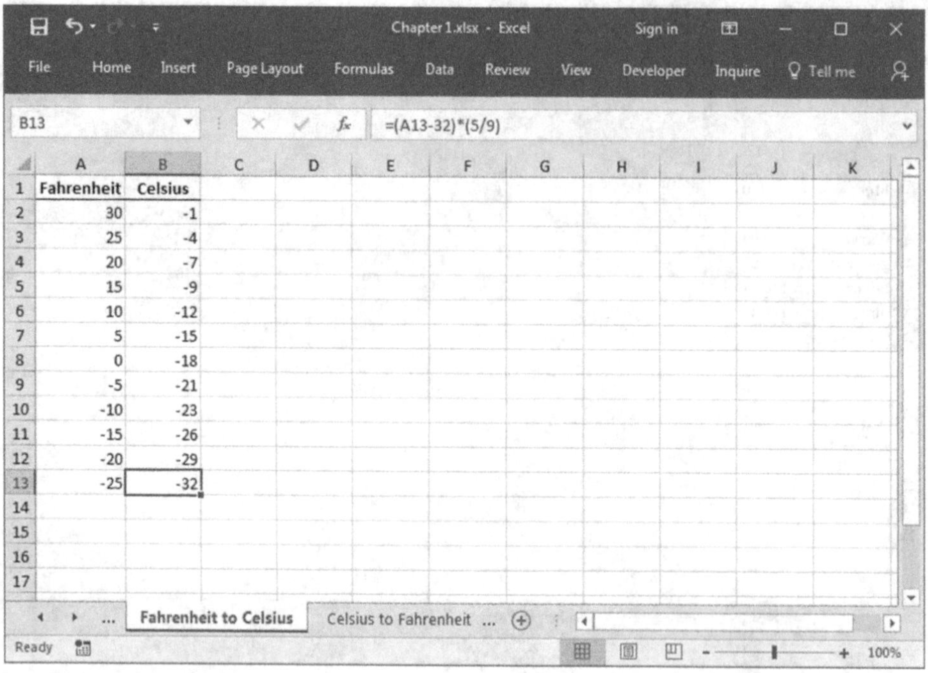

Figure 1–25

Convert from Celsius to Fahrenheit

To convert temperatures from Celsius to Fahrenheit, you can use the formula **=(Celsius *9/5)+32**, or you can use the calculation described here.

▶ To convert from Celsius to Fahrenheit:

1. In a worksheet, enter some temperatures in Celsius in column A.

2. Select cells B2:B13 and type the following formula: **=(A2*9/5)+32**.

3. Press **<Ctrl+Enter>**.

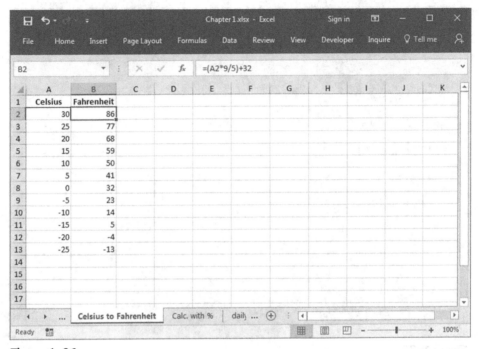

Figure 1–26

Calculate total with percentage

Let's say you want to buy a new car. The listed price of the car is $25,500, and the tax to be added is 8%. After negotiation of a sales discount of 10%, the final price needs to be calculated.

▶ To calculate the final price:

1. Select cell B1 and enter **25500**.

2. Select cell B2 to enter the tax rate of **8%**.

3. Select cell B3 and enter the discount rate of **10%**.

4. Select cell B5 and type the following formula: **=B1*(1+B2)*(1-B3)**.

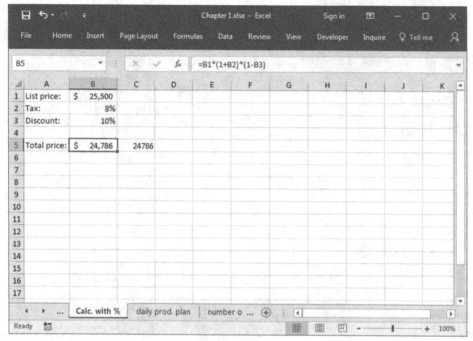

Figure 1–27

NOTE: The formula =B1*(1–B3)*(1+B2) also works for this example, as shown in the result in C5. The order of multiplication does not matter.

Monitor the daily production plan

A worksheet is used to monitor daily production. The target is defined as 1,500 pieces per day. To calculate the percentage of the daily goal produced, perform the following steps.

▶ To monitor daily production:

1. Select cell B1 and enter the predefined target: **1500**.

2. Select cells C4:C11 and type the following formula: **=B4/$B$1**.

3. Press **<Ctrl+Enter>**.

4. In the **Home** tab, go to the **Number** group and click on the % sign.

5. In the same group, click the button, **"Increase Decimal,"** twice. That way you set decimal places to 2.

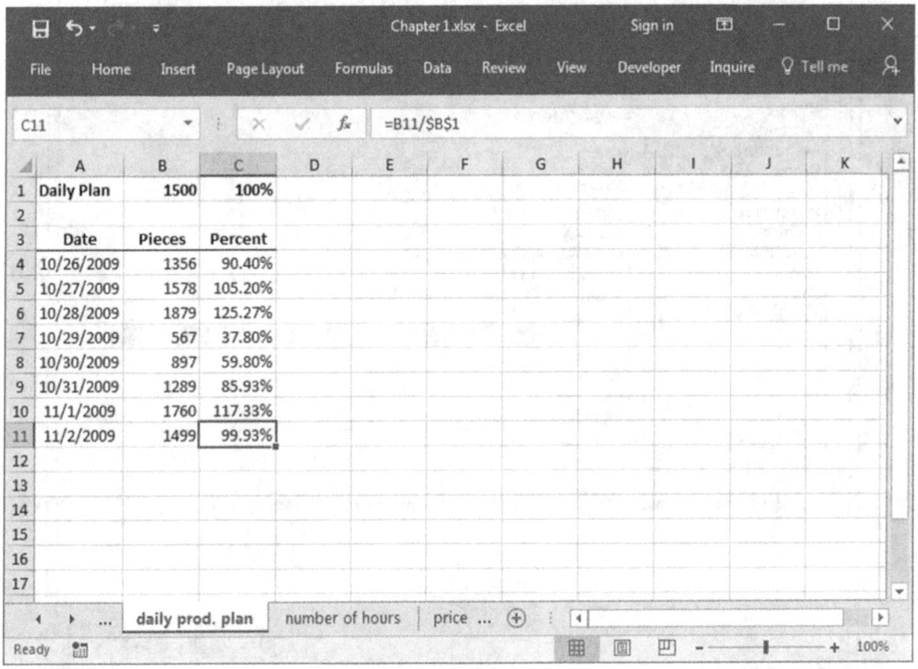

Figure 1–28

Calculate the number of hours between two dates

Excel has a problem calculating the difference between two dates in hours. You can verify this by opening a new worksheet and typing the starting date including time **(3/20/2010 1:42 p.m.)** in cell A2. In cell B2, type the end date and time **(3/24/2010 7:42 a.m.)**. Then subtract B2 from A2 in cell C2. The calculation generates 1/3/1900 6:00 p.m., which is incorrect. If the result is displayed as #####, you'll need to extend the width of column C.

Cells A2 and B2 need to be formatted as follows by selecting the expansion icon for the Numbers panel:

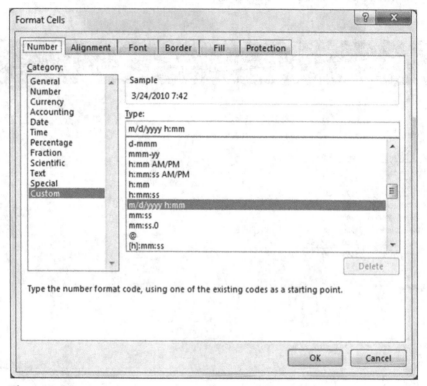

Figure 1–29

▶ To properly format the difference in hours:

1. Select cell C2.

2. In the **Home** tab, go to the **Number** group and click on the expansion icon at the lower right.

3. In the **Number** tab, click on **Custom** from **Category**.

4. Type the custom format **[he]:mm**.

5. Click **OK**. This gives the correct answer.

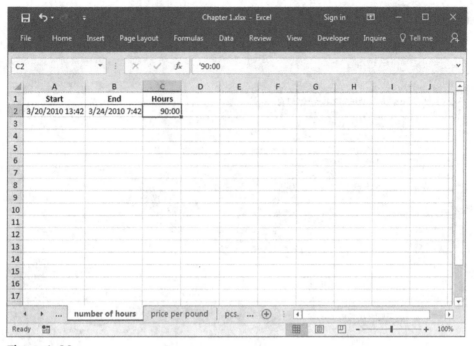

Figure 1–30

Determine the price per pound

A worksheet lists food products in column A. Column B shows the corresponding weight in pounds, and column C contains the total price. What is the price per pound?

▶ To calculate the price per pound:

1. In a workshop, enter the data shown in Figure 1–30, or use your own data.

2. Select cells D2:D8.

3. Type the following formula: **=C2/B2**.

4. Press **<Ctrl+Enter>**.

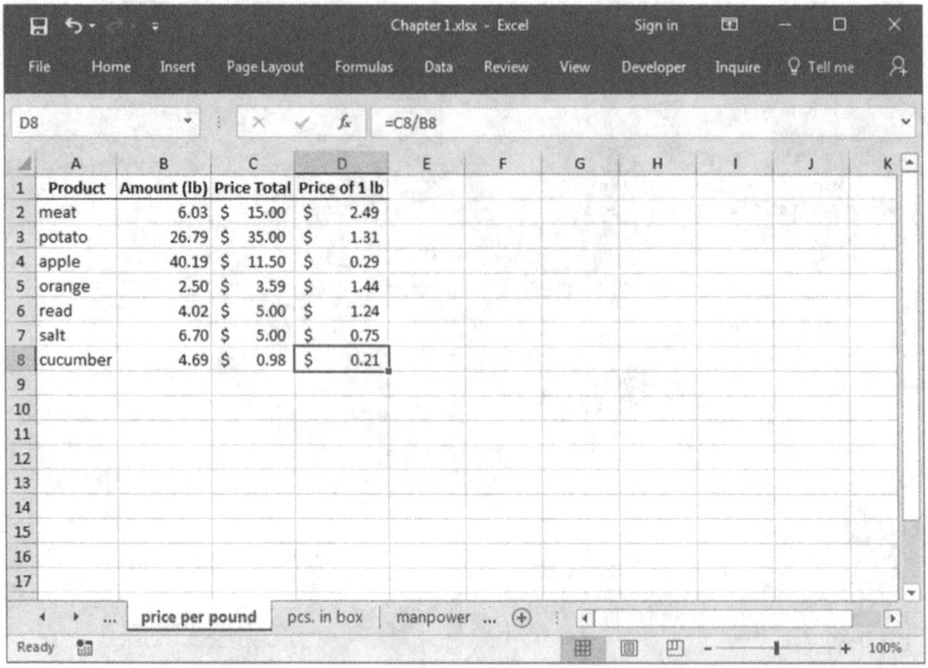

	A	B	C	D
1	Product	Amount (lb)	Price Total	Price of 1 lb
2	meat	6.03	$ 15.00	$ 2.49
3	potato	26.79	$ 35.00	$ 1.31
4	apple	40.19	$ 11.50	$ 0.29
5	orange	2.50	$ 3.59	$ 1.44
6	read	4.02	$ 5.00	$ 1.24
7	salt	6.70	$ 5.00	$ 0.75
8	cucumber	4.69	$ 0.98	$ 0.21

Figure 1–31

Determine how many pieces to put in a box

Let's say a container can hold 10 boxes and each box can hold up to 300 items. The customer requires a total of 500 items. How many items must be packed in each box, given a number of boxes?

▶ To determine the number of pieces in each box:

1. Select cell A2 and enter **10**.
2. Select cell B2 and enter **50**.
3. Select cell D2 and type **=B2*A2**.
4. In cells A4:A7 enter the number of boxes from 2 to 9.
5. Select cells B4:B7 and type the following formula: **=$B$2*($A$2/A4)**.
6. Press **<Ctrl+Enter>**.

7. Select cells D4:D7 and type the formula **=B4*A4**.

8. Press **<Ctrl+Enter>**.

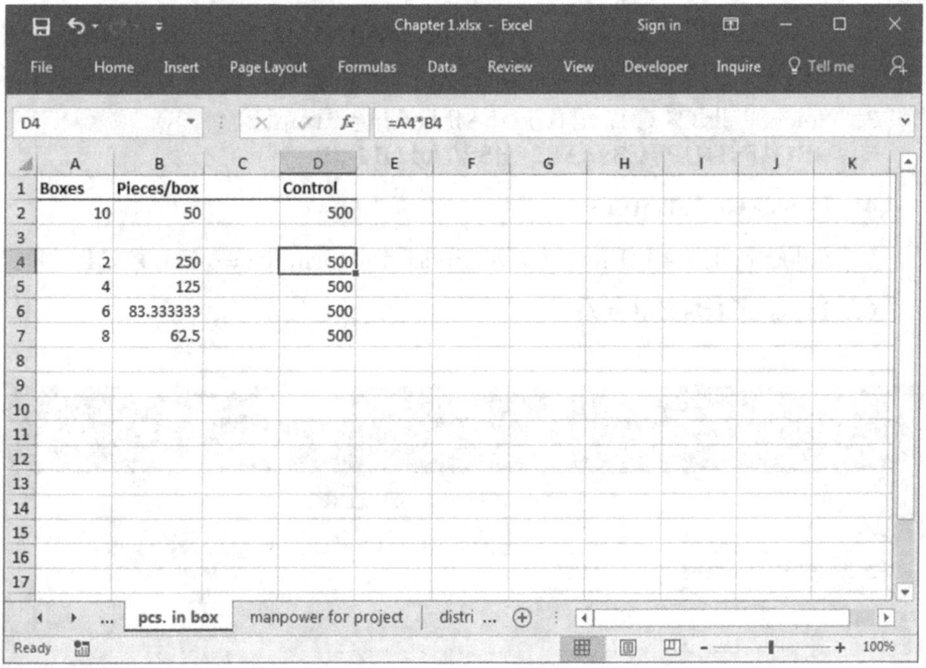

Figure 1–32

NOTE: Some entries in column A may result in a number with a decimal point in column B. These will require additional calculations on your part to determine exactly how many pieces fit in the given number of boxes so that the customer receives exactly 500 whole pieces.

Calculate the number of employees required for a project

The number of employees needed for a project needs to be calculated. To do this, enter the available time (14 days) for the project in cell A2. Cell B2 contains the number of working hours per day (8.5). Cell C2 shows the current number of employees (5). Now we can calculate how many employees are needed to reduce the project's duration or change the number of daily working hours of the employees.

▶ To calculate the desired number of employees:

1. Enter different combinations of desired days in column A and daily working hours in column B.

2. Select cell E2 and insert the formula **=A2*B2*C2** to calculate the total working hours of the project.

3. Select cells C4:C9 and type the following formula:
   =ROUNDUP (C$2*A$2*B$2/(A4*B4),0).

4. Press **<Ctrl+Enter>**.

5. Select cells E4:E9 and type the following formula: **=A4*B4*C4**.

6. Press **<Ctrl+Enter>**.

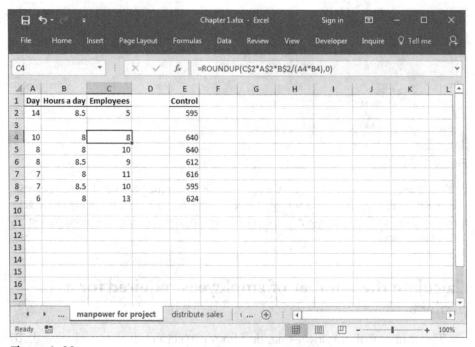

Figure 1–33

Distribute sales

In a company, each sale is assigned to a salesperson. The sale of 30 pieces totals $199,000. Each salesperson sold an individual amount of goods. Calculate the corresponding sales for each person.

▶ To calculate the total amount of sales for each employee:

1. Select cell B1 and enter the total amount of sales: **$199000**.

2. Select cell B2 and enter the total number of sold goods: **30**.

3. In columns A and B, enter the names of the salespeople and the number of pieces they sold.

4. Select cells C5:C10 and type the following formula: **=B5*$B$1/$B$2**.

5. Press **<Ctrl+Enter>**.

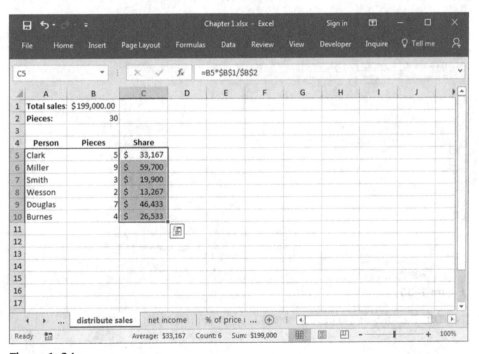

Figure 1–34

NOTE: Check out the AutoSum of the selected range in the status bar.

Calculate your net income

People often talk about their gross income. To calculate net income, it is necessary to consider the tax percentage, using the following calculation.

▶ To calculate net income:

1. Select cell B1 and enter the tax as a percentage: **33%**.

2. In cell B2, enter the gross income: **$3500**.

3. Select cell B3 and type the formula **=B2*B1** to calculate the tax amount.

4. Determine the net income in cell B4 with the formula **=B2-B3**.

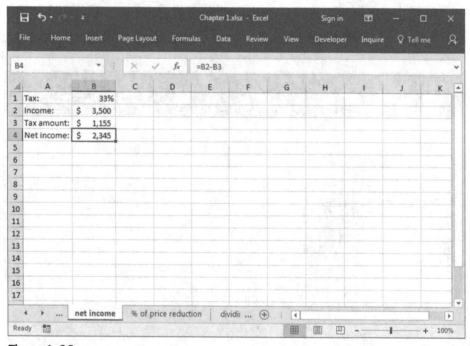

Figure 1–35

NOTE: The amounts in cells B1 and B2 can be changed.

Calculate the percentage of price reduction

A digital camera is on sale. The camera's original price is $250, but it is now available for $131. What is the percentage of the reduction?

▶ To calculate the price reduction as a percentage:

1. Select cell B2 and enter the original price: **$250**.

2. In cell B3, enter the sales price: **$131**.

3. Calculate the absolute difference in cell B4 with the formula **=B2-B3**.

4. Determine the percentage of price reduction in cell B5 using the following formula: **=B4/B2**.

5. Go to the **Number** group in the **Home** tab and select **Percentage** in the uppermost category.

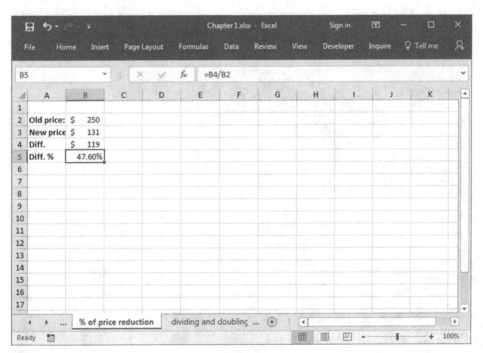

Figure 1–36

Divide and double every three hours

In an experiment, bacteria divide and double every three hours. How many bacteria will there be at the end of one day (24 hours) given a starting number?

▶ To calculate the total amount of bacteria after 24 hours:

1. Enter values from 1 to 4 in cells B2:B8.

2. Select cells C2:C8 and type the following formula: **=A2^(24/B2)**.

3. Press **<Ctrl+Enter>**.

4. Press **Ctrl+1** and select the **Number** tab and **Number** in **Category**.

5. Set Decimal Places to **0**, and tick the **Use 1000 Separator** check box.

6. Click **OK**.

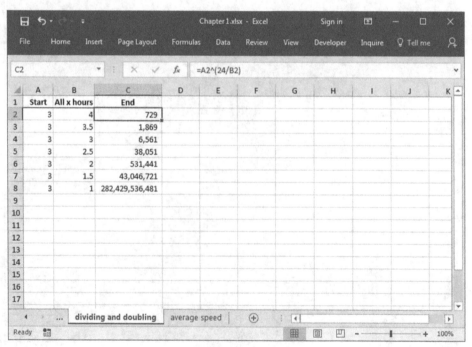

Figure 1–37

NOTE: To insert the ^ character, press the <^> key on the keyboard followed by a <Space>.

Calculate the average speed

In this example, someone travels from New York to Los Angeles with an average speed of 90 miles per hour. On the way back, the average speed is 75 miles per hour. What is the overall average speed?

To calculate the average speed, the speed in each direction needs to be taken into consideration.

▶ To calculate the overall average speed:

1. In cell C2, enter **90**.

2. In cell C3, enter **75**.

3. In cell C4, type the following formula: **=(C2+C3)/2**.

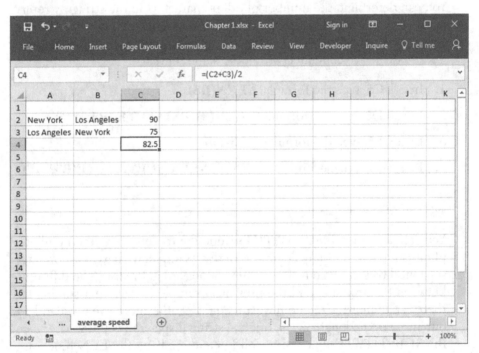

Figure 1–38

Calculate number of characters in a string

In this example, we need to calculate the number of characters in a string or the number of phrases separated by a delimiter. We are going to use the function SUBSTITUTE for this example.

To determine the number of characters in a string, simply determine the difference between what the length of the string is and what the length of the string is after you remove the characters for which you are trying to determine the count. In this example, the phrase listed in cell B5 is 44 characters long including the spaces using the LEN function. After we remove the spaces using the SUBSTITUTE function in cell D5, the length of the string is down to 35. The difference, 9, is the number of spaces in the string.

You can perform the same logic for any character (or phrase) you wish. You can determine the number of other characters in the string by replacing the space within the SUBSTITUTE function in cell D5 with any other character you wish. Row 6 contains the same logic to determine how many lower-case a's are contained within the same sentence.

1. In cell C5, type the formula: **=LEN(B5)**.

2. In cell D5, type the formula: **=LEN(SUBSTITUTE (B5," ",""))**

3. In cell F5, type the formula: **=C5-D5**

4. In cell G5, type the formula: **=LEN(B5)-LEN(SUBSTITUTE(B5," ",""))**

NOTE: Step 4 displays how to combine the previous 3 steps into one cell

You can also use the SUBSTITUTE function to determine the number of phrases separated by any delimiter. In this example, we have a list of names separated by semi-colons. How many names are in the list? The difference between this example and the previous example is that we assuming that there is one more of the item we are counting; therefore, we must add 1 to our answer. The length of the original string displays in cell B8. After using the SUBSTITUTE function in cell D8 and applying the LEN function to it in cell C8, we determine that there are four semi-colons. We further assume that the last name is not followed by a semi-colon so we add one to our final formula in cell E8. If cell B8 had ended with a semi-colon without any other names following it, then we would not include the "+1" in the F8 formula.

1. In cell C8, type the formula: **=LEN(B8)**.

2. In cell D8, type the formula: **=SUBSTITUTE (B8,";","")**

3. In cell F8, type the formula: **=C8-D8+1**

4. In cell G8, type the formula:
   =LEN(B8)-LEN(SUBSTITUTE(B8,";",""))+1

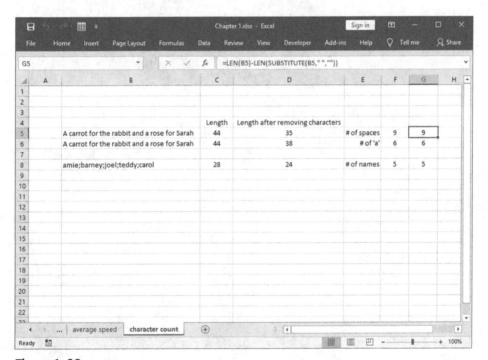

Figure 1–39

NOTE: Step 4 displays how to combine the previous 3 steps into one cell.

Logical Functions

2

Use the AND function to compare two columns

Two columns in a worksheet need to be evaluated. If the value in column A is greater than 20 and the value in column B is greater than 25, both values are valid.

▶ To compare two columns:

1. In cells A2:A10, enter values from 1 to 100.

2. In cells B2:B10, enter values from 1 to 100.

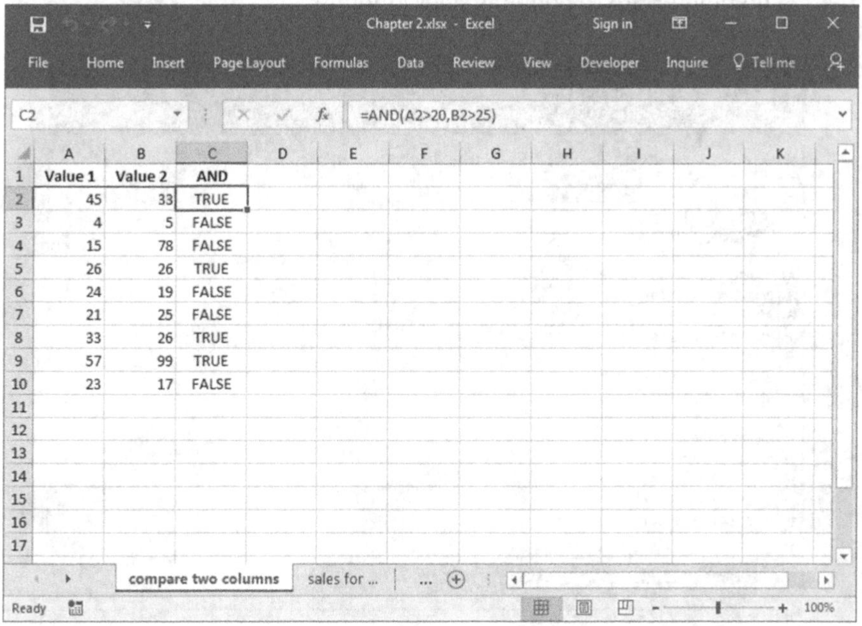

Figure 2–1

3. Select cells C2:C10 and type the following formula:
   =AND(A2>20, B2>25).

4. Press **<Ctrl+Enter>**.

NOTE: If both criteria are valid, Excel shows the value as TRUE; otherwise, it is FALSE.

Use the AND function to show sales for a specific period of time

This example checks all rows for a specific time period using the AND function. The function returns TRUE if all the arguments are TRUE and FALSE if one or more arguments are FALSE.

▶ To show sales in a period of time:

1. Select cell B1 and enter the start date.

2. Select cell B2 and enter the end date.

3. The range A5:A16 contains dates ranging from 09/11/04 to 09/22/04.

4. The range B5:B16 contains sales amounts.

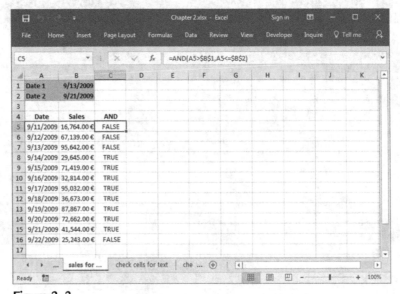

Figure 2–2

5. Select cells C5:C16 and type the following formula: **=AND(A5>B$1, A5<=$B$2)**.

6. Press **<Ctrl+Enter>**.

NOTE: Up to 30 conditions can be used in one formula.

Use the OR function to check cells for text

A worksheet contains several words in column A. Each row has to be checked for the words "new" or "actual" in column A. The OR function is used for this task. The function returns TRUE if either argument is true and FALSE if both arguments are not true.

▶ To use the OR function to check for two or more criteria:

1. Enter in range A2:A10 words like "new," "actual," and "old."

2. Select cells B2:B10 and type the following formula: **=OR(A2="New", A2="actual")**.

3. Press **<Ctrl+Enter>**.

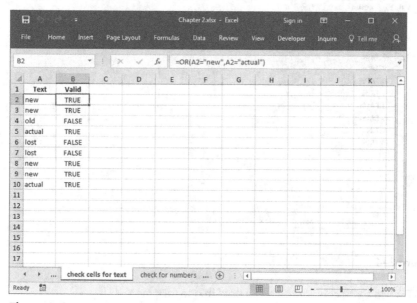

Figure 2–3

NOTE: Up to 30 conditions can be used in one formula.

Use the OR function to check cells for numbers

A worksheet contains several values in column A. Each row has to be evaluated based on certain the specific value in column A. The OR function is used for this task. The function returns TRUE if any argument is TRUE and FALSE if all arguments are FALSE.

▶ To check for two or more criteria:

1. Enter in range A2:A12 values from –43 to 100.

2. Select cells B2:B12 and type the following formula:
   =OR(A2=1, A2>=99, A2<0).

3. Press **<Ctrl+Enter>**.

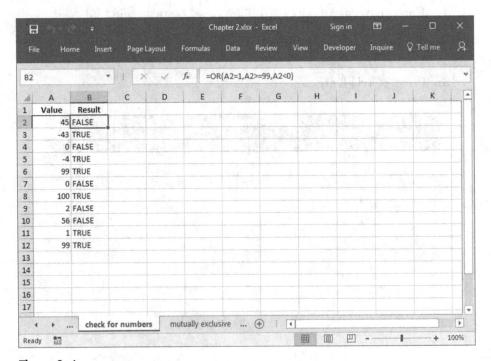

Figure 2–4

NOTE: Up to 30 conditions can be used in one formula.

Use the XOR function to check for mutually exclusive conditions

A worksheet contains several values in column A and another set of values in column B. The columns must contain in the same row one number above 900 but not both. The XOR function is used for this task. The function returns TRUE if only one argument is TRUE, FALSE if both arguments are TRUE, and FALSE if all arguments are FALSE.

▶ To check for the specified criteria:

1. Enter in range A2:A12 values from 0 to 1,000.

2. Enter in range B2:B12 values from 0 to 1,000.

3. Select cells C2:C12 and type the following formula: **=XOR(A2>=900, B2>=900)**.

4. Press **<Ctrl+Enter>**.

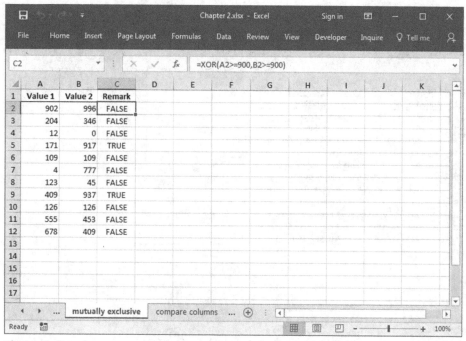

Figure 2–5

Use the IF function to compare columns and return a specific result

As shown in earlier examples, Excel returns the value TRUE or FALSE when using the OR and AND functions. The IF function can also be used to conduct conditional tests on values and formulas.

This example compares two columns and shows the result in column C.

▶ To return specific text after comparing values:

1. Enter in range A2:A12 values from 0 to 1,000.

2. Enter in range B2:B12 values from 0 to 1,000.

3. Select cells C2:C12 and type the following formula: **=IF(A2>=B2,"Column A is greater or equal","Column B is greater").**

4. Press **<Ctrl+Enter>**.

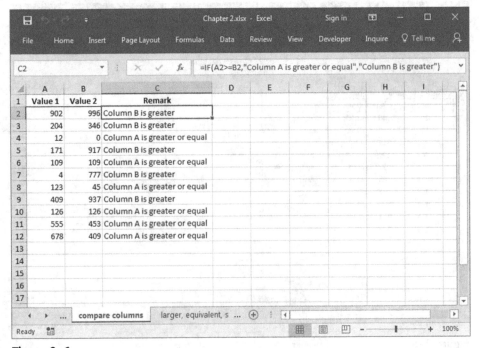

Figure 2–6

Use the IF function to check for larger, equivalent, or smaller values

In the previous example, two different messages were used as the result for comparing values. To check for three conditions in column A and present the result as "Column A is larger," "equal," or "Column A is smaller," perform the following steps.

▶ To compare columns and show the result:

1. Copy the previous example.

2. Select cells C2:C12 and type the following formula: **=IF(A2>B2,"Column A is larger",IF(A2=B2,"Equal", "Column A is smaller")).**

3. Press **<Ctrl+Enter>**.

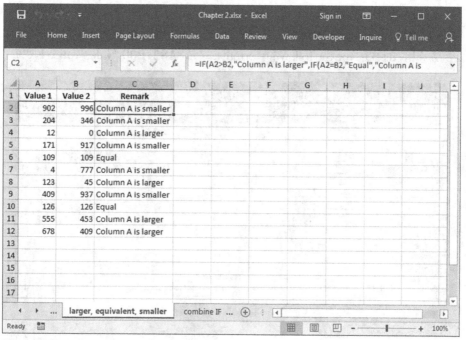

Figure 2–7

NOTE: Up to seven IF functions can be combined in one cell. To combine more than seven functions, use the customized solution near the end of this chapter.

Combine IF with AND to check several conditions

In this example, Excel evaluates which condition meets the criteria and returns the result in the same row.

▶ To combine the IF and functions:

1. Copy the content of cells C2:C5 in Figure 2–8 to your Excel table.

2. Frame the table as shown in the screenshot.

3. Select cell A2 and enter any kind of sales value, e.g., 120.

4. In cell B2, type the following formula:
   =IF(AND($A$2<=100,$A$2),"Sales value is","").

5. In cell B3, type the following formula:
   =IF(AND ($A$2>100, $A$2<=150)," Sales value is","").

6. In cell B4, type the following formula:
   =IF(AND ($A$2>150, $A$2<=200)," Sales value is","").

7. In cell B5, type the following formula: **=IF($A$2>200,"Sales value is","").**

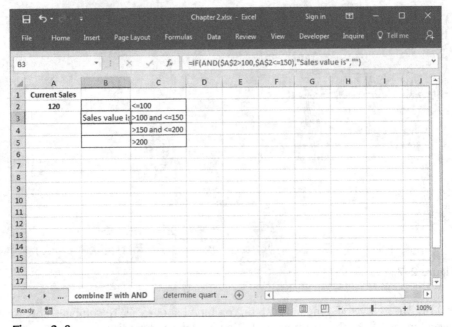

Figure 2–8

Use the IF function to determine the quarter of a year

After entering an initial value, Excel can automatically fill worksheet cells with the names of weekdays or months. Open a new worksheet and type the word "January" in cell A2. Then drag the lower-right point of this cell down to A13 to let Excel create a list containing the months of the year. In this example, we want to indicate which months fall into which quarter.

▶ To determine the quarter of a year in which a particular month falls:

1. Select cells B2:B13 and type the following formula:
   **=IF(OR(A2="January",A2="February",A2="March"),
   "1st quarter",IF(OR(A2="April",A2="May", A2="June"),"2nd
   quarter",IF(OR(A2="July", A2= "August",A2="September"),"3rd
   quarter","4th quarter"))).**

2. Press **<Ctrl+Enter>**.

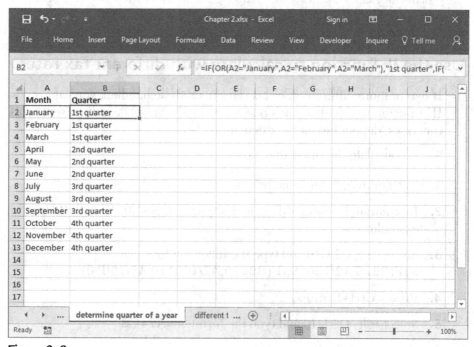

Figure 2–9

Use the IF function to check cells in worksheets and workbooks

To use an IF statement not only in a worksheet but also in a linked worksheet or workbook, start typing part of the formula, for example, "**=IF(,**" then navigate to another worksheet or open up a workbook, select the desired cell, and go back to the first worksheet to finish the formula.

▶ To use the IF function to check out cells in another worksheet:

Type **=IF(Sheet8!A2"january","wrong","OK")**.

▶ To use the IF function to check out cells in another workbook:

Type **=IF('C:\Held\Formulas\Files\[Formulas.xls] Sheet35'!$A$1<>1,"wrong","OK")**.

NOTE: For this to work, the referenced worksheets or workbooks must exist. This functionality can be checked by changing the name of the worksheet or the file reference.

Use the IF function to calculate with different tax rates

If two or more different sales tax rates need to be handled, you can use the IF function to calculate each one individually. Simply combine several IF functions, depending on the calculation.

▶ To calculate the price after tax:

1. In column A, enter some prices.

2. In column B, enter different tax percentages (0, 8, and 10 for this example).

3. Select cells C2:C10 and type the following formula:
   =IF(B2=8,A2/100*8,IF(B2=10,A2/100*10,A2/100*0)).

4. Press **<Ctrl+Enter>**.

5. Select cells D2:D10 and type the formula **=A2+C2**.

6. Press **<Ctrl+Enter>**.

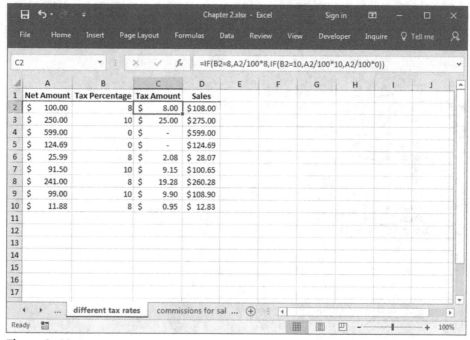

The cell reference shows **C2** with formula `=IF(B2=8,A2/100*8,IF(B2=10,A2/100*10,A2/100*0))`

	A	B	C	D
1	Net Amount	Tax Percentage	Tax Amount	Sales
2	$ 100.00	8	$ 8.00	$108.00
3	$ 250.00	10	$ 25.00	$275.00
4	$ 599.00	0	$ -	$599.00
5	$ 124.69	0	$ -	$124.69
6	$ 25.99	8	$ 2.08	$ 28.07
7	$ 91.50	10	$ 9.15	$100.65
8	$ 241.00	8	$ 19.28	$260.28
9	$ 99.00	10	$ 9.90	$108.90
10	$ 11.88	8	$ 0.95	$ 12.83

Figure 2–10

Use the IF function to calculate the commissions for individual sales

A company has a policy for individual commissions depending on sales, as shown below:

Sale < $100	3%
Sale >= $100 and < $500	5%
Sale >= $500	8%

▶ To calculate the commissions:

1. Enter different possible sales amounts in column A.

2. Select cells B2:B12 and type the following formula:
   =A2*IF(A2>=500, 0.08,IF(A2>=100,0.05,0.03)).

3. Press **<Ctrl+Enter>**.

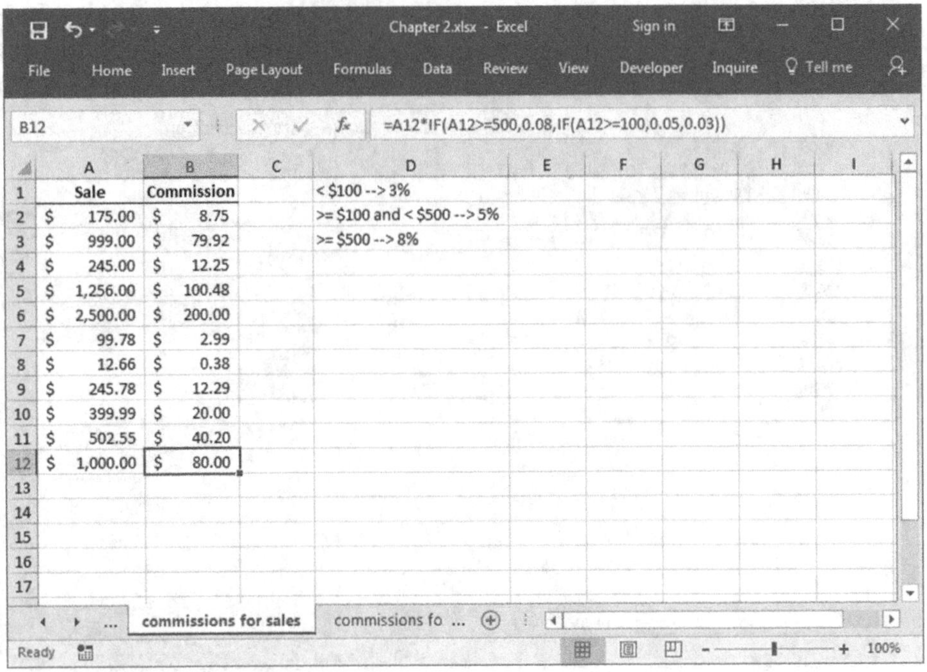

Figure 2–11

Use the IFS function to calculate the commissions for individual sales (*NEW IN EXCEL 2016*)

A company has a policy for individual commissions depending on sales, as shown below:

Sale < $100	3%
Sale >= $100 and < $500	5%
Sale >= $500	8%

▶ To calculate the commissions:

1. Enter different possible sales amounts in column A.

2. Select cells E2:E12 and type the following formula:
   =A2*IFS(A2<100, 0.03,A2<500,0.05,TRUE,0.08)

3. Press **<Ctrl+Enter>**.

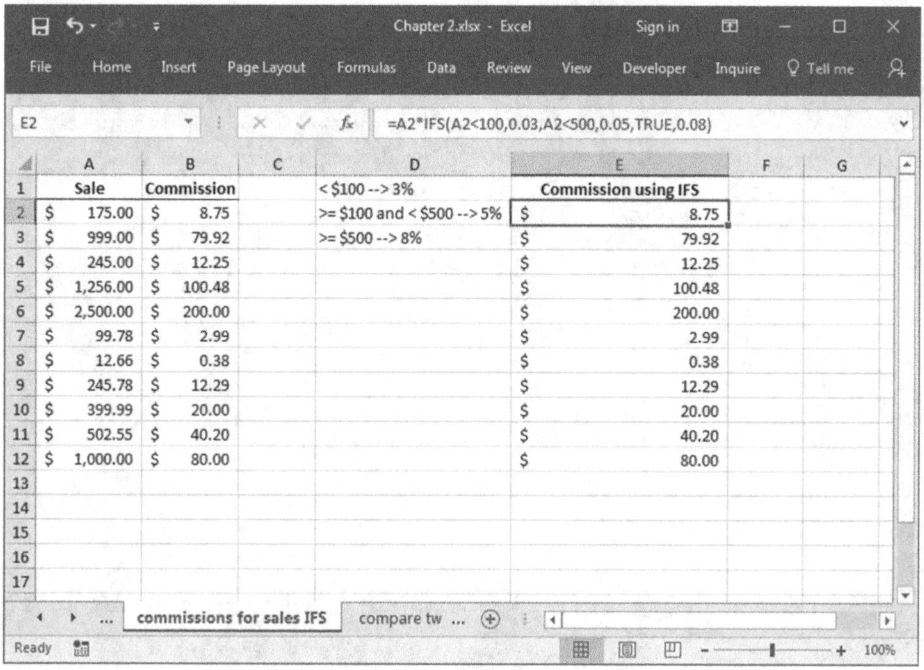

E2 =A2*IFS(A2<100,0.03,A2<500,0.05,TRUE,0.08)

	A	B	C	D	E
1	Sale	Commission		< $100 --> 3%	Commission using IFS
2	$ 175.00	$ 8.75		>= $100 and < $500 --> 5%	$ 8.75
3	$ 999.00	$ 79.92		>= $500 --> 8%	$ 79.92
4	$ 245.00	$ 12.25			$ 12.25
5	$ 1,256.00	$ 100.48			$ 100.48
6	$ 2,500.00	$ 200.00			$ 200.00
7	$ 99.78	$ 2.99			$ 2.99
8	$ 12.66	$ 0.38			$ 0.38
9	$ 245.78	$ 12.29			$ 12.29
10	$ 399.99	$ 20.00			$ 20.00
11	$ 502.55	$ 40.20			$ 40.20
12	$ 1,000.00	$ 80.00			$ 80.00

Figure 2–12

Use the IF function to compare two cells

The following tip is a solution for comparing two cells line by line. Prepare a new worksheet, filling the first two columns with the values 0 and 1 as shown in Figure 2–12.

▶ To compare cells line by line:

1. Select cells C2:C11 and type the following formula: **=IF(A2&B2="11","OK",IF(A2&B2="10","First Value is OK",IF(A2&B2="01"," Second Value is OK","Both Values are FALSE")))**.
2. Press **<Ctrl+Enter>**.

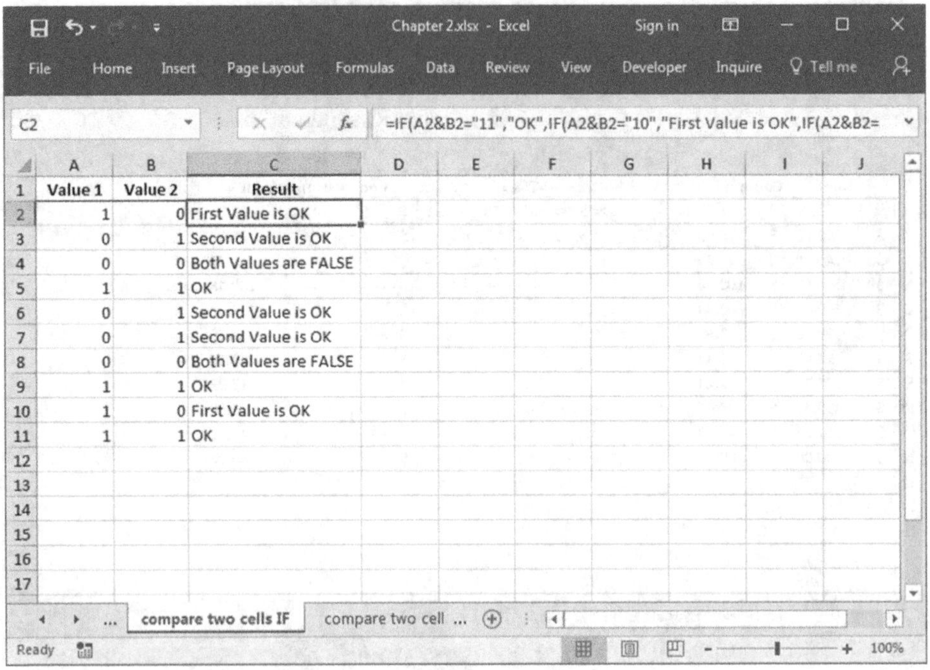

C2 =IF(A2&B2="11","OK",IF(A2&B2="10","First Value is OK",IF(A2&B2=

	A	B	C
1	Value 1	Value 2	Result
2	1	0	First Value is OK
3	0	1	Second Value is OK
4	0	0	Both Values are FALSE
5	1	1	OK
6	0	1	Second Value is OK
7	0	1	Second Value is OK
8	0	0	Both Values are FALSE
9	1	1	OK
10	1	0	First Value is OK
11	1	1	OK

Figure 2–13

Use the IFS function to compare two cells (*NEW IN EXCEL 2016*)

The following tip is a solution for comparing two cells line by line. Prepare a new worksheet, filling the first two columns with the values 0 and 1 as shown in Figure 2–12.

▶ To compare cells line by line:

1. Select cells D2:D11 and type the following formula: **=IFS(A2&B2="11","OK",A2&B2="10","First Value is OK",A2&B2="01","Second Value is OK",TRUE,"Both Values are FALSE")**

2. Press **<Ctrl+Enter>**.

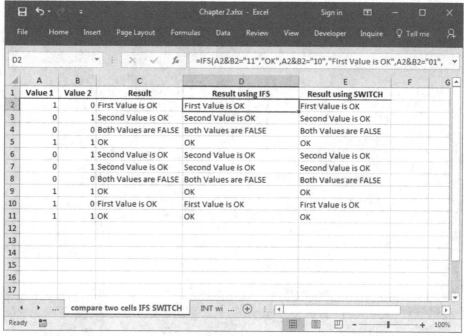

Figure 2–14

Use the SWITCH function to compare two cells (*NEW IN EXCEL 2016*)

The following tip is a solution for comparing two cells line by line. Prepare a new worksheet, filling the first two columns with the values 0 and 1 as shown in Figure 2–12.

▶ To compare cells line by line:

1. Select cells E2:E11 and type the following formula:
   =SWITCH(A2&B2,"10","First Value is OK","01","Second Value is OK","11","OK","00","Both Values are FALSE")

2. Press **<Ctrl+Enter>**.

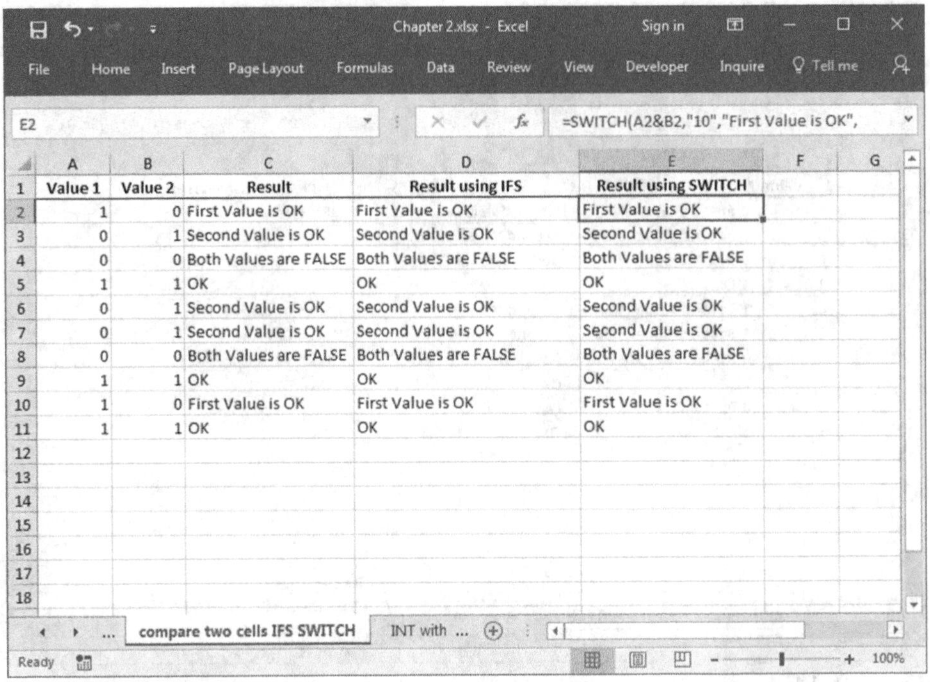

	A	B	C	D	E	F	G
1	Value 1	Value 2	Result	Result using IFS	Result using SWITCH		
2	1	0	First Value is OK	First Value is OK	First Value is OK		
3	0	1	Second Value is OK	Second Value is OK	Second Value is OK		
4	0	0	Both Values are FALSE	Both Values are FALSE	Both Values are FALSE		
5	1	1	OK	OK	OK		
6	0	1	Second Value is OK	Second Value is OK	Second Value is OK		
7	0	1	Second Value is OK	Second Value is OK	Second Value is OK		
8	0	0	Both Values are FALSE	Both Values are FALSE	Both Values are FALSE		
9	1	1	OK	OK	OK		
10	1	0	First Value is OK	First Value is OK	First Value is OK		
11	1	1	OK	OK	OK		

Figure 2–15

Use the INT function with the IF function

To see if one value is a whole number and can be evenly divided by another value, use the IF function in combination with the INT function.

▶ To see if a whole number can be evenly divided by 4:

1. Select cells B2:B10 and type the following formula: **=IF(INT(A2/4)=A2/4,"whole number divisible by 4",FALSE)**.
2. Press **<Ctrl+Enter>**.

▶ Alternately:

1. Select cells C2:C10 and type the following formula: **=IF(A2/4-INT(A2/4)=0,"whole number divisible by 4", FALSE)**.
2. Press **<Ctrl+Enter>**.

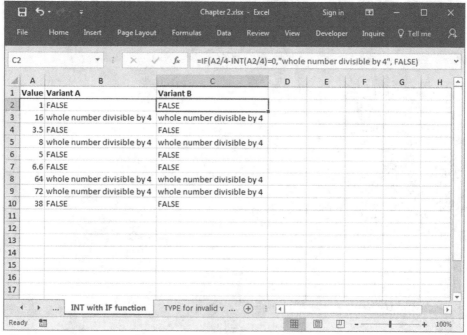

Figure 2–16

Use the TYPE function to check for invalid values

Sometimes Excel cannot interpret some values, especially imported data. As an example, let's say a cell contains an apparent value but the calculation leads to an incorrect result. To prevent this, use the IF function in combination with TYPE to check for invalid data in the worksheet. This example will enter the text "invalid value" in column B if the value entered in column A is not numeric.

▶ To show invalid values in a worksheet:

1. Enter some values or text in column A.

2. Select cells B2:B10 and type the following formula: **=IF(AND(TYPE(A2)=1,A2<>""),A2,"invalid value")**.

3. Press **<Ctrl+Enter>**.

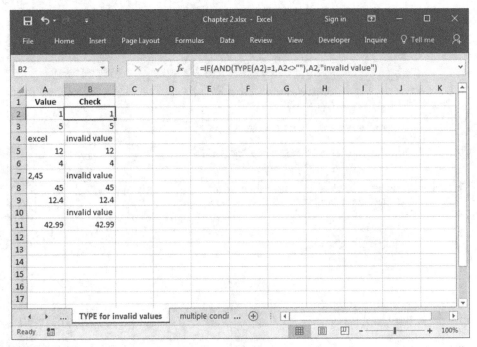

Figure 2–17

Use nested IF functions to cover multiple possibilities.

There are several methods to provide multiple results or calculations based upon a cell value. Here is one method using the basic IF function.

▶ To insert multiple conditions:

1. Select cell A2 and enter **12**.

2. Select cell B2 and type the following formula:
   **=IF(A2=1,A2,IF(A2=2,A2*2,IF(A2=3,A2*3,IF(A2=4,A2*4,
   IF(A2=5, A2*5,IF(A2=6,A2*6,IF(A2=7,A2*7,IF(A2=8,A2*8,
   IF(A2=9,A2*9,IF(A2=10,A2*10,IF(A2=11,A2*11,IF(A2=12,
   A2*12,)))))))))))))**

3. Press **<Enter>**.

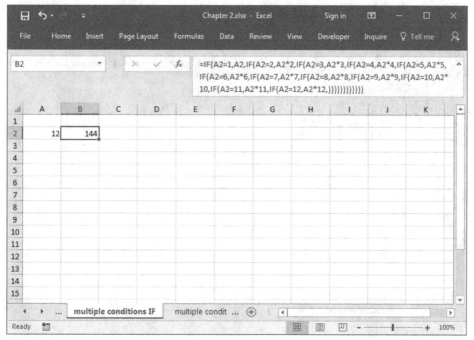

Figure 2-18

Use IFS function to cover multiple possibilities (*NEW IN EXCEL 2016*)

Another method to get the same result as the last example is new to Excel 2016. Here is one method using the IFS function.

▶ To insert multiple conditions:

1. Select cell A2 and enter **12**.

2. Select cell C2 and type the following formula:
   **=IFS(A2=1,A2,A2=2,A2*2,A2=3,A2*3,A2=4,A2*4,A2=5,A2*5,
   A2=6, A2*6,A2=7,A2*7,A2=8,A2*8,A2=9,A2*9,A2=10,A2*10,
   A2=11,A2*11,A2=12,A2*12)**

3. Press **<Enter>**.

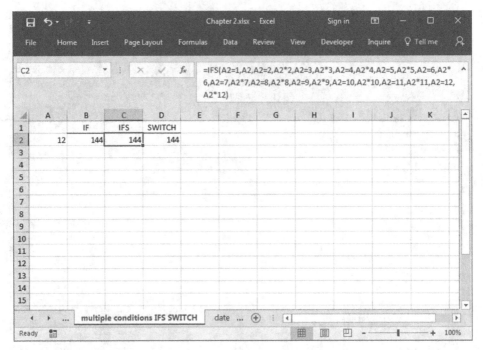

Figure 2–19

Use SWITCH function to cover multiple possibilities (*NEW IN EXCEL 2016*)

Another method to get the same result as the last two examples is new to Excel 2016. Here is one method using the SWITCH function.

▶ To insert multiple conditions:

1. Select cell A2 and enter **12**.

2. Select cell D2 and type the following formula: **=A2*SWITCH (A2,1,1,2,2,3,3,4,4,5,5,6,6,7,7,8,8,9,9,10,10,11,11,12,12)**

3. Press **<Enter>**.

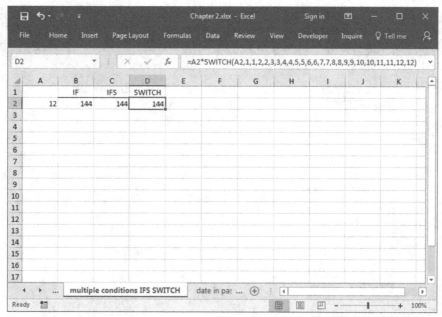

Figure 2–20

Use the IF function to check whether a date is in the past or the future

In this example, we want to check whether a particular date is in the past or the future. To do so, the TODAY() function is used with IF to compare dates with the actual date and show its result.

▶ To compare dates—variant A:

1. Select cells B2:B16 and type the following formula:
   =IF(NOT(A2>TODAY()),"Past","Future").

2. Press **<Ctrl+Enter>**.

▶ To compare dates—variant B:

1. Select cells B2:B11 and type the following formula:
   =IF(A2>=TODAY(),IF(A2=TODAY(),"Today","Future"),"Past").

2. Press **<Ctrl+Enter>**.

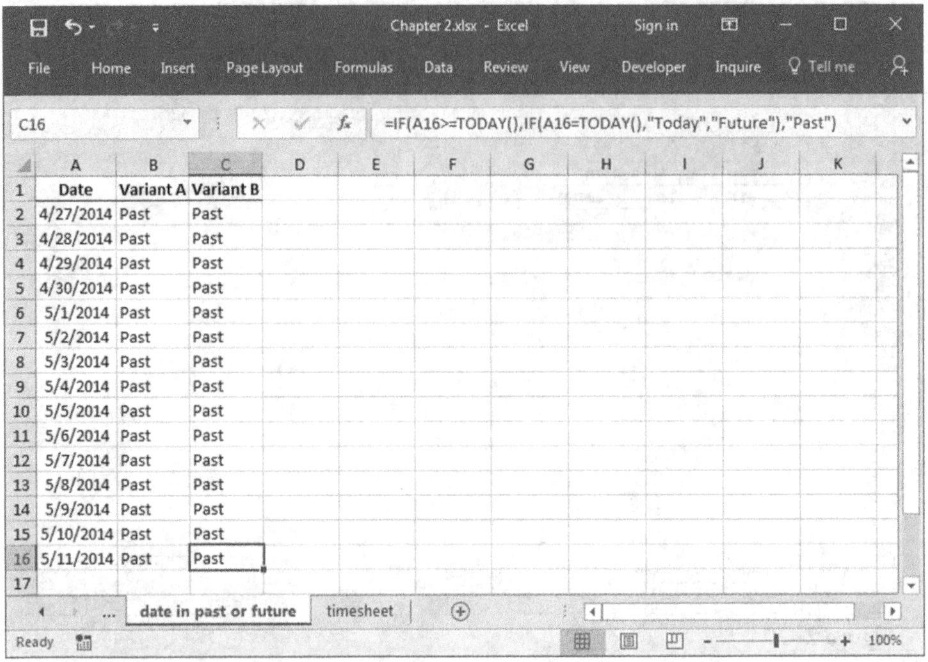

Figure 2–21

Use the IF function to create your own timesheet

In this last example we create our own timesheet, step by step. First, press **<Shift+F11>** to insert a new worksheet. Then create the following timesheet as an example:

We need to consider that the daily target of eight hours is still fulfilled when an employee is ill (IL), on holiday (HO), or in training (TR). For other days, the number of working hours must be calculated.

▶ To calculate the daily working hours:

1. Select cell F2:F6 and type the following formula: **=IF(OR(C2="TR",C2="IL",C2="HO"),E2,D2-C2)**.

2. Press **<Ctrl+Enter>**.

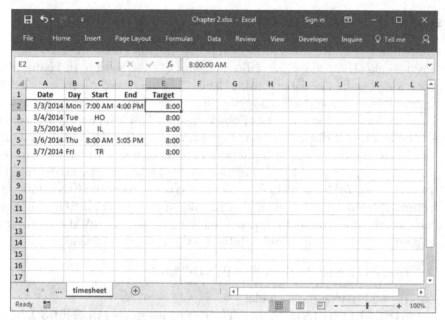

Figure 2–22

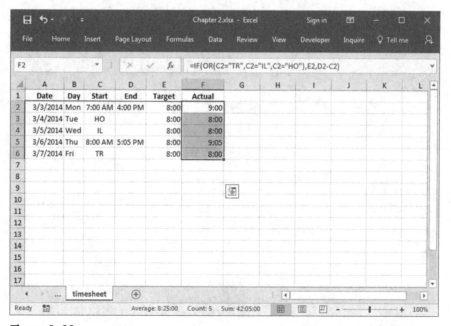

Figure 2–23

Use the IFERROR function to display a default

Sometimes when we use a formula referencing other cells, the cells contain invalid data. There are a few different approaches to tackling this issue. The best way is to fix the data by using data validation to ensure correct data is entered. But even when this is accomplished, the formula used on it can still produce an error for a variety of other reasons. You can change the format of the cell to not display the error or you can use the IFERROR function to display either nothing or a phrase that is more useful to the user. In the first example, using the FIND function we are looking for a space within the phrase "HelloToMe" in cell B3; since there is not a space, the FIND function returns an error. But if we wrap that function inside the IFERROR function, we have the opportunity to display something other than "#VALUE". In this example, we display the number 99 when the space is not found.

1. In cell D3, type the formula: **=FIND(" ",B3)**

2. In cell E3, type the formula:
    =IFERROR(FIND(" ",B3),"There are no spaces in cell B3").

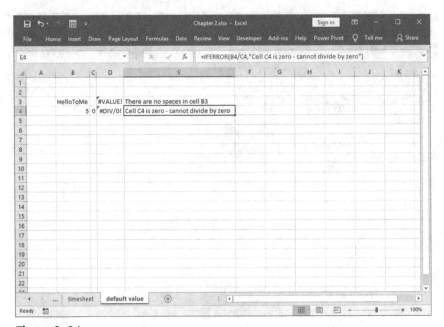

Figure 2–24

In the second example, we have a formula that divides by zero and we wish to display a more meaningful message than just "#DIV/0!" In this case, we display the message that is more descriptive.

1. In cell D4, type the formula: **=B4/C4**

2. In cell E3, type the formula:
    =IFERROR(B4/C4,"Cell C4 is zero - cannot divide by zero").

Text Functions

3

Use the LEFT and RIGHT functions to separate a text string of numbers

A worksheet contains a list of 10-digit numbers that need to be separated into two parts: a three-digit part and a seven-digit part. Use the LEFT and RIGHT functions to do this. The LEFT function returns the first character or characters in a text string, based on the number of characters specified. The RIGHT function returns the last character or characters in a text string based on the number of characters specified.

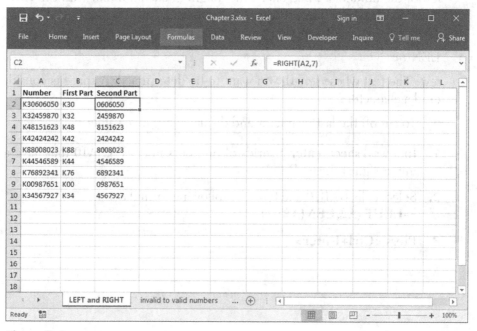

Figure 3–1

▶ To separate a text string of numbers:

1. In a worksheet, enter a series of 10-character numbers in cells A2:A10. The numbers can also contain letters.

2. Select cells B2:B10 and type the following formula: **=LEFT(A2,3)**.

3. Press **<Ctrl+Enter>**.

4. Select cells C2:C10 and type the following formula: **=RIGHT(A2,7)**.

5. Press **<Ctrl+Enter>**.

Use the LEFT function to convert invalid numbers to valid numbers

In this example, invalid numbers need to be converted to valid numbers. The invalid numbers contain a minus sign at the right end of the text. Excel cannot interpret this, so the minus sign in the text needs to be moved to the left of the numbers. First, check the length of each number with the LEN function. This function returns the number of characters in a text string. Then use the LEFT function to move the minus sign.

LEN(*text*)

text: The text whose length you want to be determined. A space is considered a character.

▶ To cut off the last character and display a negative value:

1. In a worksheet, enter a series of numbers in cells A2:A10 that have a minus sign at the end.

2. Select cells B2:B10 and type the following formula:
    =-LEFT (A2,LEN(A2)-1).

3. Press **<Ctrl+Enter>**.

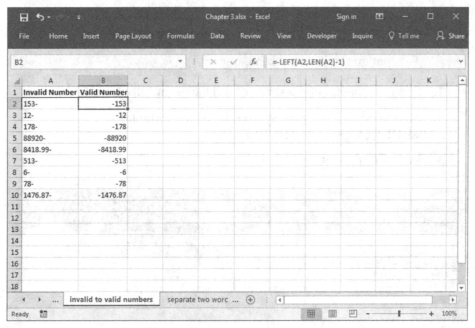

Figure 3-2

Use the SEARCH function to separate first name from last name

This task demonstrates how to separate first and last names. In a worksheet, full names are listed in column A. We want to copy the first name to column B. The SEARCH function can be used to determine the space between the parts of the text string. This function returns the position of the searched character inside a text string:

SEARCH(*find_text*, *within_text*, *start_num*)

find_text: The text or character for which you are searching. Wildcard characters, question marks (?), and asterisks (*) can be used in *find_text*. A question mark matches any single character, and an asterisk matches any sequence of characters. To find a question mark or asterisk, type a tilde (~) before the character.

within_text: The text within which you want to search for *find_text*.

start_num: The start position for the search function within the text; if there is no *start_num* defined inside the function, Excel sets it to 1.

▶ To separate the first and last names:

1. In a worksheet, enter a series of full names in cells A2:A10.

2. Select cells B2:B11 and type the following formula:
   =LEFT (A2,SEARCH(" ",A2)-1).

3. Press **<Ctrl+Enter>**.

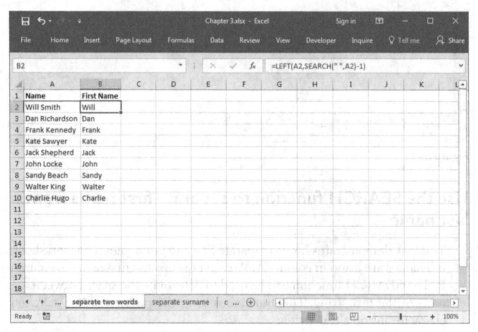

Figure 3–3

Use the MID function to separate last name from first name

In a worksheet, names are listed in column A, and the last name needs to be copied to column B. As in the previous example, the space between the first and last names needs to be determined with the SEARCH function. This function returns the position of the desired character inside a text string starting from *start_num*. The MID function then returns a specific number of characters starting from a desired position inside a text string.

MID(*text*, *start_num*, *num_chars*)

text: Text string containing the desired characters.

start_num: Position of the first character to extract from the text.

num_chars: Number of characters to be extracted.

▶ To separate the last name from the first name:

1. In a worksheet, enter a series of full names in cells A2:A10.

2. Select cells B2:B11 and type the following formula:
   =MID(A2,SEARCH (" ",A2)+1,100).

3. Press **<Ctrl+Enter>**.

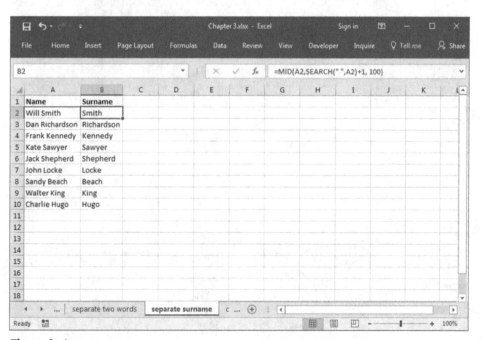

Figure 3-4

Use the MID function to sum the digits of a number

A worksheet contains four-digit numbers in column A. The four digits in each number need to be added together and the result shown in column B. To do so, the four digits of a cell are extracted by the MID function and summed.

▶ To determine the cross sum (the sum of digits in a number):

1. In a worksheet, enter a series of four-digit numbers in cells A2:A10.

2. Select cells B2:B10 and type the following formula:
   =MID(A2,1,1)+MID(A2,2,1)+MID(A2,3,1)+MID(A2,4,1).

3. Press **<Ctrl+Enter>**.

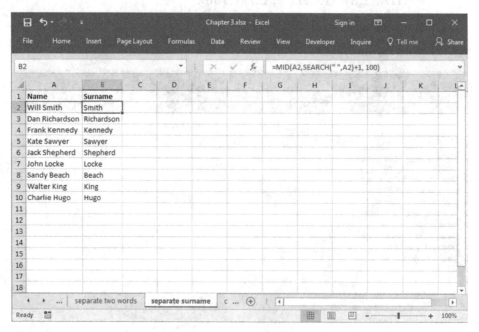

Figure 3–5

Use the EXACT function to compare two columns

There are two ways to compare two columns. With the IF function, it does not matter if the text is written in upper or lower case. The EXACT function, on the other hand, can distinguish between upper and lower case.

EXACT(*text1*, *text2*)

text1: The first text string.

text2: The second text string.

▶ To compare two columns:

1. In a worksheet, copy columns A and B from Figure 3–6.

2. Select cells C2:C8 and type the following formula:
   =EXACT(A2,B2).

3. Press **<Ctrl+Enter>**.

4. Select cells D2:D8 and type the following formula:
   =IF(A2=B2, TRUE,FALSE).

5. Press **<Ctrl+Enter>**.

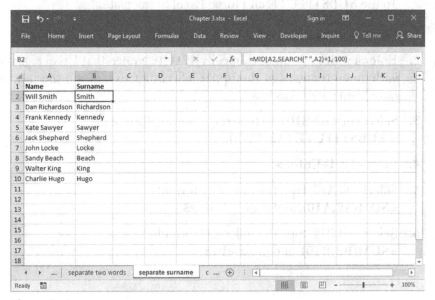

Figure 3–6

NOTE: Differences in formatting do not matter. Both functions will still work, as shown in cells A6 and B6; B6 contains the same underlying numeric value of the date in A6. Extraneous blanks in cells, as shown in row 7, also do not matter.

Use the SUBSTITUTE function to substitute characters

A worksheet contains values in column A that are formatted as text in Excel 2016. These can still be summed, because the format does not affect the content. How would these values work if converted to just text? Use the SUBSTITUTE formula to replace specific characters in text or in a cell.

SUBSTITUTE(*text, old_text, new_text, instance_num*)

text: The text or the reference to a cell containing text in which characters are to be substituted.

old_text: Text that should be replaced.

new_text: Text that replaces *old_text*.

instance_num: Specifies which instance of *old_text* is to be replaced by *new_text*. If omitted, every instance of *old_text* is replaced.

▶ To use SUBSTITUTE and force Excel to calculate:

1. Format column A as text.

2. Enter a series of numbers in cells A2:A10. Notice that Excel tags them with green triangles in the upper-left corner to indicate the numbers have been entered as text.

3. Select cells B2:B10 and type the following formula:
   = SUBSTITUTE (A2,"","")).

4. Press **<Ctrl+Enter>**.

5. Select cell A12, type the following formula:
   =SUM(A2:A10), and press **<Enter>**.

6. Select cell B12, type the following formula:
   =SUM(B2:B10), and press **<Enter>**.

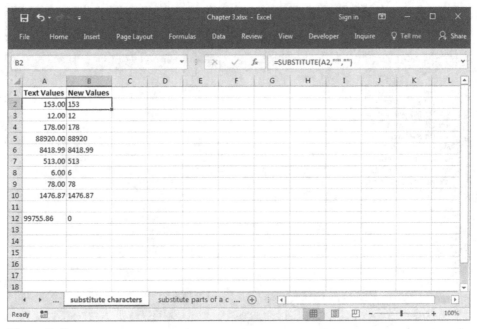

Figure 3-7

Use the SUBSTITUTE function to substitute parts of a cell

In this example, the "-" character needs to be deleted. But only the first occurrence of this character should be deleted. To do this, type any kind of text and numbers in column A, as shown in the following screenshot, using the "-" character in different positions and in a variety of occurrences.

▶ To substitute parts of a cell:

1. Select cells B2:B9 and type the following formula:
   =SUBSTITUTE (A2,"-","",1).

2. Press **<Ctrl+Enter>**.

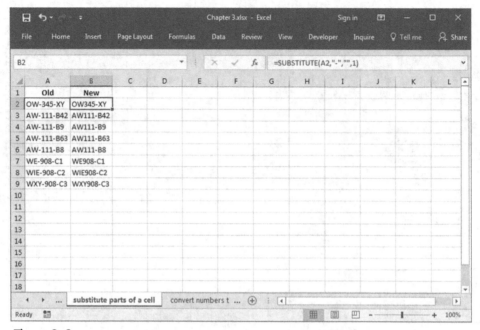

Figure 3–8

NOTE: If you want to substitute the second occurrence of this character, use the following formula: =SUBSTITUTE(A2,"-","",2).

Use the SUBSTITUTE function to convert numbers to words

A worksheet contains the numbers 1 to 5 in column A. Use the SUBSTI-TUTE function to change each number to a word. That is, change 1 to one, 2 to two, 3 to three, 4 to four, and 5 to five.

▶ To convert each number to a word:

1. In column A, type a series of numbers using 1, 2, 3, 4, and 5.

2. Select cells B2:B10 and type the following formula: **=(SUBSTITUTE (SUBSTITUTE(SUBSTITUTE(SUBSTITUTE(SUBSTITUTE (A2, 1,"one-"),2,"two-"),3,"three-"),4,"four-"),5,"five-"))**.

3. Press **<Ctrl+Enter>**.

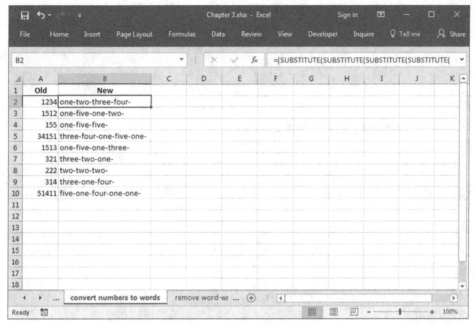

Figure 3–9

Use the SUBSTITUTE function to remove word wrapping in cells

To wrap text in a cell, you can select cells from the Home tab, select the Alignment group, and click the Wrap Text icon. Another way to do this is to type text into the first row of a cell, then press **<Alt+Enter>**, type text into the next row, and continue as desired.

If you want to disable word wrap, the SUBSTITUTE and CHAR functions can be used together. CHAR returns the character specified by a number. The ASCII character numerical equivalent for word wrap is 10.

▶ To delete word-wrap:

1. In cells A2 and A3 type text with word wraps.

2. Select cells B2:B3 and type the following formula:
   =SUBSTITUTE (A2,CHAR(10)," ").

3. Press **<Ctrl+Enter>**.

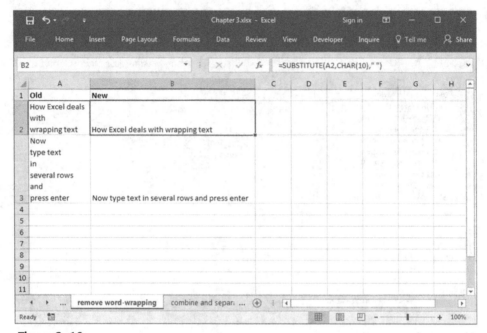

Figure 3–10

Use the SUBSTITUTE function to combine and separate columns

The & operator is used to combine several columns into one column. To include a separator between parts in addition to blank spaces, you can specify the separator just once while using the SUBSTITUTE function as follows.

▶ To combine and separate at the same time:

1. In columns A through D, type any kind of data.

2. Select cells F2:F10 and type the following formula:
   =SUBSTITUTE (A2&" "&B2&" "&C2&" "&D2&" "," - ").

3. Press **<Ctrl+Enter>**.

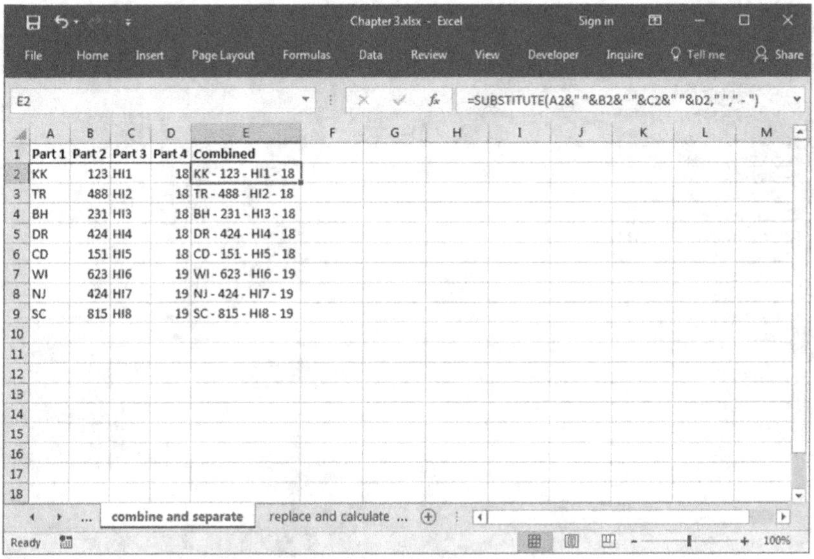

Figure 3-11

Use the REPLACE function to replace and calculate

The following worksheet contains an employee's work hours.

The format of columns B and C cannot be used to calculate time. Note that the triangle in the upper-left corner indicates the numbers have been entered as text. Rather than a period, a colon needs to be placed between the numbers to indicate time. Therefore, the period needs to be replaced using the REPLACE function in combination with SEARCH. The REPLACE function replaces part of a text string with a different text string, based on the number of characters specified. The syntax for the SEARCH function was provided earlier in this chapter.

REPLACE(*old_text*, *start_num*, *num_chars*, *new_text*)

old_text: Original text in which some characters are to be replaced.

start_num: Position of the character in old_text that is to be replaced with new_text.

num_chars: Number of characters in old_text to be replaced.

new_text: Text that will replace characters in old_text.

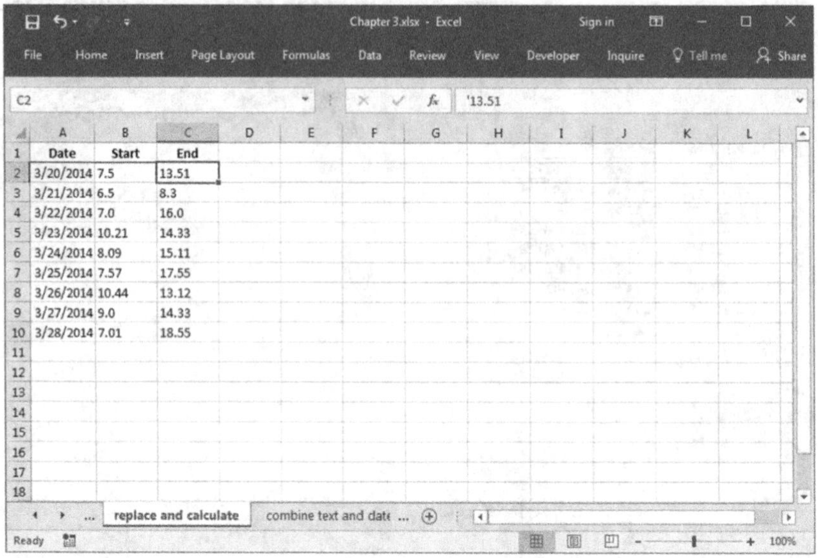

Figure 3–12

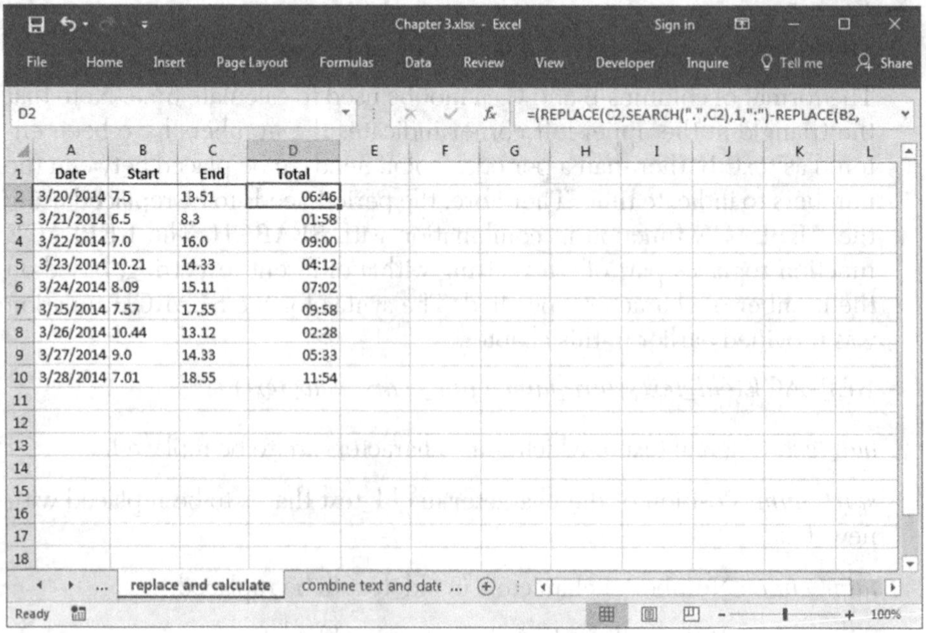

Figure 3–13

▶ To replace periods with colons and calculate:

1. In a worksheet, copy the data shown in Figure 3–13.

2. Select cells D2:D10 and type the following formula: **=(REPLACE (C2,SEARCH(".",C2),1,":")-REPLACE(B2,SEARCH(".", B2),1,":"))**.

3. Press **<Ctrl+Enter>**.

Use the FIND function to combine text and date

The following worksheet contains daily tasks in column A and their corresponding dates in column B. The task here is to combine the data and change the format of the dates. Take a closer look at the following screenshot:

The text string XXX needs to be replaced by the dates in column B. To do this, the starting position of the text string needs to be determined by using the FIND function. The REPLACE function will replace the XXX

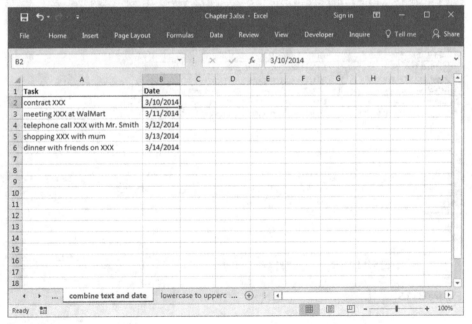

Figure 3–14

text string with the date. The string must be present for this to work, and capitalization matters.

FIND(*find_text*, *within_text*, *start_num*)

find_text: Text to find. Wildcard characters are not allowed.

within_text: Text containing find_text.

start_num: Specifies the first character in the search. If omitted, Excel sets start_num to 1.

▶ To combine and format data at the same time:

1. In a worksheet, copy the data shown in Figure 3–15.

2. Select cells C2:C6 and type the following formula: **=REPLACE(A2,FI ND("XXX",A2,1),3,TEXT(B2,"MM-DD-YYYY"))**.

3. Press **<Ctrl+Enter>**.

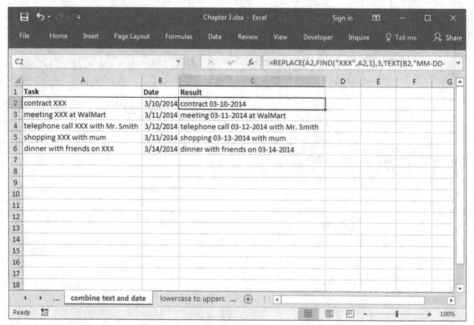

Figure 3–15

Use the UPPER function to convert text from lowercase to uppercase

The UPPER function is used to convert a text string to all uppercase letters. This function has the following syntax:

UPPER(*text*)

text: Text to be converted to all uppercase letters. The text can be either a reference or a text string.

▶ To convert a text string to uppercase:

1. In cells A2:A8, type any text in lowercase letters.

2. Select cells B2:B8 and type the following formula: **=UPPER(A2)**.

3. Press **<Ctrl+Enter>**.

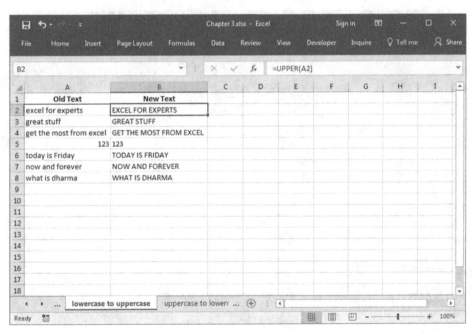

Figure 3–16

Use the LOWER function to convert text from uppercase to lowercase

To convert all letters to lowercase in a text string, use the LOWER function. This function has the following syntax:

LOWER(*text*)

text: Text to be converted to all lowercase letters. The text can be either a reference or a text string.

▶ To convert a text string to lowercase:

1. In cells A2:A8, type any text in uppercase letters.

2. Select cells B2:B8 and type the following formula: **=LOWER(A2)**.

3. Press **<Ctrl+Enter>**.

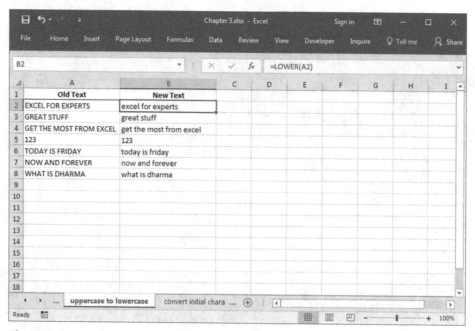

Figure 3–17

Use the PROPER function to convert initial characters from lowercase to uppercase

To convert the first letter in each word to uppercase and all other letters to lowercase, the PROPER function is used. This function capitalizes the first letter in a text string and any letters that follow characters other than a letter (such as a space). All other letters will be changed to lowercase.

This function has the following syntax:

PROPER(*text*)

text: Text enclosed in quotation marks, a formula that returns text, or a reference to a cell that contains the text that should have initial capital letters.

▶ To convert a text string to proper case:

1. In cells A2:A6 type any kind of text using different capitalization patterns.

2. Select cells B2:B7 and type the following formula: **=PROPER(A2)**.

3. Press **<Ctrl+Enter>**.

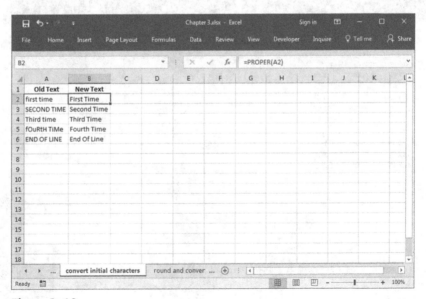

Figure 3–18

Use the FIXED function to round and convert numbers to text

To round numbers and return the result as text, use the FIXED function. This function rounds a number to the specified number of decimals, returning the result as text with or without commas.

FIXED(*number*, *decimals*, *no_commas*)

number: The number to round and convert to text.

decimals: The number of digits to the right of the decimal point. If omitted, Excel sets it to 2.

no_commas: A logical value that prevents FIXED from including commas when set to TRUE. If *no_commas* is FALSE or omitted, the returned text includes commas.

▶ To round and convert numbers to text:

1. In cells A2:A10, type values with decimals.

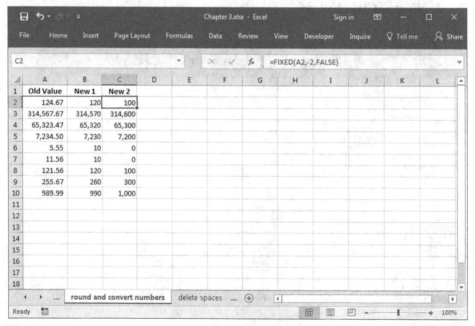

Figure 3–19

2. Select cells B2:B10 and type the following formula:
    =FIXED(A2,-1, FALSE).

3. Press **<Ctrl+Enter>**.

4. Select cells C2:C10 and type the following formula:
    =FIXED(A2,-2, FALSE).

5. Press **<Ctrl+Enter>**.

Use the TRIM function to delete spaces

Column A of a worksheet contains text with spaces at the left and right side of the text or between words. This could be a problem if, for example, data is used for evaluation and when cells are compare with other cells. Use the TRIM function to remove all spaces from a text string except for the single spaces between words.

▶ To delete unneeded spaces from text:

1. In cells A2:A5, type text with leading and trailing spaces.

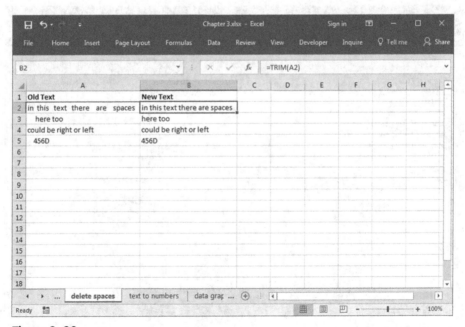

Figure 3–20

2. Select cells B2:B5 and type the following formula: **=TRIM(A2)**.

3. Press **<Ctrl+Enter>**.

Use the TRIM function to convert "text-numbers" to real numbers

In this example, numbers entered as text need to be converted to values. To do this, use the VALUE and TRIM functions in combination to get the correct result. The VALUE function converts a text string that represents a number to a number, and the TRIM function deletes all leading and trailing spaces.

▶ To convert text that represents a number to a value:

1. Format column A as text.

2. In cells A2:A10, type a series of numbers with trailing spaces.

3. Select cells B2:B10 and type the following formula: **=VALUE(TRIM (A2))**.

4. Press **<Ctrl+Enter>**.

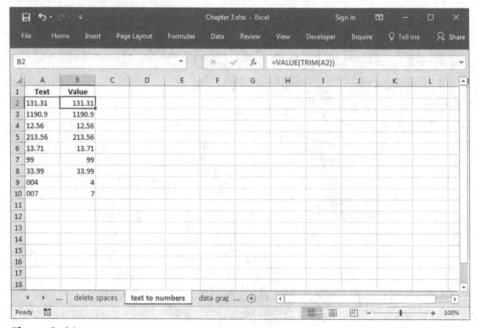

Figure 3–21

Use the CLEAN function to remove all non-printable characters

If data is imported from other applications, it is possible for this data to contain characters that may not be printable. In this case, the CLEAN function can be used to remove all non-printable characters from text.

▶ To delete non-printable characters:

1. Type any text in cells A2:A5. Make sure that some of the cells contain non-printable characters.

2. Select cells A2:A5 and type the following formula: **=CLEAN(A2)**.

3. Press **<Ctrl+Enter>**.

Use the REPT function to show data in graphic mode

To demonstrate data in a chart-like view, you can use a special character in a symbol font and repeat the character. To do so, use the REPT function. This function repeats a character a given number of times.

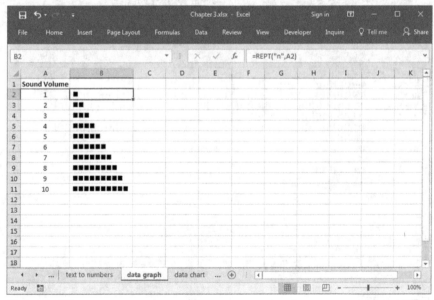

Figure 3–22

▶ To show data in a simple chart:

1. In cells A2:A11 type numbers from 1 to 10.

2. Select cells B2:B11 and type the following formula: **=REPT("n",A2)**.

3. Press **<Ctrl+Enter>**.

4. Press **Ctrl + 1**.

5. Select the **Font** tab.

6. Select **Wingdings** from the Font list.

Use the REPT function to show data in a chart

To show data in a chart-like view, you can define a character and repeat this character a specified number of times using the REPT function.

▶ To show data in a chart:

1. In cells B2:B10, type percentages in the range of 1% to 100%.

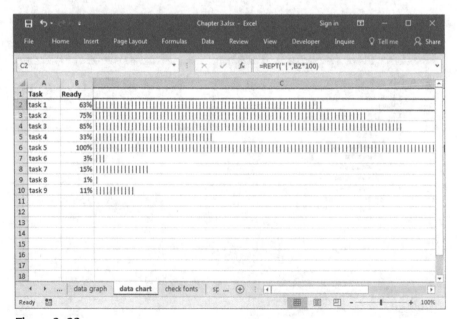

Figure 3–23

2. Select cells C2:C10 and type the following formula: **=REPT("|", B2*100)**.

3. Press **<Ctrl+Enter>**.

Use the CHAR function to check your fonts

To check a few fonts at the same time, open a new worksheet and format columns B through D with the Arial, Wingdings, Webdings, and Terminal fonts. Use the CHAR function to return the character specified by a number in column A.

▶ To check installed fonts:

1. In cell A2, type **1**.

2. Press **<Ctrl>** and drag the right corner of cell A2 down to cell A256.

3. Select cells B2:E256 and type the following formula: **=CHAR($A2)**.

4. Press **<Ctrl+Enter>**.

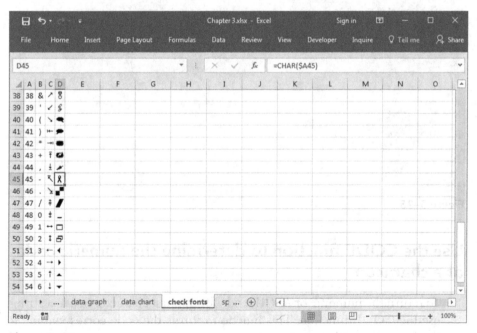

Figure 3-24

Use the CHAR function to determine special characters

To use special characters, it is necessary to figure out how to get them. The CHAR function will return the character specified by a number in column A. Note that some fonts may have different special characters.

▶ To determine special characters:

1. Copy column A as shown below to your worksheet.

2. Select cells B2:B16 and type the following formula: **=CHAR(A2)**.

3. Press **<Ctrl+Enter>**.

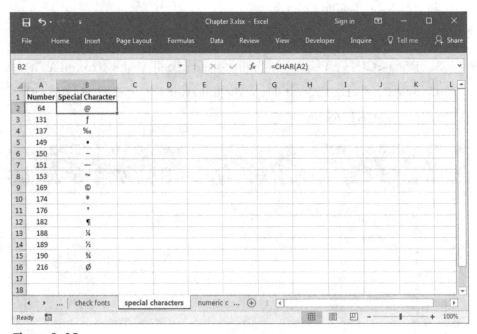

Figure 3–25

Use the CODE function to determine the numeric code of a character

To return the numeric, or ASCII, code for the first character in a text string, use the CODE function. This function returns the code corresponding to the currently used character set.

▶ To determine the numeric code of a character:

1. In cells A2:A11, type letters of the alphabet in both upper- and lower-case.

2. Select cells B2:B11 and type the following formula: **=CODE(A2)**.

3. Press **<Ctrl+Enter>**.

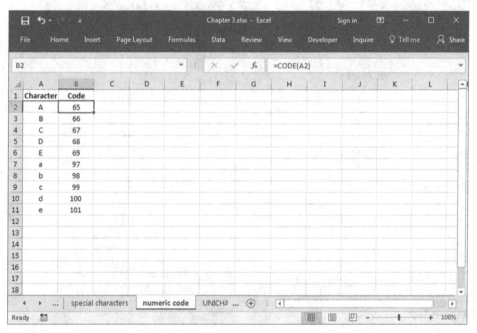

Figure 3–26

Use the UNICHAR function to determine the Unicode character from a number

Unicode is an expansion of the ASCII mapping that allows many more symbols to be interpreted by the encoding. It is becoming more popular through its integration with Java. A Unicode character can be returned from a number representing its encoding by using the UNICHAR function. Notice that the Unicode characters and numbers are the same for the ASCII subset.

▶ To determine Unicode characters:

1. Copy column A as shown below to your worksheet.

2. Select cells B2:B11 and type the following formula: **=UNICHAR(A2)**.

3. Press **<Ctrl+Enter>**.

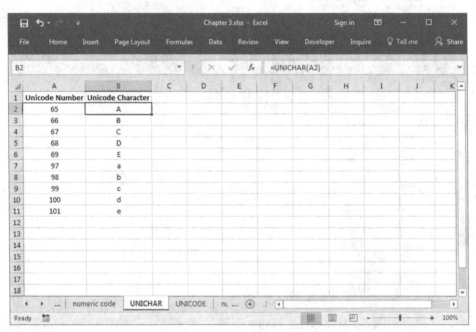

Figure 3–27

Use the UNICODE function to determine the numeric Unicode value of a character

To reverse the process shown in the previous example, use the UNICODE function to show the Unicode numeric encoding of the character.

▶ To determine the numeric Unicode value of a character:

1. In cells A2:A11, type letters of the alphabet in both upper- and lowercase.

2. Select cells B2:B11 and type the following formula: **=UNICODE(A2)**.

3. Press **<Ctrl+Enter>**.

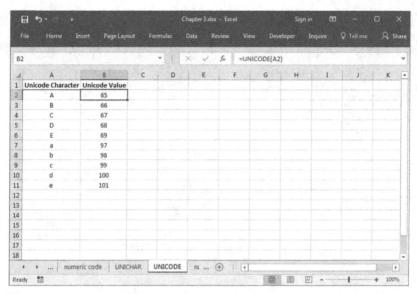

Figure 3-28

Use the DOLLAR function to convert numbers to currency in text format

The DOLLAR function converts a number to text format and applies a currency symbol. The currency format will be rounded to the specified decimal place.

DOLLAR(*number*, *decimals*)

number: A number and a reference to a cell that contains a number, or a formula that calculates a value.

decimals: The number of digits to the right of the decimal point. If negative, the number is rounded to the left of the decimal point. If omitted, Excel sets it to 2.

▶ To convert numbers to currency:

1. In cells A2:A10, type numeric values.

2. Select cells B2:B10 and type the following formula: **=DOLLAR(A2)**.

3. Press **<Ctrl+Enter>**.

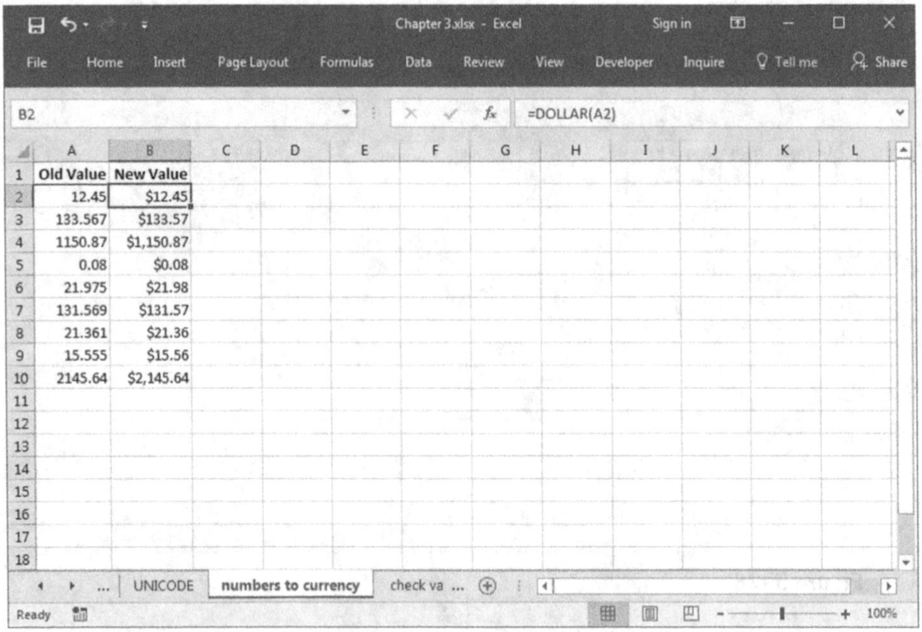

Figure 3–29

Use the T function to check for valid numbers

Reviewing Figure 3–30, you will notice that some numbers are listed, but there are also references to text and other values. You can check whether a number is a real value in an Excel worksheet by using the T function. This function checks whether a value is text. If it is text, T returns the text; if it is not, T returns empty text.

▶ To check for valid numbers:

1. Enter some values in column A and change the format for some of them to text (using the Cells option from the Format menu).

2. Select cells B2:B10 and type the following formula: **=T(A2)**.

3. Press **<Ctrl+Enter>**.

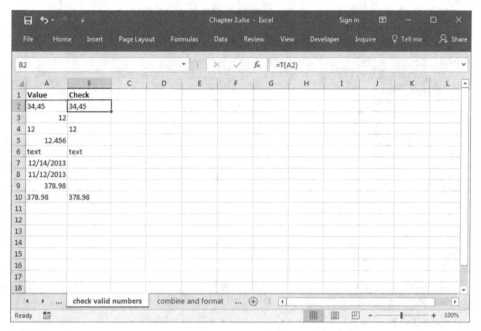

Figure 3–30

Use the TEXT function to combine and format text

In a daily sales record, employee names are listed in column A and their daily sales are entered in column B. There are two tasks here: We need to determine the percentage of the weekly sales goal ($1,000) that was met by the daily sales, and we want to combine the information from columns A and B.

▶ To combine and format text:

1. In a worksheet, copy the data shown in Figure 3–32.

2. Select cells C2:C9 and type the formula **=B2/1000**.

3. Press **<Ctrl+Enter>**.

4. Select cells D2:D9 and type the following formula: **=A2&" sold "&TEXT(B2,"$0.00")&" today. That's "&TEXT(C2,"0.0%")&" of the weekly goal."**

5. Press **<Ctrl+Enter>**.

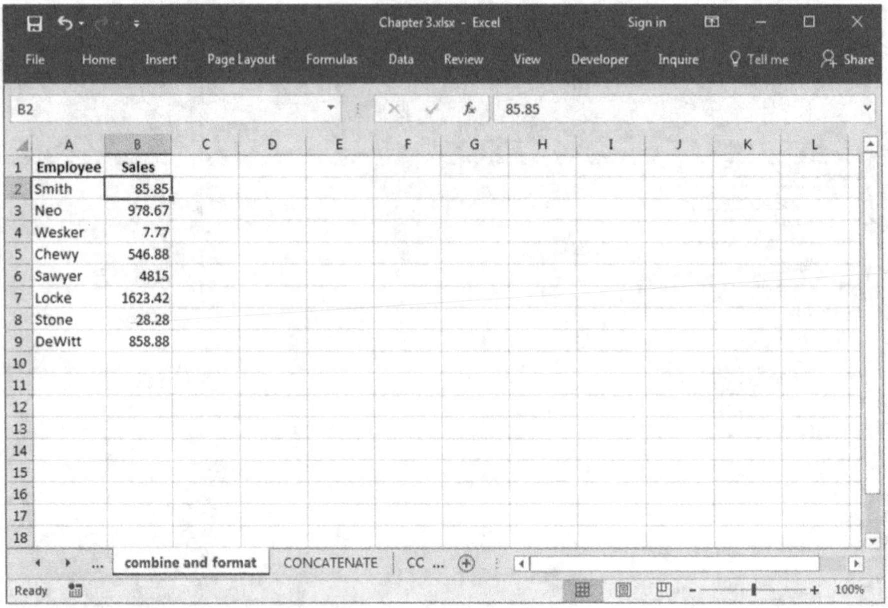

Figure 3–31

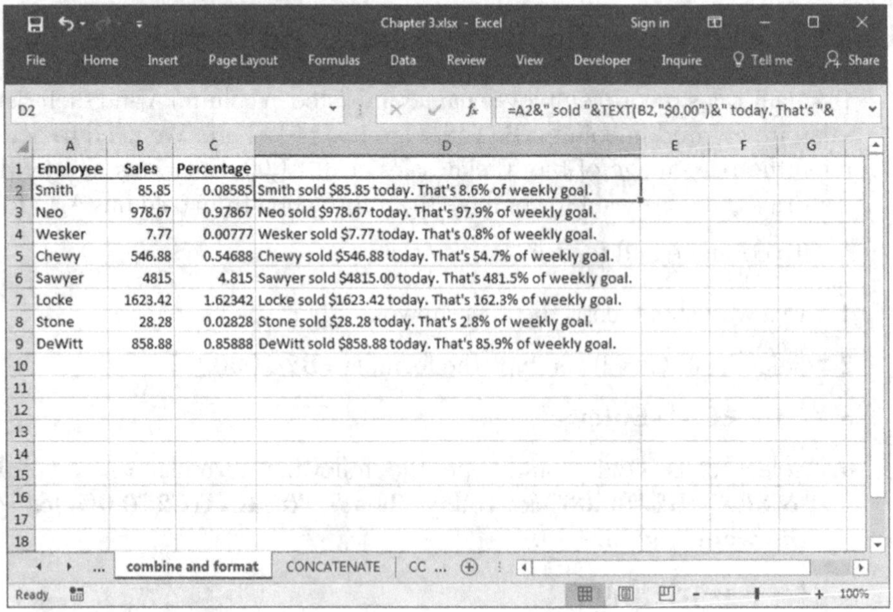

Figure 3–32

Use CONCATENATE function to combine text

In a daily sales record, employee names are listed in column A and their daily sales are entered in column B. Let us continue from the previous example only to rewrite the functions in column D. This example will be the first of three methods in combining strings. We will first use the function CONCATENATE. Go to the worksheet CONCATENATE text.

Keeping the objective in mind to create a sentence from the existing data,

▶ To combine text using CONCATENATE:

1. In a worksheet, copy the data shown in Figure 3–34.

2. Select cells D2:D9 and type the following formula: **=CONCAT-ENATE (A2," sold ",TEXT(B2,"$0.00")," today. That's ",TEXT (C2,"0.0%")," of weekly goal.")**

3. Press **<Ctrl+Enter>**.

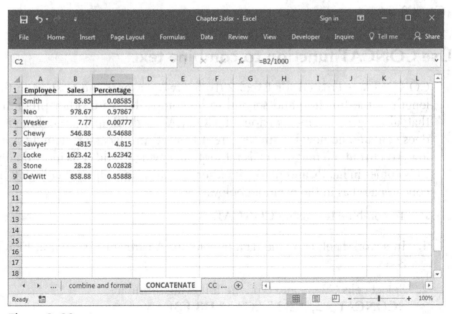

Figure 3–33

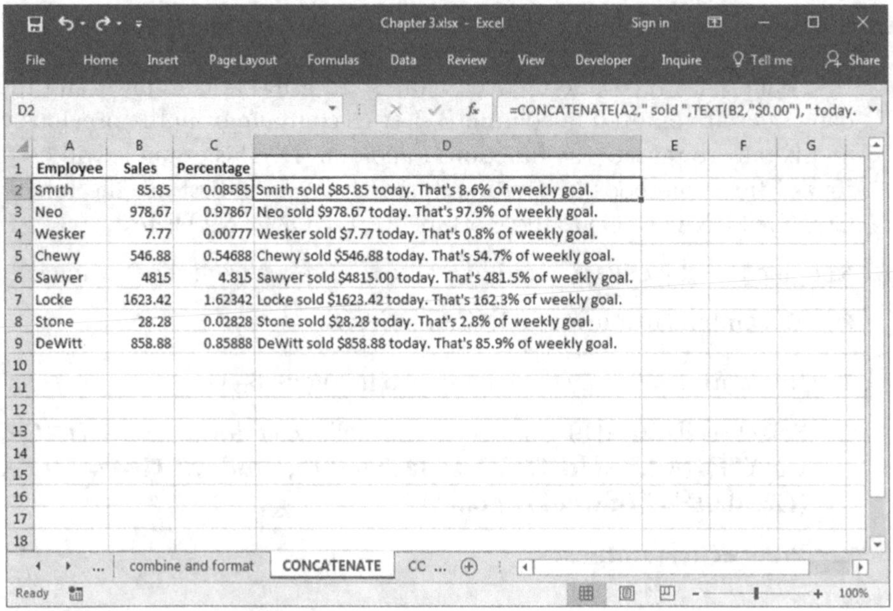

Figure 3–34

Use CONCAT function to combine text

CONCAT was created for Excel 2016 for two reasons: one to shorten the length of the function and second to be compatible with other programs that already use some version of CONCAT. Additionally, the function does contain one new feature different from its predecessor; namely, it allows you to enter a range of cells rather than having to add cells individually. This comes in handy and makes it easier to read when adjacent cells will be concatenated as in the example below.

▶ To combine text using CONCAT:

1. In a worksheet, copy the data in columns A through F shown in Figure 3–36.

2. Select cells G2:G9 and type the following formula:
   =CONCAT(A2," ",B2," ",C3," ",D3:F3)

3. Press **<Ctrl+Enter>**.

You will notice a range D3:F3 was entered as the last argument saving extra paramters passed.

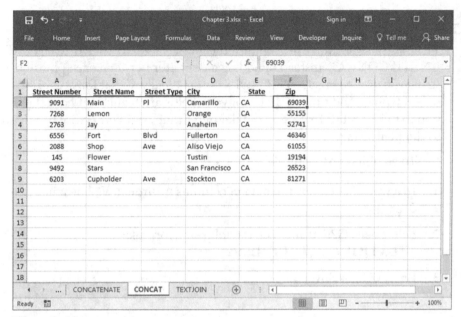

Figure 3–35

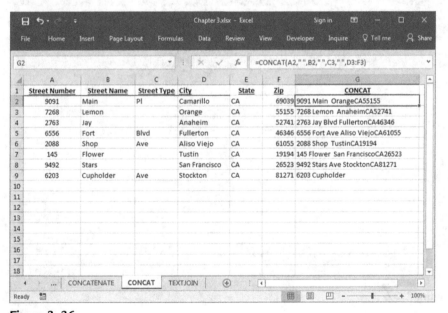

Figure 3–36

Use TEXTJOIN function to combine text

TEXTJOIN was added to simplify the most standard uses of CONCAT-ENATE/CONCAT. Instead of adding a delimiter between each phrase in a string you wish to create, TEXTJOIN automatically does it for you resulting in less typing. Additionally, if any of your fields are blank, you have the option to tell TEXTJOIN to skip the delimiter that would otherwise be added to the final string.

▶   To combine text using TEXTJOIN:

1. In a worksheet, copy the data in columns A through F shown in Figure 3–38.

2. Select cells G2:G9 and type the following formula:
    =TEXTJOIN(", ",TRUE,A2:F2)

3. Press **<Ctrl+Enter>**.

	A	B	C	D	E	F	G
1	Street Number	Street Name	Street Type	City	State	Zip	
2	5798	Main	Pl	Camarillo	CA	31338	
3	4894	Lemon		Orange	CA	97396	
4	4276	Jay		Anaheim	CA	12071	
5	9886	Fort	Blvd	Fullerton	CA	34180	
6	7017	Shop	Ave	Aliso Viejo	CA	98658	
7	8104	Flower		Tustin	CA	89624	
8	6627	Stars		San Francisco	CA	63356	
9	4070	Cupholder	Ave	Stockton	CA	91348	

Figure 3–37

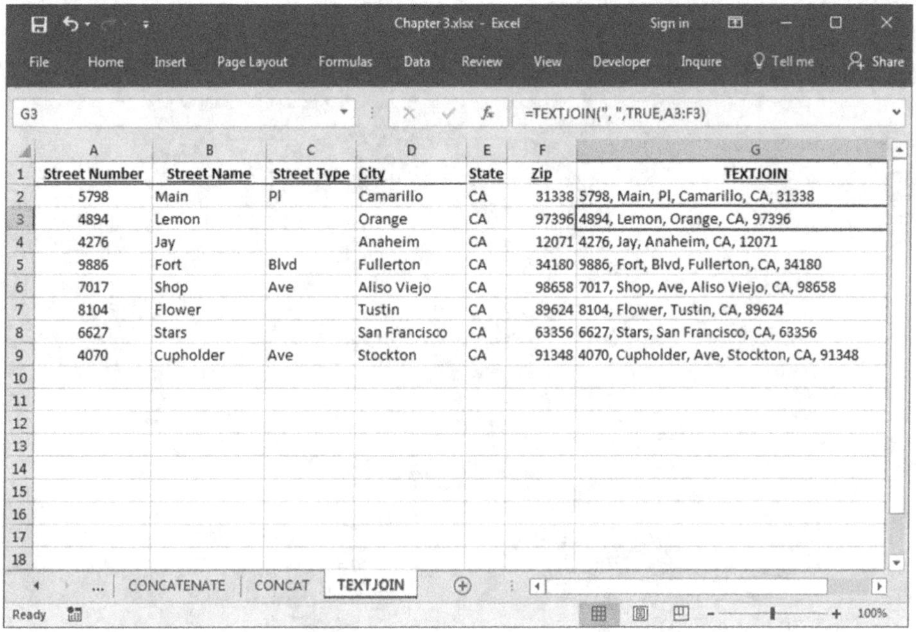

Figure 3–38

The first parameter passed is a comma and a space representating what is inserted between each cell. The second parameter TRUE tells the formula to ignore any blank cells – in other words if a cell is blank, do not place the delimiter between itself and the next cell. The final parameter is a range of cells for which to perform the function. You will notice in cell G3 that since the Street Type is blank, no delimiter is inserted reducing double delimiters.

Date and Time Functions

4

Use custom formatting to display the day of the week

A worksheet contains dates in column A. Use this tip to get the corresponding day of the week of each of these dates.

▶ To display weekdays using customized formatting:

1. Select cells B2:B10 and type the formula **=A2**.

2. Press **<Ctrl+Enter>**.

3. Press **<Ctrl + 1>**.

4. Select the **Number** tab expansion icon and click **Custom** in **Category**.

5. In the **Type** box, change the number format to **dddd**.

6. Press **OK**.

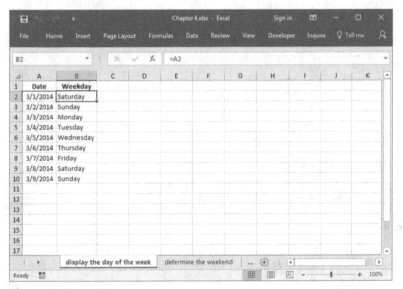

Figure 4–1

Use the WEEKDAY function to determine the weekend

How do you find out whether a date falls on a weekend? To answer this question, you can either use the previous tip or use the more convenient WEEKDAY function. This function returns the day of the week as a number corresponding to a date. The returned number is given as an integer, ranging from 1 (Sunday) to 7 (Saturday), by default.

▶ To determine the weekend:

1. Using the worksheet from the previous example, select cells C2:C10 and type the following formula: **=IF(OR(WEEKDAY(A2)=7,WEEK DAY(A2)=1),"weekend","")**.

2. Press **<Ctrl+Enter>**.

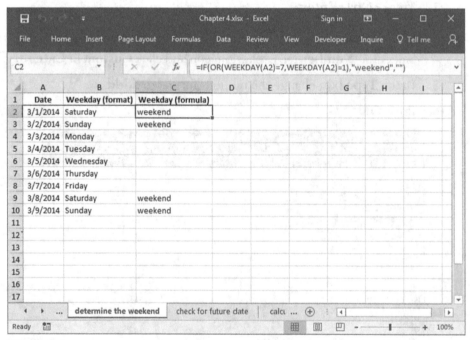

Figure 4–2

NOTE: In column B use the custom format **dddd** to check the result of column C.

Use the TODAY function to check for future dates

In a worksheet, dates in column A need to be checked to see if they are in the future. The actual date can be determined by using the TODAY function and can be compared with the dates in the worksheet using the IF function. If dates are in the future, the result in column B should be Y; otherwise, it should be N.

▶ To check for future dates:

1. In cell D1, type the formula **=TODAY()** to show the current date.

2. Select cells B2:B10 and type the following formula:
   =IF(A2<=TODAY ( ),"n","y").

3. Press **<Ctrl+Enter>**.

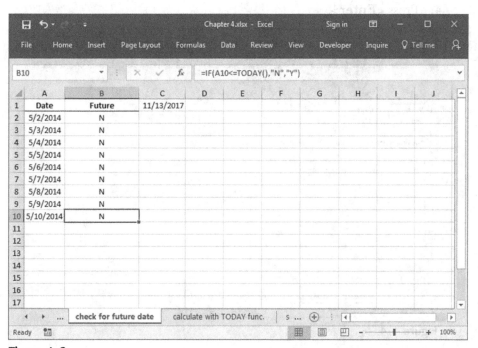

Figure 4–3

Use the TEXT function to calculate with the TODAY function

A project starts today and ends 10 days later. These dates are shown in cells B1 and B2. The end date has to be calculated based on the start date, and the dates need to be combined with additional text to form the message shown in cell A4.

▶ To calculate with the TODAY function:

1. In cell B1 type the formula **=TODAY()**.

2. In cell B2 type the formula **=TODAY()+10** to add ten days to the current date.

3. Select cell A4 and type the following formula: **="The project starts on " & TEXT(B1,"MM/DD/YYYY") & " and ends on " & TEXT(B2,"MM/DD/YYYY")**.

4. Press **<Enter>**.

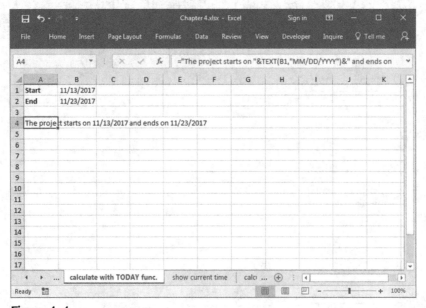

Figure 4–4

NOTE: The TEXT function (TEXT(*value, format_text*)) converts a value to text in a specific number format. In this example, format_text is shown as MM = month (two digits), DD = day (two digits), and YYYY = year (four digits).

Use the NOW function to show the current time

The previous tip described how to get the current date. Now we want to determine the current time. The NOW function returns the serial number of the current date and time. Microsoft Excel stores dates as sequential numbers so they can be used in calculations. By default, January 1, 1900, is number 1; therefore, January 1, 2006, is number 38718 because it is 38,717 days after January 1, 1900. A decimal point and numbers to its right are added to represent the time; numbers to the left of the decimal point represent the date. For example, the serial number .5 represents the time noon. The NOW() function is not updated continuously.

▶ To show the current time:

1. In cell A1 type the formula **=NOW()** and press **<Enter>**.

2. Ensure that cell A1 is selected and choose **Cells** from the **Format** menu.

3. In the **Number** tab, select **Date** under **Category**.

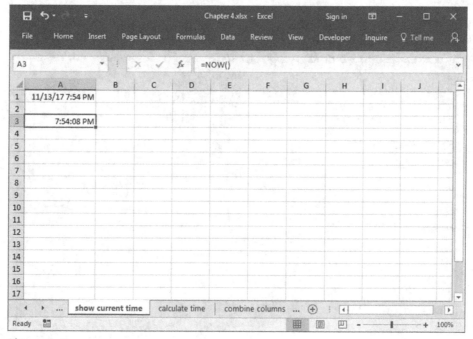

Figure 4–5

4. Select the format **3/12/14 6:30 p.m.** (This will show the current date and time when selected.)

5. Press **<Enter>**.

Use the NOW function to calculate time

To calculate with time, it is helpful to know that Excel stores the time as a decimal value. For example, 0.5 is noon, 0.75 is 6:00 a.m., and so on.

▶ To calculate with time:

1. In cell B1 type the formula **=NOW()**.

2. In cell B2 type the formula **=B1+0.25** to add six hours to the current time in cell B1.

3. Type the following formula in cell C1: **="The meeting starts at " & TEXT(B1,"hh:mm") & " and ends at " & TEXT(B2,"hh:mm")**.

4. Press **<Enter>**.

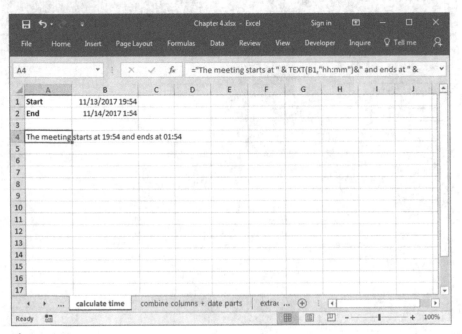

Figure 4–6

Use the DATE function to combine columns with date parts

The worksheet shown in Figure 4–7 uses three columns showing dates. Column A lists years; column B lists months, using numbers in the range 1 to 12; and column C contains the days of a month, in the range 1 to 31. These columns need to be combined to show one formatted date. To do this, use the DATE function.

DATE(*year, month, day*)

year: This argument can be from one to four digits. Microsoft Excel for Windows uses the 1900 date system.

month: A number representing the month of the year (1 to 12).

day: A number representing the day of the month (1 to 31).

▶ To combine values of cells into one date:

1. Select cells D2:D10 and type the following formula: **=DATE(A2,B2,C2)**.

2. Press **<Ctrl+Enter>**.

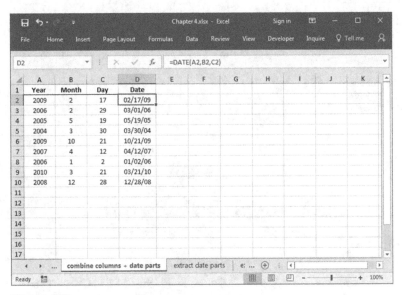

Figure 4–7

NOTE: Excel knows which years are leap years and thus provides correct results even when incorrect data is entered, as in row 3.

Use the LEFT, MID, and RIGHT functions to extract date parts

The worksheet in Figure 4–8 contains date values in column A. Excel cannot interpret these values as dates. To show the date in a correct format, the values of column A need to be extracted to year, month, and day.

▶ To extract, combine, and display the correct format:

1. Select cells B2:B10 and type the following formula: **=DATE(LEFT(A2,4), MID(A2,FIND(".",A2,1)+1,2),RIGHT(A2,2))**.

2. Press **<Ctrl+Enter>**.

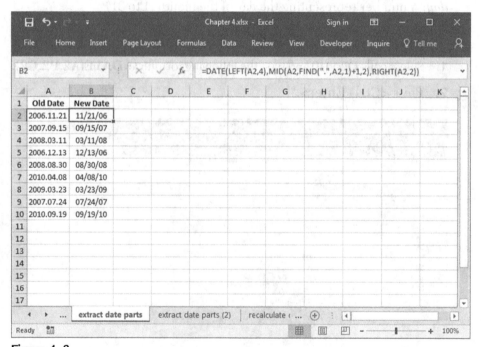

Figure 4–8

NOTE: The first four digits need to be transferred with the LEFT function. Then use the FIND function to detect the decimal point. On the right of the first decimal point (+1), two digits are interpreted as the month using the MID function. On the right side of the second decimal point, use the RIGHT function to extract two digits as the day value.

Use the TEXT function to extract date parts

A worksheet contains date values in column A as text that cannot be interpreted by Excel as date values. As in the previous example, the text has to be extracted, but the result should be specially formatted as shown in the screenshot below.

▶ To extract, combine, and show a specially formatted date:

1. Select cells B2:B10 and type the following formula: **=TEXT(DATE(RIGHT(A2,4),MID(A2,3,2),MID(A2,1,2)),"YYYY-MM-DD")**.

2. Press **<Ctrl+Enter>**.

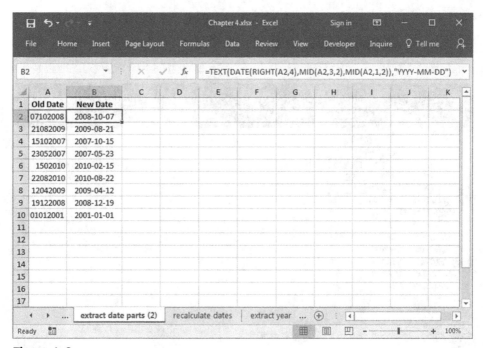

Figure 4–9

NOTE: First, transfer the last four digits with the RIGHT function. Then use the MID function twice to get the two digits for the month and those for the day. With the TEXT function, the date can be formatted individually.

Use the DATEVALUE function to recalculate dates formatted as text

Figure 4–10 shows start and end dates in columns A and B. Excel cannot interpret the columns as dates, because they are formatted as text. To convert and calculate these types of dates, use the DATEVALUE function. This function returns the serial number of the date represented by the "text date."

Let's determine the difference between start and end dates.

▶ To calculate the difference between text dates:

1. Select cells C2:C10.

2. Type the following formula: **=DATEVALUE(B2)-DATEVALUE(A2)**.

3. Press **<Ctrl+Enter>**.

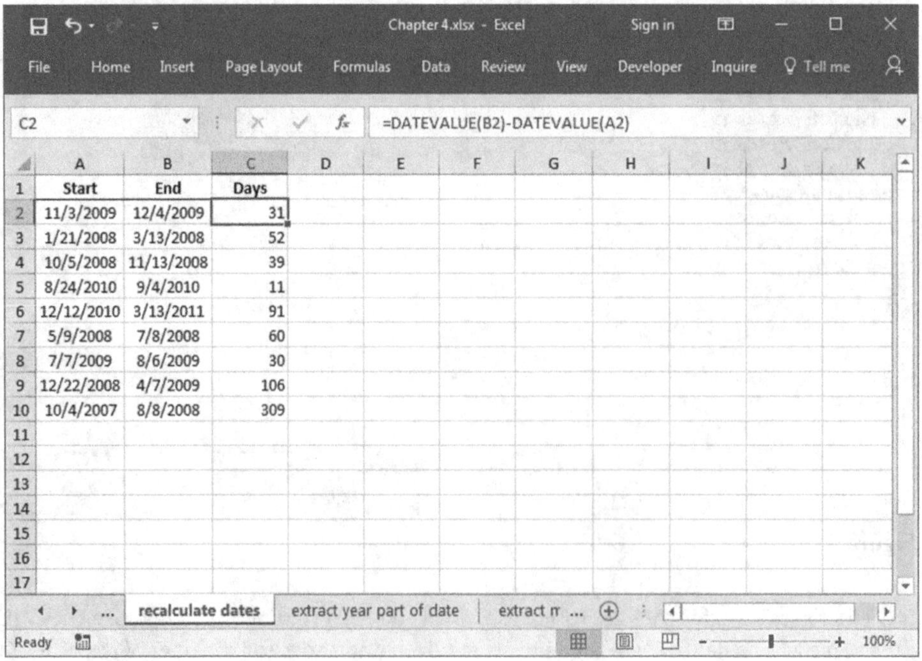

Figure 4–10

Use the YEAR function to extract the year part of a date

As shown in Figure 4–11, column A of a worksheet contains a list of dates formatted in different ways. To determine the year corresponding to a date, use the YEAR function. This function returns the year as an integer in the range 1900 to 9999. If the year is not specified, as in cell A9, the year is assumed to be the current year.

▶ To extract the year as part of a date:

1. In cells A2:A10, generate a list of dates using different formats.

2. Select cells B2:B10 and type the following formula: **=YEAR(A2)**.

3. Press **<Ctrl+Enter>**.

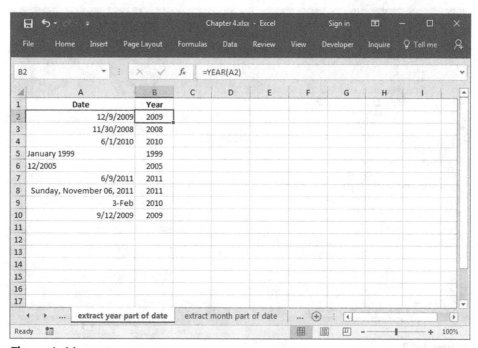

Figure 4–11

Use the MONTH function to extract the month part of a date

For this tip, use the worksheet from the previous example. Column A contains dates formatted in different ways. To determine the month part of a date, use the MONTH function. This function returns the month corresponding to a date as an integer in the range 1 to 12.

▶ To extract the month part of a date:

1. In cells A2:A10, generate a list of dates using different formats.

2. Select cells B2:B10 and type the following formula: **=MONTH(A2)**.

3. Press **<Ctrl+Enter>**.

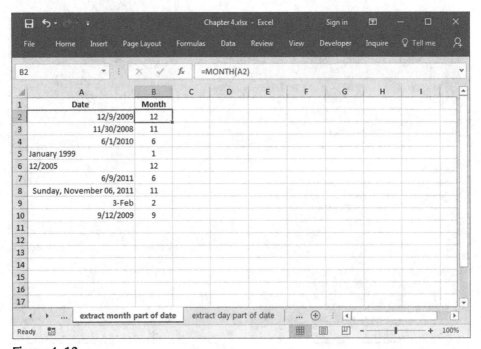

Figure 4–12

Use the DAY function to extract the day part of a date

Once again, use the worksheet from the previous two examples. Column A contains dates in different formats. To determine the day part of a date, use the DAY function. This function returns the day corresponding to a date as an integer in the range 1 to 31.

▶ To extract the day as part of a date:

1. In cells A2:A10 generate a list of dates using different formats.

2. Select cells B2:B10 and type the following formula: **=DAY(A2)**.

3. Press **<Ctrl+Enter>**.

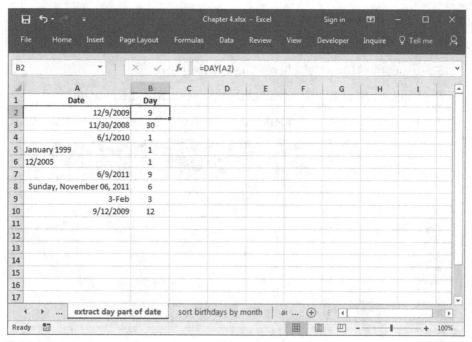

Figure 4–13

NOTE: If the day part is missing (see rows 5 and 6), the function returns the value 1.

Use the MONTH and DAY functions to sort birthdays by month

The worksheet in Figure 4–14 contains a list of employees and their birthdays. This list has to be sorted by month, which is not possible with Excel's usual sort function. Use this tip to insert a supporting column to convert the month and day dates to serial values.

▶ To sort birthdays by month:

1. In cells A2:B10 generate a list of employees and their birthdays.

2. Select cells C2:C10 and type the following formula:
   =MONTH (B2)*100+DAY(B2).

3. Press **<Ctrl+Enter>**.

4. Select cell C1.

5. From the **Home** tab choose the **Editing** bar.

6. Click on **Sort & Filter** and choose **Sort smallest to largest**.

7. Format the column as **General** to display serial values rather than dates.

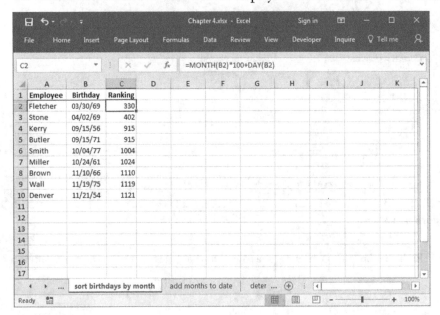

Figure 4–14

Use the DATE function to add months to a date

Let's say we want to add a number of months to a given start date. In a new worksheet, list different start dates in column A. In column B, enter the number of months to be added to or subtracted from the start date. Based on that data, the end date can be calculated.

▶ To add months to or subtract months from dates:

1. In cells A2:A10 list some start dates, as shown in Figure 4–15.

2. In cells B2:B10 list the number of months to add or subtract.

3. Select cells C2:C10 and type the following formula:
   =DATE(YEAR(A2), MONTH(A2)+B2,DAY(A2)).

4. Press **<Ctrl+Enter>**.

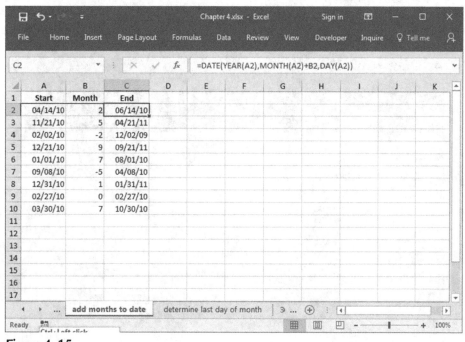

Figure 4–15

NOTE: To determine an end date in the past, put a minus sign in front of the number of months.

Use the EOMONTH function to determine the last day of a month

To find the last day of a month, use the EOMONTH function (EOMONTH(*start_date*, *offset_months*)). This function returns the date of the last day of the month that is offset_months from start_date. If the function is not available, load the Analysis ToolPak add-in. From the **File** tab, choose **Options**. Select **Add-Ins**. From the dropdown **Manage** list, select **Excel Add-Ins** and click **GO**. In the **Add-Ins** dialog, tick the **Analysis ToolPak** box and click **OK**.

▶ To determine the last day of a month:

1. In cells A2:A10, enter some dates.

2. In cells B2:B10, enter the desired offset from the start date (positive or negative values).

3. Select cells C2:C10 and type the following formula:
   =EOMONTH (A2,B2).

4. Press **<Ctrl+Enter>**.

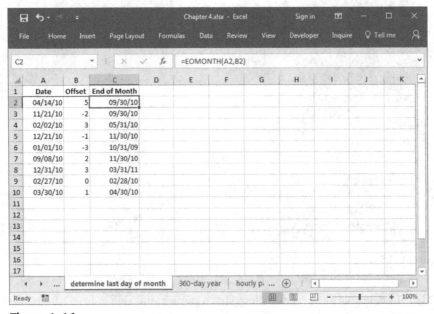

Figure 4–16

Use the DAYS360 function to calculate with a 360-day year

If there is an accounting system installed that is based on 12 30-day months, the DAYS360 function can be used. This function returns the number of days between two dates based on a 360-day year.

Here is the syntax:

DAYS360(*start_date*, *end_date*, *method*)

start_date: The start date.

end_date: The end date.

method: A logical value that specifies which method to use (U.S. or European).

U.S. (NASD) method: Used if *method* is FALSE. If the starting date is the 31st of a month, it is the 30th of the same month. If the ending date is the 31st of a month and the starting date is earlier than the 30th of the month, the ending date is the first of the next month; otherwise, the ending date is the 30th of the same month.

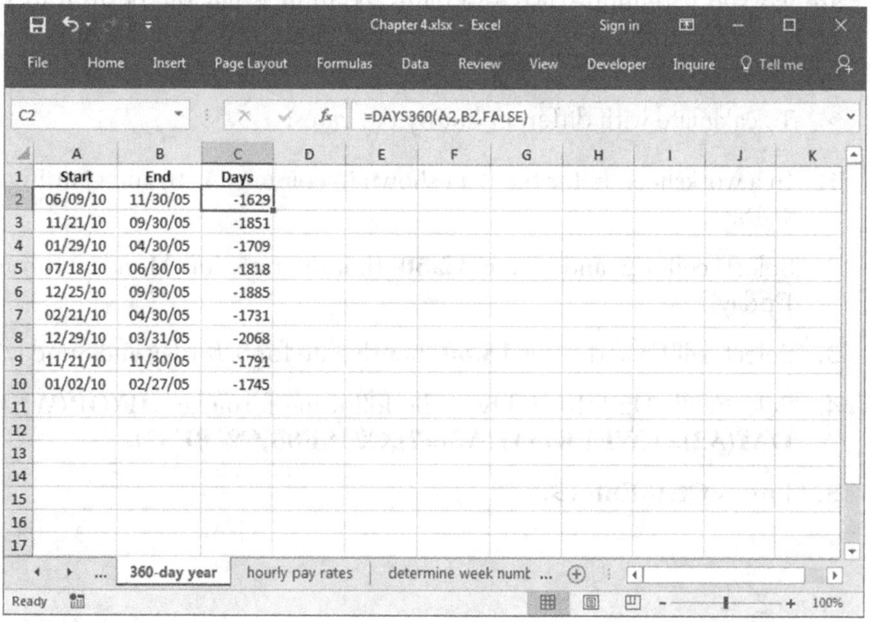

Figure 4–17

European method: Used if *method* is TRUE. Starting or ending dates on the 31st of a month are the 30th of the same month.

▶ To calculate with 360-day years:

1. In a worksheet, copy the data in columns A and B from Figure 4–17.

2. Select cells C2:C10 and type the following formula: **=DAYS360 (A2,B2,FALSE)**.

3. Press **<Ctrl+Enter>**.

Use the WEEKDAY function to calculate with different hourly pay rates

Many companies calculate payroll using hourly rates for each employee. The hourly rates depend on which days are worked, as work performed on the weekend is often paid at a higher rate than work performed Monday through Friday.

In this example, different hourly rates are defined based on which days are worked. Column A lists the dates, column B has the custom format **DDD** to show the day of the week, and column C lists the number of hours worked.

▶ To calculate with different hourly pay rates:

1. In a worksheet, enter the data shown in columns A, B, and C in Figure 4–18.

2. Select cell F2 and enter **12.50** (hourly rate for Monday through Friday).

3. Select cell F5 and enter **18.50** (hourly rate for Saturday and Sunday).

4. Select cells D2:D10 and type the following formula: **=IF(OR(WEEK DAY(A2)=1,WEEKDAY(A2)=7),C2*$F$5,C2*$F$2)**.

5. Press **<Ctrl+Enter>**.

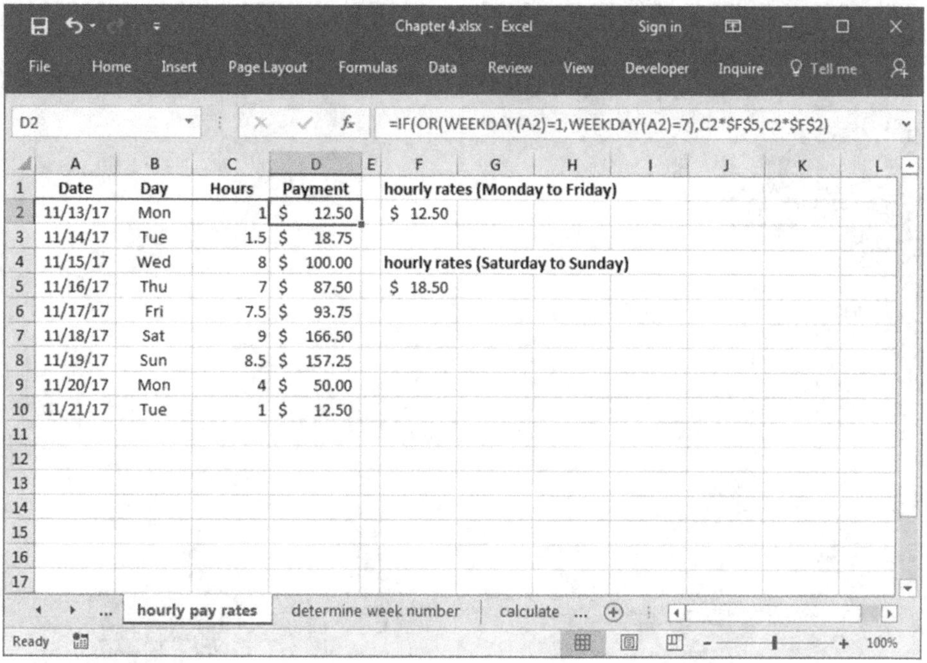

Figure 4-18

Use the WEEKNUM function to determine the week number

To determine the week number of a date (a very common practice in Europe), load the Analysis ToolPak add-in. From the **File** tab, choose **Options**. Select **Add-Ins**. From the dropdown **Manage** list, select **Excel Add-Ins** and click **GO**. In the **Add-Ins** dialog, tick the **Analysis ToolPak** box and click **OK**.

Now the WEEKNUM function is available. This function returns a number that indicates where the week falls numerically within a year.

▶ To determine the week number:

1. Type different dates of the year in cells A2:A10.

2. Select cells B2:B10 and type the following formula: **=WEEKNUM(A2)**.

3. Press **<Ctrl+Enter>**.

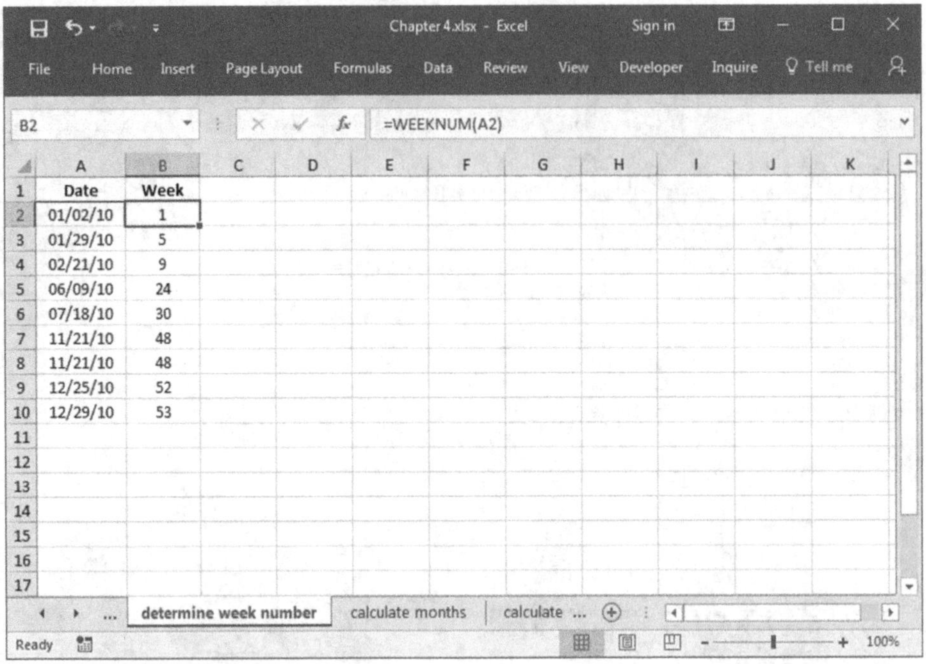

Figure 4–19

Use the EDATE function to calculate months

If a few months need to be added to or subtracted from a date, the EDATE function is very useful. This function returns a serial number that represents the date that is the indicated number of months before or after a specified date (offset).

In this example, column A of a worksheet contains the start dates. In column B, enter the offset in months to be added or subtracted. The result should show up in column C.

▶ To use EDATE and add or subtract a number of months to start dates:

1. Enter different start dates in column A.

2. Enter offset months in column B.

3. Select cells C2:C10 and type the following formula: **=EDATE(A2,B2)**.

4. Press **<Ctrl+Enter>**.

	A	B	C	D	E	F	G	H	I	J	K
1	**Start**	**Offset**	**End**								
2	09/23/10	1	10/23/10								
3	12/11/10	3	03/11/11								
4	01/01/10	6	07/01/10								
5	08/08/10	-5	03/08/10								
6	10/21/10	12	10/21/11								
7	11/17/10	1	12/17/10								
8	05/09/10	-3	02/09/10								
9	10/30/10	2	12/30/10								
10	01/09/10	10	11/09/10								

Cell C2: =EDATE(A2,B2)

Sheet tabs: calculate months | calculate workdays | number of wo...

Figure 4–20

NOTE: To use the EDATE function, the Analysis ToolPak add-in needs to be installed as described in the previous example.

Use the WORKDAY function to calculate workdays

A worksheet is used to schedule a project. The project contains the start date and five major steps. Each step is estimated to take a certain number of days to accomplish. To determine the correct end date, weekends and additional days off needs to be taken into consideration. To perform this task, use the WORKDAY function from the Analysis ToolPak add-in. This function returns a date that is the indicated number of workdays before or after a date. Workdays exclude weekends and any dates identified as holidays. The syntax is as follows:

WORKDAY(*start_date*, *days*, *holidays*)

start_date: The start date.

days: The total number of available days, not counting weekends and holidays, before or after start_date. Both positive and negative values are acceptable.

holidays: (optional) One or more dates that are to be excluded from the work schedule.

▶ To determine the end date of a project:

1. In cell C2, enter the start date of the project.

2. In column B, enter the estimated days to finish each step.

3. In cell D2, type the following formula:
   =WORKDAY(C3,B3, $F$2:$F$8).

4. In cells F1:F8, additional holidays can be listed individually.

5. In cell C3, type the formula **=D2+1**.

6. Fill cells C3 and D2 down to C6 and D6.

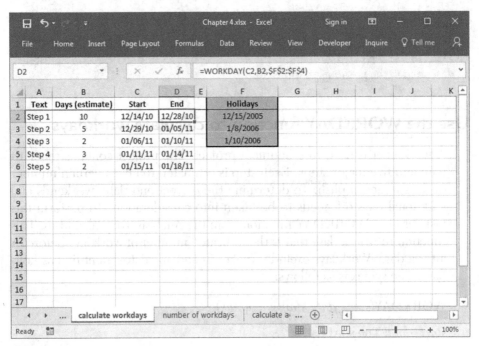

Figure 4–21

Use the NETWORKDAYS function to determine the number of workdays

In this example, a project has to be scheduled. Each of the five steps has fixed start and end dates. To determine the number of complete workdays between the start and end dates, the NETWORKDAYS function from the Analysis ToolPak add-in can be used. This function excludes weekends and any dates identified as non-workdays and holidays. The syntax is as follows:

NETWORKDAYS(*start_date*, *end_date*, *holidays*)

start_date: The start date.

end_date: The end date.

holidays: (optional) One or more dates that are to be excluded from the work schedule.

▶ To determine the number of workdays:

1. In column B, type the start date of each step.

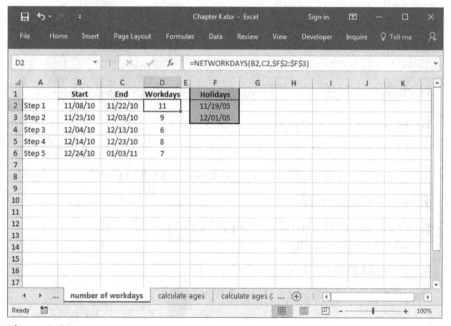

Figure 4–22

2. In column C, type the end date of each step.

3. List additional holidays in cells F2:F6.

4. Select cells D2:D6 and type the following formula:
   =NETWORKDAYS (B2,C2,$F$2:$F$6).

5. Press **<Ctrl+Enter>**.

Use the YEARFRAC function to calculate ages of employees

To calculate the difference between two dates, use the YEARFRAC function from the Analysis ToolPak add-in. This function calculates the fraction of the year represented by the number of whole days between start_date and end_date. The syntax is:

YEARFRAC(*start_date*, *end_date*, *basis*)

start_date: The start date.

end_date: The end date.

basis: The count basis to use: 0 or omitted = U.S. (NASD) 30/360, 1 = actual/actual, 2 = actual/360, 3 = actual/365, or 4 = European 30/360.

▶ To calculate the age of employees based on the current date:

1. In column A, list the names of employees.

2. In column B, enter their birthdays.

3. Select cells C2:C10 and type the formula **TODAY()**.

4. Press **<Ctrl+Enter>**.

5. Select cells D2:D10 and type the following formula:
   =YEARFRAC (B2,C2,0).

6. Press **<Ctrl+Enter>**.

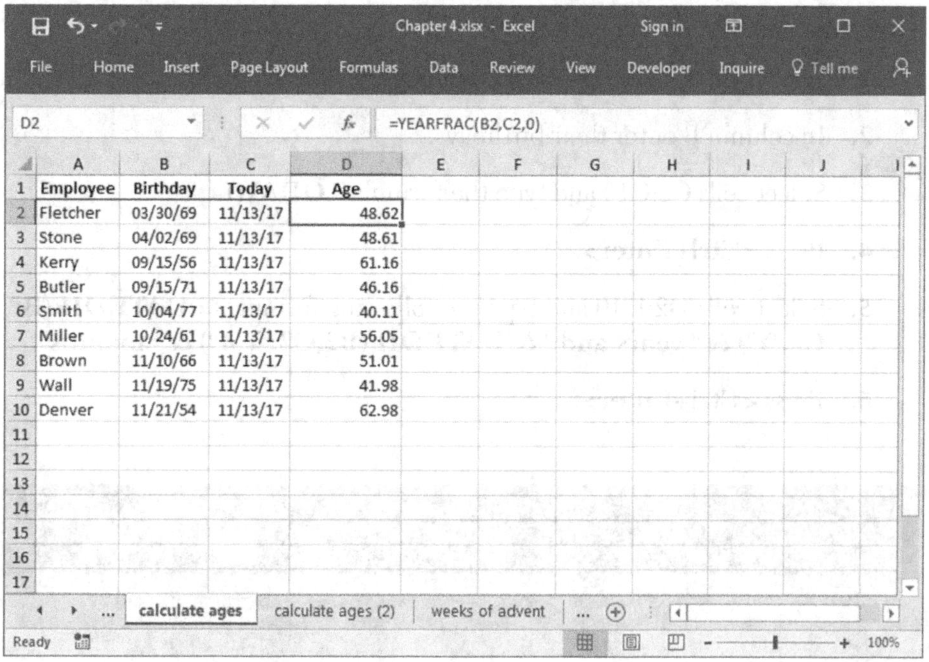

	A	B	C	D
1	Employee	Birthday	Today	Age
2	Fletcher	03/30/69	11/13/17	48.62
3	Stone	04/02/69	11/13/17	48.61
4	Kerry	09/15/56	11/13/17	61.16
5	Butler	09/15/71	11/13/17	46.16
6	Smith	10/04/77	11/13/17	40.11
7	Miller	10/24/61	11/13/17	56.05
8	Brown	11/10/66	11/13/17	51.01
9	Wall	11/19/75	11/13/17	41.98
10	Denver	11/21/54	11/13/17	62.98

Figure 4–23

Use the DATEDIF function to calculate ages of employees

To calculate the exact age of employees, use the undocumented DATEDIF function from the Analysis ToolPak add-in. This function calculates the exact number of years, months, and days between two dates. The syntax is:

DATEDIF(*start_date*, *end_date*, *format*)

start_date: The start date.

end_date: The end date.

format: Indicates the format to use. “y” gives the difference in years, “m” in months, “d” in days; “ym” gives the difference in months, ignoring the year; “yd” in days, ignoring the year; and “md” in days, ignoring the month and year.

▶ To calculate the ages of employees:

1. In column A list the names of employees.

2. In column B enter their birthdays.

3. Select cells C2:C10 and type the formula **TODAY()**.

4. Press **<Ctrl+Enter>**.

5. Select cells D2:D10 and type the following formula: **= DATEDIF(B2, C2,"Y") & " years and " & DATEDIF(B2,C2,"YM") & " months"**.

6. Press **<Ctrl+Enter>**.

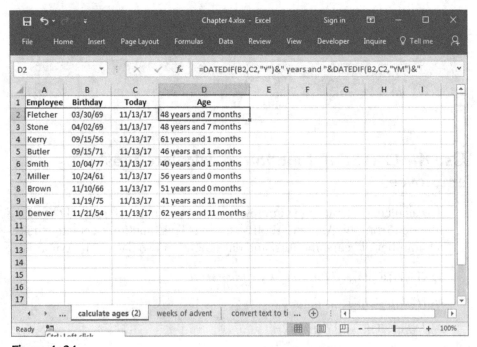

Figure 4–24

Use the WEEKDAY function to calculate the weeks of Advent

As a practical task using previously learned functions, the start date of each week of Advent can be calculated easily. Consider that Advent begins on the fourth Sunday before Christmas. Enter in a cell the date of Christmas and use the WEEKDAY function to calculate when each week of Advent begins.

▶ To calculate when the weeks of Advent begin for 2013:

1. In cell B2 enter **12/25/2013**.

2. In cell B4, enter this formula to find the first week of Advent: **=B1(WEEKDAY(B1,2))-21**.

3. Enter this formula in cell B5: **=B1-(WEEKDAY(B1,2))-14**.

4. Enter this formula in cell B6: **=B1-(WEEKDAY(B1,2))-7**.

5. Enter this formula in cell B7: **=B1-(WEEKDAY(B1,2))**.

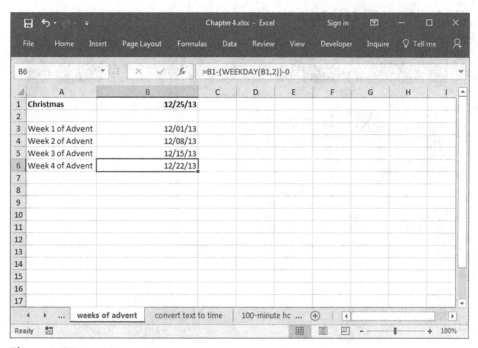

Figure 4–25

Use the TIMEVALUE function to convert text to time

In this example, a text string has to be converted to a valid time. Columns A and C contain different start and end times as part of a standardized text string. It is possible to extract the times and convert them to valid time values that can be used as the basis for calculations. To convert text into a valid time, use the TIMEVALUE function. This function returns the decimal number of the time represented by a text string. The decimal number is a value ranging from 0 to 0.99999999, representing the time from 0:00:00 (12:00:00 midnight) to 23:59:59 (11:59:59 p.m.).

▶ To extract and convert text to time:

1. Select cells B2:B10 and type the following formula: **=TIMEVALUE (MID(A2,8,5))**.

2. Press **<Ctrl+Enter>**.

3. Select cells D2:D10 and type the following formula: **=TIMEVALUE (MID(C2,6,5))**.

4. Press **<Ctrl+Enter>**.

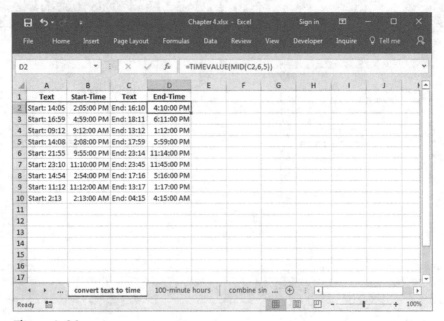

Figure 4–26

5. Select cells B2:B10 and D2:D10.

6. Press **Ctrl + 1** and select the **Number** tab, click **Time** under **Category**, then select the **1:30:55 p.m.** option in the **Type** box.

7. Click **OK**.

Use a custom format to create a time format

When you enter time values in cells, you need to type the colon between the hours and minutes. However, this is unnecessary if you use a custom format.

▶   To create a customized time format:

1. Enter time values without colons and select the cells.

2. Press **Ctrl + 1**, select the **Number** tab, and click on **Custom** under **Category**.

3. Type **00":"00** as the custom format.

4. Click **OK**.

Figure 4–27

NOTE: You can also use the AutoCorrect options. Click the **File** tab and then click **Options**. Then click **Proofing** and afterwards click **AutoCorrect Options**. Type two commas in the **Replace** field and type the colon in the **With** field. Click **Add** to insert this option. Test this by typing **1200** in a cell. Excel corrects the input to 12:00.

Use the HOUR function to calculate with 100-minute hours

Some companies record working time in 100-minute hours. For example, the time 6:45 a.m. is converted to 6:75, which sometimes makes further calculations easier. To convert to this format, extract the minutes from the time and divide them by 60 using the MINUTE function. This function returns the minutes of a time value. The minute is given as an integer, ranging from 0 to 59. The hours can be extracted with the HOUR function. This function returns the hour of a time value as an integer ranging from 0 (12:00 a.m.) to 23 (11:00 p.m.).

▶ To convert normal time to 100-minute hours:

1. In cells A2:A10, list work dates.

2. In cells B2:B10, enter the start time for each day.

3. In cells C2:C10, record the end time for each day.

4. Select cells D2:D10 and type the following formula:
    =HOUR(C2-B2)+ MINUTE(C2-B2)/60.

5. Press **<Ctrl+Enter>**.

	A	B	C	D
1	Date	Start	End	Time
2	11/08/04	8:30	16:45	8.25
3	11/09/04	7:15	15:30	8.25
4	11/10/04	7:59	17:06	9.12
5	11/11/04	9:11	18:34	9.38
6	11/12/04	8:00	17:00	9.00
7	11/15/04	8:05	19:01	10.93
8	11/18/04	8:55	17:01	8.10
9	11/19/04	9:12	15:02	5.83
10	11/20/04	8:34	14:55	6.35

Figure 4–28

Use the TIME function to combine single time parts

The worksheet in Figure 4–29 shows single time parts in each column. Column B contains hours, column C contains minutes, and column D contains seconds. All three columns need to be combined into one time, as shown in column E. To do this, use the TIME function. This function returns the decimal number for a particular time. The syntax is:

TIME(*hour, minute, second*)

hour: A number from 0 to 23 that represents the hour. Any value greater than 23 will be divided by 24, and the remainder will be treated as the hour value.

minute: A number from 0 to 59 that represents minutes. Any value greater than 59 will be converted to hours and minutes.

second: A number from 0 to 59 that represents seconds. Any value greater than 59 will be converted to hours, minutes, and seconds.

▶ To combine single time parts into a valid time:

1. Select cells E2:E10 and type the formula **=TIME(B2,C2,D2)**.

2. Press **<Ctrl+Enter>**.

3. From the **Format** menu, select **Cells**.

4. Select the **Number** tab and click **Custom** under **Category**.

5. Enter **hh:mm:ss** as the custom format.

6. Click **OK**.

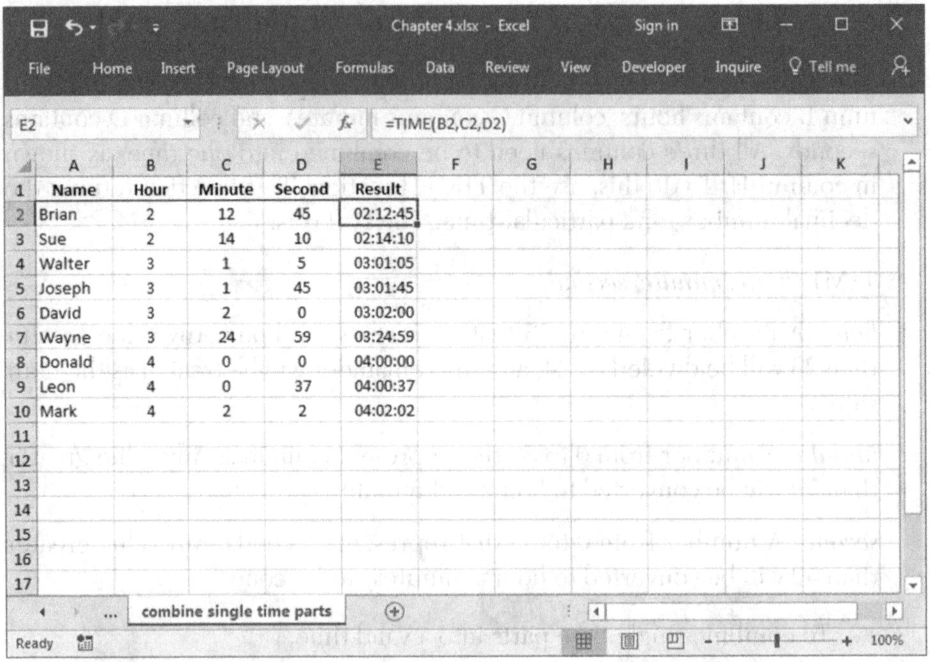

Figure 4–29

Basic Statistical Functions

5

Use the MAX function to determine the largest value in a range

This example finds the largest value in the range A3:D11 by using the MAX function. The function's return value is the largest value in a set.

MAX(*number1*, *number2*, ...)

number1, *number2*, ...: From 1 to 30 numbers for which you want to find the largest value. It is possible to use a cell reference; however, the cells must contain numbers or values that can be converted to numbers.

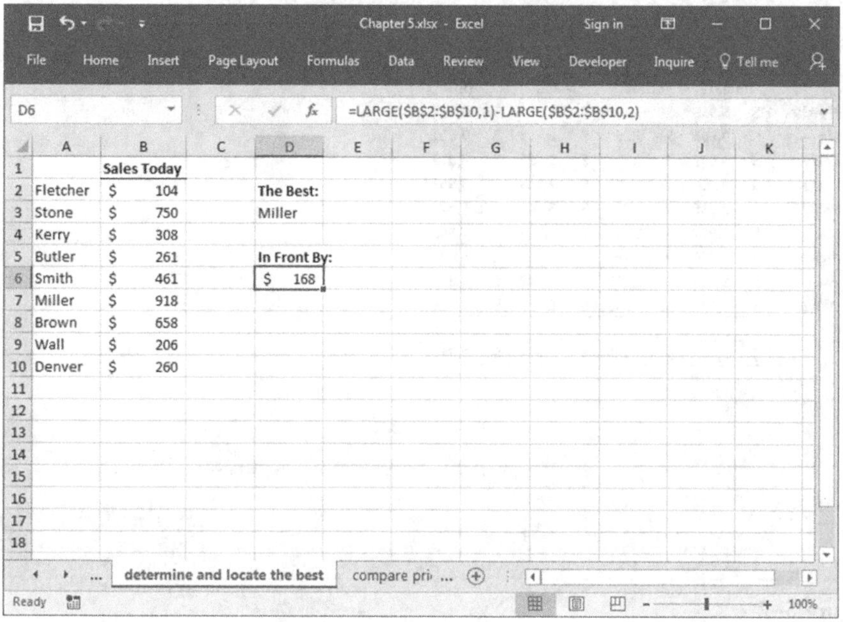

Figure 5–1

NOTE: In Chapter 10, you will learn how to automatically mark and shade the largest value in a range.

▶ To determine the largest value:

1. In cells A3:D11 type any values.

2. In cell B1 type the formula **=MAX(A3:D11)**.

3. Press **<Enter>**.

Use the MIN function to discover the lowest sales volume for a month

In a company, employee sales are monitored. Columns B to E contain the sales for the first four months of the year. To determine the lowest sales for a given month, use the MIN function. The function's return value is the smallest value in a set.

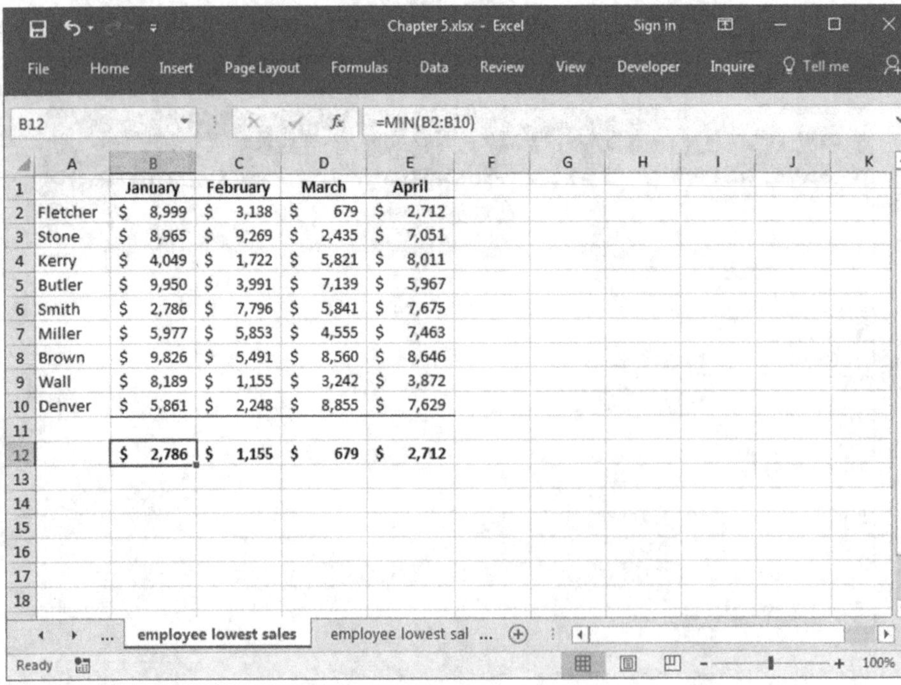

	A	B	C	D	E
		January	February	March	April
2	Fletcher	$ 8,999	$ 3,138	$ 679	$ 2,712
3	Stone	$ 8,965	$ 9,269	$ 2,435	$ 7,051
4	Kerry	$ 4,049	$ 1,722	$ 5,821	$ 8,011
5	Butler	$ 9,950	$ 3,991	$ 7,139	$ 5,967
6	Smith	$ 2,786	$ 7,796	$ 5,841	$ 7,675
7	Miller	$ 5,977	$ 5,853	$ 4,555	$ 7,463
8	Brown	$ 9,826	$ 5,491	$ 8,560	$ 8,646
9	Wall	$ 8,189	$ 1,155	$ 3,242	$ 3,872
10	Denver	$ 5,861	$ 2,248	$ 8,855	$ 7,629
11					
12		$ 2,786	$ 1,155	$ 679	$ 2,712

Cell B12: =MIN(B2:B10)

Figure 5–2

NOTE: In Chapter 10, you will learn how to automatically shade the smallest value in each column.

MIN(*number1, number2, ...*)

number1, number2, ...: From 1 to 30 numbers for which you want to find the smallest value. It is possible to use a cell reference; however, the cells must contain numbers or values that can be converted to numbers.

▶ To determine the lowest monthly sales:

1. In a worksheet, copy the range A1:E10 shown in Figure 5–2.

2. elect cells B12:E12 and type the following formula: **=MIN(B2:B10)**.

3. Press **<Ctrl+Enter>**.

Use the MINIFS function to discover the lowest sales volume for a month based on criteria

Similar scenario to the previous example with the addition of the Region column. Column B contains the region in which the sales people work. Columns C to F contain the sales for the first four months of the year. To determine the lowest sales for a given month in the "West" region, use the MINIFS function. The function's return value is the smallest value in a set based upon criteria.

MINIFS(min_range,criteria_range1, criteria1,[criteria_range2, criteria2],...)

Min_range is the range of values (must be numbers) from which to determine the minimum. Up to 126 criteria can be placed in the function after the min_range. In this example, we only use one – the region with a value of "West"

▶ To determine the lowest monthly sales for the West region:

1. In a worksheet, copy the range A1:F10 shown in Figure 5–3.

2. Select cells C13:F13 and type the following formula:
   =MINIFS(C2: C10,$B$2:$B$10,"West")

3. Press **<Ctrl+Enter>**.

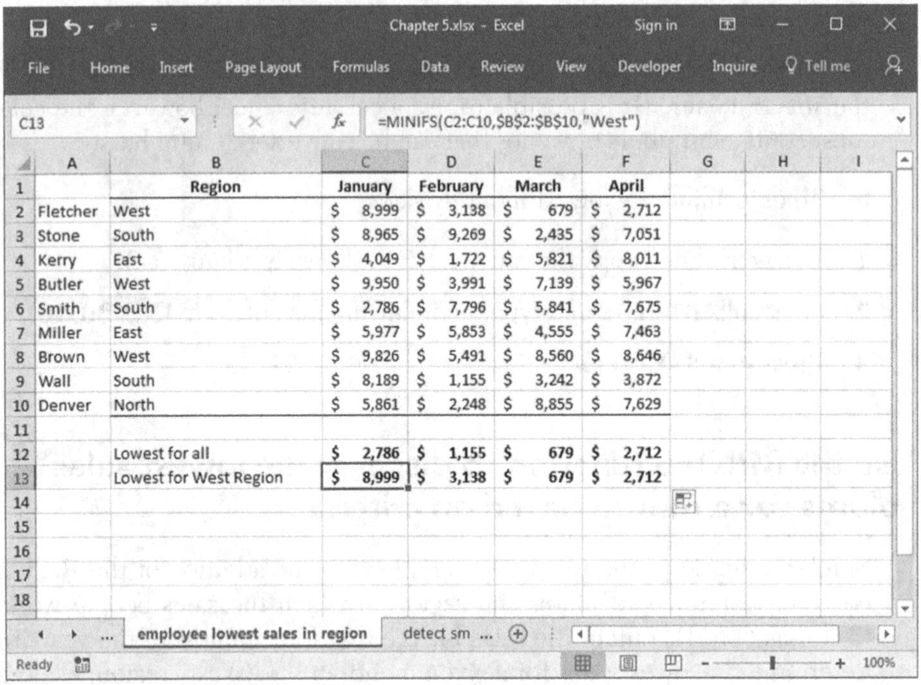

	A	B	C	D	E	F
1		Region	January	February	March	April
2	Fletcher	West	$ 8,999	$ 3,138	$ 679	$ 2,712
3	Stone	South	$ 8,965	$ 9,269	$ 2,435	$ 7,051
4	Kerry	East	$ 4,049	$ 1,722	$ 5,821	$ 8,011
5	Butler	West	$ 9,950	$ 3,991	$ 7,139	$ 5,967
6	Smith	South	$ 2,786	$ 7,796	$ 5,841	$ 7,675
7	Miller	East	$ 5,977	$ 5,853	$ 4,555	$ 7,463
8	Brown	West	$ 9,826	$ 5,491	$ 8,560	$ 8,646
9	Wall	South	$ 8,189	$ 1,155	$ 3,242	$ 3,872
10	Denver	North	$ 5,861	$ 2,248	$ 8,855	$ 7,629
11						
12		Lowest for all	$ 2,786	$ 1,155	$ 679	$ 2,712
13		Lowest for West Region	$ 8,999	$ 3,138	$ 679	$ 2,712

Figure 5-3

Use the MAXIFS function to discover the highest sales volume for a month based on criteria

Similar scenario to the previous example but seeking the highest sales amount. Column B contains the region in which the sales people work. Columns C to F contain the sales for the first four months of the year. To determine the highest sales for a given month in the "West" region, use the MAXIFS function. The function's return value is the highest value in a set based upon criteria.

MAXIFS(max_range,criteria_range1, criteria1,[criteria_range2, criteria2],...)

Max_range is the range of values (must be numbers) from which to determine the maximum. Up to 126 criteria can be placed in the function after the Max_range. In this example, we only use one – the region with a value of "West"

▶ To determine the highest monthly sales for the West region:

1. In a worksheet, copy the range A1:F10 shown in Figure 5–4.
2. Select cells C13:F13 and type the following formula: **=MAXIFS(C2: C10,$B$2:$B$10,"West")**
3. Press **<Ctrl+Enter>**.

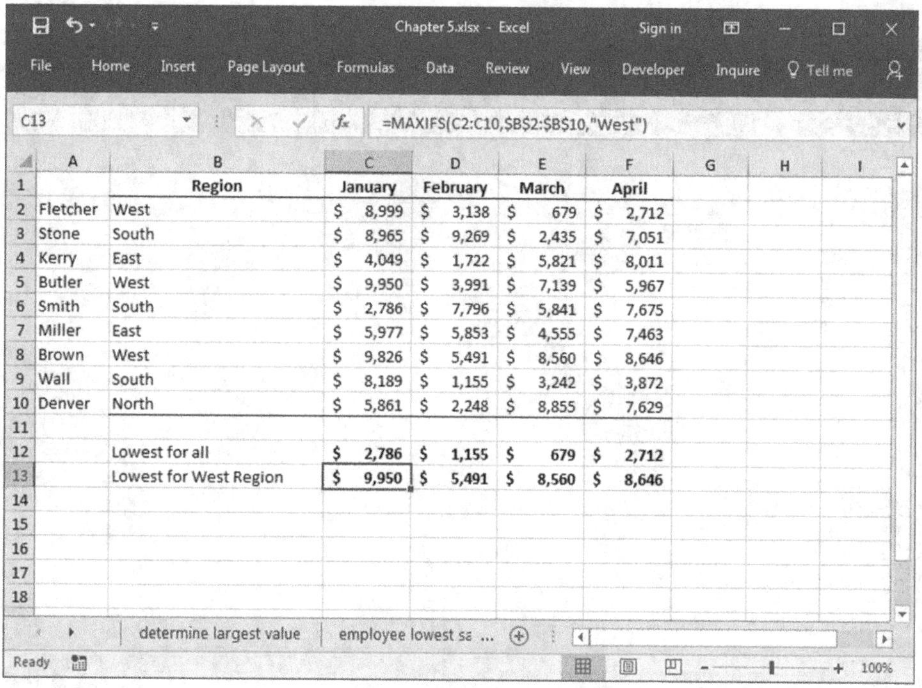

	A	B	C	D	E	F
1		Region	January	February	March	April
2	Fletcher	West	$ 8,999	$ 3,138	$ 679	$ 2,712
3	Stone	South	$ 8,965	$ 9,269	$ 2,435	$ 7,051
4	Kerry	East	$ 4,049	$ 1,722	$ 5,821	$ 8,011
5	Butler	West	$ 9,950	$ 3,991	$ 7,139	$ 5,967
6	Smith	South	$ 2,786	$ 7,796	$ 5,841	$ 7,675
7	Miller	East	$ 5,977	$ 5,853	$ 4,555	$ 7,463
8	Brown	West	$ 9,826	$ 5,491	$ 8,560	$ 8,646
9	Wall	South	$ 8,189	$ 1,155	$ 3,242	$ 3,872
10	Denver	North	$ 5,861	$ 2,248	$ 8,855	$ 7,629
11						
12		Lowest for all	$ 2,786	$ 1,155	$ 679	$ 2,712
13		Lowest for West Region	$ 9,950	$ 5,491	$ 8,560	$ 8,646

Figure 5–4

Use the MIN function to detect the smallest value in a column

To determine the smallest value in a single column, the MIN function is used. This function returns the smallest value in a set of values. The syntax is described in the previous tip.

▶   To determine the smallest value in a column:

1.   In column A, type any values down to cell A10.

2.   Select cell B1 and type the following formula: **=MIN(A1:A10)**.

3.   Press **<Enter>**.

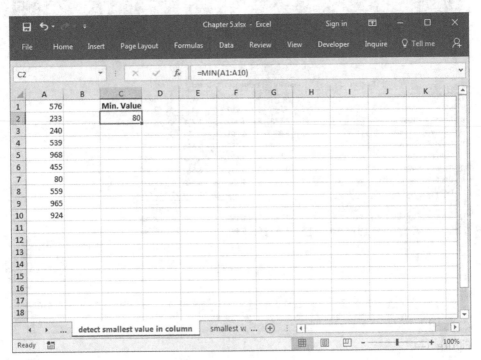

Figure 5–5

NOTE: The MIN function can be used to determine the smallest value in a row. For the smallest value in the first row, use the formula =MIN(1:1). To get the smallest value of the first three rows, use the following function: =MIN(1:3).

Use the SMALL function to find the smallest values in a list

To determine the smallest value in a list, we can use the MIN function. However, the easiest way to find multiple small values of a range is by using the SMALL function. This function returns the *n*th smallest value in a set of data.

SMALL(*array*, *n*)

array: An array or range of numerical data in which you want to find the *n*th smallest value.

n: The position from the smallest in the array or range of data to return.

▶ To determine the three smallest values of a range:

1. In cells A1:A10, enter any values from 100 to 999.

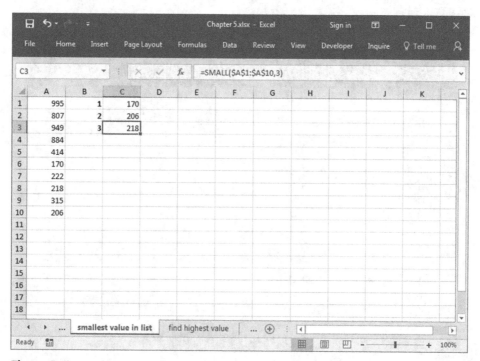

Figure 5–6

2. Select cell C1 and type the following formula **=SMALL($A$1:$A$10,1)** to get the smallest value.

3. In cell C2 type the formula **=SMALL($A$1:$A$10,2)** to get the second smallest value.

4. In cell C3 type the formula **=SMALL($A$1:$A$10,3)** to get the third smallest value.

Use the LARGE function to find the highest values

To determine the highest value in a list, we use the MAX function. To find out multiple high values of a range, the LARGE function can be used. This function returns the *n*th highest value in a set of data.

LARGE(*array*, *n*)

array: Array or range of numerical data in which we want to find the *n*th highest value.

n: The position from the highest in the array or range of data to return.

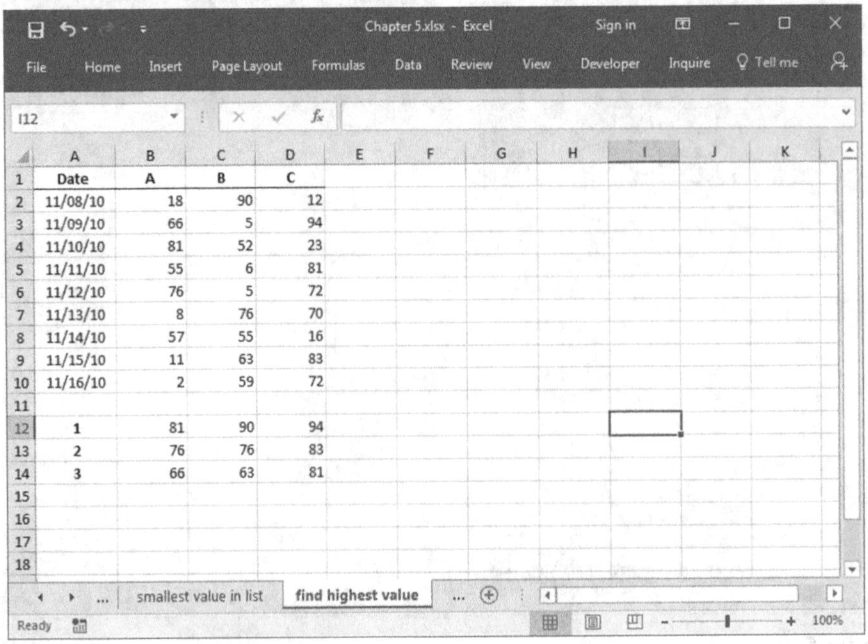

	A	B	C	D
1	Date	A	B	C
2	11/08/10	18	90	12
3	11/09/10	66	5	94
4	11/10/10	81	52	23
5	11/11/10	55	6	81
6	11/12/10	76	5	72
7	11/13/10	8	76	70
8	11/14/10	57	55	16
9	11/15/10	11	63	83
10	11/16/10	2	59	72
11				
12	1	81	90	94
13	2	76	76	83
14	3	66	63	81

Figure 5-7

▶ To determine the three highest values of a range:

1. In cells A2:C10, type any values from 0 to 99.

2. Number cells A12, A13, and A14 with 1, 2, and 3.

3. Select cells B12:D14 and type the following formula:
   =LARGE (B$2:B$10,$A12).

4. Press **<Ctrl+Enter>**.

Use the INDEX, MATCH, and LARGE functions to determine and locate the best salesperson

As seen in the previous tips, it is easy to find out the highest value in a list. But how do you find the one person on a sales team who sold the most? And how do you find out how much ahead of the others he or she is?

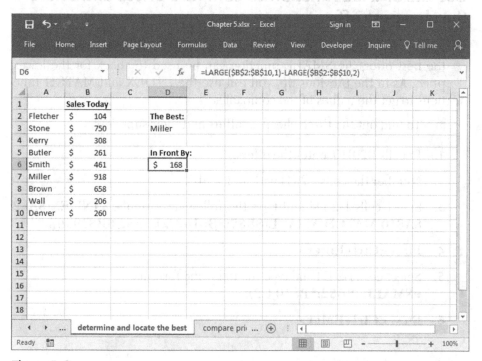

Figure 5–8

Start with the LARGE function to determine the highest sales. Then use the INDEX and MATCH functions to retrieve the name of the employee.

▶ To determine and locate the employee with the most sales:

1. In cells B2:B10 type the daily sales of the employees.

2. Select cell D3 and type the following formula: **=INDEX($A$2:$A$10, MATCH(LARGE($B$2:$B$10,1),$B$2:$B$10,0))**.

3. Press **<Enter>**.

4. Select cell D6 and type the following formula: **=LARGE($B$2:$B$10,1) -LARGE($B$2:$B$10,2)**.

5. Press **<Enter>**.

Use the SMALL function to compare prices and select the cheapest offer

A worksheet lists offers from different suppliers. To decide as to which is the best offer, the SMALL function can be used to check for the lowest price. As in the previous tip, you can use the INDEX and MATCH functions to get the names of the companies.

▶ To find out the three cheapest offers and their suppliers:

1. In cells B2:B10, enter the offers.

2. Number the cells C2:C4 with 1, 2, and 3.

3. Select cells D2:D4 and type the following formula: **=INDEX($A$2: $A$10,MATCH(SMALL($B$2:$B$10,C2),$B$2:$B$10,0))**.

4. Press **<Ctrl+Enter>**.

5. Select cells E2:E4 and type the following formula: **=SMALL ($B$2:$B$10,C2)**.

6. Press **<Ctrl+Enter>**.

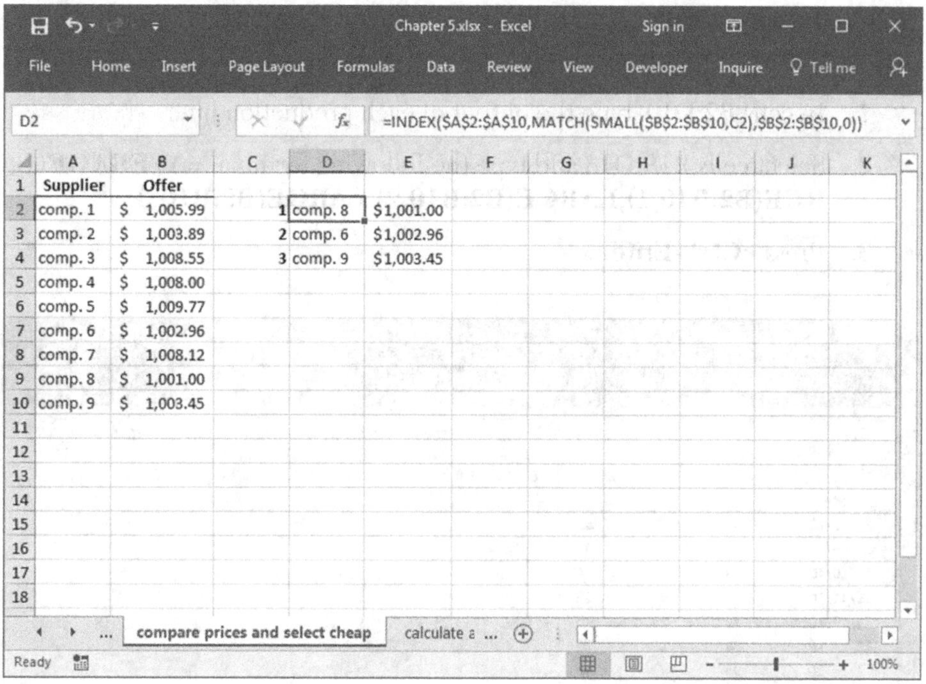

Figure 5-9

Use the AVERAGE function to calculate the average output

In this example, the output of three production lines has been recorded for several days. Now the average of the three highest outputs of each line must be calculated. For this task, Excel provides the AVERAGE function, which returns the average, or arithmetic mean, of the arguments.

AVERAGE(*number1, number2, ...*)

number1, number2, ...: From 1 to 30 numeric arguments for which you want to determine the average. It is also possible to use a cell reference, as shown in this example.

▶ To calculate the average of the three highest capacities of each production line:

1. In cells B2:D10, type the output of each production line.

2. Select cells B13:D13 and type the following formula: **=AVERAGE(LARGE(B2:B10,1),LARGE(B2:B10,2),LARGE(B2:B10,3))**.

3. Press **<Ctrl+Enter>**.

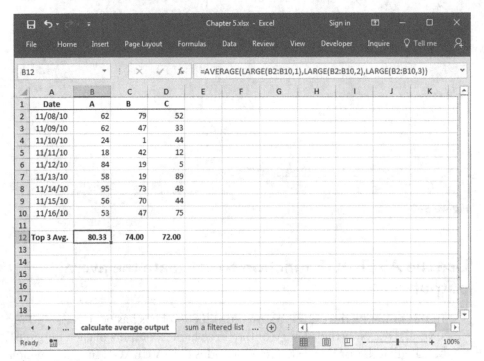

Figure 5–10

Use the SUBTOTAL function to sum a filtered list

When using the Filter option in the Data menu, it is not advisable to use the SUM function to sum filtered rows, because it sums all rows, including those that are hidden. Instead, use the SUBTOTAL function to get the subtotal of a list or database that is visible.

SUBTOTAL(*function_num, ref1, ref2, …*)

function_num: A number from 1 to 11 that specifies a particular function to use for calculating subtotals. (1 = AVERAGE, 2 = COUNT, 3 = COUNTA , 4 = MAX, 5 = MIN, 6 = PRODUCT, 7 = STDEV, 8 = STDEVP, 9 = SUM, 10 = VAR, and 11 = VARP.)

ref1, *ref2*, ...: From 1 to 29 ranges or references for which a subtotal is desired.

▶ To sum a filtered list:

1. In cells B2:B10, type group numbers from 1 to 3.

2. In cells C2:C10, type the daily sales for each group.

3. From the Data menu, select **Filter | AutoFilter**.

4. Select group 1 in the column B filter.

5. Select cell C12 and type the following formula:
   =SUBTOTAL (9,C2:C10).

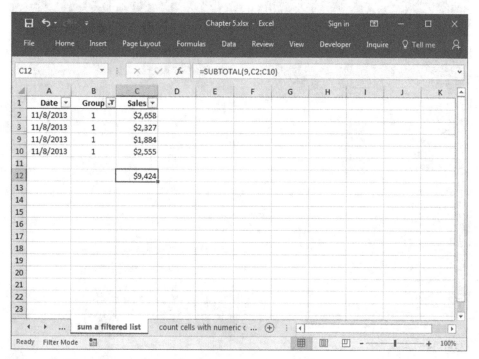

Figure 5–11

Use the COUNT function to count cells containing numeric data

To count all cells that contain numbers, use the COUNT function. Empty cells, logical values, text, and error values are ignored.

COUNT(*value1*, *value2*, ...)

value1, *value2*, ...: From 1 to 30 arguments of any type of data. However, all but numeric data is ignored.

▶ To count the number of cells that contain numbers:

1. In cells A1:A10, type data (numeric and text).

2. Select cell C1 and type the following formula: **=COUNT(A1:A10)**.

3. Press **<Enter>**.

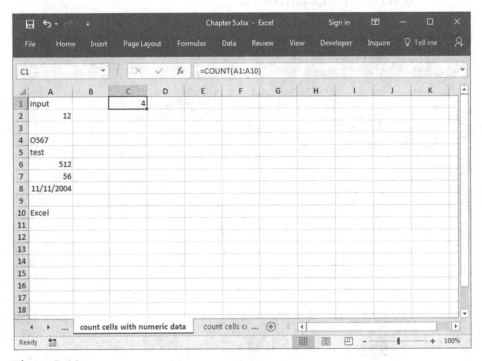

Figure 5–12

NOTE: Arguments that are date and time values are counted as numeric, too.

Use the COUNTA function to count cells containing data

To count all cells that are not empty and contain data in a range or array, use the COUNTA function.

COUNTA(*value1, value2, ...*)

value1, value2, ...: 1 to 30 arguments representing the values to be counted.

▶ To count all cells containing data:

1. In cells A1:A10, type any kind of data (numeric and text).

2. Select cell C1 and type the following formula: **=COUNTA(A1:A10)**.

3. Press **<Enter>**.

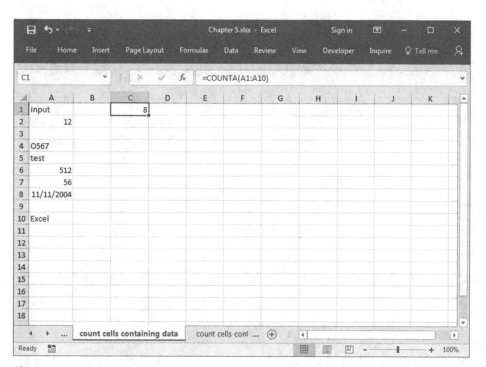

Figure 5–13

NOTE: The COUNTA function does not count empty cells.

Use the COUNTA function to count cells containing text

To count all cells that contain text data, use a combination of functions in one formula. The number of cells with any kind of data is counted with the COUNTA function. All numeric cells are counted with the COUNT function. Just subtract the results of the COUNT function from the results of the COUNTA function, using the same range, to get all cells containing text.

▶ To count only cells with text:

1. In cells A1:A10 type any kind of data (numeric and text).

2. Select cell C1 and type the following formula: **=COUNTA(A1:A10)-COUNT(A1:A10)**.

3. Press **<Enter>**.

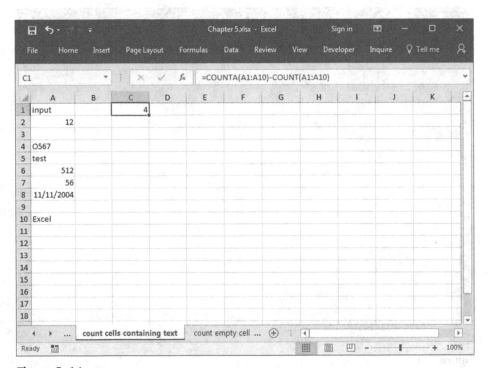

Figure 5–14

Use the COUNTBLANK function to count empty cells

Occasionally it may be useful to determine how many cells in a range are empty. You can use the COUNTBLANK function to count all empty cells in a range of cells.

COUNTBLANK(*range*)

range: The range in which to count blank cells.

▶ To count all empty cells in a specified range:

1. In cells A1:A10 type data (numeric and text). Be sure to leave some of the cells empty.

2. Select cell C1 and type the following formula: **=COUNTBLANK (A1:A10)**.

3. Press **<Enter>**.

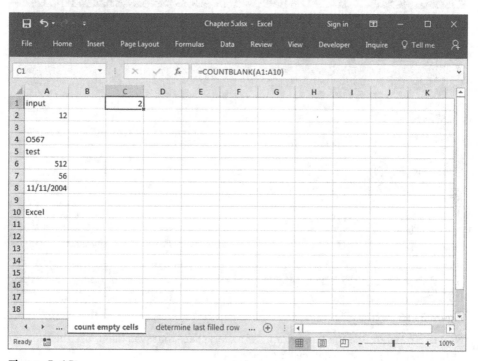

Figure 5–15

Use the COUNTA function to determine the last filled row

In this example, the last row that was filled in on a worksheet needs to be determined. If all cells of a column contain data and are not empty, the COUNTA function can be used. Define as the range the entire column in order to count all filled cells.

▶ To determine the last filled row:

1. In cells A1:A10 type data (numeric and text).

2. Select cell B1 and type the following formula: **=COUNTA(A:A)**.

3. Press **<Enter>**.

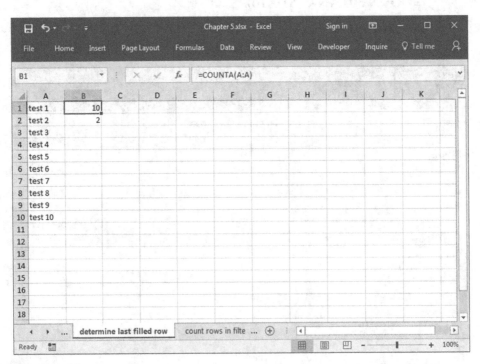

Figure 5–16

NOTE: To determine the last column of a worksheet that was filled, use the function =COUNTA(1:1), as shown in cell B2.

Use the SUBTOTAL function to count rows in filtered lists

When using the Filter option in the Data menu, it is recommended that the COUNT and COUNTA functions not be used, because in a filtered worksheet they count both visible and hidden rows. Instead, use the SUBTOTAL function to get the subtotal of a list or database that is visible. The syntax for the SUBTOTAL function was presented earlier in this chapter.

▶ To count rows in a filtered list:

1. In cells B2:B10, type group numbers from 1 to 3.

2. In cells C2:C10, type the daily sales of each group.

3. From the **Data** menu, select **Filter | AutoFilter**.

4. Select group 1 in the column B filter.

5. Select cell C12 and type the following formula:
   =SUBTOTAL(2,C2:C10) & " rows in filter".

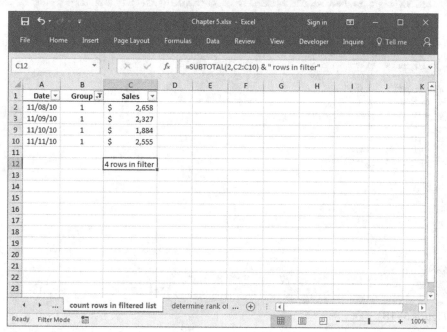

Figure 5–17

NOTE: Use the function =SUBTOTAL(3,B2:B10) & " rows in filter" in cell B12 to count the filtered cells as seen in Figure 5–17.

Use the RANK function to determine the rank of sales

To compare sales of several days and rank them, use the RANK function. This function returns a number that is the rank of a value. In this example, the list can be sorted to display sales in rank order.

1. RANK(*number, ref, order*)

number: The number for which we want to find the rank.

ref: A reference to a list of numbers. Only numeric values are considered.

order: A number that specifies the ranking method. If *order* is 0 or omitted, the numbers are ranked in descending order. If *order* is a nonzero value, the numbers are ranked in ascending order.

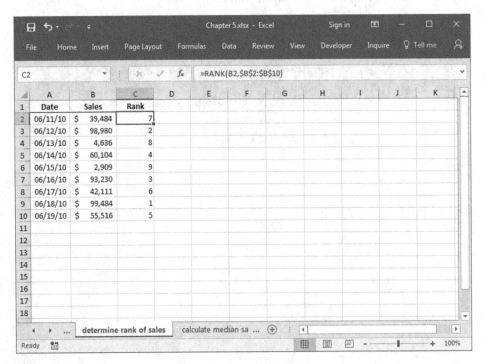

Figure 5–18

NOTE: If you want to rank in ascending order, use this formula:
=RANK(B2,$B$2:$B$10,1).

▶ To rank a list in descending order:

1. In cells A2:A10, enter dates.
2. In cells B2:B10, enter the sales for each date.
3. Select cells C2:C10 and type the following formula: **=RANK(B2, $B$2:$B$10)**.
4. Press **<Ctrl+Enter>**.

Use the MEDIAN function to calculate the median sales

In this example, the average and median sales for a month need to be determined. Use the data shown in Figure 5–19 and calculate the average sales in cell E2. To calculate the median of the sales, use the MEDIAN function.

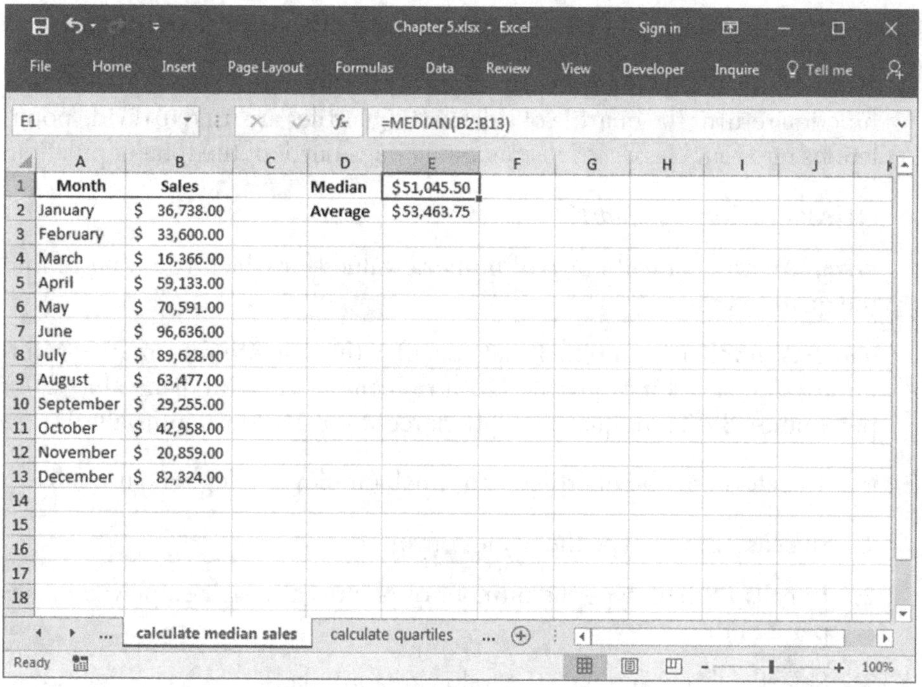

	A	B	C	D	E
1	Month	Sales		Median	$51,045.50
2	January	$ 36,738.00		Average	$53,463.75
3	February	$ 33,600.00			
4	March	$ 16,366.00			
5	April	$ 59,133.00			
6	May	$ 70,591.00			
7	June	$ 96,636.00			
8	July	$ 89,628.00			
9	August	$ 63,477.00			
10	September	$ 29,255.00			
11	October	$ 42,958.00			
12	November	$ 20,859.00			
13	December	$ 82,324.00			

Figure 5–19

NOTE: You can find the average, as shown in cell E2, by using the formula =AVERAGE(B2:B13).

The median is a value in the middle of a set of values; i.e., half the values are above the median and half the values are below it.

MEDIAN(*number1, number2, ...*)

number1, number2,...: From 1 to 30 numbers for which you want to find the median.

▶ To calculate the median sales:

1. In cells A2:A13, type the months.

2. In cells B2:B13, type the monthly sales.

3. Select cell E1 and type the following formula: **=MEDIAN(B2:B13)**.

4. Press **<Enter>**.

Use the QUARTILE function to calculate the quartiles

In this example, the quartile of a list must be determined. The QUARTILE function returns the quartile of a data set. Quartiles are used to divide populations into four classes, each containing one-fourth of the total population.

QUARTILE(*array, quart*)

array: An array or cell range of numeric values for which you want to find the quartile value.

quart: A number from 0 to 4 that specifies the value to return. (0 = Minimum value, 1 = First quartile (25th percentile), 2 = Median value (50th percentile), 3 = Third quartile (75th percentile), 4 = Maximum value).

▶ To determine the quartiles into which employee telephone use falls:

1. In cells A2:A10, type the names of your employees.

2. In cells B2:B10, type the number of phone calls each employee makes per month.

3. Select cells D2 and type the following formula:
   =QUARTILE ($B$2:$B$10,0).

4. Select cells D3 and type the following formula:
   =QUARTILE ($B$2:$B$10,1).

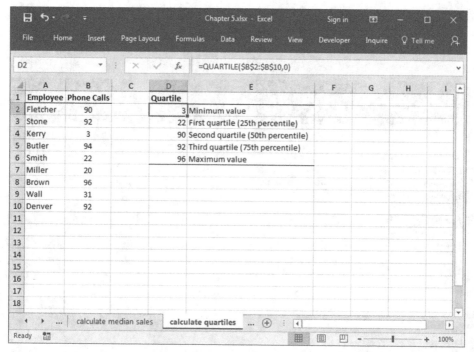

Figure 5-20

Use the STDEV function to determine the standard deviation

In this example, the standard deviation of the number of phone calls must be determined. Use the STDEV function for this purpose. This function measures how widely values in a set differ from the average, or mean, value.

STDEV(*number1, number2, ...*)

number1, number2, ...: From 1 to 30 numerical arguments that represent a population sample.

▶ To determine the standard deviation for employee phone calls:

1. In cells A2:A10, type the names of your employees.

2. In cells B2:B10, type the number of phone calls each employee makes per month.

3. Select cells E2 and type the following formula: **=STDEV(B2:B10)**.

4. Press **<Enter>**.

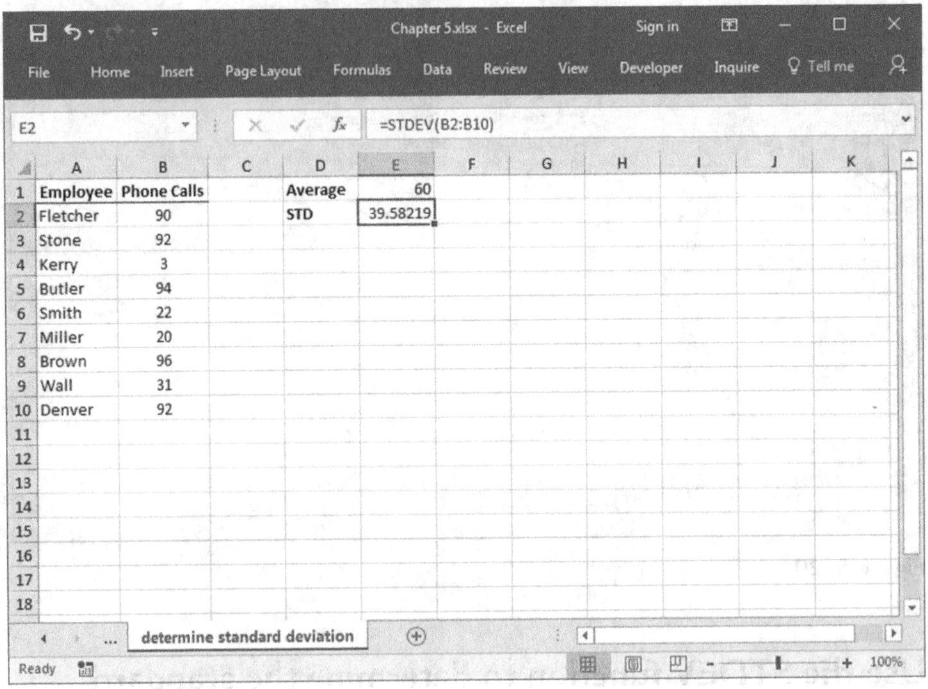

Figure 5–21

Use the FORECAST.LINEAR function to determine future values

In this example, a farm sells milk by the gallons and in order to estimate how much they require in future months, the FORECAST.LINEAR function can be used. By inputting the gallons that have been sold (demand) in past months, the farm can determine an estimate of how many gallons will be demanded in the months ahead. This is a simple estimation and ahead in the chapter, we can determine the confidence of the accuracy of this estimation, but for now we simply get a starting estimate for the rest of the year. As so, we will use a "linear" type of forecast which assumes each month will following a linear pattern of the previous months.

FORECAST.LINEAR(*X,Known_ys,Known_xs*)

X is the point, in this case a date, for which you wish to predict a value. The point must be a natural progression from its previous values. In other words, a numeric progression that is even with the rest; follow a pattern a consistent time period. Known_ys are the gallons sold in the past and Known_xs are the dates.

▶ To determine the number of gallons that will be demanded from September 2017 to December 2017, assume the farm just completed August and have real data of the number of gallons sold from January to August.

1. In cells A2:13, type a period of time – in this example we used the first day of each month in the year.

2. In cells B2:B9, type in the number of gallons sold for each month from January to August. Leave September thru December blank as we will be predicting the gallons sold for each of these months.

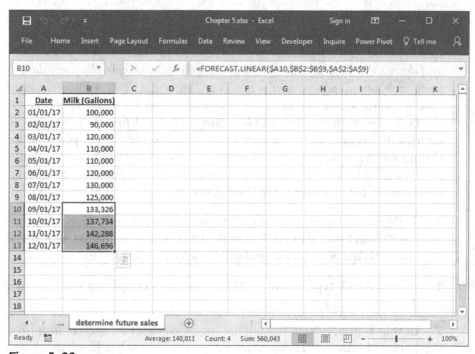

Figure 5–22

3. Highlight cells B10 to B13 and type the following formula in the formula bar: **==FORECAST.LINEAR($A10,$B$2:$B$9,$A$2:$A$9)**.

4. Press **\<Ctrl-Enter\>**.

Use the FORECAST.ETS function to determine future values

Using the same example of gallons of milk sold over time in the previous example, Instead of using a linear forecasting model which assumes generally the same trend in the future as in the past, we now use an exponential forecasting tool which forecasts the future based upon greater attention to the ups and downs of the past. By using the exponential method, we are assuming in this example that the values will not always increase in future months.

FORECAST.ETS(Target_date, Values, Timeline, [Seasonality], [Data_completion])

Target_date is the current date for which we are determining a future value, the Values are the known gallons sold in previous month and the Timeline is the previous months in which we know the number of gallons sold. Seasonality is an optional value that helps determine previous groupings of ups and downs. It's default value is 1 meaning in this example the formula will treat each month as a 'season' – you could enter a 2, 3, or 4 for example to look at several months as a season. The final parameter which is optional is the Data_completion which will be either 1 or 0: a 1 forces the formula to interpolate a value for a given date that is blank or zero; if you place a 0 for this parameter, it will use a zero value which can, at least in our example, produce wide variances in future predictions. For this example, we will use the defaults for Seasonality and Data_completion

▶ To determine the number of gallons that will be demanded from September 2017 to December 2017, assume the farm just completed August and have real data of the number of gallons sold from January to August.

1. In cells A2:13, type a period of time – in this example we used the first day of each month in the year.

2. In cells B2:B9, type in the number of gallons sold for each month from January to August. Leave September thru December blank as we will be predicting the gallons sold for each of these months.

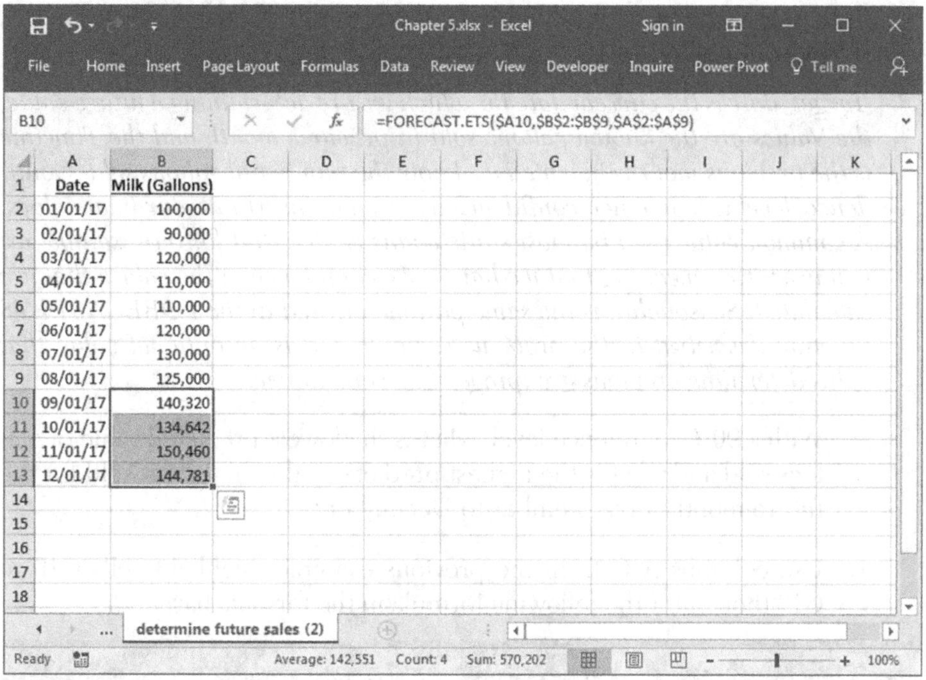

Figure 5–23

3. Highlight cells B10 to B13 and enter the following formula in the formula bar: **==FORECAST.ETS($A10,$B$2:$B$9,$A$2:$A$9)**.

4. Press **<Ctrl-Enter>**.

Use the FORECAST.ETS.CONFINT function to determine confidence in future values

Using the previous example, we arrive at future values based on previous values. But how accurate are these future numbers? What confidence do we have in using these predictions for our farm business? For this confidence determination, we use the FORECAST.ETS.CONFINT which contains in it a confidence level. The values derived are essentially a plus or minus range based upon a confidence interval. For example, we wish to determine with a 90% confidence level the lowest or highest number of gallons that are sold for future months.

FORECAST.ETSCONFINT(Target_date, Values, Timeline, [Seasonality], [Data_completion])

Target_date is the current date for which we are determining a future value, the Values are the known gallons sold in previous month and the Timeline is the previous months in which we know the number of gallons sold. Confidence_level is how much confidence we wish to insert into our final values. A common value used by most statisticians is 95%, but for our example we will use 90% - meaning that we have 90% confidence in the values that are calculated. Seasonality is the same parameter used in the FORECAST.ETS function described in the previous example and is an optional value that helps determine previous groupings of ups and downs.

▶ With a 90% confidence level, what is the lowest predicted value of gallons sold and what is the highest predicted value of gallons sold for the future months of September to December?

1. Use columns A-C from the previous example, highlight cells C10 to C13 then enter the following formula in the formula bar:

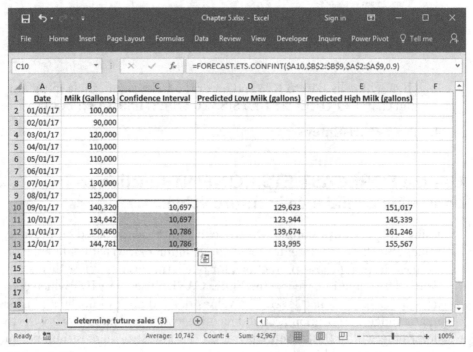

Figure 5-24

2. =FORECAST.ETS.CONFINT($A10,$B$2:$B$9,$A$2:$A$9,0.9).

3. Press **<Ctrl-Enter>**.

4. Highlight cells D10 to D13, enter the formula =B10-C10

5. Highlight cells E10 to E13, enter the formula =B10+C10.

Columns D and E now display the mininum and maximum number of gallons predicted to be sold based upon a 90% confidence level.

Use the FORECAST.ETS.SEASONALITY function to future value patterns

Using the previous example with the future values entered in for the months from September to December, let us determine if there are any patterns during the entire period. We can then use this as a number for the Seasonality parameter that is optional in the other FORECAST.ETS functions. Since many times patterns are not month to month (or period to period), we can attain a more accurate future value if we know the time length of a pattern. Sometimes it can be one month and sometimes it can mimic the weather patterns of roughly three months. Whatever the case, the FORECAST.ETS.SEASONALITY function assists us in determining a pattern for a more accurate prediction of the future.

FORECAST.ETS.SEASONALITY(Values, Timeline, [Data_completion], [Aggregation])

Values are the known gallons sold in previous month and the Timeline is the previous months in which we know the number of gallons sold. Data_completion is used to fill in blanks or zeros of missing data or to exclude them. Aggregation is to either aggregate or average values with the same date. In this case, we have different dates for each value.

▶ In this example, we know the number of gallons of Milk sold from January to August. So what is the pattern from month to month? Does it increase, decrease or is the pattern grouped by a number of months?

1. Enter the following formula for cell E2 in the formula bar:

2. =FORECAST.ETS.SEASONALITY(B$2:$B$9,$A$2:$A$9).

3. Press **<Ctrl-Enter>**.

Cell E2 tells us that, in general, the pattern of number of gallons sold repeats itself every two periods (in this case months). We can then input this number in the optional Seasonality parameter of the previously explained FORECAST functions.

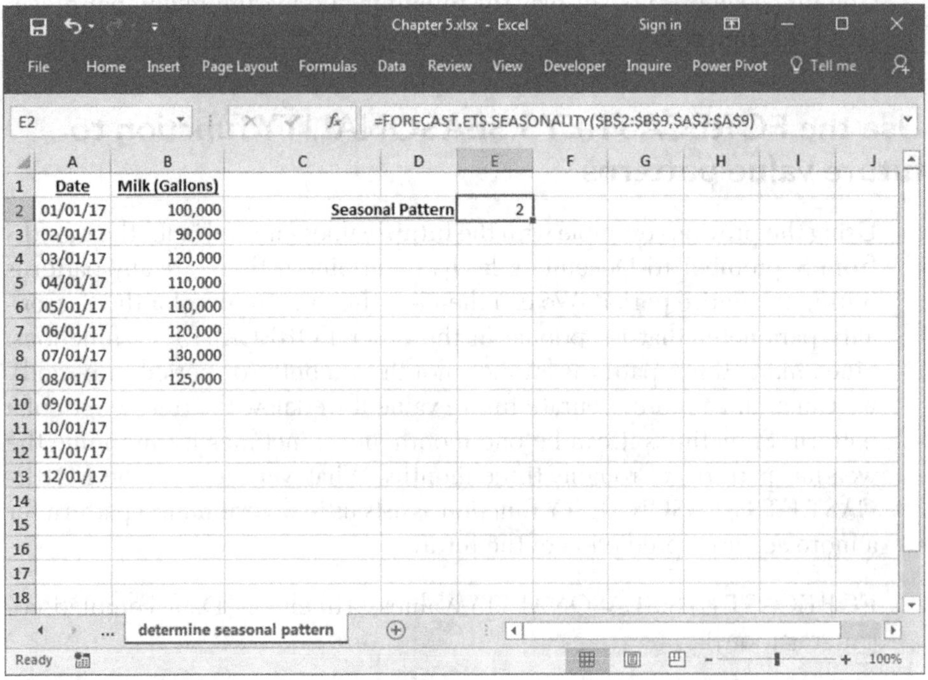

Figure 5–25

Use the CORREL function to determine data correlation

Sometimes we need to know how accurate a forecasting model is or how accurately we can predict values in a formula. In order to determine this, we can measure the correlation between two data sets. In other words, how accurate does one set of data points determine the value of another set of data points. We use three examples to show the value of correlation.

When determining a correlation between two sets of numbers, the range in correlation will be between -1 and 1. The closer to either -1 or 1, the better the predictability of the data set. The closer to zero, means the two sets of data are not at all related. Furthermore, if the two sets of data approach 1 or -1, the two data sets are highly correlated and either data set will be a good predictor of the other data set when used in a forecasting model. The difference between 1 and -1 is positive or negative correlation. In other words, if two data sets have a correlation of 1, they are positively correlated in the same direction. If the two data sets approach -1, they are correlated in opposite directions and are said to be negatively correlated. The examples will clarify. In each example, you are comparing two sets of numbers to determine how much the X numbers can predict a Y number.

1. In cell D4, type the formula: **=CORREL(B4:B8,C4:C8)**

2. In cell H4, type the formula: **=CORREL(F4:F8,G4:G8)**

3. In cell L4, type the formula: **=CORREL(J4:J8,K4:K8)**

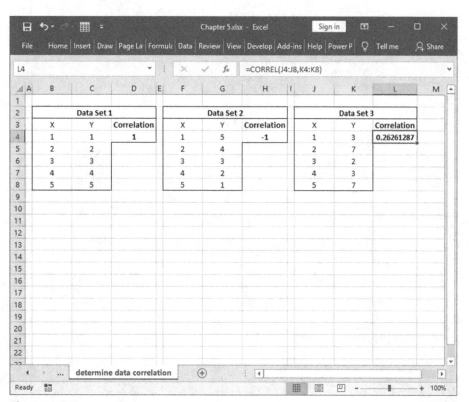

Figure 5–26

In the first example, the numbers are highly correlated in the positive direction. In other words, if we plug a 6 as an X in the formula used to calculate Y using X, there is a high probability that Y will be a 6 also.

Data Set 2 shows us how two sets of numbers are negatively correlated. If we enter another number such as 6 in the formula that links X to Y, chances are the value of Y will be 0. They are highly correlated, but in the opposite direction.

Data Set 3 group of numbers are not at all correlated meaning that whatever number we enter for X, it will be difficult to estimate a Y. This is usually the case when the correlation value is between -.5 and 5.

Mathematical Functions

6

Use the SUM function to sum a range

In this example, all values of a range in a worksheet need to be added, with the sum appearing in cell A11. To do this, use the SUM function, which returns the sum of all numbers in a range of cells.

SUM(*number1, number2, ...*)

number1, number2, ...: From 1 to 30 arguments to be summed. Cell references are also valid.

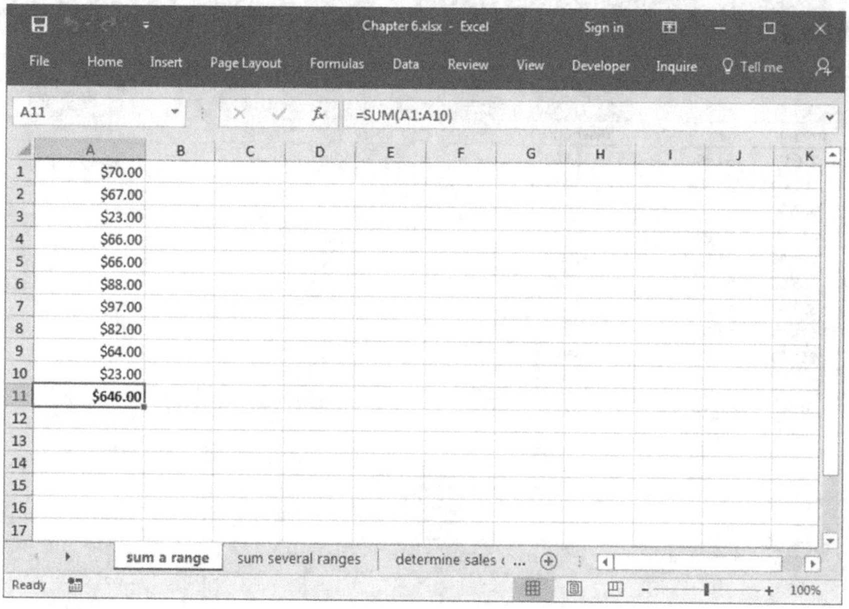

Figure 6–1

NOTE: To perform this task a little faster, just select cell A11 and click on the Σ icon (AutoSum) in the **Editing** bar under the **Home** tab. Then press **<Enter>** to display the result of the calculation.

▶ To sum a range:

1. In cells A2:A10, enter any values from 1 to 100. Figure 6–1 shows that we used dollar amounts.

2. In cell A11, type the following formula: **=SUM(A1:A10)**.

3. Press **<Enter>**.

Use the SUM function to sum several ranges

To sum several ranges, simply refer to each of them, separated by commas, using the SUM function from the previous tip.

▶ To sum several ranges:

1. In cells A2:A10, enter prices from $1 to $100.

	A	B	C	D
1	Price	Tax		Discount
2	$56.00	$4.48		-$2.00
3	$80.00	$6.40		-$2.50
4	$57.00	$4.56		-$2.50
5	$26.00	$2.08		-$1.50
6	$82.00	$6.56		-$2.00
7	$36.00	$2.88		-$3.00
8	$57.00	$4.56		-$1.50
9	$44.00	$3.52		-$1.75
10	$64.00	$5.12		-$3.00
11				
12	Total:	$522.41		

Cell B12: =SUM(A2:A10,B2:B10,D2:D10)

Figure 6–2

NOTE: To place a border around all cells used in the function, select cell B12 and press <F2>. The function will be displayed as well.

2. Select cells B2:B10 and type the formula **=A2*8%** to calculate the tax amount.

3. Press **<Ctrl+Enter>**.

4. In cells D2:D10, type some discount values from −1 to −3.

5. In cell B12 sum all three columns with the following function: **=SUM(A2:A10,B2:B10,D2:D10)**.

6. Press **<Enter>**.

Use the SUMIF function to determine sales of a team

In this example, all the sales of different teams need to be summed. You can use the SUMIF function to add all cells in a range, specified by a given criterion.

SUMIF(*range, criteria, sum_range*)

range: A range of cells to be evaluated.

criteria: The criteria that specifies which cells to add. This can be a number, expression, or text.

sum_range: The actual cells to be summed.

▶ To sum specified data:

1. In cells A2:A10, enter a team number from 1 to 3.

2. List all team members in cells B2:B10.

3. In cells C2:C10, enter the daily sales of each employee.

4. List the numbers 1, 2, 3 for each team in cells E2:E4.

5. Select cells F2:F4 and type the following formula: **=SUMIF($A$2:$A$10,E2,$C$2:$C$10)**.

6. Press **<Ctrl+Enter>**.

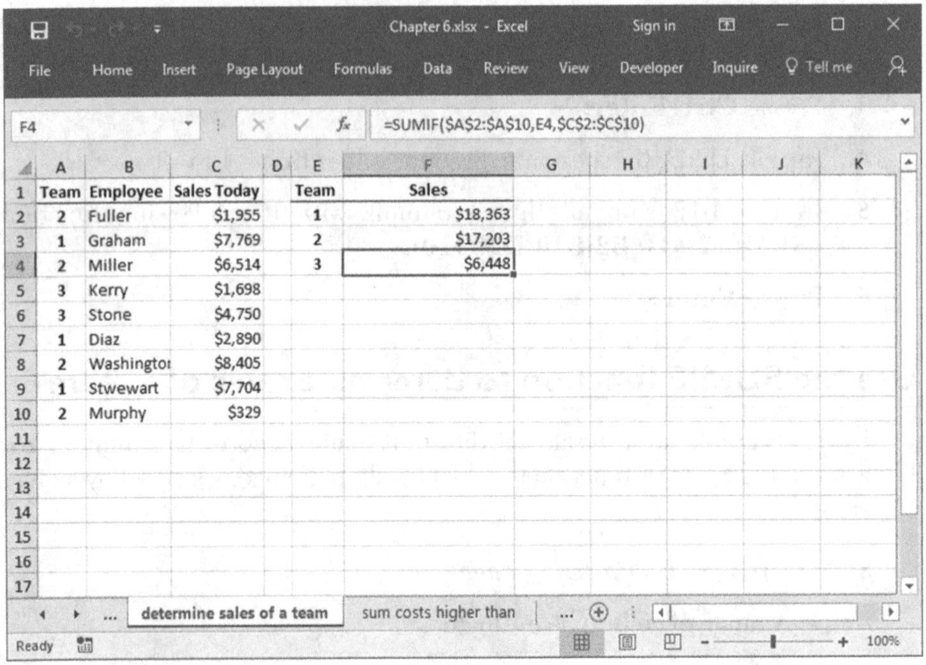

Figure 6–3

NOTE: At the end of Chapter 6 you will find a further example called SUMIFS, which has been available since Excel 2007.

Use the SUMIF function to sum costs higher than $1,000

This tip can be used to determine the sum of all phases for which costs are higher than $1,000. To sum just those cells, use the SUMIF function. It adds the cells that are specified by a given criterion.

▶ To sum specified costs:

1. In cells A2:A11, enter the different phases.

2. Enter the cost of each phase in cells B2:B11.

3. In cell D1, enter **1000** as the given criterion.

4. Select cell D2 and type the following formula: **=SUMIF(B2:B11,">" & D1)**.

5. Press **<Enter>**.

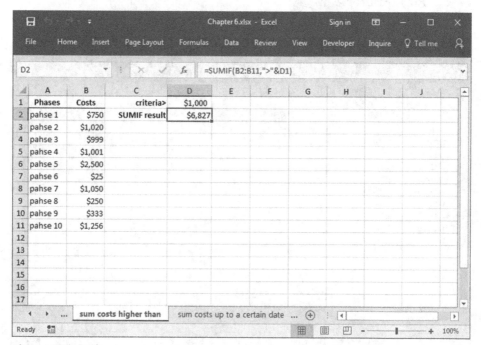

Figure 6–4

NOTE: If the criteria should not be linked to a cell reference, use this formula: =SUMIF(B2:B11,">1000").

Use the SUMIF function to sum costs up to a certain date

Figure 6–5 contains a dynamic worksheet with daily costs. To sum all costs in a specified timeframe, use the SUMIF function.

▶ To sum costs up to a certain date:

1. In cells A2:A11, list dates from 11/09/10 to 11/18/10.

2. In cells B2:B11, enter the corresponding costs for each day.

3. In cell E1, enter the date **11/16/10.**

4. Select cell E2 and type the following formula:
   =SUMIF(A2:A11,"<=" & E1,B2:B11).

5. Press **<Enter>**.

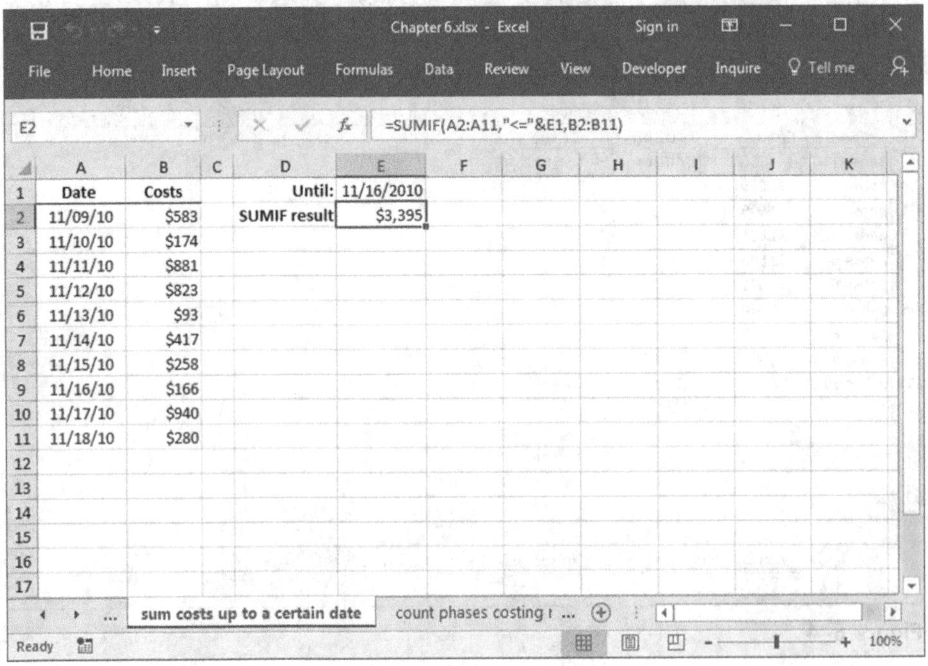

Figure 6–5

NOTE: To check the calculated result, select cells B2:B9 and watch the displayed sum in the Excel status bar.

Use the COUNTIF function to count phases that cost more than $1,000

In this example, some project phases are listed in a worksheet. To determine how many phases cost more than $1,000, use the COUNTIF function. This function counts the number of cells in a range that meet the specified criteria.

COUNTIF(*range*, *criteria*)

range: The range of cells.

criteria: The criterion that specifies which cells to count. This can be a number, expression, or text.

▶ To count specified phases:

1. In cells A2:A11, enter the different phases.

2. Enter the costs of each phase in cells B2:B11.

3. In cell D1 enter **1000** as the given criterion.

4. Select cell D2 and type the following formula:
   =COUNTIF(B2:B11,">" & D1).

5. Press **<Enter>**.

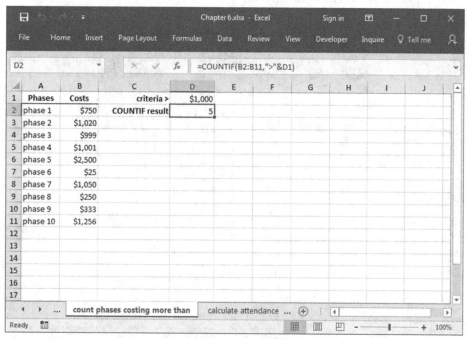

Figure 6–6

NOTE: If the criteria should not be linked to a cell reference, use this formula: =COUNTIF(B2:B11,">1000").

NOTE: At the end of Chapter 6 you will find a further example called COUNTIFS, which has been available since Excel 2007.

Use the COUNTIF function to calculate an attendance list

For this task, an attendance list needs to be generated and the number of those who are present each day determined. Generate the list shown in Figure 6–7. Column A contains the dates, and column B uses the user-defined format **DDD** to determine the day of the week. In columns C to G, the letter "X" is entered for each person in attendance.

▶ To calculate the attendance for each day:

1. Select cells H2:H11 and type the formula **=COUNTIF(C2:G2,"X")** to get the attendance for each day.

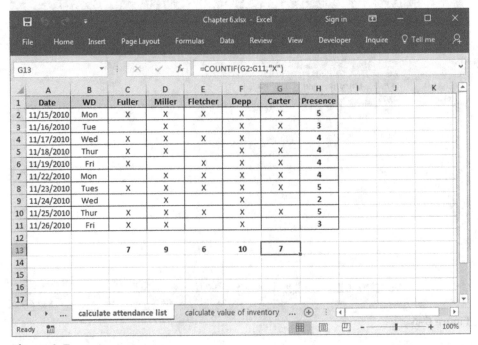

Figure 6–7

2. Press **<Ctrl+Enter>**.

3. Select cells C13:G13 and type the formula **=COUNTIF(G2:G11,"X")** to count the attendance of each employee.

4. Press **<Ctrl+Enter>**.

Use the SUMPRODUCT function to calculate the value of the inventory

In this example, the costs of all products in a warehouse need to be summed to obtain the value of the entire inventory. To do this, use the SUMPRODUCT function. This function multiplies corresponding components in the given arrays and returns the sum of those products.

SUMPRODUCT(*array1, array2, array3, ...*)

array1, array2, array3, ...: From 2 to 30 arrays whose components are to be multiplied and then added.

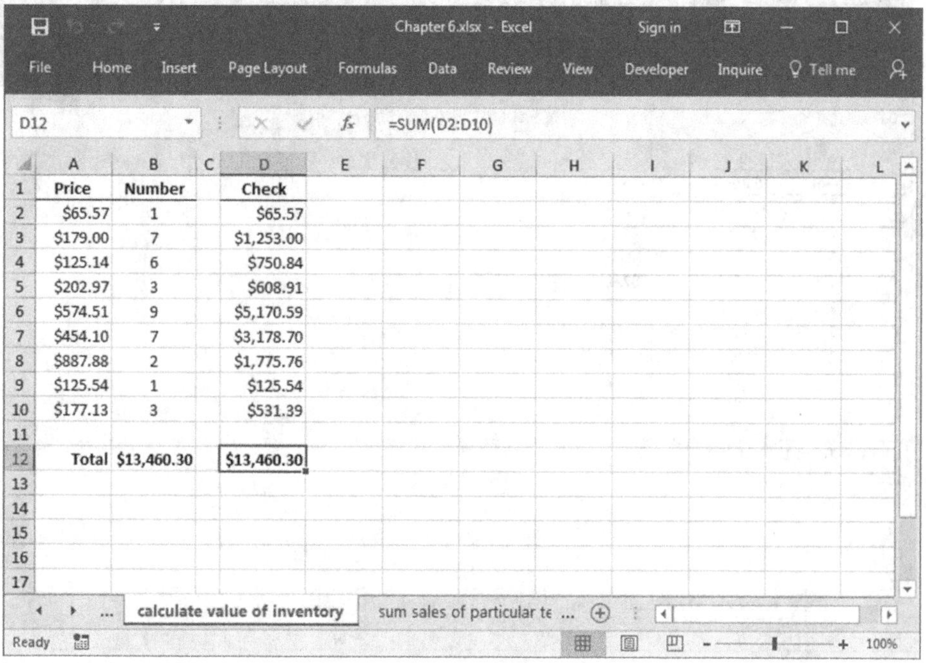

Figure 6–8

▶ To calculate the inventory value:

1. Enter the data shown in columns A and B in Figure 6–8. The quantity of each product is listed along with the cost of each unit.
2. Select cell B12 and type the following formula: **=SUMPRODUCT (B2:B10,A2:A10)**.
3. Check the result by selecting cells D2:D10 and typing the following formula: **=A2*B2**.
4. Press **<Ctrl+Enter>**.
5. Sum this range in cell D12.

Use the SUMPRODUCT function to sum sales of a team

The worksheet below contains the sales of different teams. As discussed earlier, summing the sales of each team can be done with the SUMIF function. Another way to get a result is by using the SUMPRODUCT function.

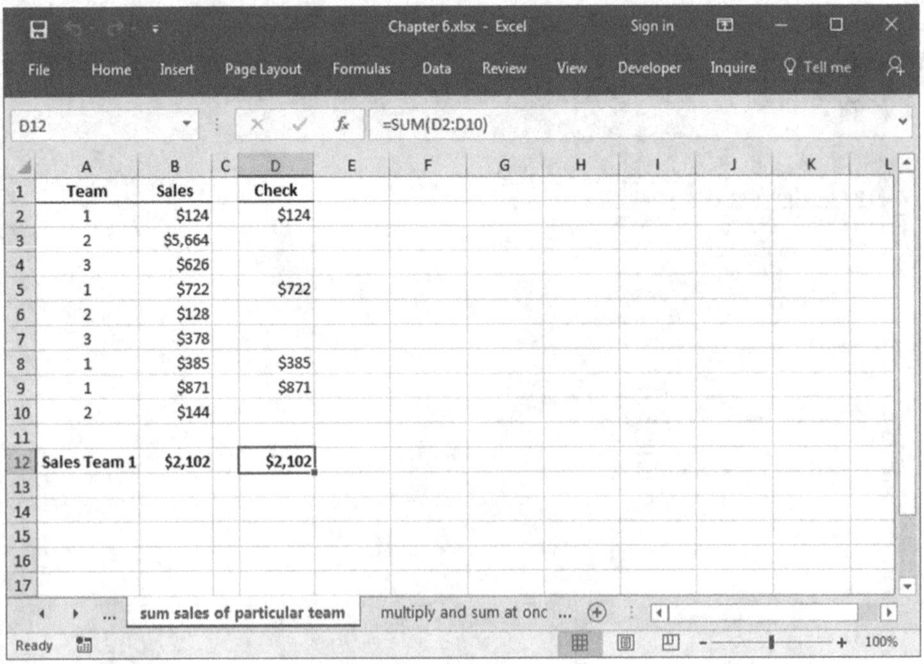

	A	B	C	D
1	Team	Sales		Check
2	1	$124		$124
3	2	$5,664		
4	3	$626		
5	1	$722		$722
6	2	$128		
7	3	$378		
8	1	$385		$385
9	1	$871		$871
10	2	$144		
11				
12	Sales Team 1	$2,102		$2,102

Figure 6–9

▶ To sum the sales of Team 1:

1. Use the values in Figure 6–9 to fill in columns A and B.

2. Select cell B12 and type the following formula:
   =SUMPRODUCT((A2:A10=1)*(B2:B10)).

3. To check the result, select cells D2:D10 and type the following formula:
   =IF(A2=1,B2,"").

4. Press **<Ctrl+Enter>** to enter the formula in the selected range of cells.

5. Select cell D12 and enter the following formula: **=SUM(D2:D10)**.

Use the SUMPRODUCT function to multiply and sum at the same time

The salary of each team needs to be calculated. The teams' numbers, daily working hours, and daily payment are recorded in a table. To calculate the total salary for each team, the working hours need to be multiplied by

	A	B	C	D	E
1	Date	WD	Team	Hours	Payment
2	11/15/10	Mon	2	6	$294
3	11/16/10	Tues	1	7	$343
4	11/17/10	Wed	3	9	$441
5	11/18/10	Thur	1	3	$147
6	11/19/10	Fri	2	1	$49
7	11/22/10	Mon	1	1	$49
8	11/23/10	Tues	1	3	$147
9	11/24/10	Wed	3	6	$294
10	11/25/10	Thur	2	7	$343
11	11/26/10	Fri	1	9	$441
12					
13	Team	1	$1,127		
14		2	$686		
15		3	$735		

Formula bar: C15 =SUMPRODUCT(($C$2:$C$11=B15)*($E$2:$E$11))

Figure 6–10

the payment and summed for each day worked. Use the SUMPRODUCT function to get the result.

▶ To multiply and sum in one operation for each team:

1. In a worksheet, copy the range A2:E11 shown in Figure 6–10.

2. Select cells C13:C15 and type the following formula:
   =SUMPRODUCT ((($C$2:$C$11=B13)* ($E$2:$E$11))).

3. Press **<Ctrl+Enter>**.

Use the ROUND function to round numbers

In this example, all numbers need to be rounded. Use the Excel built-in ROUND function to round a number to a specified number of digits.

ROUND(*number, num_digits*)

number: The number to be rounded.

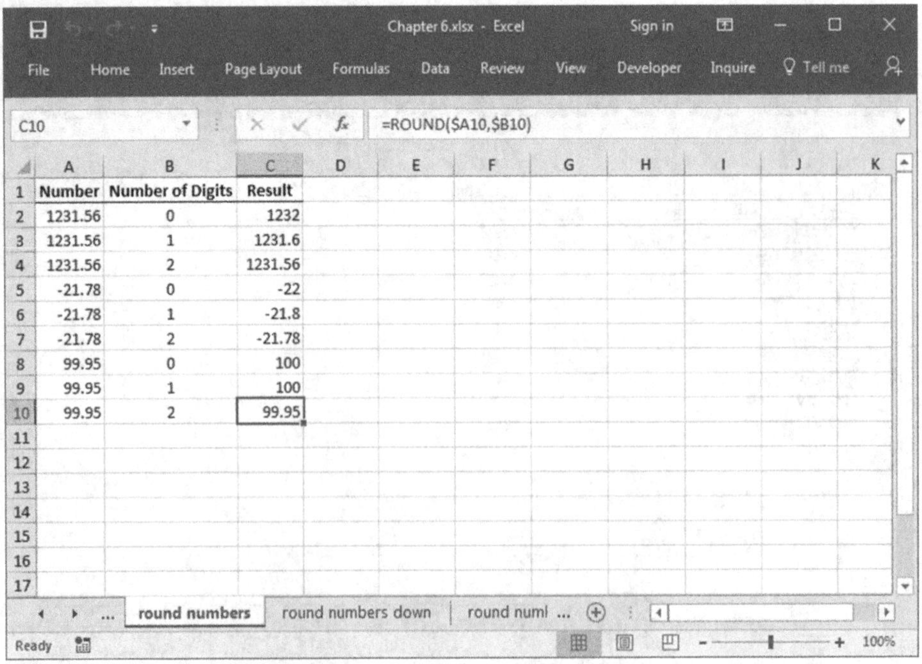

	A	B	C	D
1	Number	Number of Digits	Result	
2	1231.56	0	1232	
3	1231.56	1	1231.6	
4	1231.56	2	1231.56	
5	-21.78	0	-22	
6	-21.78	1	-21.8	
7	-21.78	2	-21.78	
8	99.95	0	100	
9	99.95	1	100	
10	99.95	2	99.95	

C10 = ROUND($A10,$B10)

Figure 6–11

num_digits: The number of digits the number will be rounded to. If greater than 0, the number is rounded to num_digits decimal places. If 0, the number is rounded to the nearest integer. If less than 0, the number is rounded to the left of the decimal point.

▶ To round numbers:

1. In cells A2:A10, enter numbers with a decimal point.

2. In cells B2:B10, enter the number of decimal places the number should be rounded to.

3. Select cells C2:C10 and type the following formula: **=ROUND ($A2,$B2)**.

4. Press **<Ctrl+Enter>**.

Use the ROUNDDOWN function to round numbers down

To cut off numbers to a specific decimal place or round numbers down in a worksheet, use the ROUNDDOWN function. This function rounds a number down, toward zero.

ROUNDDOWN(*number, num_digits*)

number: Any real number to be rounded down.

num_digits: The number of digits the number will be rounded down to. If greater than 0, the number is rounded to num_digits decimal places. If 0, the number is rounded to the nearest integer. If less than 0, the number is rounded to the left of the decimal point.

▶ To round down numbers:

1. In cells A2:A10, enter numbers with a decimal point.

2. In cells B2:B10, enter the number of decimal places the number should be rounded down to.

3. Select cells C2:C10 and type the following formula: **=ROUNDDOWN ($A2,$B2)**.

4. Press **<Ctrl+Enter>**.

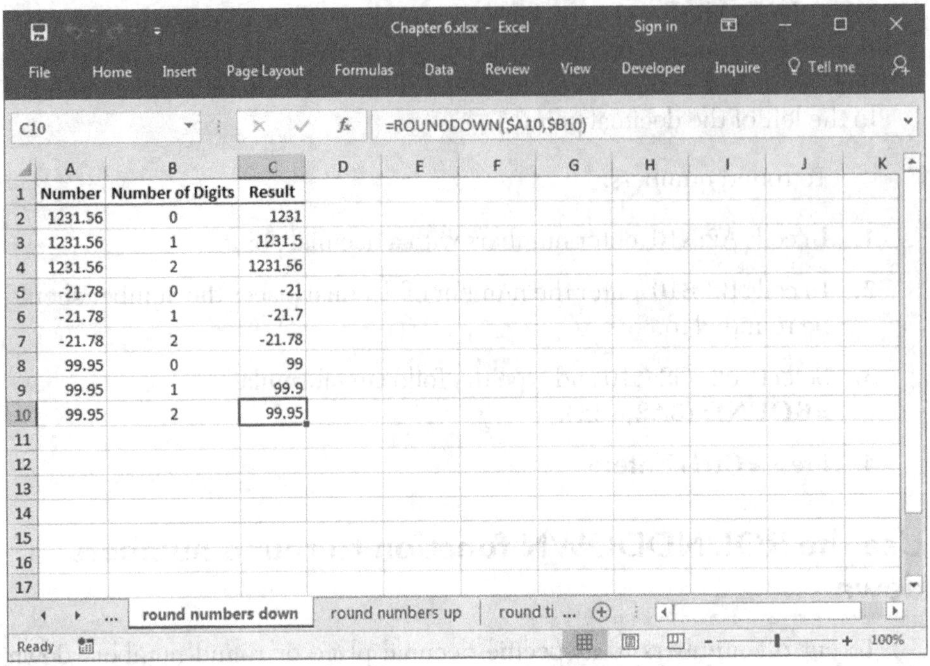

Figure 6–12

Use the ROUNDUP function to round numbers up

Like the ROUNDDOWN function explained in the previous tip, the ROUNDUP function can be used to round up numbers in a worksheet.

ROUNDUP(*number, num_digits*)

number: Any real number to be rounded up.

num_digits: The number of digits the number will be rounded up to. If greater than 0, the number is rounded to num_digits decimal places. If 0, the number is rounded to the nearest integer. If less than 0, the number is rounded to the left of the decimal point.

▶ To round up numbers:

1. In cells A2:A10, enter numbers with a decimal point.

2. In cells B2:B10, enter the number of decimal places the number should be rounded up to.

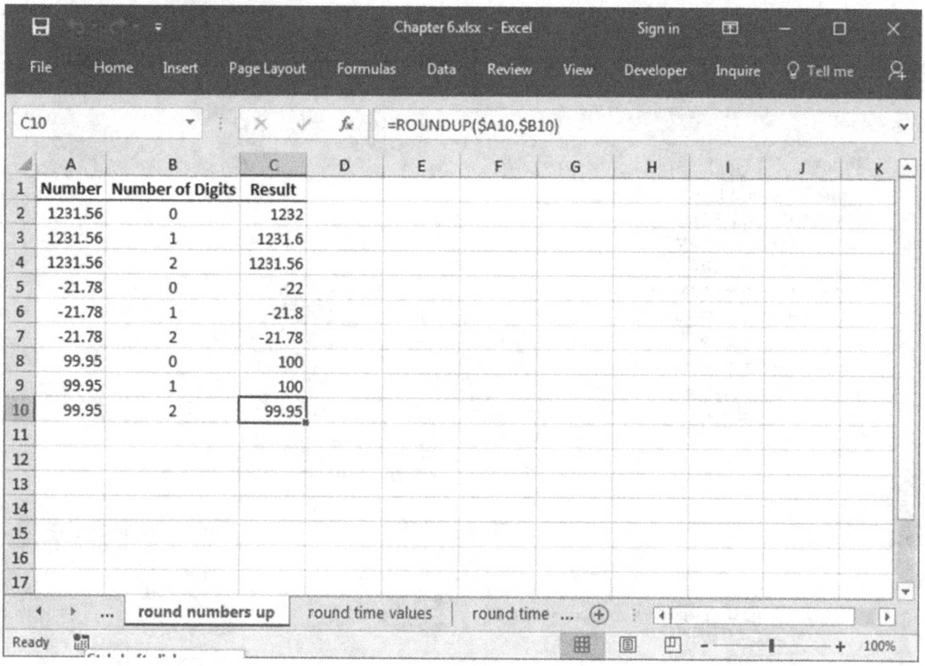

Figure 6–13

3. Select cells C2:C10 and type the following formula:
   =ROUNDUP ($A2,$B2).

4. Press **<Ctrl+Enter>**.

Use the ROUND function to round time values to whole minutes

A worksheet contains time values including hours, minutes, and seconds as shown in Figure 6–14. The task is to round the minutes to whole minutes by using the standard ROUND function. Note that a day has 24 hours, which is 1,440 minutes.

▶ To round different time values to whole minutes:

1. In cells A2:A10, list some time values in this format: 12:02:59 a.m.

2. Select cells B2:B10 and type the following formula:
   =ROUND (A2*1440,0)/1440.

3. Press **<Ctrl+Enter>**.

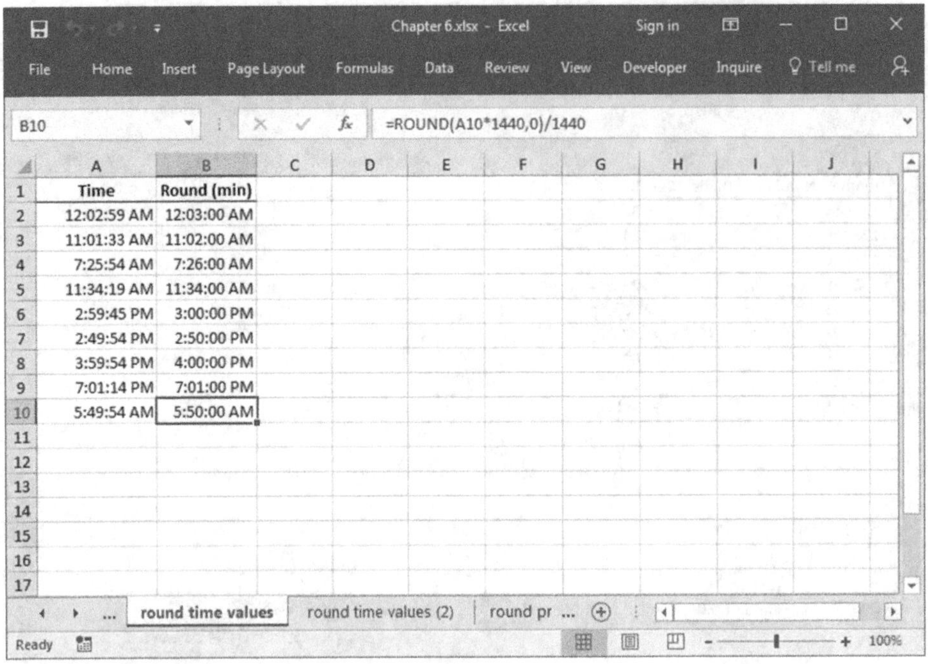

Figure 6–14

Use the ROUND function to round time values to whole hours

As in the previous tip, a worksheet contains time values including hours, minutes, and seconds as shown in Figure 6–15. To round these time values to whole hours, use the standard ROUND function. Recall that a day has 24 hours.

▶ To round time values to whole hours:

1. In cells A2:A10 list some time values in this format: 12:02:59 a.m.

2. Select cells B2:B10 and type the following formula:
   =ROUND (A2*24,0)/24.

3. Press **<Ctrl+Enter>**.

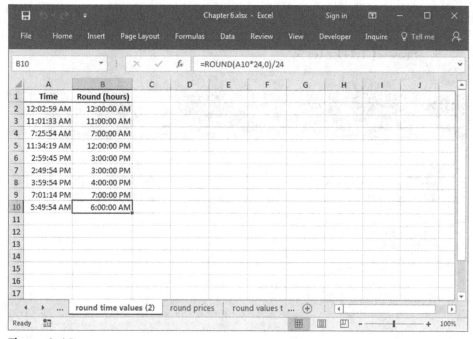

Figure 6–15

Use the MROUND function to round prices to 5 or 25 cents

In this example, prices need to be rounded to the nearest 5 or 25 cents. Use the MROUND function, which returns a number rounded to the desired multiple.

MROUND(*number, multiple*)

number: The value to be rounded.

multiple: The multiple to which the number will be rounded.

▶   To round prices to a multiple of 5 or 25 cents:

1.   In cells A2:A10, list some prices with a decimal point.

2.   Select cells B2:B10 and type the following formula:
     =MROUND (A2,0.05).

3.   Press **<Ctrl+Enter>**.

4. Select cells C2:C10 and type the following formula: **=MROUND (A2,0.25)**.

5. Press **<Ctrl+Enter>**.

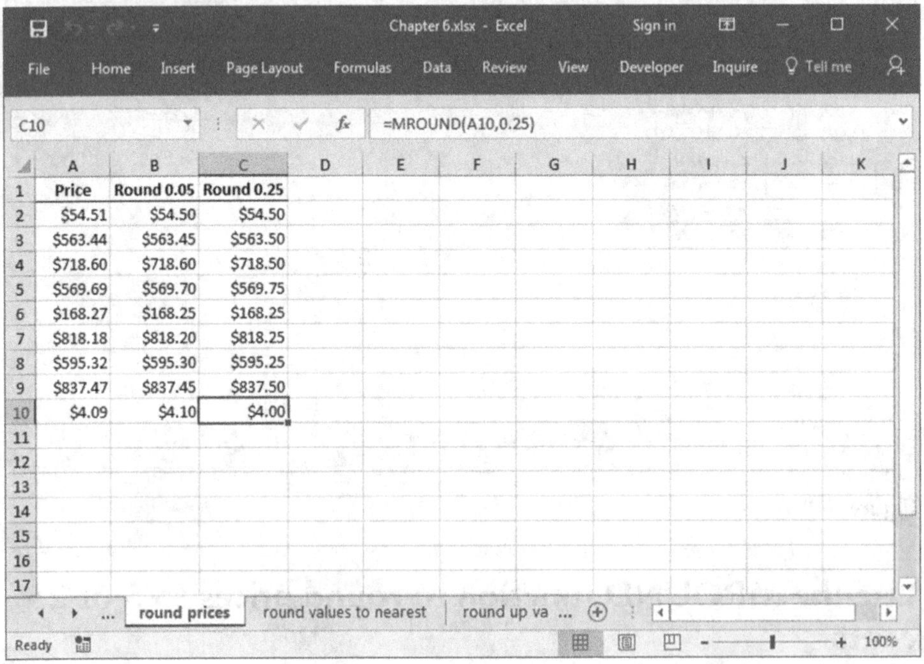

Figure 6–16

NOTE: To use this function, you need to have the Analysis ToolPak installed and loaded. From the **Tools** menu, select the **Add-Ins** option. Select the desired add-in and click **OK**.

Use the MROUND function to round values to the nearest multiple of 10 or 50

Sometimes it is necessary to round up values to the nearest multiple of 10 or 50. To perform this task, use the MROUND function from the Analysis ToolPak add-in. MROUND returns a number rounded to the desired multiple.

▶ To round values to the nearest multiple of 10 or 50:

1. In cells A2:A10, list any kind of values.

2. Select cells B2:B10 and type the following formula: **=MROUND (A2,10)**.

3. Press **<Ctrl+Enter>**.

4. Select cells C2:C10 and type the following formula: **=MROUND (A2,50)**.

5. Press **<Ctrl+Enter>**.

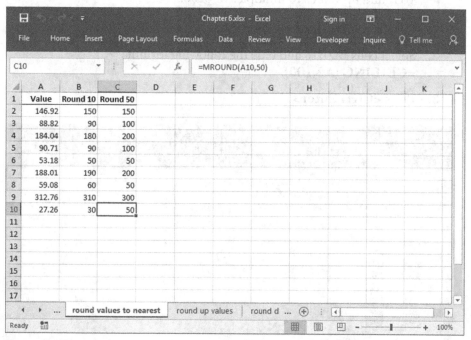

⊿	A	B	C	D
1	Value	Round 10	Round 50	
2	146.92	150	150	
3	88.82	90	100	
4	184.04	180	200	
5	90.71	90	100	
6	53.18	50	50	
7	188.01	190	200	
8	59.08	60	50	
9	312.76	310	300	
10	27.26	30	50	

Figure 6–17

NOTE: To use this function, you need to have the Analysis ToolPak installed and loaded as described in the previous tip.

Use the CEILING function to round up prices to the nearest $100

For this example, all prices need to be rounded up to whole $100 units. To do this, use the CEILING function. This function returns a number that is rounded up to the nearest multiple of significance.

CEILING(*number*, *significance*)

number: The value to be rounded.

significance: The multiple to which the number will be rounded up.

▶ To round up values to multiples of $100:

1. In cells A2:A10, list some prices.

2. Select cells B2:B10 and type the following formula:
   =CEILING (A2,100).

3. Press **<Ctrl+Enter>**.

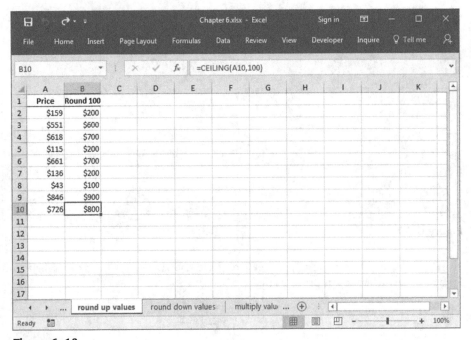

Figure 6–18

Use the FLOOR function to round down prices to the nearest $100

As seen in the previous example, it is easy to round up prices to multiples of $100. To round numbers down to the nearest multiple of significance, use the FLOOR function.

FLOOR(*number, significance*)

number: The value to be rounded.

significance: The multiple to which the number will be rounded down.

▶ To round down values to multiples of $100:

1. In cells A2:A10, list some prices.

2. Select cells B2:B10 and type the following formula: **=FLOOR(A2,100)**.

3. Press **<Ctrl+Enter>**.

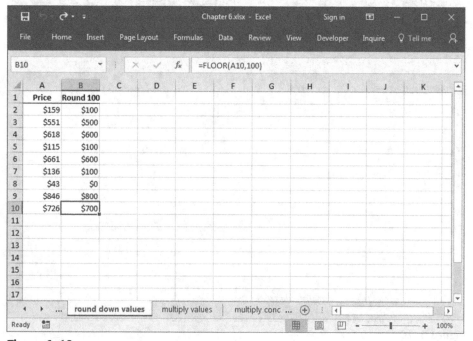

Figure 6–19

Use the PRODUCT function to multiply values

Normally, values in a worksheet are multiplied with the * operator in formulas like **=A1*B1**. However, Excel also provides a useful function to do the same calculation. Use the PRODUCT function to multiply all the given numbers and return the product.

PRODUCT(*number1, number2, ...*)

number1, number2, ...: From 1 to 30 numbers to be multiplied.

As an example, calculate a price reduction with the PRODUCT function using a standard factor in cell D1.

▶ To calculate the price reduction:

1. In cells A2:A10, list some prices.

2. Enter in cell D1 the value **0.15** to calculate a 15% price reduction.

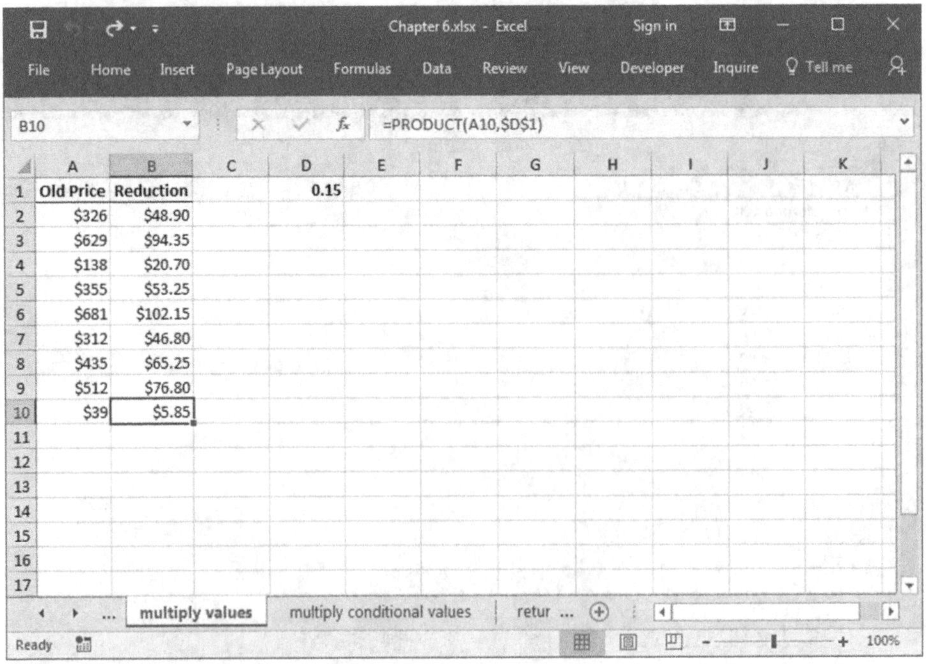

Figure 6–20

3. Select cells B2:B10 and type the following formula: **=PRODUCT (A2,$D$1)**.

4. Press **<Ctrl+Enter>**.

Use the PRODUCT function to multiply conditional values

In this example, values are listed in columns A and B. Excel should calculate the product of each value in a row, but only if both values exist. If one or both values are missing, the result is an empty cell, as shown in column C. To get the desired results, use the PRODUCT function in combination with the IF and OR functions as described below.

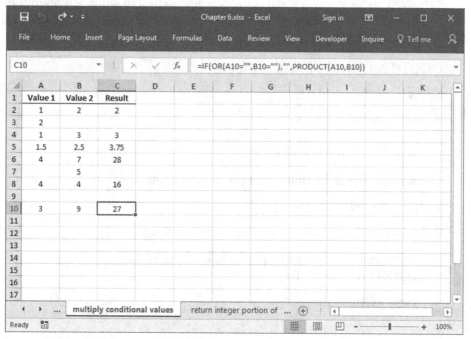

Figure 6–21

NOTE: The following formula produces the same result: =IF(OR(A2="",B2=""),"", A2 * B2).

▶ To multiply conditional values:

1. In cells A2:A10 enter some numbers for value 1.

2. In cells B2:B10 enter some numbers for value 2.

3. Select cells C2:C10 and type the following formula: **=IF(OR(A2="",B2="")," ",PRODUCT(A2,B2))**.

4. Press **<Ctrl+Enter>**.

Use the QUOTIENT function to return the integer portion of a division

The opposite of PRODUCT, which was used in the previous tip, is QUOTIENT. This function calculates the integer portion of a division operation and discards the remainder. To use this function, you must first install and load the Analysis ToolPak add-in.

QUOTIENT(*numerator, denominator*)

numerator: The dividend.

denominator: The divisor.

▶ To calculate the integer portion:

1. Select cells A2:A10 and enter the number **100**.

2. Press **<Ctrl+Enter>**.

3. In cells B2:B10, enter any values as the divisors.

4. Select cells C2:C10 and type the following formula: **=QUOTIENT (A2,B2)**.

5. Press **<Ctrl+Enter>**.

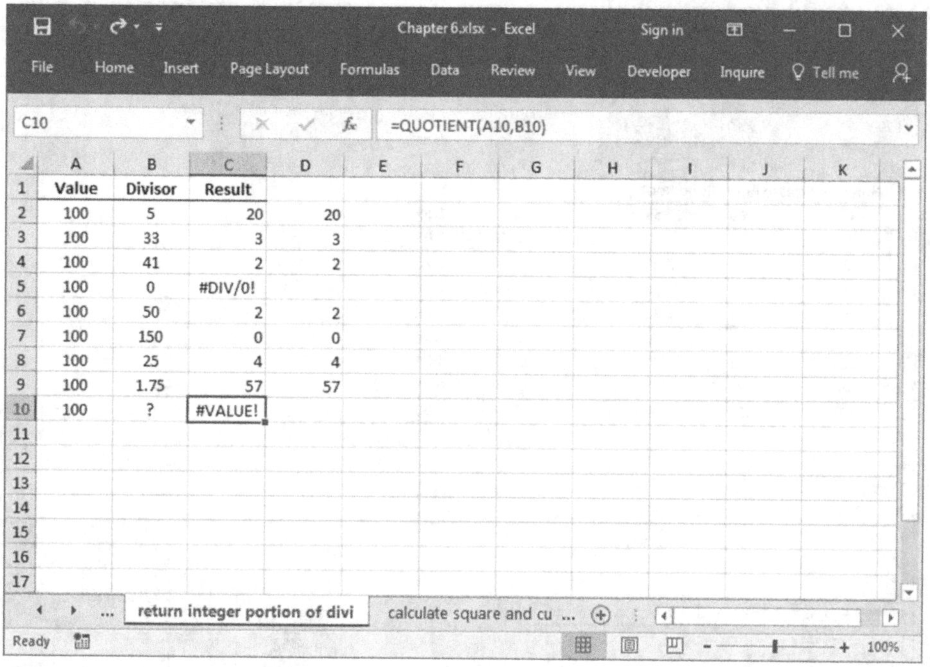

	A	B	C	D
1	Value	Divisor	Result	
2	100	5	20	20
3	100	33	3	3
4	100	41	2	2
5	100	0	#DIV/0!	
6	100	50	2	2
7	100	150	0	0
8	100	25	4	4
9	100	1.75	57	57
10	100	?	#VALUE!	

Figure 6-22

NOTE: To avoid incorrect calculations (division with zero) and the error value shown in cells C5 and C10, use the following formula: **=IF(ISERROR(QUOTIENT(A10,B10)), " ",QUOTIENT(A10,B10)).**

Use the POWER function to calculate square and cube roots

To raise numbers to the power of another number, the POWER function is used. It can also be used to calculate the root.

POWER(*number*, *power*)

number: The base number, which can be any real number.

power: The exponent.

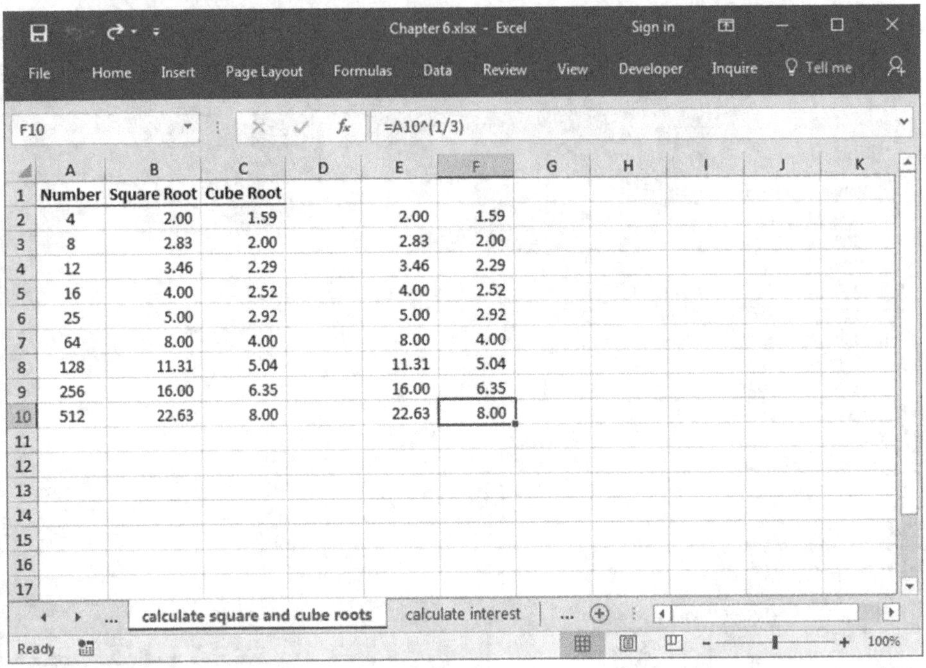

Figure 6–23

NOTE: The operator ^ can be used instead of POWER, so =POWER(3,2) could be written like this: =3^2

NOTE: To use the ^ operator, type =A2^(1/2) to calculate the square root and =A2^(1/3) to determine the cube root.

▶ To calculate roots using the POWER function:

1. In cells A2:A10, list some values.

2. Select cells B2:B10 and type the formula **=POWER((A2),1/2)** to calculate the square root.

3. Press **<Ctrl+Enter>**.

4. Select cells C2:C10 and type the formula **=POWER((A2),1/3)** to calculate the cube root.

5. Press **<Ctrl+Enter>**.

Use the POWER function to calculate interest

Imagine you won $1,000 and wanted to save it in a bank account. Depending on the bank, the account could earn 2.5% to 5% in interest compounded annually. How many dollars would be in the bank account after several years if you saved it and didn't touch it? Follow along with this example to find out.

▶ To calculate the total amount of money saved depending on the interest rate:

1. Select cells A2:A10 and enter **$1,000** as the starting amount.

2. Press **<Ctrl+Enter>**.

3. In cells B2:B10, enter different interest rates.

4. In cells C2:C10, enter the number of years the money will be saved.

5. Select cells D2:D10 and enter the following formula:
   =A2*POWER ((1+B2/100),C2).

6. Press **<Ctrl+Enter>**.

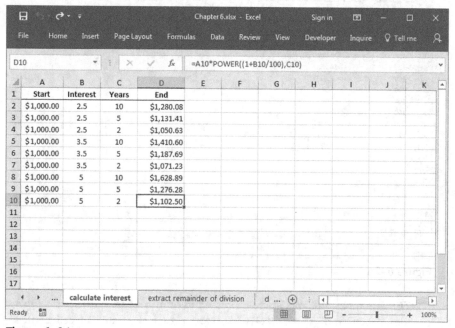

Figure 6–24

Use the MOD function to extract the remainder of a division

This example contains the value 100 in cells A2:A10 and divisors in column B. The MOD function is used here to find the remainder of a division operation. The result has the same sign as the divisor.

MOD(*number, divisor*)

number: The number to find the remainder for.

divisor: The number to divide number by.

▶ To extract the remainder of a division operation:

1. Select cells A2:A10 and enter **100**.
2. Press **<Ctrl+Enter>**.

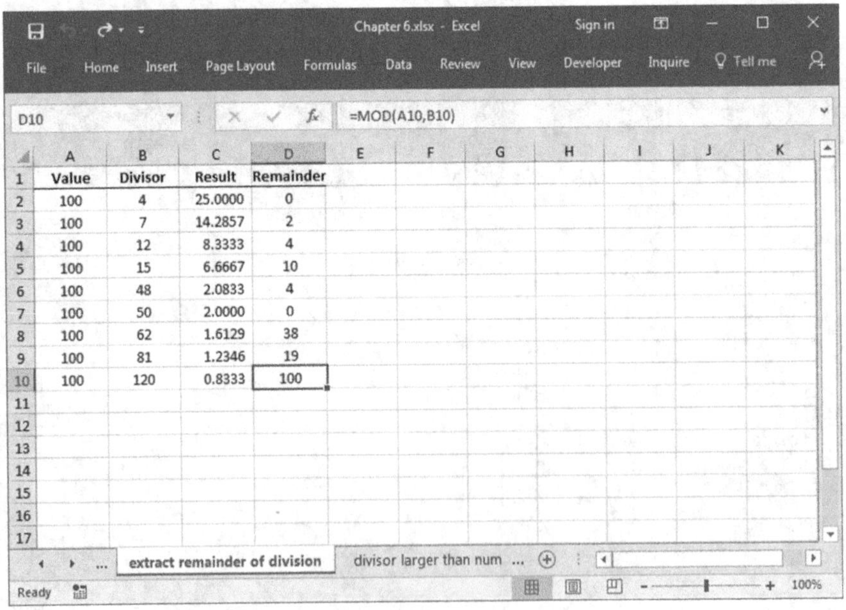

Value	Divisor	Result	Remainder
100	4	25.0000	0
100	7	14.2857	2
100	12	8.3333	4
100	15	6.6667	10
100	48	2.0833	4
100	50	2.0000	0
100	62	1.6129	38
100	81	1.2346	19
100	120	0.8333	100

Figure 6-25

NOTE: The function can also be expressed in terms of the mathematical INT function: MOD(n,d) = n-d*INT(n/d). Notice that the value in cell D10 is incorrect. See the following tip for a way to avoid this.

3. In cells B2:B10, enter different divisors.

4. Select cells C2:C10 and type the formula **=A2/B2**.

5. Press **<Ctrl+Enter>**.

6. Select cells D2:D10 and type the formula **=MOD(A2,B2)**.

7. Press **<Ctrl+Enter>**.

Modify the MOD function for divisors larger than the number

As seen in the previous tip, a problem occurs when the divisor is larger than the number for which you want to find the remainder. The result will always be the number itself. To handle this using the MOD function, follow these steps.

▶ Handling divisors that are larger than the number:

1. Select cells A2:A10 and enter **100**.

2. Press **<Ctrl+Enter>**.

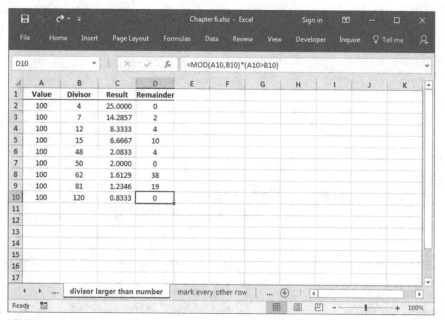

Figure 6–26

3. In cells B2:B10, enter different divisors.

4. Select cells C2:C10 and type this formula: **=A2/B2**.

5. Press **<Ctrl+Enter>**.

6. Select cells D2:D10 and type this formula: **=MOD(A2,B2)*(A2>B2)**.

7. Press **<Ctrl+Enter>**.

Use the ROW function to mark every other row

Sometimes it is necessary to mark every other row in a worksheet. Several functions can be used in combination to do this. Use the MOD, ROW, and IF functions together as described below.

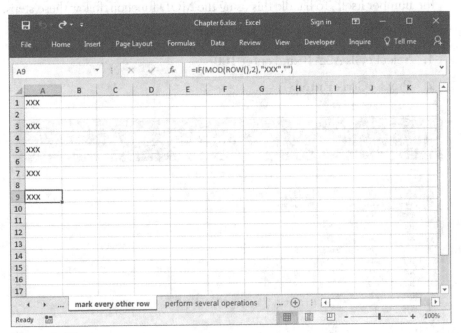

Figure 6–27

NOTE: If every other column needs to be marked, use the following formula: =IF(MOD(COLUMN(),2),"XXX"," ").

NOTE: See Chapter 10, "Conditional Formatting with Formulas," for additional tips on using the MOD function.

▶ To mark every other row:

1. Select cells A1:A10 and type the following formula: **=IF(MOD (ROW(),2),"XXX"," ")**.

2. Press **<Ctrl+Enter>**.

Use the SUBTOTAL function to perform several operations

The SUBTOTAL function can be used to calculate subtotals in a list or database. There are different subtotal operations available that are all covered by just one function. The syntax is provided."

▶ To use the SUBTOTAL function for multiple calculations:

1. Copy the data shown in columns A and B in Figure 6–28.

2. Select cells C2:C10 and enter the daily sales of each team.

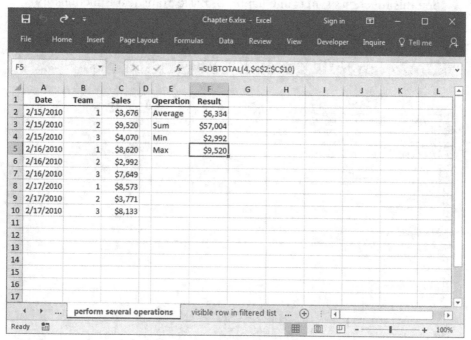

Figure 6–28

3. Calculate the average in cell F2 with the following formula:
   =SUBTOTAL (1,$C$2:$C$10).

4. Calculate the sum in cell F3 with the following formula:
   =SUBTOTAL (9,$C$2:$C$10).

5. Calculate the lowest sales value in cell F4 with the following formula:
   =SUBTOTAL(5,$C$2:$C$10).

6. Calculate the maximum value in cell F5 with the following formula:
   =SUBTOTAL(4,$C$2:$C$10).

Use the SUBTOTAL function to count all visible rows in a filtered list

This example shows a filtered list. The task is to count all visible and used rows. Note that the COUNT and COUNTA functions can also be used in a non-filtered list. However, they also count hidden rows. To get the right result, use the SUBTOTAL function and use "3" as the function_num value. (See this function's syntax in Chapter 5, Basic Statistical Functions.)

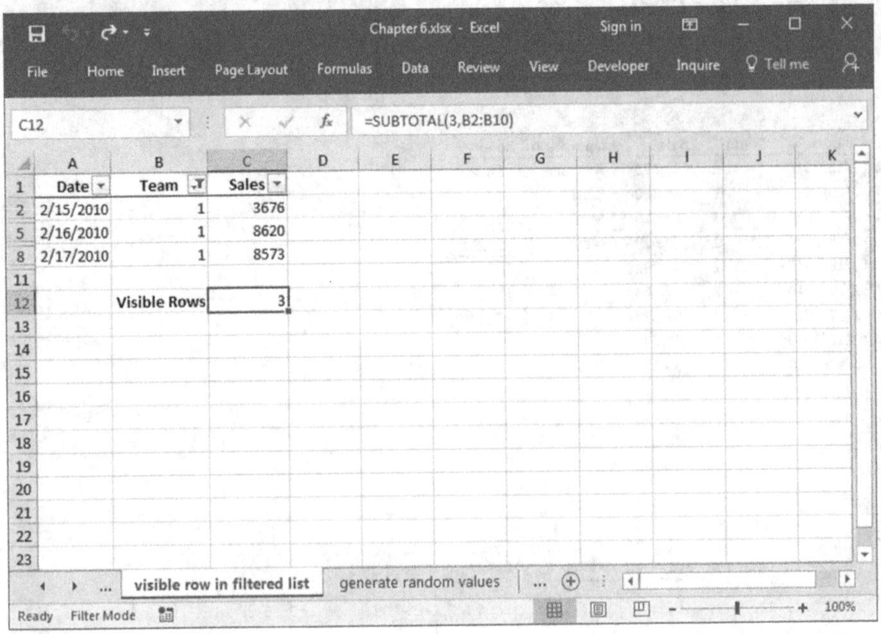

Figure 6–29

▶ To count all visible rows in a filtered list:

1. Generate a filtered list like the one shown in Figure 6–29.

2. Select cell C13 and type the following formula: **=SUBTOTAL (3,B2:B10)**.

3. Press **<Enter>**.

Use the RAND function to generate random values

To generate randomized values, Excel provides the RAND function. This function returns a random number greater than or equal to 0 and less than 1. Each time the worksheet is calculated, a new random number is generated. This example generates randomized integer values from 1 to 999 in cells A2:D10 and then replaces the formulas with calculated values.

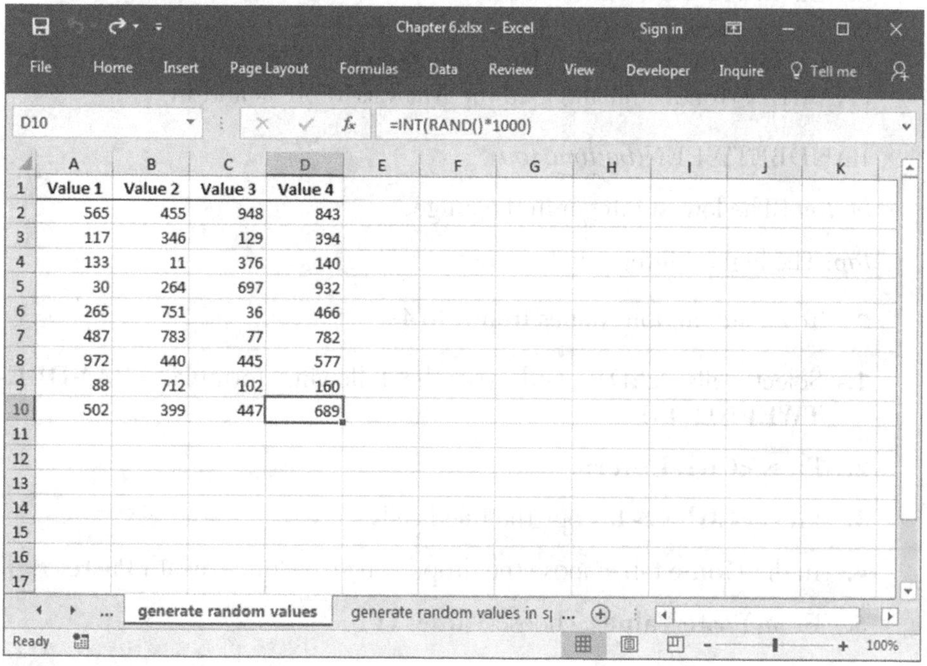

Figure 6–30

NOTE: The values appearing in Figure 6-30 above will be different than the values you see on your worksheet since the RAND function displays different values each time it is re-calculated. To see new random values, press F9.

▶ To generate integer random values:

1. Select cells A2:D10 and type the following formula: **=INT(RAND ()*1000)**.

2. Press **<Ctrl+Enter>**.

3. Press **<Ctrl+C>** to copy the filled cells.

4. In the **Home** tab, choose the dropdown arrow underneath **Paste**.

5. From **Paste Values,** choose **Values (V)**.

Use the RANDBETWEEN function to generate random values in a specified range

To generate randomized values in a specified range, such as from 1 to 49, use the RANDBETWEEN function. This function returns a random number in the range you specify, returning a new random number every time the worksheet is calculated. If this function is not available and returns the #NAME? error, install and load the Analysis ToolPak add-in.

RANDBETWEEN(*bottom, top*)

bottom: The lowest integer in the range.

top: The highest integer in the range.

▶ To create random values from 1 to 49:

1. Select cells A2:D10 and type the following formula: **=RANDBE-TWEEN(1,49)**.

2. Press **<Ctrl+Enter>**.

3. Press **<Ctrl+C>** to copy the filled cells.

4. In the **Home** tab, choose the dropdown arrow underneath **Paste**.

5. From **Paste Values,** choose **Values (V)**.

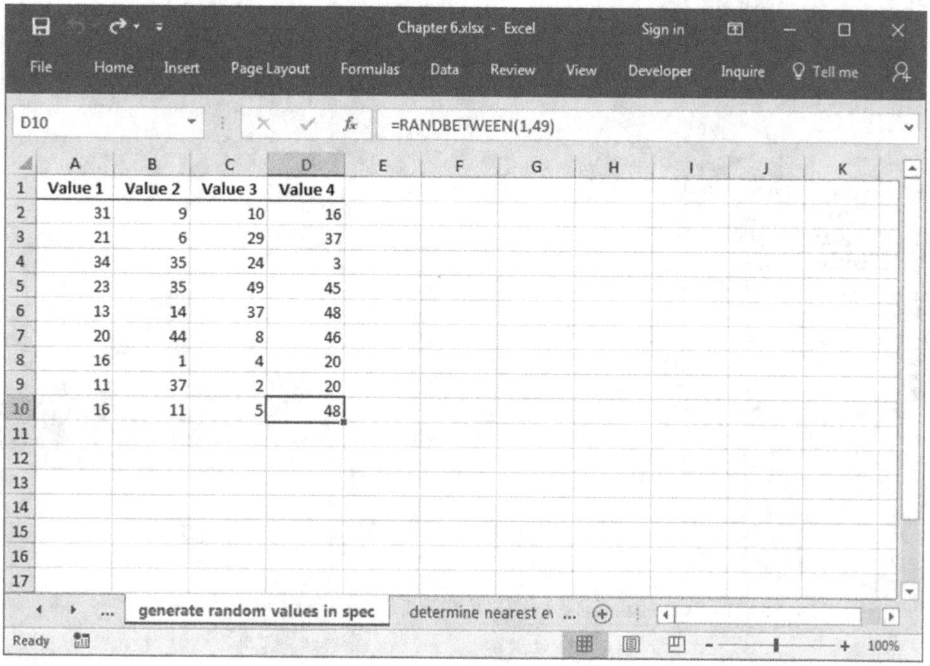

Value 1	Value 2	Value 3	Value 4
31	9	10	16
21	6	29	37
34	35	24	3
23	35	49	45
13	14	37	48
20	44	8	46
16	1	4	20
11	37	2	20
16	11	5	48

Figure 6-31

NOTE: The values appearing in Figure 6-31 above will be different than the values you see on your worksheet since the RANDBETWEEN function displays different values each time it is re-calculated. To see new random values, press F9.

Use the EVEN and ODD functions to determine the nearest even/odd value

In addition to the standard functions for rounding up a number, there are other functions available, like EVEN and ODD. For example, to round up a number to the nearest even integer, use the EVEN function.

EVEN(*number*)

number: The value to be rounded.

To round up a number to the nearest odd value, use the ODD function.

ODD(*number*)

number: The value to be rounded.

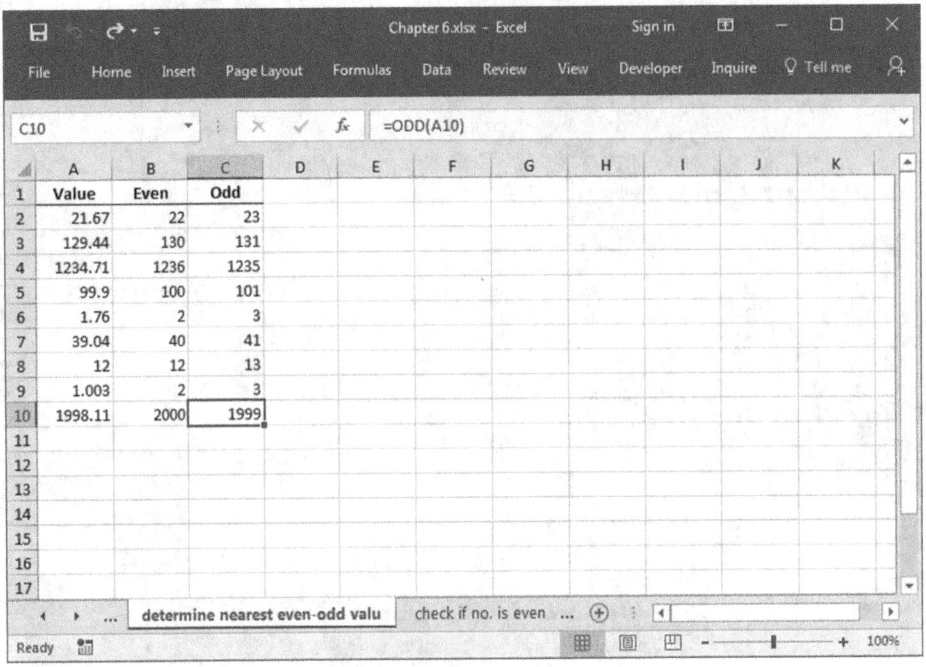

Figure 6–32

▶ To determine the nearest even/odd value:

1. In cells A2:A10, list some valid numbers with decimal points.

2. Select cells B2:B10 and enter the following function: **=EVEN(A2)**.

3. Press **<Ctrl+Enter>**.

4. Select cells C2:C10 and enter the following function: **=ODD(A2)**.

5. Press **<Ctrl+Enter>**.

Use the ISEVEN and ISODD functions to check if a number is even or odd

To find out whether numbers are even or odd, use the ISEVEN or ISODD functions. ISEVEN returns TRUE if the number is even and FALSE if the number is odd, while ISODD returns TRUE if the number is odd and FALSE if the number is even.

ISEVEN(*number*)

ISODD(*number*)

number: The value to be tested. Non-integer values are truncated.

▶ To check if a number is even or odd:

1. In cells A2:A10, enter some numbers.

2. Select cells B2:B10 and type the following formula:
=IF(ISEVEN(A2),"X","").

3. Press **<Ctrl+Enter>**.

4. Select cell C2:C10 and type the following formula:
=IF(ISODD (A2),"X","").

5. Press **<Ctrl+Enter>**.

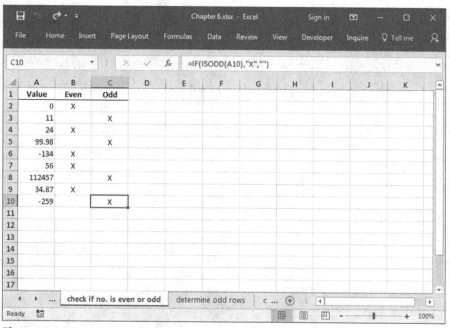

Figure 6–33

NOTE: To use these functions, you will need to install and load the Analysis ToolPak add-in as described earlier.

Use the ISODD and ROW functions to determine odd rows

In this example, we need to determine whether a row number in a range is even or odd and then fill each odd row with the character "X." Use the ISODD function in combination with IF and ROW() to get the result shown in Figure 6–34.

If this function is not available and returns an error, install and load the Analysis ToolPak add-in.

▶ To determine odd rows and mark them:

1. Select cells A1:E11 and type the following formula: **=IF(ISODD (ROW()),"X","")**.

2. Press **<Ctrl+Enter>**.

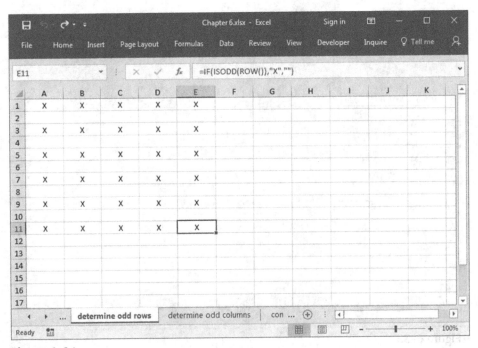

Figure 6–34

NOTE: To mark all even rows, use the following formula: =IF(ISEVEN(ROW()),"X","").

Use the ISODD and COLUMN functions to determine odd columns

In this example, we want to determine whether a column's index in a range is even or odd and then fill each odd row with the character "X." Use the ISODD function in combination with IF and COLUMN() to get the result shown in Figure 6–35. If this function is not available and returns an error, install and load the Analysis ToolPak add-in.

▶ To determine odd columns:

1. Select cells A1:E11 and type the following formula:
=IF(ISODD (COLUMN()),"X","").

2. Press **<Ctrl+Enter>**.

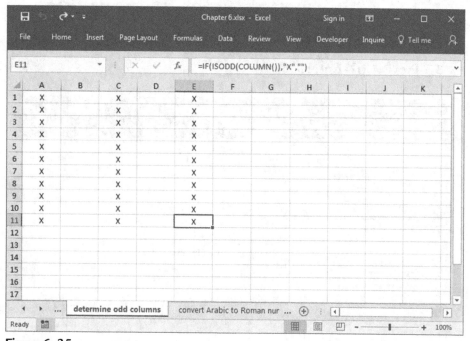

Figure 6–35

NOTE: To mark even columns, type the following formula:
=IF(ISEVEN(COLUMN()), "X","").

Use the ROMAN function to convert Arabic numerals to Roman numerals

This tip explains how to convert an Arabic numeral to a Roman numeral. To get this result, use the ROMAN function, which returns the Roman value as text.

ROMAN(*number*, *form*)

number: The Arabic numeral to be converted.

form: (optional) A number from 0 to 4 that specifies the type of Roman numeral. Styles range from Classic to Simplified and become more concise (using fewer characters) as the value of form increases. If omitted, the Classic type is used.

▶ To convert Arabic numerals to Roman numerals:

1. In cells A2:A10, enter valid numbers from 1 to 3999.

2. Select cells B2:B10 and type the following formula: **=ROMAN(A2,0)**.

3. Press **<Ctrl+Enter>**.

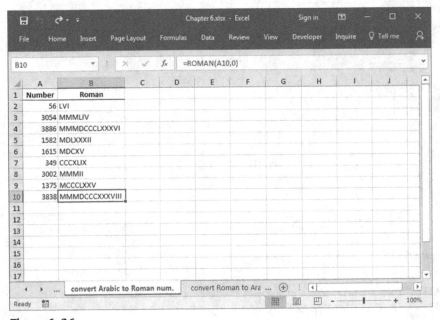

Figure 6–36

Use the ARABIC function to convert Roman numerals to Arabic numerals

This tip explains how to convert a Roman numeral to an Arabic numeral. To get this result, use the ARABIC function, which returns the Arabic value as a number.

ARABIC(*text*)

text: The Roman numeral to be converted.

▶ To convert Roman numerals to Arabic numerals:

1. In cells A2:A10, enter valid Roman numerals like those shown in Figure 6-37.

2. Select cells B2:B10 and type the following formula: **=ARABIC(A2)**.

3. Press **<Ctrl+Enter>**.

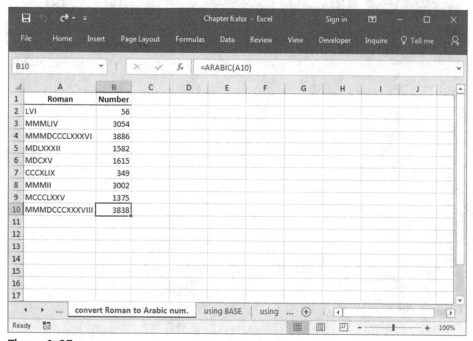

Figure 6–37

Use the BASE function to convert decimal numbers to binary numbers

This tip explains how to convert the numeric base of a number, for example, from decimal to binary. To get this result, use the BASE function, which returns the numeric value as text in the new base.

BASE(*number, radix, min_length*)

number: The number value to be converted.

radix: The number representing the base into which the number should be converted. This must be a value from 2 to 36.

min_length: (optional) The minimum length of the returned string. This must be greater than 0.

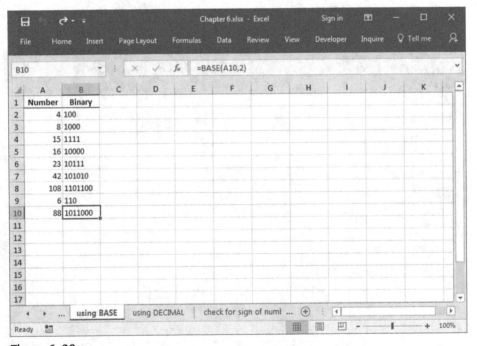

Figure 6–38

▶ To convert decimal (base 10) numbers to binary (base 2) numbers:

1. In cells A2:A10, enter valid numbers.

2. Select cells B2:B10 and type the following formula: **=BASE(A2,2)**.

3. Press **<Ctrl+Enter>**.

Use the DECIMAL function to convert binary numbers to decimal numbers

This tip explains how to convert a value in a different numeric base to a decimal number. To get this result, use the DECIMAL function, which returns the decimal numeric value from a number in a different base.

DECIMAL(*number, radix*)

number: The number value to be converted.

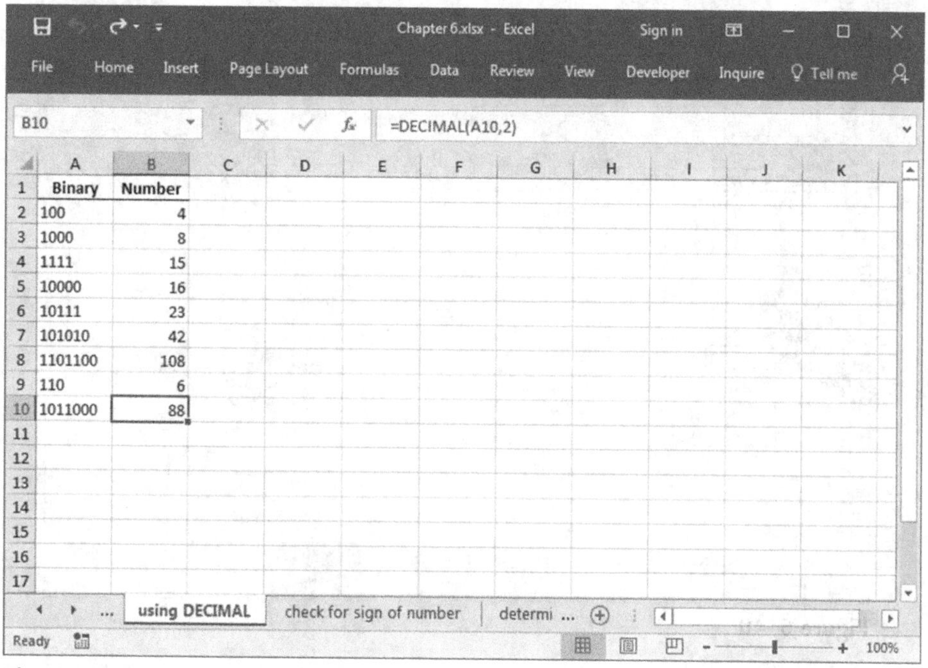

Figure 6–39

radix: The number representing the base in which the number is represented. This value must be an integer.

▶ To convert binary (base 2) numbers to decimal (base 10) numbers:

1. In cells A2:A10, enter binary numbers such as those used in Figure
   6-39.

2. Select cells B2:B10 and type the following formula: **=DECIMAL(A2,2)**.

3. Press **<Ctrl+Enter>**.

Use the SIGN function to check for the sign of a number

Excel provides the SIGN function to check the sign of a number. This function returns 1 if the number is positive, 0 if the number is 0, and –1 if the
number is negative. If the user enters text instead of a number, the SIGN
function returns the error code #VALUE!.

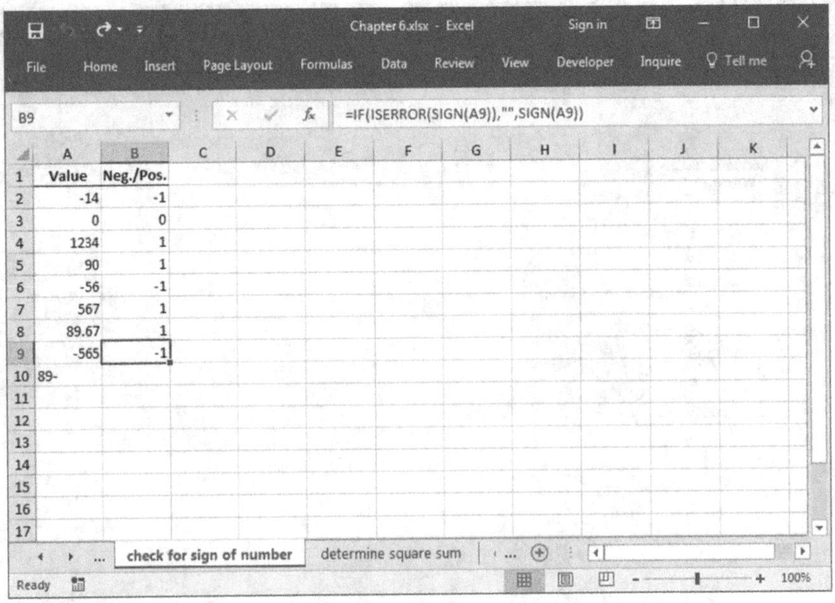

Figure 6-40

NOTE: The same result for numeric values can also be generated by combining
IF functions. Use this formula: =IF(A1>0;1;IF(A2<0;–1;0)).

SIGN(*number*).

number: Any real number.

▶ To check for the sign of a number:

1. In cells A2:A10, list numbers or text.

2. Select cells B2:B10 and type the following formula:
   =IF(ISERROR(SIGN(A2)),"",SIGN(A2)).

3. Press **<Ctrl+Enter>**.

Use the SUMSQ function to determine the square sum

Excel provides the SUMSQ function to sum the squares of the arguments.

SUMSQ(*number1, number2, ...*)

number1, number2, ...: From 1 to 30 arguments that will have their squares summed. Instead of values, you can use a single array or a reference to an array separated by commas.

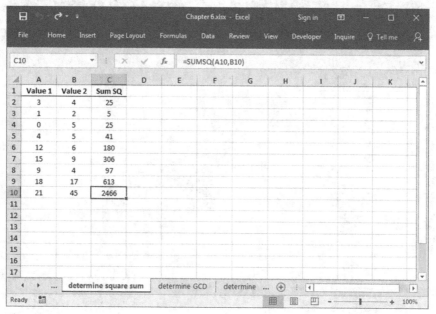

Figure 6–41

▶ To determine the square sum:

1. In cells A2:A10, list valid numbers.

2. In cells B2:B10, list valid numbers.

3. Select cells C2:C10 and type the following formula: **=SUMSQ(A2,B2)**.

4. Press **<Ctrl+Enter>**.

Use the GCD function to determine the greatest common divisor

In this example, the greatest common divisor (GCD) of two integers needs to be determined. To do so, use the GCD function. This function is available only if you have the Analysis ToolPak add-in installed.

GCD(*number1*, *number2*, ...)

number1, number2, ...: From 1 to 29 values for which you want to find the greatest common divisor. Non-integer values are truncated.

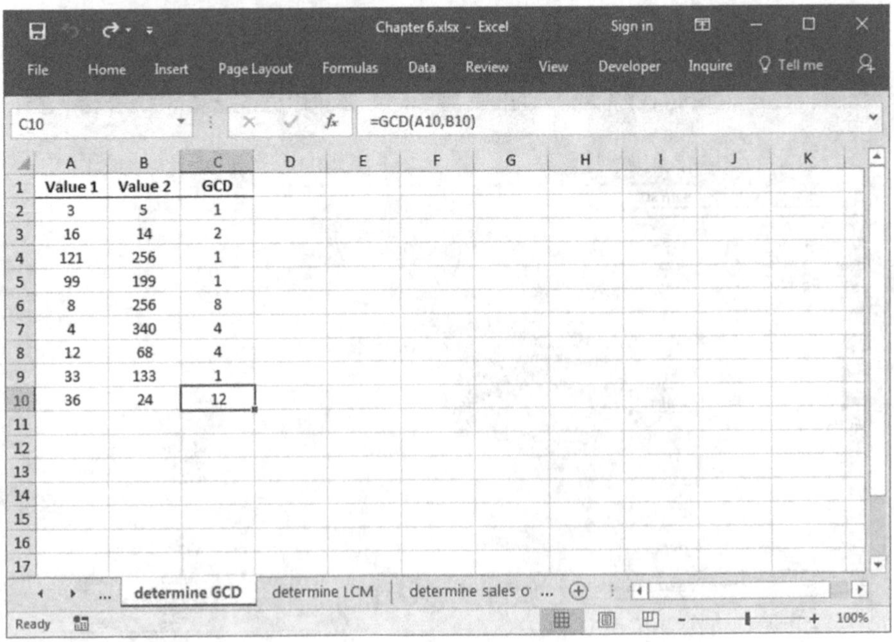

Figure 6–42

▶ To determine the greatest common divisor:

1. In cells A2:A10 list any valid numbers.

2. In cells B2:B10 list any valid numbers.

3. Select cells C2:C10.

4. Type the following formula: **=GCD(A2,B2)**.

5. Press **<Ctrl+Enter>**.

Use the LCM function to determine the least common multiple

This example shows how to determine the least common multiple (LCM) of two integers. Excel provides the LCM function through the Analysis ToolPak add-in. You will need to install and load the add-in to perform these steps.

LCM(*number1, number2, ...*)

number1, number2, ...: From 1 to 29 values for which you want to find the least common multiple. Non-integer values are truncated.

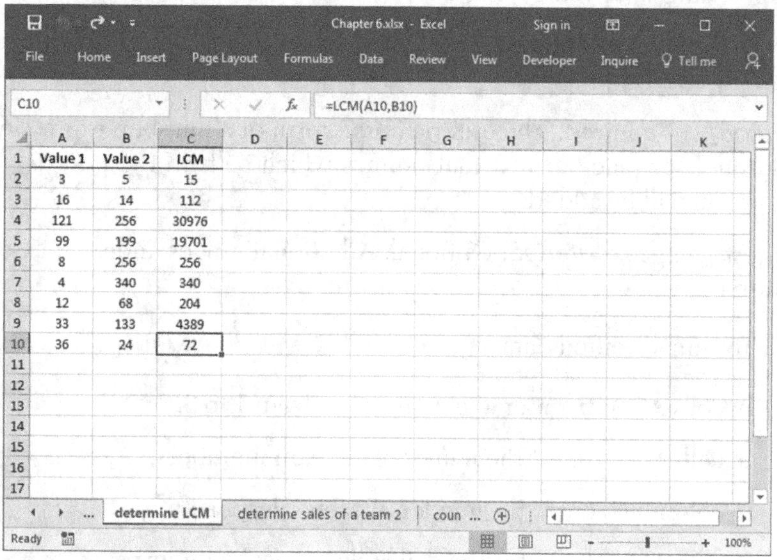

Figure 6–43

▶ To determine the least common multiple:

1. In cells A2:A10, list any valid numbers.

2. In cells B2:B10, list any valid numbers.

3. Select cells C2:C10 and type the following formula: **=LCM(A2,B2)**.

4. Press **<Ctrl+Enter>**.

Use the SUMIFS function to determine sales of a team and gender of its members

This example uses the worksheet referred to in Figure 6–3; however, the table not only sums the sales of different teams but also sums the sales of each team by the gender of each member. You can use the SUMIFS function to add all cells in a range that are specified by several criteria.

The SUMIFS function syntax has the following arguments:

SUMIFS(sum_range, criteria_range1, criteria1, [criteria_range2, criteria2], ...)

sum_range: Required. One or more cells to sum, including numbers or names, ranges, or cells.

criteria_range1: Required. The first range in which to evaluate the associated criteria.

criteria_1: Required. The criteria in the form of a number, expression, cell reference, or piece of text that defines which cells in the *criteria_range1* argument will be added.

criteria_range2, criteria2: Optional. Additional ranges and their associated criteria.

▶ To sum specified data:

1. In cells A2:A10, enter a team number from 1 to 3.

2. In cells B2:B10, list the names of all team members.

3. In column C, enter the gender of each salesperson.

4. In cells D2:D10, enter the daily sales of each employee.

5. List the numbers 1, 2, 3, and the sales broken down by gender for each team in cells F2:F7 as shown in Figure 6–44.

6. Select cells H2:H7 and type the following formula: **=SUMIFS($D$2:$D$10,$A$2:$A$10,F2,$C$2:$C$10,G2)**

7. Press **<Ctrl+Enter>**.

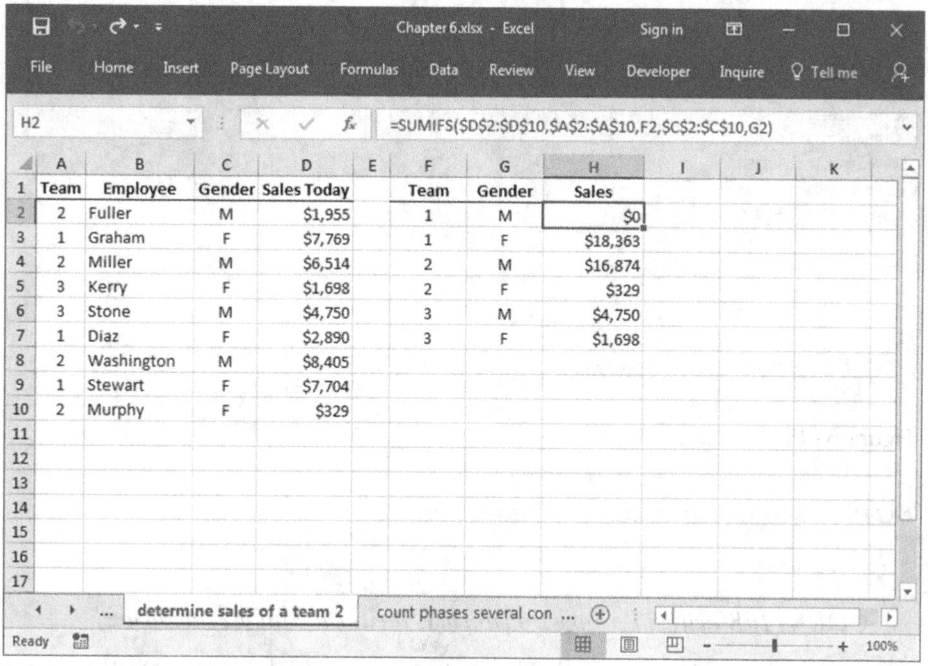

Figure 6–44

NOTE: Up to 127 range/criteria pairs are allowed.

Use the COUNTIF function to count phases that cost more than $1,000 within a certain duration

This example uses the worksheet referred to in Figure 6–6 with the addition of the duration of each project phase. To determine how many phases cost more than $1,000 and take two days or less, use the COUNTIFS function. This function counts the number of cells in a range that meet the specified criteria.

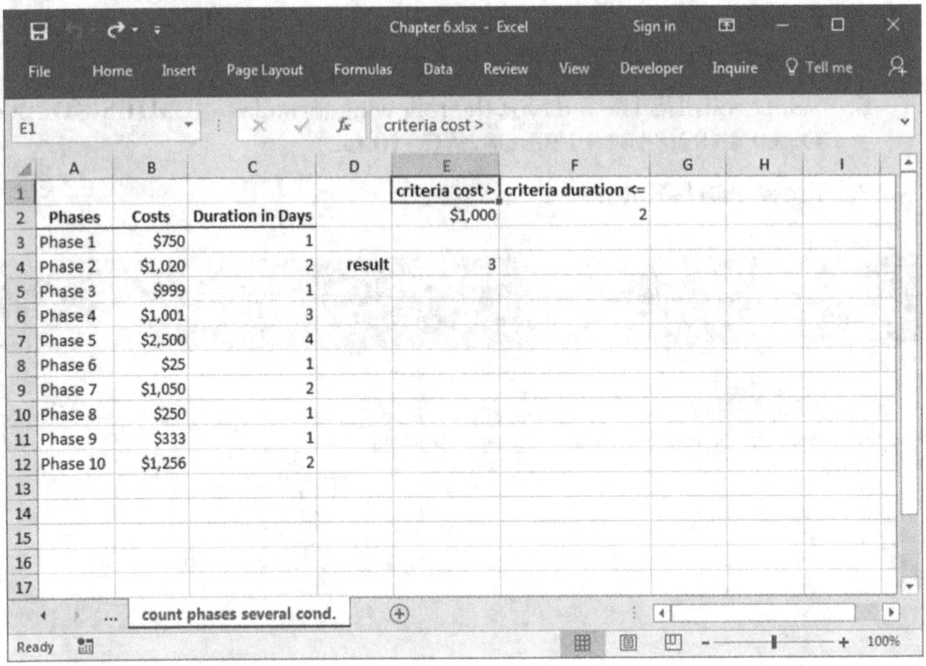

Figure 6–45

NOTE: Up to 127 range/criteria pairs are allowed.

COUNTIFS(*criteria_range1, criteria1, [criteria_range2, criteria2],...*)

criteria_range1: Required. The first range in which to evaluate the associated criteria.

criteria1: Required. The criteria in the form of a number, expression, cell reference, or piece of text that defines which cells will be counted.

criteria_range2, criteria2, ... Optional. Additional ranges and their associated criteria.

▶ To count specified phases:

1. In cells A3:A12, enter the different phases.

2. In cells B3:B12, enter the costs of each phase.

3. In cells C3:C12, enter the duration of each phase.

4. Enter **1000** in cell E2 and **2** in cell F2 as the given criteria.

5. Select cell E4 and type the following formula:
    =COUNTIFS (B3:B12,">" & E2,C3:C12,"<=" & F2).

6. Press **<Enter>**.

Compare the INT, TRUNC, and ROUND functions

There are different methods in displaying numbers based on the accuracy required. Many financial functions depend on a high degree of accuracy especially when money is involved. Some programs calculate decimals out the the thousands or even further. Other programs do not require as much detail.

In this example, we will detail the differences between the INT, TRUNC, and ROUND functions. First the INT function simply cuts off all decimals and displays the number left of the decimal. The TRUNC functions cuts off all decimal places to the right of where you tell it. The ROUND functions rounds up or down at the decimal place you tell it.

For this example, we have three numbers on which to perform these functions in column B. The numbers across in row 3 are the number of decimals we are including in the TRUNC and ROUND functions. (In this example, we are using the "$" to make it easier to copy and paste formulas without having to change the formulas.)

1. In cell D5, type the formula =**INT($B5)**

2. In cell E5, type the formula: =**TRUNC($B5,E$3)** – this tells the cell to cutoff all values to the right of the decimal point listed in cell E3.

3. In cell F5, type the formula: =**ROUND($B5,F$3)** – this tells the cell to round the value at the decimal point listed in cell E3.

4. Highlight cells D5 to F5, place the cursor over the lower right corner of cell F5 and drag the contents down to cell F7.

5. Highlight cells D5 to F7, right-click and copy.

6. Click in cell H5 and paste

7. Click in cell L5 an paste

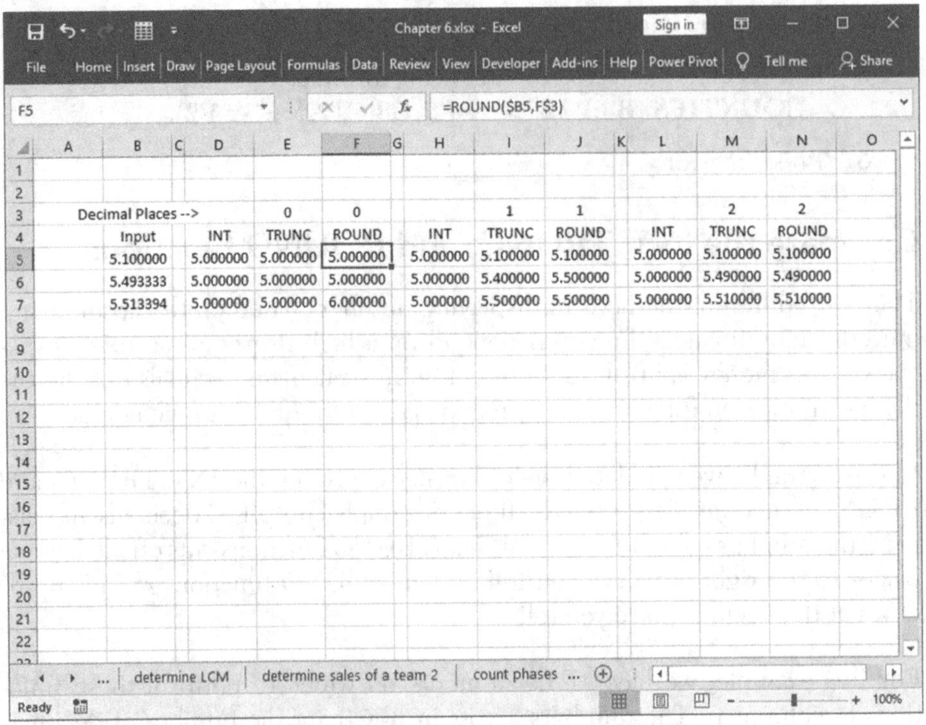

	A	B	C	D	E	F	G	H	I	J	K	L	M	N	O
3		Decimal Places -->			0	0			1	1			2	2	
4		Input	INT	TRUNC	ROUND		INT	TRUNC	ROUND		INT	TRUNC	ROUND	
5		5.100000	5.000000	5.000000	5.000000		5.000000	5.100000	5.100000		5.000000	5.100000	5.100000	
6		5.493333	5.000000	5.000000	5.000000		5.000000	5.400000	5.500000		5.000000	5.490000	5.490000	
7		5.513394	5.000000	5.000000	6.000000		5.000000	5.500000	5.500000		5.000000	5.510000	5.510000	

Figure 6–46

You can see that in some instances TRUNC acts like an INT while in other instances TRUNC acts like a ROUND. And yet in other instances such as in our example of truncating to one decimal, it treats numbers in its own manner apart from the other two.

Basic Financial Functions

7

Use the SYD function to calculate depreciation

In this tip, we calculate the depreciation of an investment. To do so, use the SYD function, which returns the sum-of-years' digits depreciation of an asset for a specified period.

SYD(*cost*, *salvage*, *life*, *per*)

cost: The asset's initial cost.

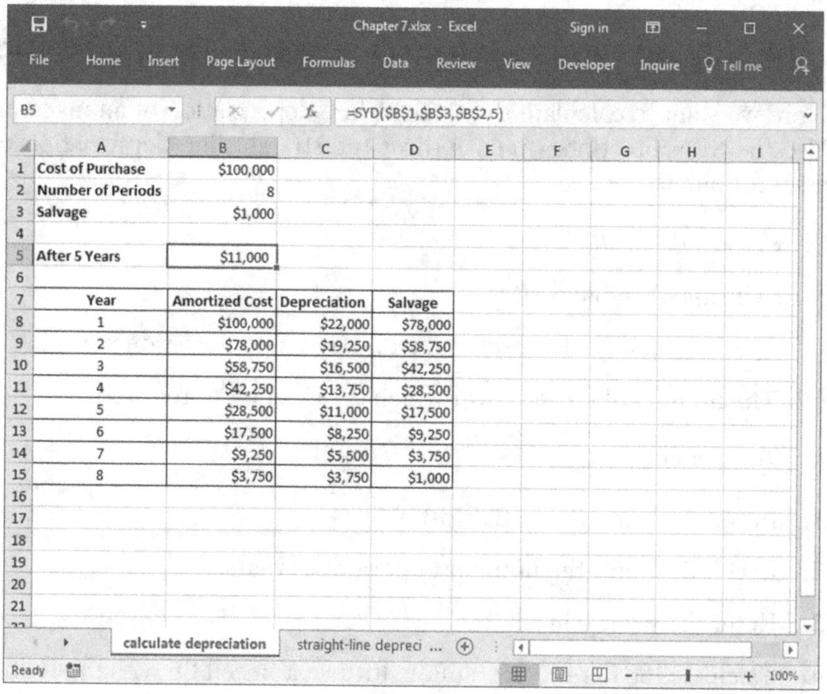

	A	B	C	D
1	Cost of Purchase	$100,000		
2	Number of Periods	8		
3	Salvage	$1,000		
4				
5	After 5 Years	$11,000		
6				
7	Year	Amortized Cost	Depreciation	Salvage
8	1	$100,000	$22,000	$78,000
9	2	$78,000	$19,250	$58,750
10	3	$58,750	$16,500	$42,250
11	4	$42,250	$13,750	$28,500
12	5	$28,500	$11,000	$17,500
13	6	$17,500	$8,250	$9,250
14	7	$9,250	$5,500	$3,750
15	8	$3,750	$3,750	$1,000

Cell B5: =SYD($B$1,$B$3,$B$2,5)

Figure 7-1

NOTE: SYD is calculated as follows: = ((cost–salvage)* (life–per+1)*2) / (life*(life+1)).

salvage: The value of the asset at the end of the depreciation period.

life: The number of periods over which the asset is depreciated.

per: The period. *per* must use the same units as *life*.

▶ To calculate depreciation:

1. In cell B1 enter the cost of purchase.

2. In cell B2 enter in years the number of periods over which the purchase will be depreciated.

3. Enter the salvage value in cell B3.

4. Calculate the depreciation in the fifth year in cell B5 with the following formula: **=SYD($B$1,$B$3,$B$2,5)**.

5. Press **<Enter>**.

Use the SLN function to calculate straight-line depreciation

Here we want to calculate the straight-line depreciation of an investment. Use the SLN function, which returns the straight-line depreciation of an asset for one period.

SLN(*cost, salvage, life*)

cost: The asset's initial cost.

salvage: The value of the asset at the end of the depreciation period.

life: The number of periods over which the asset is depreciated.

▶ To calculate depreciation:

1. In cell B1, enter the initial cost.

2. In cell B2, enter the number of periods as years.

3. Enter the salvage in cell B3.

4. Calculate the depreciation in the fifth year in cell B5 with the following formula: **=SLN($B$1,$B$3,$B$2)**.

5. Press **<Enter>**.

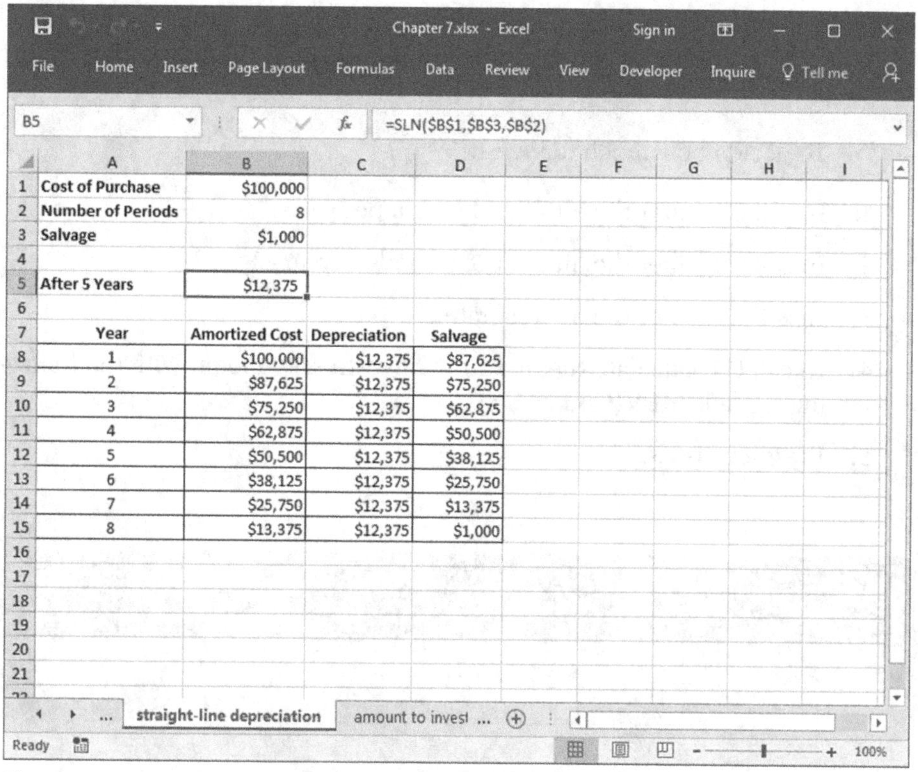

	A	B	C	D
1	Cost of Purchase	$100,000		
2	Number of Periods	8		
3	Salvage	$1,000		
4				
5	After 5 Years	$12,375		
6				
7	Year	Amortized Cost	Depreciation	Salvage
8	1	$100,000	$12,375	$87,625
9	2	$87,625	$12,375	$75,250
10	3	$75,250	$12,375	$62,875
11	4	$62,875	$12,375	$50,500
12	5	$50,500	$12,375	$38,125
13	6	$38,125	$12,375	$25,750
14	7	$25,750	$12,375	$13,375
15	8	$13,375	$12,375	$1,000

Figure 7-2

Use the PV function to decide an amount to invest

In this example, you need to decide on an amount of money you want to invest. To solve this problem, you use the PV function, which returns the present value of an investment. This is the total amount that a series of future payments is worth now.

PV(*rate*, *nper*, *pmt*, *fv*, *type*)

rate: The interest rate per period.

nper: The total number of payment periods in an annuity.

pmt: The payment made each period, which is a constant value.

fv: The future value. This is the amount you want after the last payment is made.

type: A number that indicates when payments are due. 0 or omitted indicates the end of the period, and 1 indicates the beginning of the period.

▶ To decide how much to invest:

1. In cell C1, enter the estimated return per year.

2. In cell C2, enter the number of periods in years.

3. In cell C3, enter the interest rate.

4. In cell C4, calculate the maximum investment amount with the following formula: **=PV(C3,C2,C1)**.

5. Press **<Enter>**.

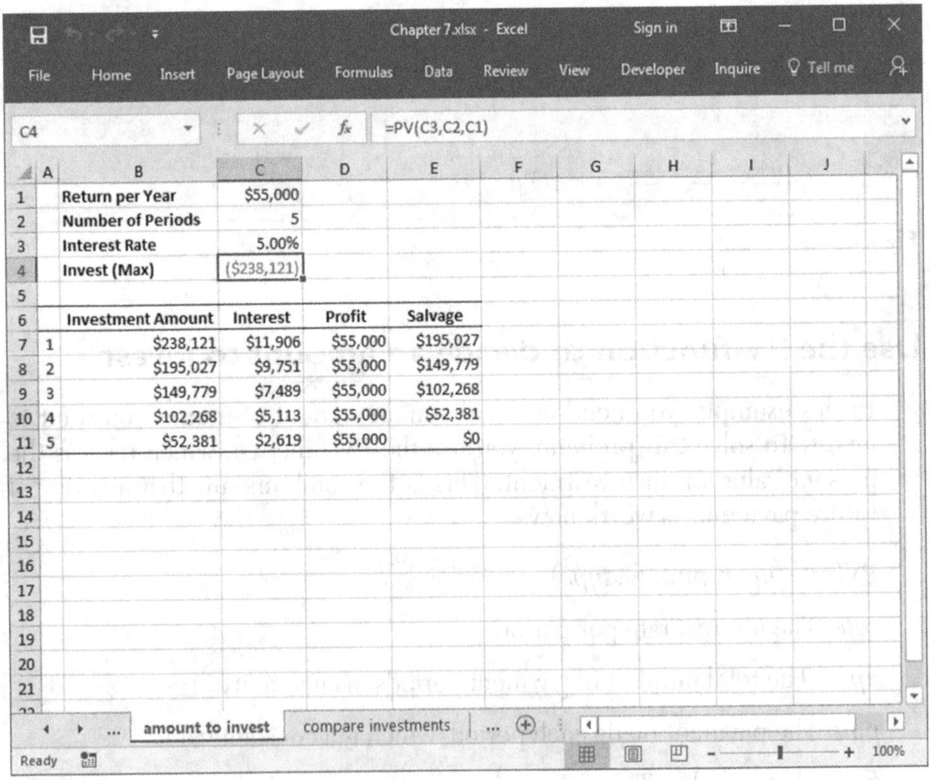

	A	B	C	D	E	F	G	H	I	J
1		Return per Year	$55,000							
2		Number of Periods	5							
3		Interest Rate	5.00%							
4		Invest (Max)	($238,121)							
5										
6		Investment Amount	Interest	Profit	Salvage					
7	1	$238,121	$11,906	$55,000	$195,027					
8	2	$195,027	$9,751	$55,000	$149,779					
9	3	$149,779	$7,489	$55,000	$102,268					
10	4	$102,268	$5,113	$55,000	$52,381					
11	5	$52,381	$2,619	$55,000	$0					

C4 = =PV(C3,C2,C1)

Figure 7–3

Use the PV function to compare investments

Two investments need to be compared. The amount of each investment, the number of periods, the interest, and the estimated return are given. To calculate and compare, use the PV function as described below.

▶ To compare investments:

1. In cells B2 and C2, enter the investment amounts.

2. In cells B3 and C3, enter the interest rates.

3. In cells B4 and C4, enter the number of periods.

4. In cells B5 and C5, enter the estimated return of each investment.

5. Select cells B7:C7 and type the following formula: **=-PV(B3,B4,B5)**.

6. Press **<Ctrl+Enter>**.

7. Select cells B8:C8 and type the formula **=B7-B2**.

8. Press **<Ctrl+Enter>**.

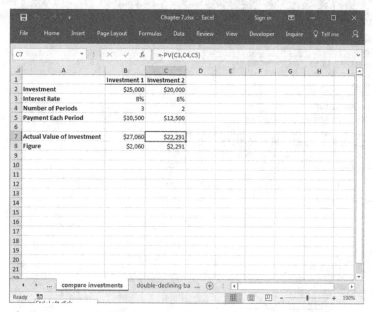

Figure 7-4

NOTE: Investment 2 is more expensive than Investment 1.

Use the DDB function to calculate using the double-declining balance method

The DDB function returns the depreciation of an asset for a specified period, using the double-declining balance method or some other method that can be specified.

DDB(*cost, salvage, life, period, factor*)

cost: The asset's initial cost.

salvage: The value of the asset at the end of the depreciation period.

life: The number of periods over which the asset is being depreciated.

period: The period for which the depreciation is being calculated.

factor: The rate at which the balance declines. If *factor* is omitted, it is assumed to be 2, which specifies the double-declining balance method.

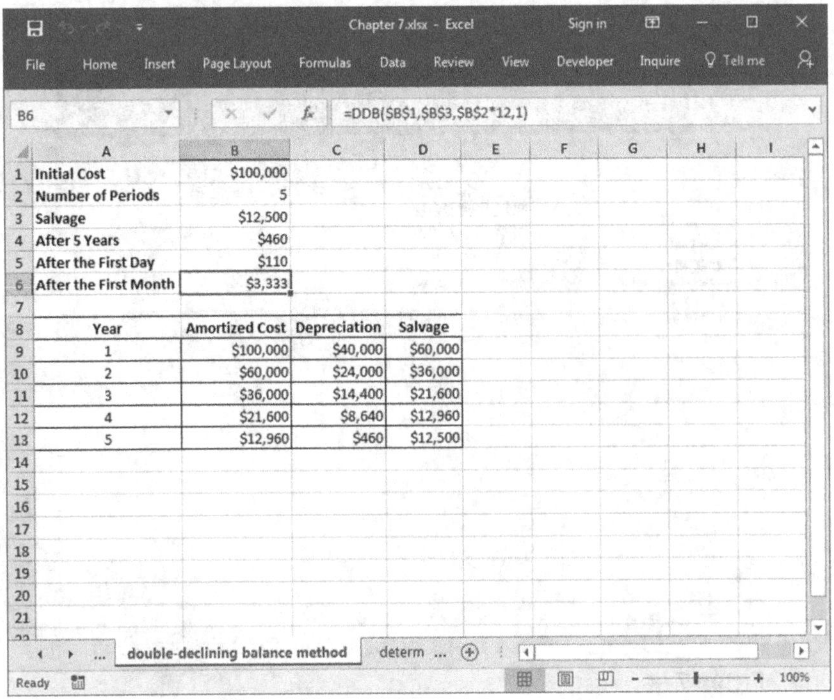

	A	B	C	D
1	Initial Cost	$100,000		
2	Number of Periods	5		
3	Salvage	$12,500		
4	After 5 Years	$460		
5	After the First Day	$110		
6	After the First Month	$3,333		
7				
8	Year	Amortized Cost	Depreciation	Salvage
9	1	$100,000	$40,000	$60,000
10	2	$60,000	$24,000	$36,000
11	3	$36,000	$14,400	$21,600
12	4	$21,600	$8,640	$12,960
13	5	$12,960	$460	$12,500

Figure 7-5

▶ To use the double-declining balance method:

1. Enter the initial cost in cell B1, the number of periods in cell B2, and the salvage in cell B3.

2. Calculate the depreciation in the fifth year in cell B4 with the following formula: **=DDB($B$1,$B$3,$B$2,5)**.

3. To calculate the depreciation after one day, type this formula in cell B5: **=DDB($B$1,$B$3,$B$2*365,1)**.

4. To calculate the depreciation after the first month, use this formula in cell B6: **=DDB($B$1,$B$3,$B$2*12,1)**.

Use the PMT function to determine the payment of a loan

To determine the payment amount for a loan based on constant payments and a constant interest rate, use the PMT function.

PMT(*rate, nper, pv, fv, type*)

rate: The interest rate of the loan.

nper: The total number of payments for the loan.

pv: The present value. This is also referred to as the principal.

fv: The future value. This is the amount you want after the last payment is made. If *fv* is omitted, it is assumed to be 0.

type: A number that indicates when payments are due. 0 or omitted indicates the end of the period, and 1 indicates the beginning of the period.

▶ To determine the payment for a loan:

1. In cell B1, enter the interest rate.

2. In cell B2, enter the number of periods in months.

3. In cell B3, enter the amount of the loan.

4. In cell B5, calculate the payment after one month with the following formula: **=-PMT($B$1/12,$B$2,$B$3)**.

5. Press **<Enter>**.

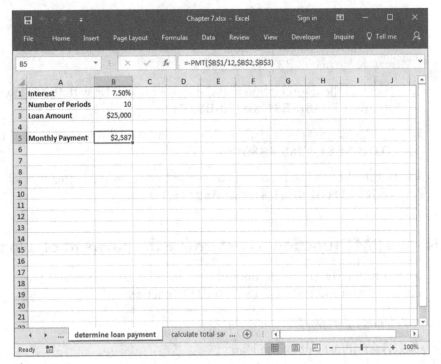

Figure 7–6

Use the FV function to calculate total savings account balance

In this example, you want to save money for five months. The interest rate is 3.5%. Every month you deposit $500 in the bank. How much money is in your bank account after five months? This question can be answered by using the FV function. It returns the future value of an investment based on periodic, constant payments and a constant interest rate.

FV(*rate, nper, pmt, pv, type*)

rate: The interest rate per period.

nper: The total number of payment periods in an annuity.

pmt: The payment made each period, which is a constant value.

pv: The present value. This is the amount that a series of future payments is worth right now.

type: A number that indicates when payments are due. 0 indicates the end of the period, and 1 indicates the beginning of the period.

▶ To calculate the total balance of an account with regular deposits and a constant interest rate:

1. Enter the current interest rate in cell B1 and the number of periods in cell B2.

2. In cell B3 enter the monthly amount to be put in the savings account.

3. In cell B4 type the formula **=-FV(B1/12,B2,B3)**.

4. Press **<Enter>**.

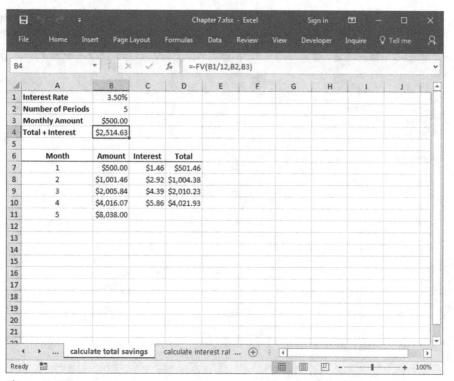

Figure 7–7

Use the RATE function to calculate interest rate

Let's say a bank advertises that if you deposit $500 each month for 12 years, you will have $100,000 at the end of the period. What is the interest rate the bank is paying? To answer this question, use the RATE function, which returns the interest rate per period of an annuity.

RATE(*nper, pmt, pv, fv, type, guess*)

nper: The total number of payment periods in an annuity.

pmt: The payment made each period, which is a constant value.

pv: The present value. This is the amount that a series of future payments is worth right now.

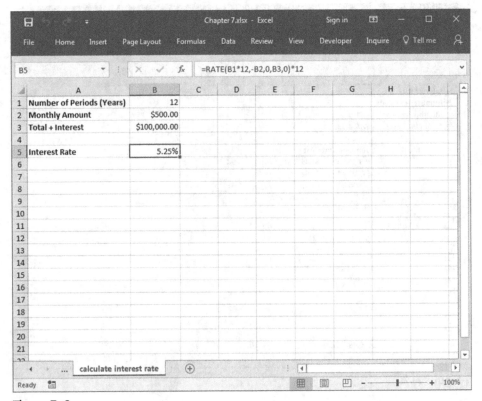

Figure 7–8

fv: The future value. This is the amount you want after the last payment is made.

type: A number that indicates when payments are due. 0 or omitted indicates the end of the period, and 1 indicates the beginning of the period.

guess: A guess for what the interest rate will be. If omitted, Excel uses 10%.

▶ To calculate the interest rate:

1. In cell B1, enter the number of periods in years.

2. In cell B2, enter the monthly amount to deposit.

3. In cell B3, enter the final value the bank has advertised.

4. In cell B5, type the following formula:
   =RATE(B1*12,-B2,0,B3,0)*12.

5. Press **<Enter>**.

Database Functions 8

Use the DCOUNT function to count special cells

Using this tip, cells in a list can be counted by specific criteria. Use the DCOUNT function to count all cells that contain numbers in a column of a list or database that match specified conditions.

DCOUNT(*database*, *field*, *criteria*)

database: The range of cells in the list or database. The first row of the list contains column headings.

field: Indicates the column to use in the function. *field* can be provided as text with the column heading enclosed in double quotation marks or as a number representing the position of the column within the list: 1 for the first column, 2 for the second column, and so on.

No.	Name	Category	Size	Price
12	carrots	vegetable	lb	$1.79
13	salad	vegetable	each	$2.99
14	bananas	fruit	lb	$0.49
15	bread	bread	lb	$1.99
16	apples	fruit	lb	$0.89
17	cabbage	vegetable	each	$0.79
18	beef steak	meat	lb	$6.99
19	chicken	meat	each	$4.99
20	cherries	fruit	lb	$3.99

Figure 8-1

criteria: The range of cells containing the specified conditions. Any range can be used for the *criteria* argument, as long as it includes at least one column heading and at least one cell below the column heading to specify a condition.

Use the following data for this tip.

You can manually count all products in the vegetable category with a price less than or equal to $2.50, or you can let Excel do the counting, as described next:

▶ To count special cells:

1. Copy the range A1:E1, as shown in the preceding figure.

2. Select cell A14 and press **<Ctrl+V>**.

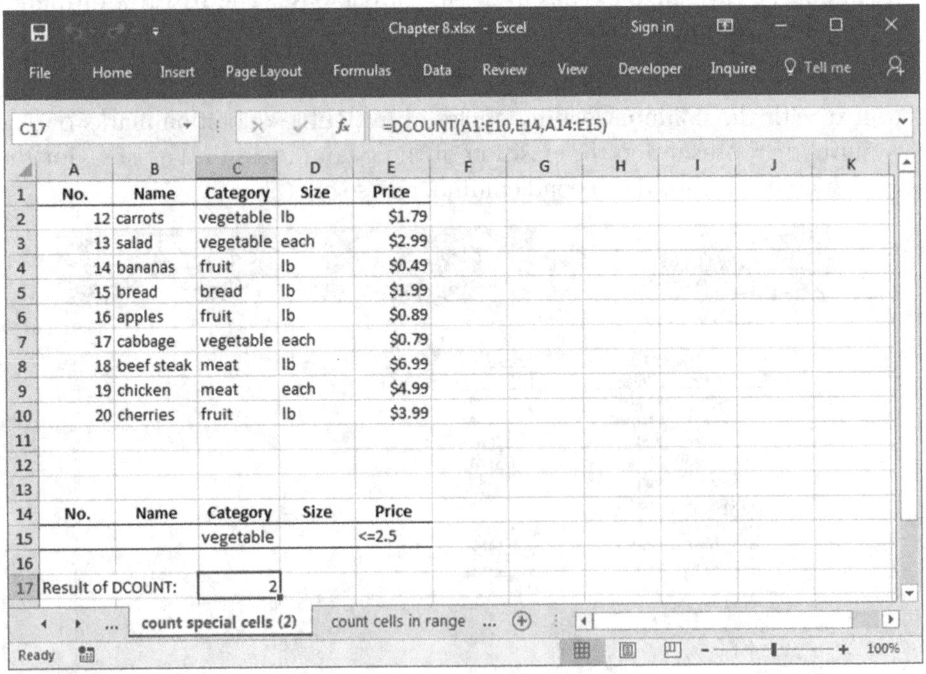

Figure 8–2

NOTE: The category in cell C15 can be changed. To count several categories, just type "meat" in cell C16 and change the formula in cell A17 to this:
=DCOUNT (A1:E10,E14,A14:E16).

3. Select cell C15 and type **vegetable**.

4. In cell E15, type **<=2.50** to define the search criteria.

5. In cell C17, type the following formula:
   =DCOUNT(A1:E10, E14,A14:E15).

6. Press **<Enter>**.

Use the DCOUNT function to count cells in a range between x and y

Use the data in the previous example to continue working with the DCOUNT function. Here we want to count all products in the vegetable category that cost more than $1.75 but no more than $2.50.

▶ To count cells in a specific range between x and y:

1. Copy the range A1:E1.

2. Select cell A14 and paste the copied cells with **<Ctrl+V>**.

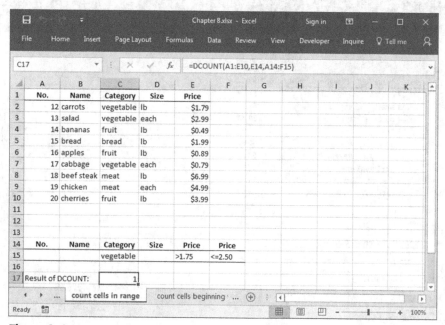

Figure 8–3

3. Select cell C15 and type **vegetable**.

4. In cell E15 type **>1.75**.

5. In cell F15 type **<=2.50**.

6. In cell C17 type the following formula:
   =DCOUNT(A1:E10, E14,A14:F15).

7. Press **<Enter>**.

Use the DCOUNTA function to count all cells beginning with the same character

Continuing with the previous example, now we want to count all cells that begin with the letter "b," like bread, beef steak, and bananas. To do this, use the DCOUNTA function, which counts the non-blank cells in a column of a list or database that match the specified conditions.

The arguments are the same as those used with the DCOUNT function.

	A	B	C	D	E	F	G	H	I	J	K
1	No.	Name	Category	Size	Price						
2	12	carrots	vegetable	lb	$1.79						
3	13	salad	vegetable	each	$2.99						
4	14	bananas	fruit	lb	$0.49						
5	15	bread	bread	lb	$1.99						
6	16	apples	fruit	lb	$0.89						
7	17	cabbage	vegetable	each	$0.79						
8	18	beef steak	meat	lb	$6.99						
9	19	chicken	meat	each	$4.99						
10	20	cherries	fruit	lb	$3.99						
11											
12											
13											
14	No.	Name	Category	Size	Price	Price					
15		b*									
16											
17	Result of DCOUNT:		3								

Figure 8–4

▶ To count cells beginning with the letter "b:"

1. Copy the range A1:E1.

2. Select cell A14 and press **<Ctrl+V>**.

3. In cell B15, type **b***.

4. In cell C17, type the following formula:
   =DCOUNTA(A1:E10,E14, A14:E15).

5. Press **<Enter>**.

Use the DGET function to search for a product by number

In this example, enter a product number to let Excel search a list for the corresponding product. To do so, use the DGET function, which selects a value from a column of a list or database that matches specified conditions. This is like the VLOOKUP function used to lookup a value in a range or table a return associated information.

DGET(*database, field, criteria*)

database: The range of cells in the list or database. The first row of the list contains column headings.

field: Indicates the column to use in the function. *field* can be provided as text with the column heading enclosed in double quotation marks or as a number representing the position of the column within the list.

criteria: The range of cells containing the specified conditions.

▶ To search for a product number:

1. Copy the range A1:B1.

2. Select cell D1 and press **<Ctrl+V>**.

3. In cell D2, enter the number **13**.

4. In cell E2, type the following formula: **=DGET(A1:B10,E1,D1:D2)**.

5. Press **<Enter>**.

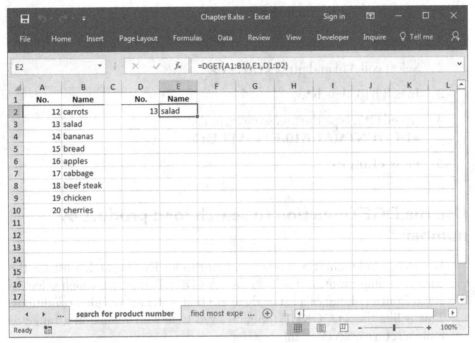

Figure 8–5

Use the DMAX function to find the most expensive product in a category

This tip shows how to determine the most expensive product in a list specified by a category using the DMAX function. This function returns the largest number in a column of a list or database that matches specified conditions.

DMAX(*database, field, criteria*)

database: The range of cells in the list or database. The first row of the list contains column headings.

field: Indicates the column to use in the function.

criteria: The range of cells containing the specified conditions.

▶ To find the most expensive vegetable:

1. Copy the range A1:E1.

2. Select cell A14 and press **<Ctrl+V>**.

3. In cell C15, enter **vegetable** as the search criteria.

4. In cell C17, type the following formula:
=DMAX(A1:E10,E14, A14:E15).

5. Press **<Enter>**.

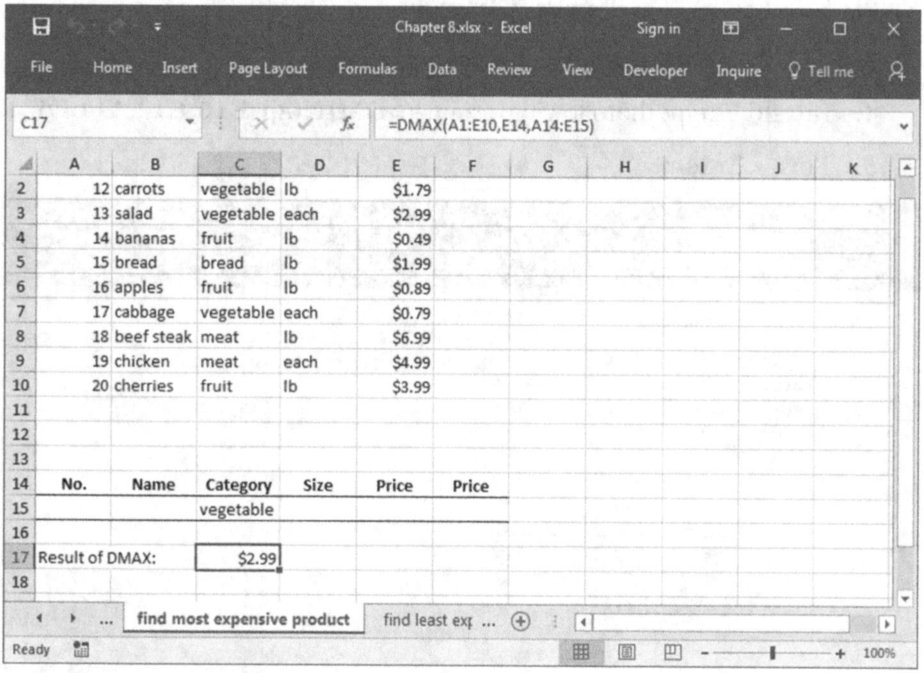

Figure 8-6

Use the DMIN function to find the least expensive product in a category

For this example, use the same list of food products to determine the least expensive fruit. To do so, use the DMIN function to return the smallest number in a column of a list or database that matches specified conditions.

DMIN(*database, field, criteria*)

database: The range of cells in the list or database. The first row of the list contains column headings.

field: Indicates the column to use in the function.

criteria: The range of cells containing the specified conditions.

▶ To find the least expensive fruit:

1. Copy the range A1:E1.

2. Select cell A14 and press **<Ctrl+V>**.

3. In cell C15, enter **fruit** as the search criteria.

4. In cell C17, type the following formula: **=DMIN(A1:E10,E14,A14:E15)**.

5. Press **<Enter>**.

▲	A	B	C	D	E	F	G	H	I	J	K	▲
2	12	carrots	vegetable	lb	$1.79							
3	13	salad	vegetable	each	$2.99							
4	14	bananas	fruit	lb	$0.49							
5	15	bread	bread	lb	$1.99							
6	16	apples	fruit	lb	$0.89							
7	17	cabbage	vegetable	each	$0.79							
8	18	beef steak	meat	lb	$6.99							
9	19	chicken	meat	each	$4.99							
10	20	cherries	fruit	lb	$3.99							
11												
12												
13												
14	No.	Name	Category	Size	Price	Price						
15			fruit									
16												
17	Result of DMIN:		$0.49									
18												

find least expensive product | find oldest pe ...

Figure 8–7

Use the DMIN function to find the oldest person on a team

The oldest member of a team can be found by using the DMIN function. (To find the youngest person, use DMAX.) Dates are stored in Excel as integer values beginning with 1 for January 1, 1900, and incrementing by

1 for each subsequent day. For example, the date 11/16/2004 has the value 38307. The syntax for DMIN is described in the previous tip.

▶ To find the oldest person on a team:

1. Copy to a worksheet cells A1:C10 as shown in Figure 8–8.

2. Copy the range A1:C1.

3. Select cell A12 and press **<Ctrl+V>**.

4. In cell C13, enter **1** to search just inside team 1.

5. In cell C15, type the following formula: **=DMIN(A1:C10,B1,A12:C13)**.

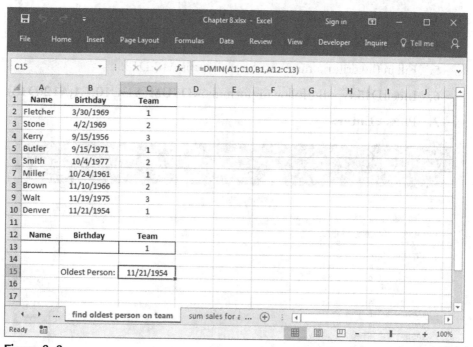

Figure 8–8

Use the DSUM function to sum sales for a period

Sometimes a list has to be summed up if it matches particular conditions. For example, you might want to sum sales in a certain category or for a specified time period. Use the DSUM function, which adds the numbers in a column of a list or database that matches specified conditions.

DSUM(*database*, *field*, *criteria*)

database: The range of cells in the list or database. The first row of the list contains column headings.

field: Indicates the column to use in the function.

criteria: The range of cells containing the specified conditions.

▶ To sum sales for a particular time period:

1. Copy to a worksheet cells A2:C10 as shown in Figure 8–9.

2. Copy the range A1:C1.

3. Select cell A12 and press **<Ctrl+V>**.

4. In cell D12, type **Date**.

5. Fill in the criteria range as shown in cells A13:D13.

6. In cell D15, type the following formula: **=DSUM(A1:C10,C1,A12:D13)**.

7. Press **<Enter>**.

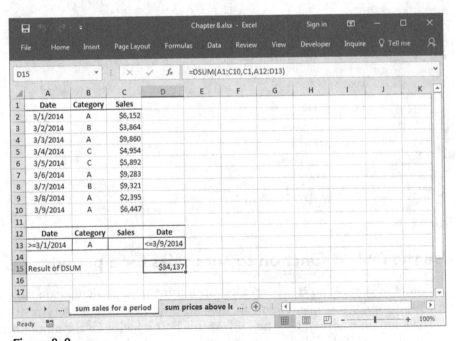

Figure 8–9

Use the DSUM function to sum all prices in a category that are above a particular level

The list in the following figure shows the prices of a number of goods in different categories. To sum all prices in one category that are above a particular price, use the DSUM function. Here we will sum all prices in category A that are above $100.

▶ To sum all prices in category A above $100:

1. Copy to a worksheet cells A1:C10 as shown in Figure 8–10.

2. Copy range A1:C1.

3. Select cell A12 and press **<Ctrl+V>**.

4. In cell B13, enter **A** to search inside category A.

5. In cell C13, type the argument **>100**.

6. In cell C15, type the following formula:
   =DSUM(A1:C10,C1,A12:C13).

7. Press **<Enter>**.

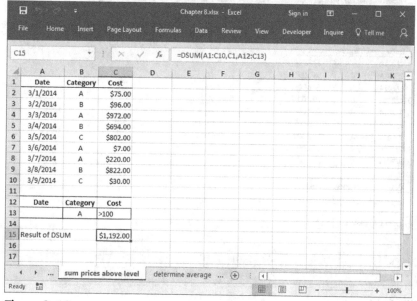

Figure 8–10

Use the DAVERAGE function to determine the average price in a category

To determine the average price in a category, use the DAVERAGE function. This function averages the values in a column of a list or database that match specified conditions.

DAVERAGE(*database, field, criteria*)

database: The range of cells in the list or database. The first row of the list contains column headings.

field: Indicates the column to use in the function.

criteria: The range of cells containing the specified conditions.

▶ To determine the average price of a category:

1. Copy to a worksheet cells A1:C10 as shown in Figure 8–11.

2. Copy range A1:C1.

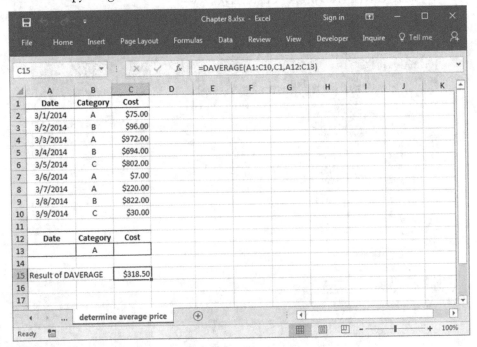

Figure 8–11

3. Select cell A12 and press **<Ctrl+V>**.

4. In cell B13, enter **A** to search inside category A.

5. In cell C15, type the following formula: **=DAVERAGE(A1:C10,C1, A12:C13)**.

6. Press **<Enter>**.

Lookup and Reference Functions 9

Use the ADDRESS, MATCH, and MAX functions to find the position of the largest number

We learned in previous tips how to look up a single value in a list. Now we want to determine the position of the largest value in a list by combining three Excel functions. First, we use the MAX function to get the largest value, then we use the MATCH function to find its relative position, and finally we use the ADDRESS function to determine the exact cell address.

NOTE: The MAX function was described in Chapter 5.

MATCH(*lookup_value, lookup_array, match_type*)

lookup_value: The value that corresponds to the entry to be found in a table.

lookup_array: A contiguous range of cells that contain possible *lookup* values.

match_type: Specifies how *Excel matches lookup_*value with values in *lookup_array*. 1 specifies that MATCH is to find the largest value that is less than or equal to *lookup_value*; 0 specifies that MATCH is to find the first value equal to *lookup_value*; and −1 specifies that MATCH is to find the smallest value that is greater than or equal to *lookup_value*.

The ADDRESS function returns the exact cell address as text.

ADDRESS(*row_num, column_num, abs_num, sheet_text*)

row_num: The row number to be used in the cell reference.

column_num: The column number to be used in the cell reference.

abs_num: The type of reference to return. 1 or omitted indicates absolute, 2 indicates absolute row and relative column, 3 indicates relative row and absolute column, and 4 indicates relative.

sheet_text: The name of the worksheet to be used as the external reference. If omitted, no sheet name is used.

For example:

=*ADDRESS(5,2)* is an absolute reference to cell $B$5.

=*ADDRESS(4,4,2)* is an absolute row reference and relative column reference to cell D$4.

=*ADDRESS(1,1,3)* is a relative row reference and an absolute column reference to cell $A1.

Take a look at the following example.

▶ To search for the cell reference of the greatest number:

1. In cells A2:A10, enter some numbers.

2. Select cell C2 and type the following formula:
   =ADDRESS(MATCH(MAX(A1:A10),A1:A10),1,4).

3. Press **<Enter>**.

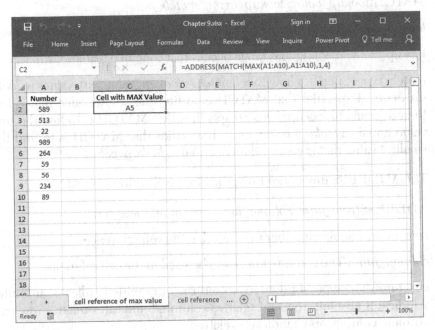

Figure 9–1

Use the ADDRESS, MATCH, and MIN functions to find the position of the smallest number

As with the previous tip, we can find the cell address for the smallest value in a list. We will again use the ADDRESS and MATCH functions, but this time in combination with MIN.

The MIN function finds the smallest value in a list. MATCH returns the relative position of the value 2, which will be transferred to the ADDRESS function to determine the cell address as shown in the following figure.

▶ To search for the smallest number:

1. In cells A2:A10, list some numbers.

2. Select cell C2 and type the following formula:
   =ADDRESS(MATCH (MIN(A1:A10),A1:A10,0),1).

3. Press **<Enter>**.

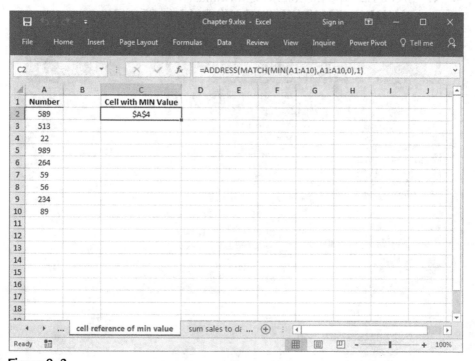

Figure 9–2

Use the ADDRESS, MATCH, and TODAY functions to sum sales up to today's date

In a worksheet, daily sales are recorded. To sum all listed sales until today's date, use the functions learned from previous tips, including the TODAY function, which returns the actual date. MATCH returns the relative position of TODAY, which will be transferred to the ADDRESS function to determine the cell address, as seen in cell E2 of Figure 9-3. With the SUM and INDIRECT functions, you can sum all sales up to today and get the desired result.

▶   To sum sales up to today:

1.   In cells A2:A7 list dates in ascending order.

2.   In cells B2:B7, enter the daily sales amounts.

3.   Select cell E1 and type the formula **=TODAY()** to get the current date.

4.   In cell E2, type the following formula:
     =ADDRESS(MATCH(TODAY(),$A$1:$A$7,1),2).

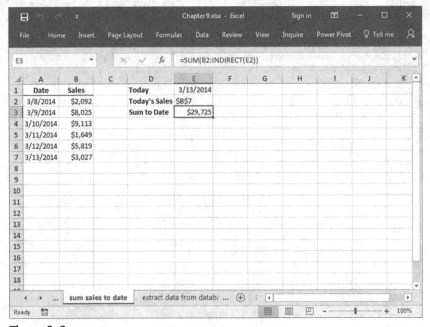

Figure 9-3

5. Determine the sum in cell E3 with the following formula: **=SUM (B2:INDIRECT(E2))**.

6. Press **<Enter>**.

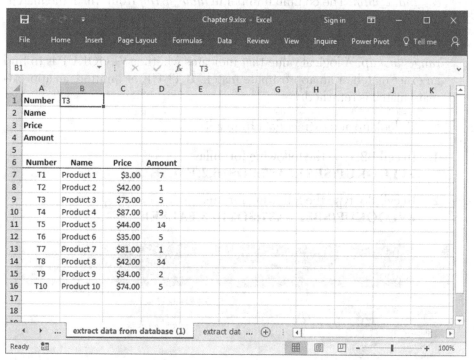

Figure 9–4

NOTE: INDIRECT(ref_text) returns the reference specified by a text string.

Use the VLOOKUP function to look up and extract data from a database

This tip explains how to search for a certain product in a list. First, take a look at the data in Figure 9-4:

Typing a valid product number in cell B1 fills cells B2 to B4 with the corresponding data from the list. To do this, use the VLOOKUP function, which searches for a value in the left-hand column of a table and returns a value in the same row from a column specified in the table.

VLOOKUP(*lookup_value*, *table_array*, *col_index_num*, *range_lookup*)

lookup_value: The value to be found in the left-hand column of the array.

table_array: The table in which data is looked up.

col_index_num: The column number in *table_array* from which the matching value must be returned. 1 returns the value in the first column in *table_array*, 2 returns the value in the second column in *table_array*, and so on.

range_lookup: A logical value that indicates whether VLOOKUP is to find an exact match or an approximate match. If TRUE or omitted, an approximate match is returned.

▶ To look up and extract data from a list:

1. In cell B2, type the following formula:
   =VLOOKUP($B$1,$A$7:$D$16,2,FALSE).

2. In cell B3, type the following formula:
   =VLOOKUP($B$1,$A$7:$D$16,3,FALSE).

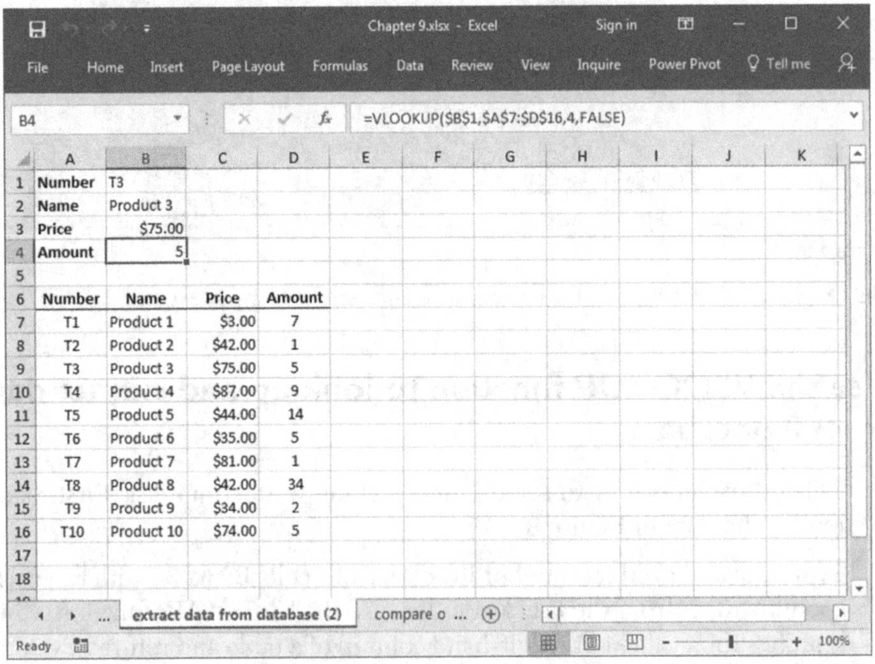

Figure 9–5

3. In cell B4, type the following formula:
   =VLOOKUP($B$1,$A$7:$D$16, 4,FALSE).

4. Press **<Enter>**.

Use the VLOOKUP function to compare offers from different suppliers

This example contains a table with offers from different suppliers for a product listed vertically. To search for the best offer, use the built-in MIN function in combination with VLOOKUP to display the supplier with the lowest price.

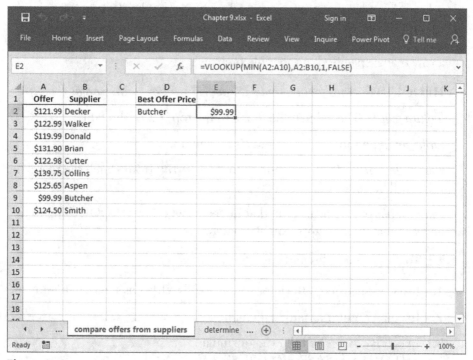

Figure 9–6

NOTE: To determine the lowest offer, use the function MIN(A2:A10), the result of which is shown in cell E2.

▶ To find the supplier with the lowest price:

1. In cells A2:A10, enter the offers.

2. In cells B2:B10, enter the names of the suppliers.

3. Select cell D2 and type the following formula:
    =VLOOKUP(MIN (A2:A10),A2:B10,1,FALSE).

4. Press **<Enter>**.

Use the HLOOKUP function to determine sales and costs for a team

The costs and sales for a team need to be looked up in a table. Each team is listed by column with its costs and sales. To get the desired information, use the HLOOKUP function, which searches for a value in the top row of a table or an array of values and then returns a value in the same column from a row that is specified in the table or array.

HLOOKUP(*lookup_value, table_array, row_index_num, range_lookup*)

lookup_value: The value to be found in the top row of the table.

table_array: A table in which data is looked up.

row_index_num: The row number in *table_array* from which the matching value will be returned.

range_lookup: A logical value that indicates whether HLOOKUP is to find an exact match or an approximate match.

▶ To determine sales and costs for a team:

1. In a worksheet, copy the information in cells A1:E3, as shown in Figure 9–7.

2. In cell A7, enter a valid team name.

3. In cell B7, type the following formula:
    =HLOOKUP($A$7,$B$1:$E$3,2,FALSE).

4. Press **<Enter>**.

5. Select cell C7 and type the following formula:
    =HLOOKUP($A$7, $B$1:$E$3,3,FALSE).

6. Press **<Enter>**.

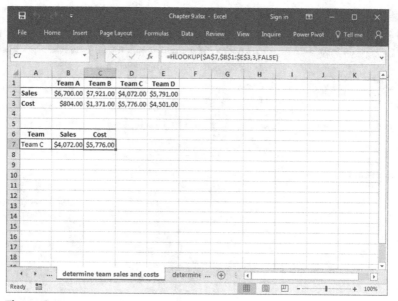

Figure 9–7

Use the HLOOKUP function to determine sales for a particular day

In this example, all sales for a certain day need to be listed in the first column of a table. In addition, all sales need to be summed in cell A7 to show the total amount of sales for this day.

▶ To determine the total amount of sales for one day:

1. In a worksheet, copy the information in cells C1:G5 as shown in Figure 9–8.

2. In cell A1, enter the desired day for which the sales of each team need to be listed.

3. Select cells A2:A5 and type the following formula:
   =HLOOKUP($A$1, $D$1:$G$5,(ROW())).

4. Press **<Ctrl+Enter>**.

5. Select cell A7 and type the following formula:
   ="SUM = " & TEXT (SUM(A2:A5),"$#,000.00").

6. Press **<Enter>**.

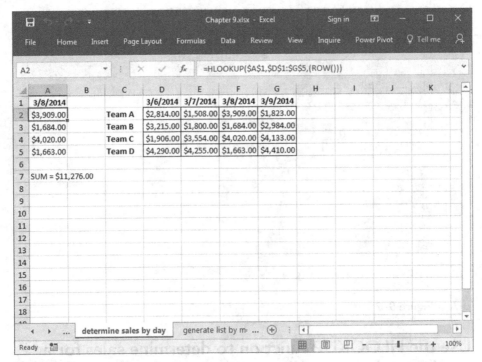

Figure 9–8

NOTE: The ROW function returns the active row number.

Use the HLOOKUP function to generate a list for a specific month

The dates on which errors occur in a system are recorded each month in an Excel table as shown in the Figure 9-9. The first column lists the dates of all errors that occurred in a certain month. Enter the month in cell A1 and use a combination of functions based on HLOOKUP to return all recorded dates.

▶ To generate a list for a specific month:

1. In a worksheet, copy cells C2:F5, as shown in Figure 9–9.

2. In cell A1, type the month **11**.

3. Select cells A3:A5 and type the following formula: **=IF (HLOOKUP ($A$1,$C$2:$F$11,ROW()-1,FALSE)=0,"",HLOOKUP($A$1, $C$2:$F$11,ROW()-1,FALSE)).**

4. Press **<Ctrl+Enter>**.

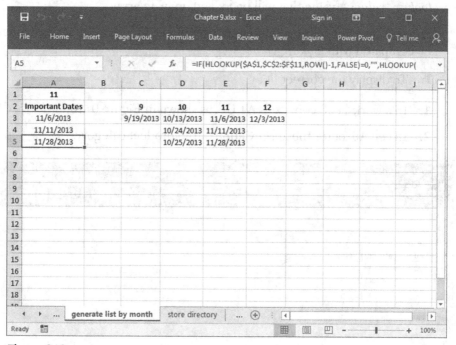

Figure 9–9

NOTE: You may need to format cells A3:A8 with a date format.

Use the LOOKUP function to get the directory of a store

A store sells different products in a big warehouse. Each floor contains different categories of products. For example, the customer can find software on the first floor and hardware on the second floor. Each category is assigned a combination of two letters, such as software = SO, hardware = HA, food = FO, indoor = IN, and outdoor = OU. The task now is to find which products are sold on which floor by entering the category abbreviation in cell A9. Do this by using the array form of the LOOKUP function to return a value from a one-row or one-column range or from an array.

LOOKUP(*lookup_value*, *array*)

lookup_value: A value that will be looked up in an array.

array: A range of cells containing text, numbers, or logical values that are to be compared with *lookup_value*.

▶ To display the correct floor:

1. In a worksheet, copy cells A1:C6, as shown in Figure 9–10.

2. In cell A9, enter the abbreviation of the product category.

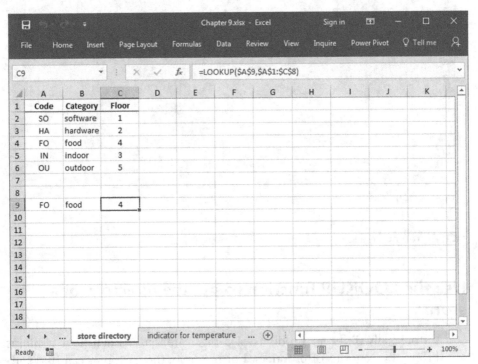

Figure 9–10

NOTE: The array form of the LOOKUP function is provided for compatibility with other spreadsheet programs. VLOOKUP can also be used in this situation, provided that the values in the first column are sorted in ascending order.

3. Select cell B9 and type the following formula:
   =LOOKUP ($A$9, $A$1:$B$8).

4. Press **<Enter>**.

5. Select cell C9 and type the following formula:
   =LOOKUP($A$9,$A$1:$C$8).

6. Press **<Enter>**.

Use the LOOKUP function to get the indicator for the current temperature

The following list contains indicators like cold, cool, warm, or hot for different temperature ranges. Enter the current temperature in one cell and let Excel determine the corresponding indicator with the vector form of the LOOKUP function.

LOOKUP(*lookup_value, lookup_vector, result_vector*)

lookup_value: A value that will be searched for in the first vector.

lookup_vector: A range containing only one row or one column.

result_vector: A range containing only one row or one column. *result_vector* and *lookup_vector* must be the same size.

If LOOKUP can't find the *lookup_value*, it matches the largest value in *lookup_vector* that is less than or equal to it, which is quite useful for our task, because we have just four indicators.

They are defined as follows:

- From –50°F to 31°F = icy

- From 32°F to 49°F = cold

- From 50°F to 76°F = warm

- 77°F and above = hot

▶ To add an indicator for the temperature:

1. In a worksheet, copy the information in cells A1:B5, as shown in Figure 9–11.

2. In cell D2, enter the current temperature.

3. cell E2 and type the following formula:
   = LOOKUP ($D$2,B2:B5, A2:A5).

4. Press **<Enter>**.

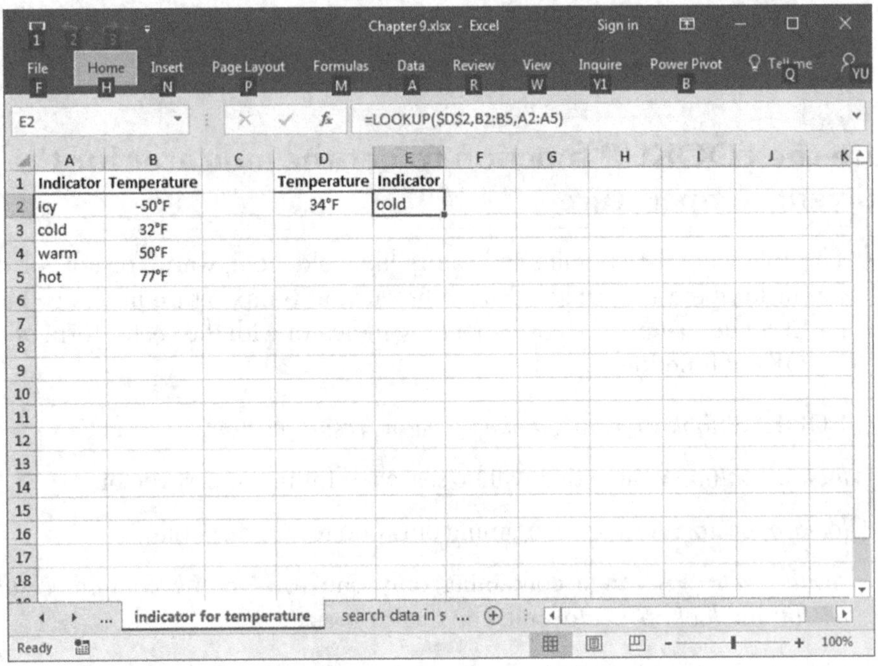

Figure 9–11

Use the INDEX function to search for data in a sorted list

In addition to VLOOKUP, the INDEX function can be used to search for data in a sorted list. Copy the table below to a new worksheet and enter in cell A2 the team number for which you want to search. Let Excel search for the team name and corresponding costs with the INDEX or VLOOKUP functions as described in the next steps.

▶ To search for data in a list:

1. In cells A2 and A3, enter valid numbers between 1 and 7.

2. cell B2 and type the following formula:
   =INDEX($A$6:$C$12,MATCH($A$2,$A$6:$A$12,0),2).

3. In cell B3, type the following formula:
   =VLOOKUP($A$3,$A$5: $C$12,2,FALSE).

4. Select cell C2 and type the following formula:
   =INDEX($A$6:$C$12,MATCH($A$2,$A$6:$A$12,0),3).

5. In cell C3, type the following formula:
   =VLOOKUP($A$3,$A$5:$C$12, 3,FALSE).

6. Press **<Enter>**.

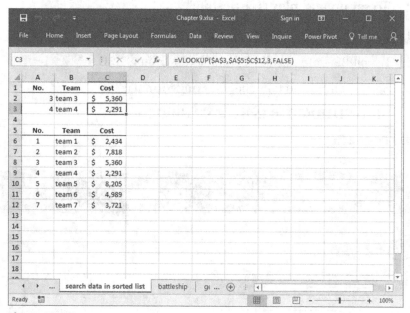

Figure 9–12

Use the INDIRECT function to play "Battleship"

Why not take a break and play "Battleship?" It's easy to create, and when you're finished reading this tip, you can enjoy playing.

In a new worksheet, define the range C1:E10 as the battlefield and border it as desired. Place some Xs to define the location of the ships and enter in cells B1 and B2 the coordinates of the cell to be fired on. Use the INDIRECT function to get the functionality that returns the reference, specified by a text string (e.g., "HIT").

INDIRECT(*ref_text*, *a1*)

ref_text: A reference to a cell containing an A1-style reference, an R1C1-style reference, a name defined as a reference, or a reference to a cell as a text string.

a1: A logical value specifying the type of reference that is contained in the cell *ref_text*. If *a1* is TRUE or omitted, *ref_text* will be an A1-style reference. If *a1* is FALSE, *ref_text* will be an R1C1-style reference.

▶ **To set up and play "Battleship:"**

1. In cell B1, enter a valid row number from 1 to 10.

2. In cell B2, enter a valid column letter from C to E.

3. Select cell B3 and type the following formula:

    =IF(INDIRECT(B2&B1)="X","Hit","").

4. Press **<Enter>**.

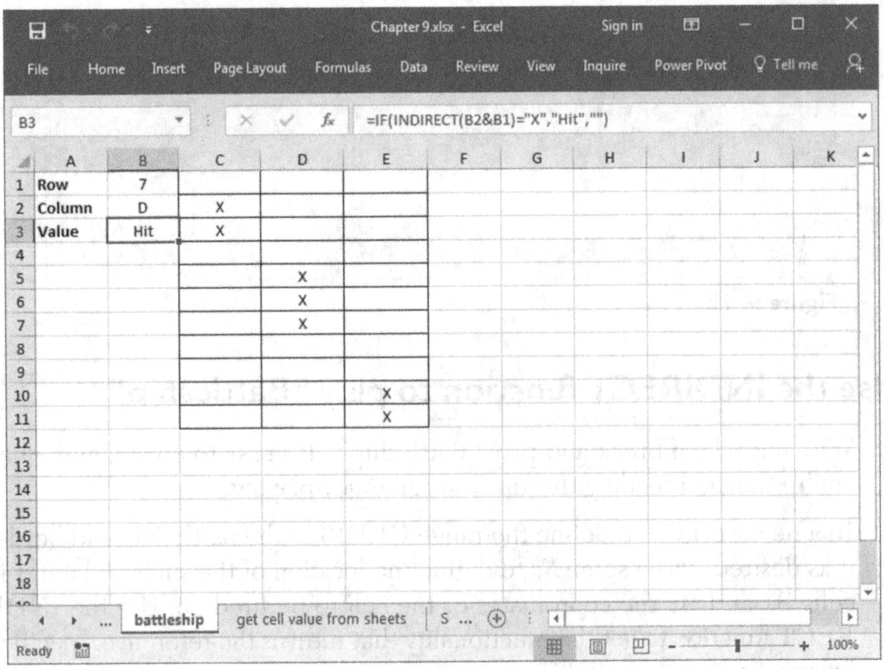

Figure 9–13

Use the INDIRECT function to copy cell values from different worksheets

The INDIRECT function can also be used to address cells in other worksheets and copy their values to the current sheet. Column A lists the names of worksheets, and column B lists cell references. With the INDIRECT function, the value of each cell reference can be copied to the current worksheet.

▶ To copy cell values of different worksheets:

1. In a worksheet, copy cells A1:B10, as shown in Figure 9–14.

2. Select cells C2:C10 and type the following formula:
   =INDIRECT(A2& "!"&B2).

3. Press **<Ctrl+Enter>**.

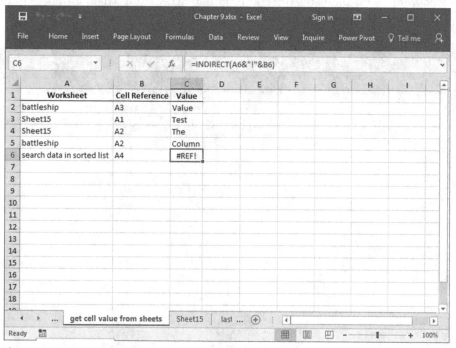

Figure 9–14

NOTE: If you rename the worksheets, make sure not to use blanks (see row 6 in the previous example).

Use the INDEX function to determine the last number in a column

Sometimes it is very useful to let Excel automatically determine the last value in a list. Use the INDEX function in combination with COUNTA and COUNT-BLANK to determine the last number in a column. The INDEX function returns the value of an element in a table or an array that is selected by the row and column number indexes.

INDEX(*array*, *row_num*, *column_num*)

array: A range of cells or an array constant.

row_num: Indicates the row in an array from which a value will be returned. If omitted, *column_num* is required.

column_num: Indicates the column in an array from which a value will be returned. If omitted, *row_num* is required.

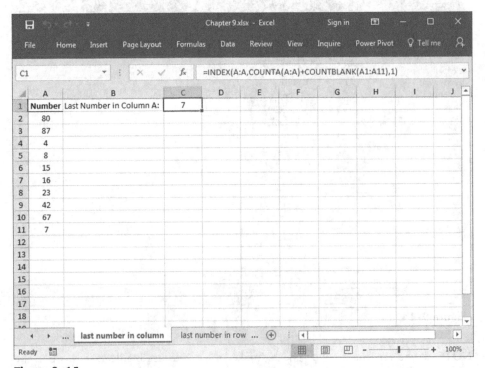

Figure 9–15

▶ To determine the last number in a column:

1. In cells A2:A11, list any kind of numbers.
2. Select cell C1 and type the following formula: **=INDEX (A:A, COUNTA(A:A) + COUNTBLANK (A1:A11),1)**.
3. Press **<Enter>**.

Use the INDEX and COUNTA functions to determine the last number in a row

In the previous tip, we learned how to determine the last value for each column. Use the INDEX function in combination with COUNTA to determine the last number in a row. The INDEX function will return the value of an element in a table or an array, selected by the row and column number indexes.

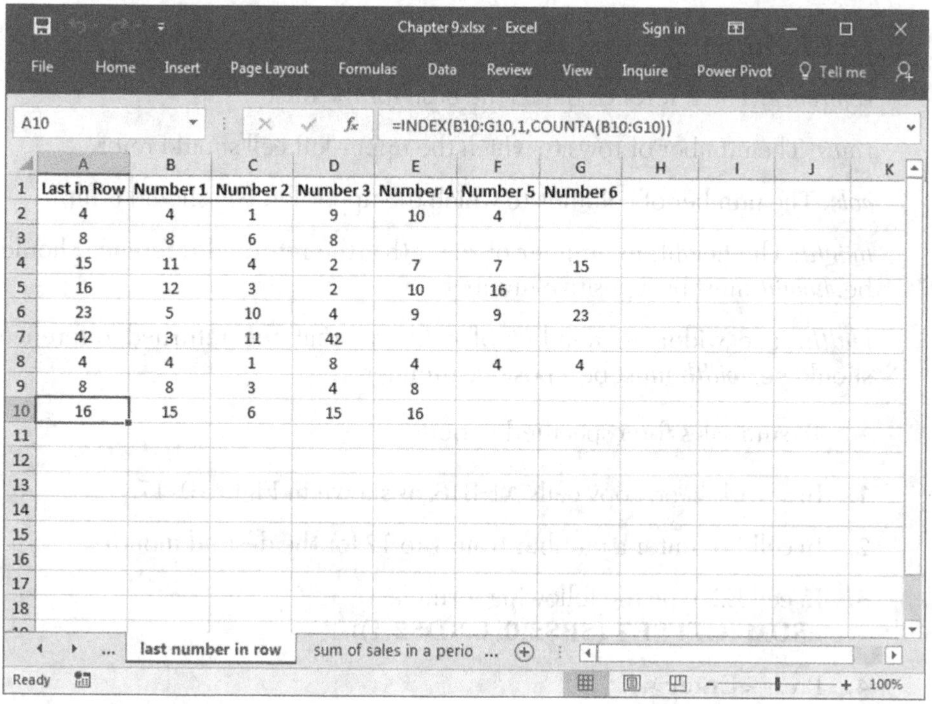

	A	B	C	D	E	F	G
1	Last in Row	Number 1	Number 2	Number 3	Number 4	Number 5	Number 6
2	4	4	1	9	10	4	
3	8	8	6	8			
4	15	11	4	2	7	7	15
5	16	12	3	2	10	16	
6	23	5	10	4	9	9	23
7	42	3	11	42			
8	4	4	1	8	4	4	4
9	8	8	3	4	8		
10	16	15	6	15	16		

Figure 9–16

▶ To determine the last number in a row:

1. In cells B2:G10, enter some numbers, leaving some cells empty.

2. Select cells A2:A10 and type the following formula:
   =INDEX (B2:G2,1,COUNTA(B2:G2)).

3. Press **<Ctrl+Enter>**.

Use the OFFSET function to sum sales for a specified period

Figure 9–17 gives an overview of the monthly sales figures from the previous year. Let's sum the sales from January to November. To do so, use the OFFSET function in combination with SUM. OFFSET returns a reference to a range that is a specific number of rows and columns from a cell or range of cells.

The syntax is:

OFFSET(*reference, rows, cols, height, width*)

reference: The reference that is the base for the offset.

rows: The number of rows to which the upper-left cell should refer.

cols: The number of columns to which the upper-left cell should refer.

height: The height, in number of rows, that the returned reference should be. *height* must be a positive number.

width: The width, in number of columns, that the returned reference should be. *width* must be a positive number.

▶ To sum sales for a specified period:

1. In a worksheet, copy cells A1:B13, as shown in Figure 9–17.

2. In cell D1, enter a number from 1 to 12 for the desired month.

3. In cell E2, type the following formula:
   =SUM (OFFSET ($B$2,0, 0,$D$2,1)).

4. Press **<Enter>**.

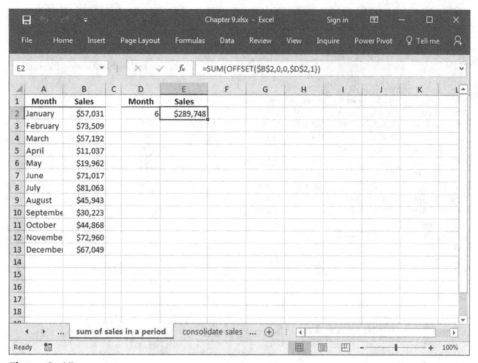

Figure 9–17

Use the OFFSET function to consolidate sales for a day

This tip shows an effective way of summing all the sales of each team for one specific day. The tricky part of the task is that the dates appear more than once. To calculate all sales for each team on one specific date, use the OFFSET function in combination with SUMIF.

▶ To consolidate sales per day and team:

1. In a worksheet, copy cells A1:E12, as shown in Figure 9–18.

2. In cell H1, enter a desired date.

3. In cells G3:G6, type the team names.

4. Select cells H3:H6 and type the following formula: **=SUMIF ($A$2:$A$12, $H$1, OFFSET ($A$2:$A$12, 0, MATCH (G3,$1:$1,)-1)).**

5. Press **<Ctrl+Enter>**.

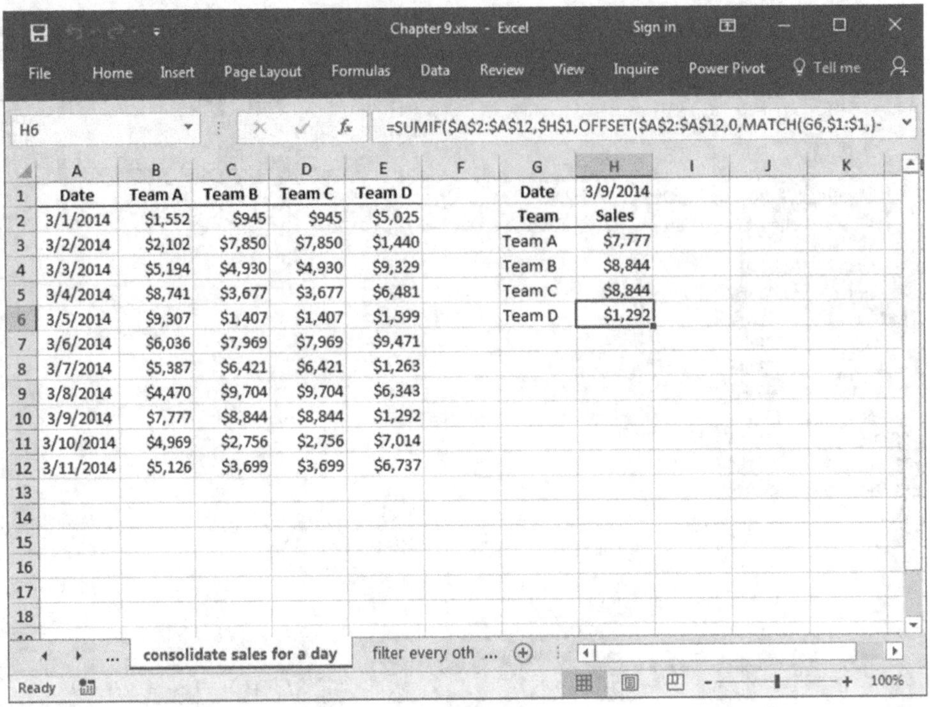

Figure 9–18

Use the OFFSET function to filter every other column

This example shows a table where every other column has to be filtered. Use the COLUMN function to get the current column and combine it with the OFFSET function to reach the goal.

▶ To extract every other column:

1. In cells A2:G6, type numbers from 1 through 6.

2. Select cells A9:D13 and type the following formula:
   = OFFSET ($A2,0, (COLUMN()-1)*2).

3. Press **<Ctrl+Enter>**.

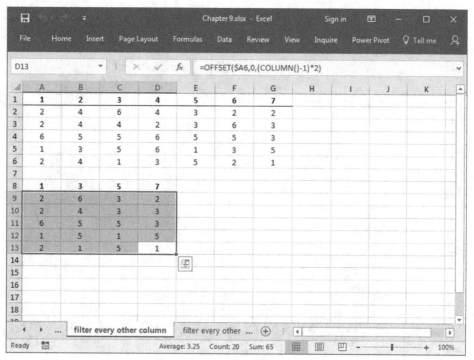

Figure 9–19

Use the OFFSET function to filter every other row

In the previous example, we filtered every other column. To do the same with rows, use the ROW function to get the current row and combine it with the OFFSET function to get the result shown below.

▶ To extract every other row:

1. In cells A2:A16, type any numbers.

2. Select cells B2:D9 and type the following formula:
   = OFFSET ($A$2, (ROW()-2)*COLUMN(),0).

3. Press **<Ctrl+Enter>**.

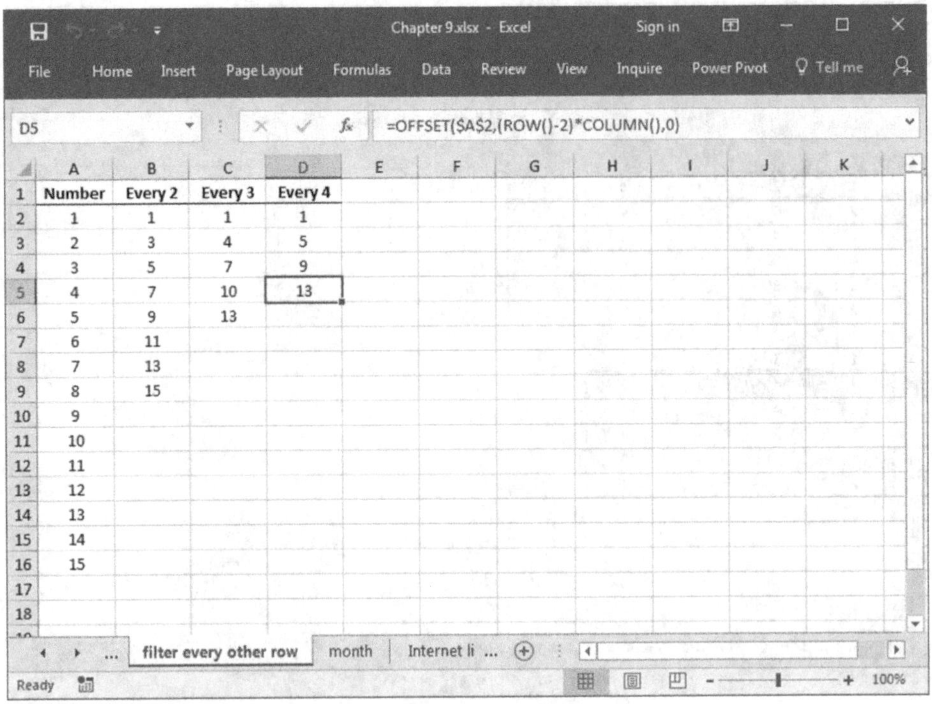

Figure 9–20

NOTE: To hide all cells containing 0, select **Options** from the **Tools** menu, click the **View** tab, and deactivate **Zero values**.

Use the HYPERLINK function to jump directly to a cell inside the current worksheet

Hyperlinks are usually used to navigate through the Internet or link different Office documents. You can also use the HYPERLINK function to jump directly to a specific cell in your worksheet with one mouse click. This function normally creates a shortcut to a document stored on a network server or located in an intranet or the Internet. When a user clicks on a cell that contains the HYPERLINK function, Excel opens the file stored at *link_location*.

HYPERLINK(*link_location*, *friendly_name*)

link_location: The path and file name of the document to be opened.

friendly_name: The text or numeric value that is displayed in the cell and that the user must select.

In this example, we insert a hyperlink that jumps to the already opened file and its cell containing the current month.

▶ To jump with one mouse click to the current month:

1. In cell A1, enter **January**.

2. Drag the right corner of this cell down to A12.

3. In cell C1, type the following formula: **=HYPERLINK("month!A"&MONTH(TODAY()),"Jump to actual month")**.

4. Press **<Enter>**.

5. Click with the mouse on the displayed hyperlink in cell C1.

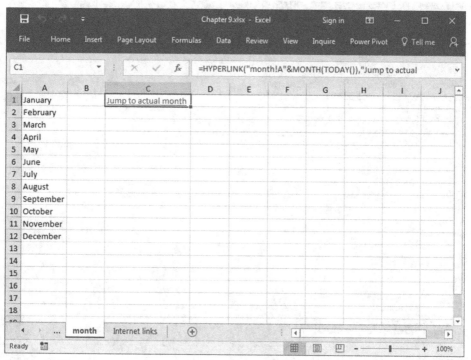

Figure 9–21

Use the HYPERLINK function to link to the Internet

This final tip in Chapter 9 shows how the HYPERLINK function is normally used to create links to the Internet. You can jump directly from your Excel application to predefined Web sites using the HYPERLINK function.

▶ To link to the Internet:

1. In column A, type the URLs of the Web sites to which you want to link.

2. In column B, type the captions of the hyperlinks.

3. Select cells C2:C5 and type the following formula: **= HYPERLINK ("http://" & A2,"Click to " & B2)**.

4. Press **<Ctrl+Enter>**.

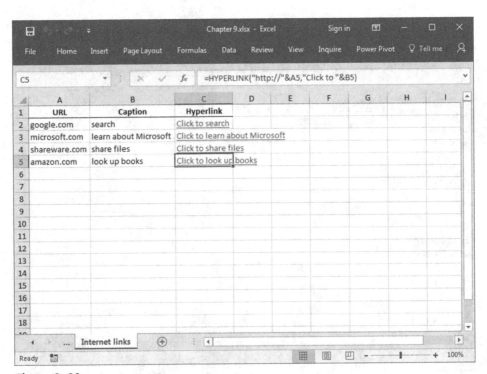

Figure 9–22

Use the CHOOSE function to lookup values

There are many instances where one value depends on the value of another value. In order to yield the correct value, we can use VLOOKUP, IF, IFS or a combination of MATCH/INDEX. In the case where a simple reference to a list is all that is required, we can use the CHOOSE function. It is simpler than using nested IF statements.

1. In cell C4, type the formula: =CHOOSE(C2,"Red,""Blue,""Green,""Yellow,""Orange")

2. In cell C2, enter a number between 1 and 5.

The number you enter in cell C2 which tell the CHOOSE function to select value represented by the number in the list of colors. What happens if you enter a number below 1 or above 5 in this instance? The function yields an error because there are no values represented by those indices. There are only colors listed for 1 through 5.

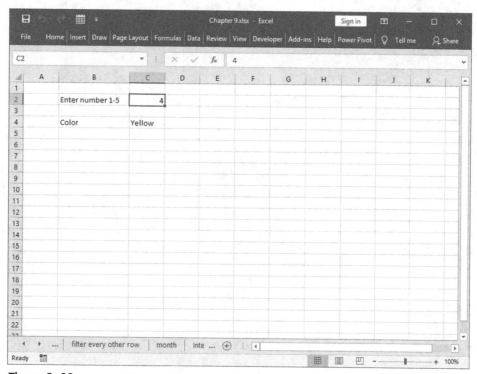

Figure 9–23

Conditional Formatting with Formulas

10

Use the WEEKDAY function to determine weekends and shade them

With the help of the WEEKDAY function, we can find out the day of the week for a particular date. This function returns the days as an integer ranging from 1 (Sunday) to 7 (Saturday) by default. You can also use this function in conditional formatting. In this example, some dates are listed in column A and the weekends are then marked as shown.

▶ To detect and shade weekends:

1. Copy cells A1 and B1 into a new worksheet, as shown in Figure 10–1.

2. Enter **= TODAY()** in cell A2 and **= A2+1** in cell A3. For the remaining cells A4:A12, enter **= Ax+1**, where x is the previous cell number.

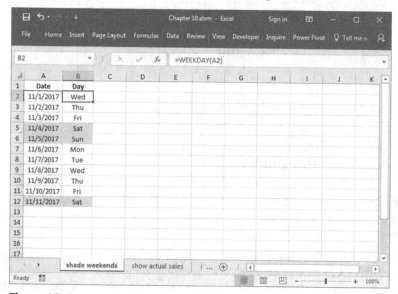

Figure 10–1

3. Select cells B2:B12 and enter the function **= WEEKDAY(A2)**.

4. Press **<Ctrl+Enter>**.

5. Select cells A2:B12.

6. From the **Home** tab, go to the **Styles** bar and click on **Conditional Formatting**.

7. Choose **New Rule**.

8. In the **Select a Rule Type** dialog, select **Use a formula to determine which cells to format**.

9. In the **Edit** box, type the following formula to mark Saturday: **=WEEKDAY($A2) = 7** as depicted in Figure 10-1

10. Click **Format** to select the desired formatting to apply when the cell value meets the condition.

Figure 10–2

NOTE: To display the short versions of the days of the week rather than the integers returned by the function, highlight cells B2:B12, select **Cells** from the **Format** menu, and enter **ddd** in the **Type** box. Click **OK**.

You can also enter one conditional formatting rule instead of two. Instead of typing in **=WEEKDAY($A2)=1** and **=WEEKDAY ($A2)=7** in separate conditional formatting rules you can use the **OR** function explained in chapter two to create only one rule. **=OR (WEEKDAY ($A2)=1, WEEKDAY ($A2)=7).**

11. Select a color from the **Fill** tab and click **OK**.

12. Click **OK**.

13. Repeat steps 2 through 6 and choose **Manage Rule**.

14. Click **New Rule** and insert the following formula (to mark Sunday): = WEEKDAY ($A2) = 1.

15. Repeat step 10.

16. Click **OK**.

Use the TODAY function to show completed sales

All daily sales are listed in an Excel table. The list contains estimated sales as well, which are assigned this status as shown in column C. We need to mark all completed sales by using conditional formatting, being sure to exclude the estimated sales.

▶ To show completed sales:

1. In a worksheet, copy cells A1:C13, as shown in Figure 10–3.

2. In cell E1, enter the function **TODAY()**.

3. Select cells A2:C13.

4. From the **Home** tab, go to the **Styles** bar and click on **Conditional Formatting**.

5. Choose **New Rule**.

6. In the **Select a Rule Type** dialog, select **Use a formula to determine which cells to format**.

7. In the **Edit** box, type the following formula to mark the days that either match today's date or are before today's date: = $A2 < = $E$1.

8. Click **Format** to select the desired formatting to apply when the cell value meets the condition.

9. Select a color from the **Fill** tab and click **OK**.

10. Go to the **Font** tab and select **Bold** in the **Font Style**.

11. Click **OK**.

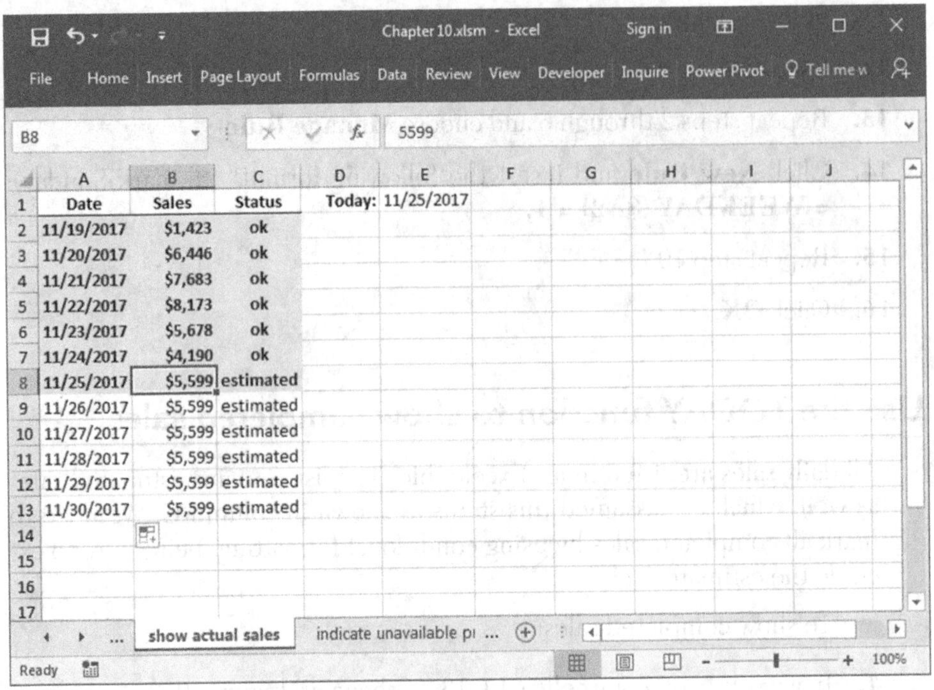

Figure 10–3

NOTE: The Status column used in this example is meant to be used as a verification. Therefore, as the days go by, the colored formatting you accomplished in this example will be automatic depending on what today's date is. The Status column is to be used by someone to manually verify that the sales are correct. Once correct, the person types in "ok." If the cell contains "estimated," it means that the sales have not been confirmed as final for that day.

Another way to accomplish this is to automate the Status column by comparing today's date with the date in column A using the IF statement and the formula used above in the conditional formatting rule to yield either "ok" or "estimated."

Use conditional formats to indicate unavailable products

When checking the existing inventory of a warehouse, it needs to be determined which products are out of stock so they can be ordered. To get a better overview of the inventory, all products that are unavailable need to be marked by using conditional formatting. The formatting criterion is taken from column D, which indicates whether a product is available.

▶ To mark all products that are out of stock:

1. Copy the table shown in Figure 10–4 into a worksheet and select cells A2:D13.

2. From the **Home** tab, go to the **Styles** bar and click on **Conditional Formatting**.

3. Choose **New Rule**.

4. In the **Select a Rule Type** dialog, select **Use a formula to determine which cells to format**.

5. In the **Edit** box, type the following formula: **= $D2 = "no"**.

6. Click **Format** to select the desired formatting to apply when the cell value meets the condition.

7. Select a color from the **Fill** tab and click **OK**.

8. Click **OK**.

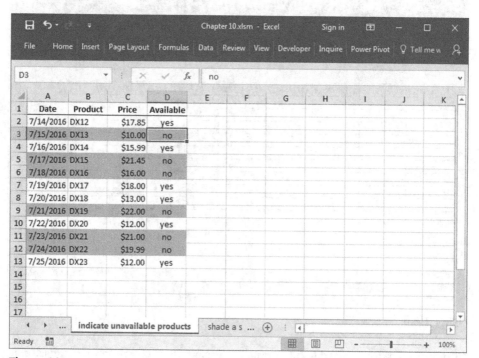

Figure 10–4

Use the TODAY function to shade a specific column

A project schedule can be generated quite easily through Excel. To make it easier to read at a glance, the current day can be colored automatically. Use the TODAY function to determine the actual date and define it as the criterion for conditional formatting.

▶ To shade the column for the current day:

1. In cell H1, enter the function **TODAY()**.

2. Select cells A3:H12.

3. From the **Home** tab, go to the **Styles** bar and click on **Conditional Formatting**.

4. Choose **New Rule**.

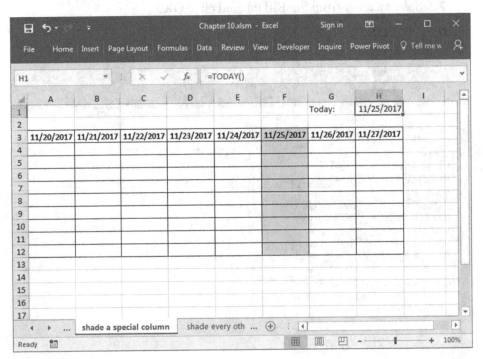

Figure 10–5

NOTE: To remove all conditional formats as well as all other cell formats for selected cells, do as described in step 3 and choose **Clear Rules**.

5. In the **Select a Rule Type** dialog, select **Use a formula to determine which cells to format**.

6. In the **Edit** box, type the following formula: **= A\$3 = TODAY()**.

7. Click **Format** to select the desired formatting to apply when the cell value meets the condition.

8. Select a color from the **Fill** tab and click **OK**.

9. Click **OK**.

Use the WEEKNUM and MOD functions to shade every other Tuesday

The table shown in Figure 10–6 is part of a schedule for the purchasing department. Purchases are made every other Tuesday. Create a schedule and color every other Tuesday as a reminder. Use the WEEKNUM function (introduced in Chapter 4) from the Analysis ToolPak add-in. This function returns a number that indicates where the week falls numerically within a

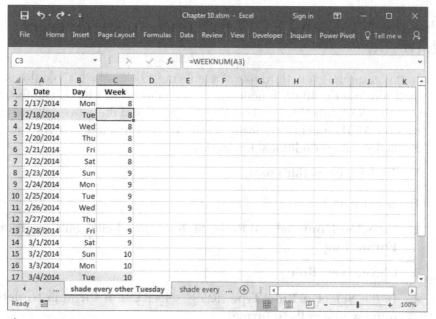

Figure 10–6

year. In combination with the MOD function, it can be determined if the week number is even or odd.

▶ To mark every second Tuesday:

1. Select cells A2:C20.

2. From the **Home** tab, go to the **Styles** bar and click on **Conditional Formatting**.

3. Choose **New Rule**.

4. In the **Select a Rule Type** dialog, select **Use a formula to determine which cells to format**.

5. In the **Edit** box, type the following formula:
   =AND(WEEKDAY($A3)=3, MOD($C3,2)<>1).

6. Click **Format** to select the desired formatting to apply when the cell value meets the condition.

7. Select a color from the **Fill** tab and click **OK**.

8. Click **OK**.

Use the MOD and ROW functions to shade every third row

In this example, every third row of a table must be marked. To do this automatically, use the ROW function in combination with MOD. The formula uses the ROW function to return the row number of the active cell and then uses the MOD function to divide it by 3. If the remainder is 0, the row can be shaded using conditional formatting.

▶ To shade every third row:

1. Select rows 1 to 20.

2. From the **Home** tab, go to the **Styles** bar and click on **Conditional Formatting**.

3. Choose **New Rule**.

4. In the **Select a Rule Type** dialog, select **Use a formula to determine which cells to format**.

5. In the **Edit** box, type the following formula: **=MOD(ROW(),3)=0**.

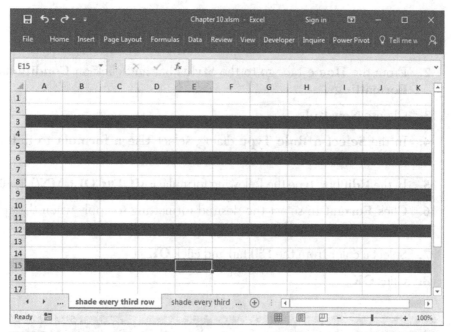

Figure 10–7

6. Click **Format** to select the desired formatting to apply when the cell value meets the condition.

7. Select a color from the **Fill** tab and click **OK**.

8. Click **OK**.

NOTE: Up to three conditions can be specified as conditional formats. If none of the specified conditions are true, the cells keep their existing formats.

Use the MOD and COLUMN functions to shade every third column

The previous tip showed how to mark every third row. Now let's find out how to automatically mark every third column in a range. Use the COLUMN function in combination with MOD by entering a formula that uses the COLUMN function to return the column number of the active cell and the MOD function to divide that number by 3. If the remainder is zero, the column can be shaded through conditional formatting.

▶ To shade every third column:

1. Select range A1:P14.

2. From the **Home** tab, go to the **Styles** bar and click on **Conditional Formatting**.

3. Choose **New Rule**.

4. In the **Select a Rule Type** dialog, select **Use a formula to determine which cells to format**.

5. In the **Edit** box, type the following formula: **=MOD(COLUMN(),3)=0**.

6. Click **Format** to select the desired formatting to apply when the cell value meets the condition.

7. Select a color from the **Fill** tab and click **OK**.

8. Click **OK**.

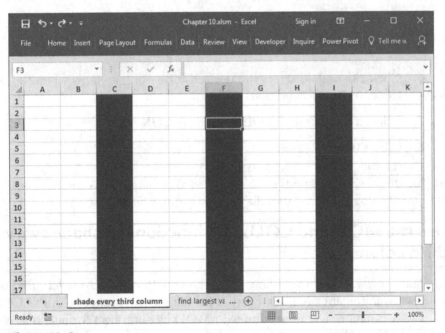

Figure 10–8

NOTE: Because conditional formatting causes the document file size to grow very quickly, you should format only the ranges where it is really needed.

Use the MAX function to find the largest value

This example shows how to find and automatically mark the largest value in a range. All occurrences of the largest value will be shaded. Use the MAX function to determine the largest value in a range and then use that value as the formatting criterion for conditional formatting.

▶ To search for and shade the largest value:

1. In a worksheet, enter numbers in cells A1:E10 (or copy the values in Figure 10–9) and select the range.

2. From the **Home** tab, go to the **Styles** bar and click on **Conditional Formatting**.

3. Choose **New Rule**.

4. In the **Select a Rule Type** dialog, select **Use a formula to determine which cells to format**.

5. In the **Edit** box, type the following formula: **=A1=MAX($A$1:$E$10)**.

6. Click **Format** to select the desired formatting to apply when the cell value meets the condition.

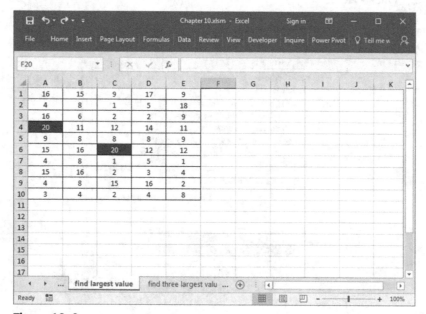

Figure 10–9

7. Select a color from the **Fill** tab and click **OK**.

8. Click **OK**.

Use the LARGE function to find the three largest values

The three largest values in a range need to be found and shaded, regardless of how many times they appear. Use the LARGE function to determine the three largest values in a range and specify those three conditions as criteria for conditional formatting.

▶ To search for and shade the three largest values:

1. In a worksheet, enter numbers in cells A1:E10 (or copy the values in Figure 10–10) and select the range.

2. From the **Home** tab, go to the **Styles** bar and click on **Conditional Formatting**.

3. Choose **Format only top or bottom ranked values.**

4. In the dialog box choose 3 and the required cell format.

5. Click **OK**.

Figure 10–10

Use the MIN function to find the month with the worst performance

Salespeople usually do some market analysis to find their current share of the market. Before you can investigate the reasons for a bad fiscal year, you need to find the worst month of sales and then shade it. Use the MIN function to get the lowest value in a range and use it as the formatting criterion for conditional formatting.

▶ To search for the worst month:

1. In a worksheet, enter the months in cells A2:A13 and the sales amounts in cells B2:B13 (or copy the values in Figure 10–11) and select the range.

2. From the **Home** tab, go to the **Styles** bar and click on **Conditional Formatting**.

3. Choose **New Rule**.

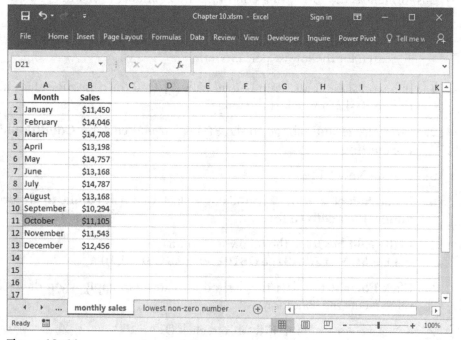

Figure 10–11

4. In the **Select a Rule Type** dialog, select **Use a formula to determine which cells to format**.

5. In the **Edit** box, type the following formula:
    = **$B2 = MIN ($B$2:$B$13)**.

6. Click **Format** to select the desired formatting to apply when the cell value meets the condition.

7. Select a color from the **Fill** tab and click **OK**.

8. Click **OK**.

Use the MIN function to search for the lowest nonzero number

In this example, the smallest nonzero number in a range must be found and marked automatically. Use the MIN function to get the lowest value in a range, then use the IF function to check that the number is not zero. Insert this formula as the formatting criterion for conditional formatting, and the lowest numbers will be colored as desired. This function finds the lowest number, whether it is positive or negative.

▶ To search for the lowest nonzero number:

1. In a worksheet, enter numbers in cells A1:D10 (or copy the values in Figure 10–12) and select the range.

2. From the **Home** tab, go to the **Styles** bar and click on **Conditional Formatting**.

3. Choose **New Rule**.

4. In the **Select a Rule Type** dialog, select **Use a formula to determine which cells to format**.

5. In the **Edit** box, type the following formula:
    = **A1 = MIN (IF($A$1: $D$10<>0, $A$1:$D$10))**.

6. Click **Format** to select the desired formatting to apply when the cell value meets the condition.

7. Select a color from the **Fill** tab and click **OK**.

8. Click **OK**.

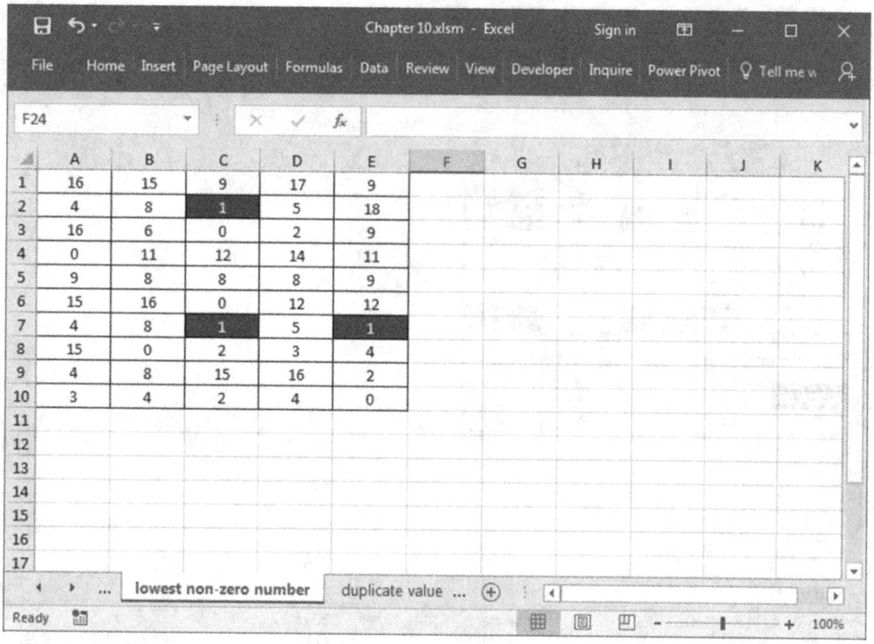

Figure 10–12

Use the COUNTIF function to mark duplicate input automatically

Sometimes a list must be checked for duplicate entries. This example creates a randomized list and then finds all duplicate values and marks them. Use the COUNTIF function to count numbers that are repeated in a range and then use this function with conditional formatting to shade all duplicate values as desired.

▶ To mark duplicate entries automatically:

1. Select the range A1:D10.

2. Type the following formula to generate randomized numbers from 1 to 300: = **RANDBETWEEN (1,300)** (as a result of the RANDBETWEEN function, the numbers displayed in Figure 10-13 will be different than the numbers displayed in your worksheet.

3. Press **<Ctrl+Enter>**.

4. In the **Format** menu, click **Conditional Formatting**.

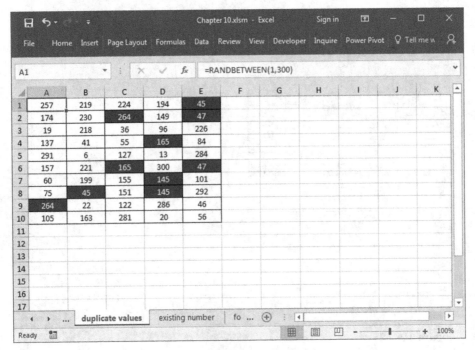

Figure 10–13

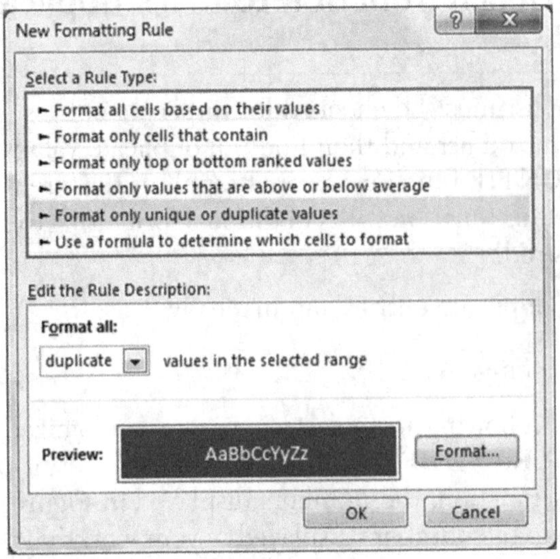

Figure 10–14

NOTE: Press <F9> to recalculate and generate new randomized numbers for the range.

5.   Select **Format only unique or duplicate values** or use the following
     formula in the formula option for defining rules:
     = COUNTIF ($A$1:$D$12,A1) >1.

6.   Click **Format**.

7.   From the **Patterns** tab, choose a color and click **OK**.

8.   Click **OK**.

Use the COUNTIF function to check whether a number exists in a range

From this example, you can learn how to check whether a specific number
is found in a range and have Excel automatically mark each cell of the range
that contains the number. Use the COUNTIF function to check whether
the range contains the number in cell B1 and combine it with conditional
formatting to shade the specific value as desired.

▶   To check whether a number exists in a range:

1.   Copy cells A1:D10 as shown in Figure 10–15, or use your own data.

2.   Select cell B1.

3.   From the **Home** tab, go to the **Styles** bar and click on **Conditional
     Formatting**.

4.   Choose **New Rule**.

5.   In the **Select a Rule Type** dialog, select **Use a formula to deter-
     mine which cells to format**.

6.   In the **Edit** box, type the following formula:
     = COUNTIF ($A$3: $D$10, $B$1) > 0.

7.   Click **Format** to select the desired formatting to apply when the cell
     value meets the condition.

8.   Select a color from the **Fill** tab and click **OK**.

9.   Click **OK**.

10. Select cells A3:D10.

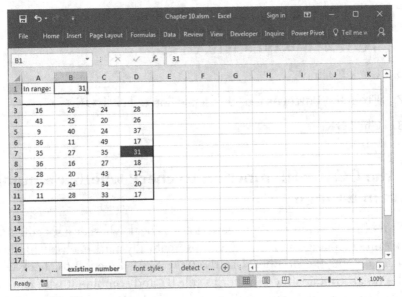

Figure 10–15

11. Repeat step 3 and choose **Manage Rule**.

12. Click **New Rule** and insert the following formula: **= $B$1 = A3**.

13. Repeat steps 7–8.

14. Click **OK**.

Use conditional formatting to control font styles in a specific range

Conditional formatting can also be used to control font styles in a specified range. Use cell E1 to enter letters like "i" for italic, "b" for bold, and "s" for strikethrough. Use conditional formatting to format the range as desired based on the input in cell E1.

▶ To control font styles in a specified range:

1. In a worksheet, enter numbers in cells A1:D10 (or copy the values in Figure 10–16) and select the range A1:D10.

2. From the **Home** tab, go to the **Styles** bar and click on **Conditional Formatting**.

3. Choose **New Rule**.

4. In the **Select a Rule Type** dialog, select **Use a formula to determine which cells to format**.

5. In the **Edit** box, type the following formula: =$E$1="i".

6. Click **Format** to select the desired formatting to apply when the cell value meets the condition.

7. On the **Font** tab, select **Italic** from the **Font style** box.

8. Click **OK**.

9. In cell E1, enter the character **i** to indicate that you want to italicize all the items in the range.

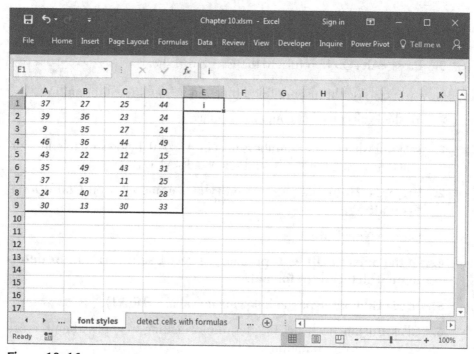

Figure 10–16

NOTE: You can add further font styles to the Conditional Formatting dialog using different conditions.

Use a user-defined function to detect cells with formulas

This example requires you to be familiar with the VBA Editor. Here we want to mark all cells in a specific range that contain a formula. First, you need to write a user-defined function:

1. Press **<Alt+F11>** to open the VBA window.

2. On the **Insert** menu, click **Module** and enter the following function:
   Function HF(rng)As Boolean

   HF = rng. HasFormula

   'returns TRUE if rng contains

   'a formula

   End Function

   (The lines above that begin with an apostrophe indicate the information that follows is a comment.)

3. Press **<Alt+Q>** to return to the Excel worksheet.

Now you can use this user-defined function in conditional formatting.

▶ To shade all cells that contain formulas:

1. In a worksheet, enter numbers in cells A1:D10, being sure to enter formulas in some of the cells, and select cells A1:D10.

2. From the **Home** tab, go to the **Styles** bar and click on **Conditional Formatting**.

3. Choose **New Rule**.

4. In the **Select a Rule Type** dialog, select **Use a formula to determine which cells to format**.

5. In the **Edit** box, type the following formula: **=HF(A1)**.

6. Click **Format** to select the desired formatting to apply when the cell value meets the condition.

7. Select a color from the **Fill** tab and click **OK**.

8. Click **OK**.

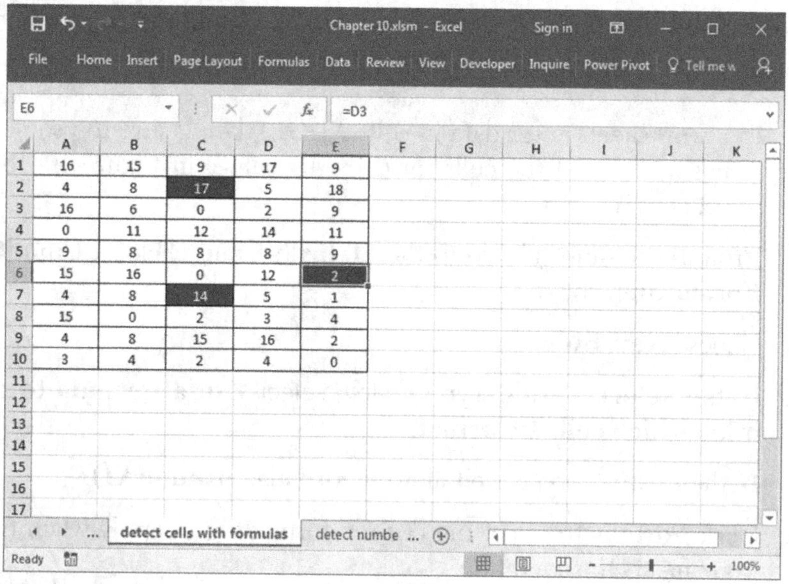

Figure 10–17

Use a user-defined function to detect cells with valid numeric values

Continuing with the previous tip, let's now mark all cells in a range that contain valid numeric values. First, you need to write a user-defined function:

1. Press **<Alt+F11>** to open up the VBA window.

2. On the **Insert** menu, click **Module** and enter the following function:
   Function ISNUM(rng) As Boolean

   If rng.Value <> "" Then

   ISNUM = IsNumeric(rng.Value)

   End If

   'returns TRUE if rng contains

   'numeric values

   End Function

3. Press **<Alt+Q>** to return to the Excel worksheet.

Now you can use this user-defined function in conditional formatting.

▶ To shade cells with valid numeric values:

1. In a worksheet, enter data in cells A1:C10, being sure to use numeric values in some of the cells (or copy the values in Figure 10–18), and select cells A1:C10.

2. From the **Home** tab, go to the **Styles** bar and click on **Conditional Formatting**.

3. Choose **New Rule**.

4. In the **Select a Rule Type** dialog, select **Use a formula to determine which cells to format**.

5. In the **Edit** box, type the following formula: **=isnum(A1)**.

6. Click **Format** to select the desired formatting to apply when the cell value meets the condition.

7. Select a color from the **Fill** tab and click **OK**.

8. Click **OK**.

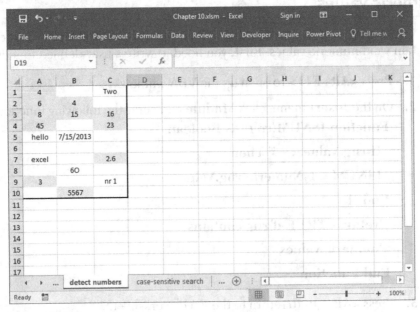

Figure 10–18

Use the EXACT function to perform a case-sensitive search

Usually Excel doesn't differentiate between uppercase and lowercase letters. To search for a string that has the same case, use the EXACT function. The search string is entered in cell B1. With the support of conditional formatting, all cells within a specified range will be formatted if they contain the exact search string.

▶ To perform a case-sensitive search on text:

1. In a worksheet, enter a variety of values in cells A3:E13, being sure to use both "Excel" and "excel" in several cells (or copy the values in Figure 10–19).

2. In cell B1, enter **Excel**.

3. Select cells A3:E13.

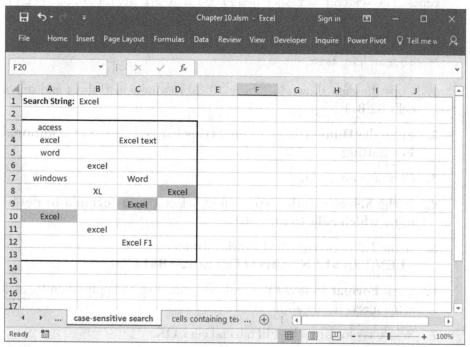

Figure 10–19

4. From the **Home** tab, go to the **Styles** bar and click on **Conditional Formatting**.

5. Choose **New Rule**.

6. In the **Select a Rule Type** dialog, select **Use a formula to determine which cells to format**.

7. In the **Edit** box, type the following formula: **=EXACT(A3,$B$1)**.

8. Click **Format** to select the desired formatting to apply when the cell value meets the condition.

9. Select a color from the **Fill** tab and click **OK**.

10. Click **OK**.

Use the SUBSTITUTE function to search for text

This tip can help you look for specific text in a list and mark each occurrence. The search text is specified in cell B13. Specify the SUBSTITUTE function as a condition to search for and shade each cell where the text string is found.

▶ To search for text:

1. Copy the data shown in Figure 10–20 to a new worksheet and select cells B2:B11.

2. From the **Home** tab, go to the **Styles** bar and click on **Conditional Formatting**.

3. Choose **New Rule**.

4. In the **Select a Rule Type** dialog, select **Use a formula to determine which cells to format**.

5. In the **Edit** box, type the following formula:
    =LEN(B2)<>LEN(SUBSTITUTE(B2,$B$13,"")).

6. Click **Format** to select the desired formatting to apply when the cell value meets the condition.

7. Select a color from the **Fill** tab and click **OK**.

8. Click **OK**.

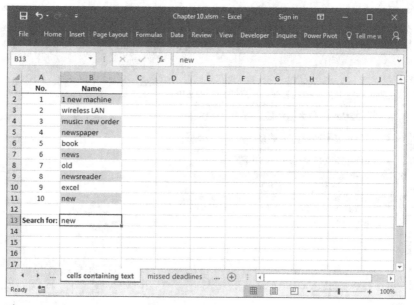

Figure 10–20

Use conditional formatting to shade project steps with missed deadlines

The project schedule shown in Figure 10–21 contains different steps and their starting and projected ending dates. The actual end dates are listed in column E. Use conditional formatting to search for all steps that ended late by comparing the dates in columns D and E. As usual, select the desired formatting to apply when the cell value meets the condition.

▶ To shade project steps with missed deadlines:

1. In a worksheet, copy the values shown in Figure 10–21 and select cells A2:E11.

2. From the **Home** tab, go to the **Styles** bar and click on **Conditional Formatting**.

3. Choose **New Rule**.

4. In the **Select a Rule Type** dialog, select **Use a formula to determine which cells to format**.

5. In the **Edit** box, type the following formula: **=$E2>$D2**.

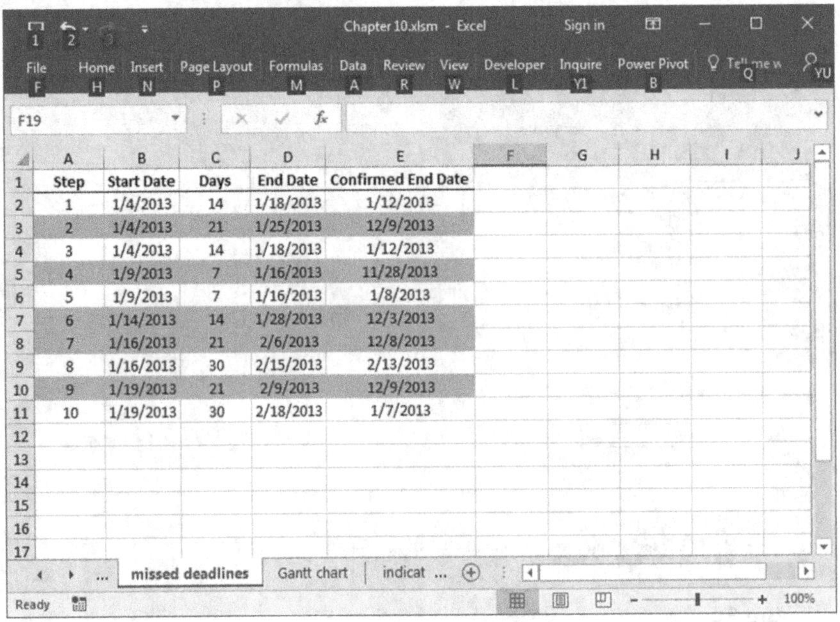

	A	B	C	D	E
1	Step	Start Date	Days	End Date	Confirmed End Date
2	1	1/4/2013	14	1/18/2013	1/12/2013
3	2	1/4/2013	21	1/25/2013	12/9/2013
4	3	1/4/2013	14	1/18/2013	1/12/2013
5	4	1/9/2013	7	1/16/2013	11/28/2013
6	5	1/9/2013	7	1/16/2013	1/8/2013
7	6	1/14/2013	14	1/28/2013	12/3/2013
8	7	1/16/2013	21	2/6/2013	12/8/2013
9	8	1/16/2013	30	2/15/2013	2/13/2013
10	9	1/19/2013	21	2/9/2013	12/9/2013
11	10	1/19/2013	30	2/18/2013	1/7/2013

Figure 10–21

6. Click **Format** to select the desired formatting to apply when the cell value meets the condition.

7. Select a color from the **Fill** tab and click **OK**.

8. Click **OK**.

Use conditional formatting to create a Gantt chart in Excel

With the help of this tip, you can easily create a project plan that includes a Gantt chart in Excel. Begin by inserting a new worksheet and then copy the header row as shown in Figure 10–22.

▶ To create a project plan and Gantt chart step by step:

1. Copy the data in cells A2:C11, as shown in Figure 10–22.

2. Select cells D2:D11 and type the formula = **C2-D2**.

3. Press **<Ctrl+Enter>**.

4. Select cell E1 and type the formula = **B2**.

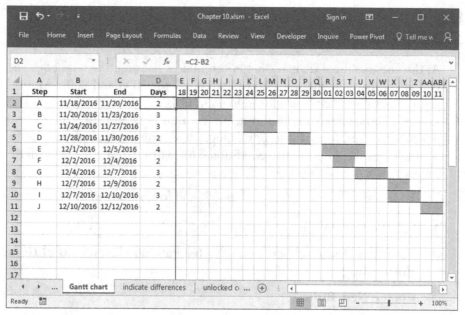

Figure 10-22

5. Select cells F1:AB1 and type the formula **= E1+1**.

6. Press **<Ctrl+Enter>**.

7. Select cells E2:AB11.

8. From the **Home** tab, go to the **Styles** bar and click on **Conditional Formatting**.

9. Choose **New Rule**.

10. In the **Select a Rule Type** dialog, select **Use a formula to determine which cells to format**.

11. In the **Edit** box type the following formula:
    = AND (E$1 > = $ B2, E$1 < $C2).

12. Click **Format** to select the desired formatting to apply when the cell value meets the condition.

13. Select a color from the **Fill** tab and click **OK**.

14. Click **OK**.

Use the OR function to indicate differences higher than 5% and lower than −5%

At the end of a fiscal year, a company compares the monthly sales of the last two years. Look at the following sales report for 2008 and 2009. Monthly sales of fiscal year 2008 are listed in column B, and column C contains the sales for 2009. Check the difference in column D by inserting the formula **=(C2/B2)-1** and format it to percentages with one decimal place. The following steps show how to use conditional formatting to shade each cell that meets the desired condition.

▶ To shade differences higher than 5% and lower than −5%:

1. Select cells C2:C13.

2. From the **Home** tab, go to the **Styles** bar and click on **Conditional Formatting**.

3. Choose **New Rule**.

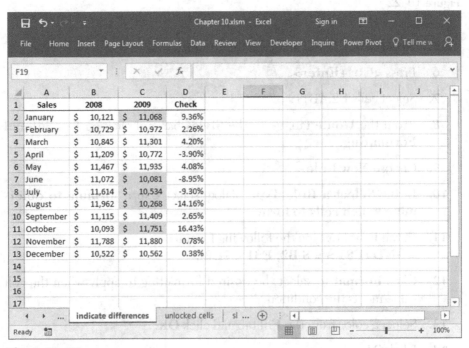

	A	B	C	D
1	Sales	2008	2009	Check
2	January	$ 10,121	$ 11,068	9.36%
3	February	$ 10,729	$ 10,972	2.26%
4	March	$ 10,845	$ 11,301	4.20%
5	April	$ 11,209	$ 10,772	-3.90%
6	May	$ 11,467	$ 11,935	4.08%
7	June	$ 11,072	$ 10,081	-8.95%
8	July	$ 11,614	$ 10,534	-9.30%
9	August	$ 11,962	$ 10,268	-14.16%
10	September	$ 11,115	$ 11,409	2.65%
11	October	$ 10,093	$ 11,751	16.43%
12	November	$ 11,788	$ 11,880	0.78%
13	December	$ 10,522	$ 10,562	0.38%

Figure 10–23

4. In the **Select a Rule Type** dialog, select **Use a formula to determine which cells to format**.

5. In the **Edit** box type the following formula: **=OR ((C2/B2)-1>5%, (C2/B2)-1<-5%)**.

6. Click **Format** to select the desired formatting to apply when the cell value meets the condition.

7. Select a color from the **Fill** tab and click **OK**.

8. Click **OK**.

Use the CELL function to detect unlocked cells

If a worksheet has been protected, all cells are locked by default. The protection for each cell must be unlocked before activating sheet protection. If a sheet is protected, usually it is not possible to see at one glance which cells are locked and which are unlocked. Use conditional formatting to shade all unlocked cells in a range.

▶ To shade unlocked cells:

1. Create the worksheet shown in Figure 10–24 and unlock cells B2, B4, B6, and B8.

2. Select cells A1:D10.

3. From the **Home** tab, go to the **Styles** bar and click on **Conditional Formatting**.

4. Choose **New Rule**.

5. In the **Select a Rule Type** dialog, select **Use a formula to determine which cells to format**.

6. In the **Edit** box, type the following formula: **=CELL("protect",A1)=0**.

7. Click **Format** to select the desired formatting to apply when the cell value meets the condition.

8. Select a color from the **Fill** tab and click **OK**.

9. Click **OK**.

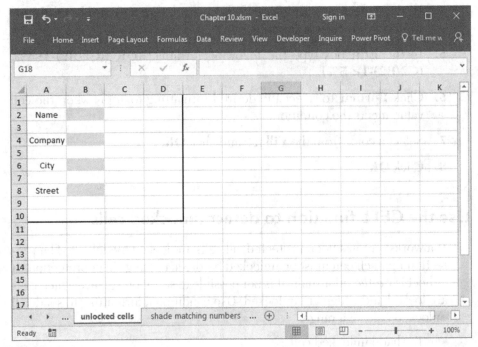

Figure 10–24

Use the COUNTIF function to shade matching numbers in column B

Cells A2:A4 in Figure 10–25 contain numbers that need to be found in column B. If values in column B match values in column A, the cells should be marked. Use the COUNTIF function in combination with conditional formatting to shade each cell that meets the desired condition.

▶ To shade values in column B that correspond to values in column A:

1. Create the worksheet shown in Figure 10–25 and select cells B1:B10.

2. From the **Home** tab, go to the **Styles** bar and click on **Conditional Formatting**.

3. Choose **New Rule**.

4. In the **Select a Rule Type** dialog, select **Use a formula to determine which cells to format**.

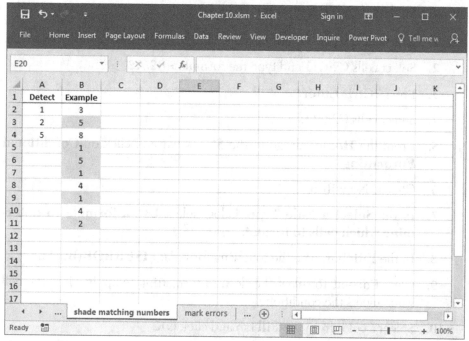

Figure 10-25

5. In the **Edit** box, type the following formula: **= COUNTIF ($A$2: $A$4,B2) > = 1**.

6. Click **Format** to select the desired formatting to apply when the cell value meets the condition.

7. Select a color from the **Fill** tab and click **OK**.

8. Click **OK**.

Use the ISERROR function to mark errors

In this example, the value in column B is divided by the value in column A and the result is displayed in column C. If the result of this operation is invalid, an error appears in column C. Use the ISERROR function in combination with conditional formatting to shade each cell that contains an error.

▶ To detect and shade errors:

1. In a worksheet, enter numbers in cells A2:B11, as shown in Figure 10–26.

2. Select cells C2:C11 and type the formula **=B2/A2**.

3. Press **<Ctrl+Enter>**.

4. Select cells C2:C11.

5. From the **Home** tab, go to the **Styles** bar and click on **Conditional Formatting**.

6. Choose **New Rule**.

7. In the **Select a Rule Type** dialog, select **Use a formula to determine which cells to format**.

8. In the **Edit** box, type the following formula: **=ISERROR(B2/A2)**.

9. Click **Format** to select the desired formatting to apply when the cell value meets the condition.

10. Select a color from the **Fill** tab and click **OK**.

11. Click **OK**.

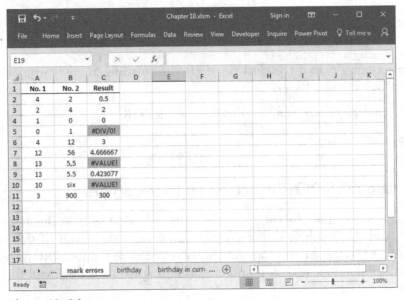

Figure 10–26

Use the DATEDIF function to determine all friends younger than 30

You have the birth dates of your friends listed in a worksheet and want to shade those who are currently younger than 30 years old. Use the TODAY function to determine the current date and the DATEDIF function to calculate each friend's exact age, then combine those functions with conditional formatting.

▶ To determine all friends younger than 30:

1. In a worksheet, enter data in cells A2:B10, as shown in Figure 10–27.

2. Select cells A2:B10.

3. From the **Home** tab, go to the **Styles** bar and click on **Conditional Formatting**.

4. Choose **New Rule**.

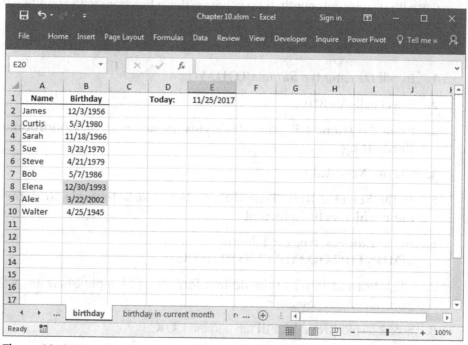

Figure 10–27

5. In the **Select a Rule Type** dialog, select **Use a formula to determine which cells to format**.

6. In the **Edit** box, type the following formula:
   =DATEDIF ($B2, TODAY(),"Y") < 30.

7. Click **Format** to select the desired formatting to apply when the cell value meets the condition.

8. Select a color from the **Fill** tab and click **OK**.

9. Click **OK**.

Use the MONTH and TODAY functions to find birthdays in the current month

Use the same list from the previous tip to determine whose birthday falls in the current month. Use the TODAY function to determine the current date and the MONTH function to compare the month of everyone's birthday with the current month, then combine those functions with conditional formatting.

▶ To determine all friends whose birthday is in the current month:

1. In cell D1 enter the formula **TODAY()**.

2. Select cells A2:B10.

3. From the **Home** tab, go to the **Styles** bar and click on **Conditional Formatting**.

4. Choose **New Rule**.

5. In the **Select a Rule Type** dialog, select **Use a formula to determine which cells to format**.

6. In the **Edit** box, type the following formula:
   =(MONTH(TODAY()) =MONTH($B2)).

7. Click **Format** to select the desired formatting to apply when the cell value meets the condition.

8. Select a color from the **Fill** tab and click **OK**.

9. Click **OK**.

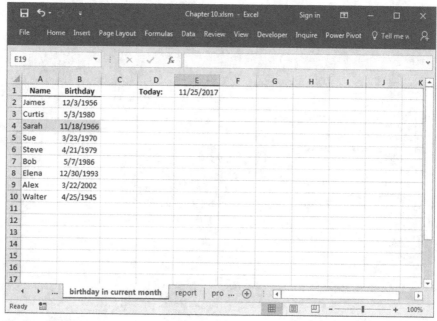

Figure 10-28

Use conditional formatting to border summed rows

Enhance worksheets with this tip for placing a border on special cells. The worksheet contains daily sales for different teams. After a certain period, team sales are summed. To enhance the visibility of each sum, we want to border it automatically through conditional formatting. Use a simple instruction as the condition for conditional formatting and border the row of each cell that meets the desired condition.

▶ To border all rows containing a sum:

1. In a worksheet, enter data in cells A1:C11, as shown in Figure 10–29, and select the range A2:C11.

2. From the **Home** tab, go to the **Styles** bar and click on **Conditional Formatting**.

3. Choose **New Rule**.

4. In the **Select a Rule Type** dialog, select **Use a formula to determine which cells to format**.

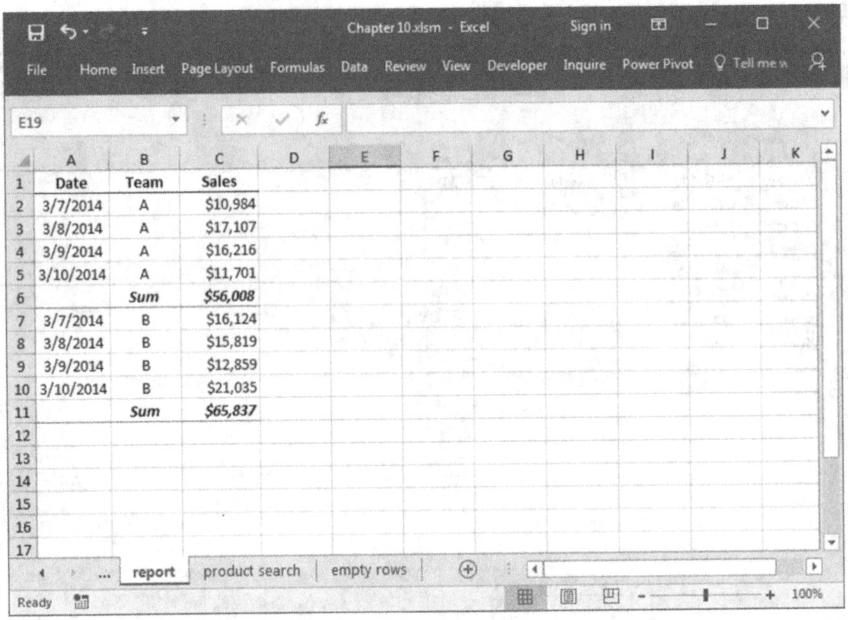

Figure 10–29

5. In the **Edit** box, type the following formula: **=$B2="sum"**.

6. Click **Format**.

7. On the **Border** tab, click the bottom line in the **Border** field.

8. Select **Red** from the **Color** drop-down box.

9. Click **OK**.

Use the LEFT function in a product search

In this example, you need to find all the product numbers that contain the same first three characters. Enter the product number as the search criterion in cell A2 and let Excel find each product that corresponds to the same first three characters. The first three characters of the numbers can be extracted by the LEFT function. The name of the first product appears automatically in cell B2 with the use of the following formula: **=VLOOKUP ($A$2,$A$5:$B$15,2,FALSE)**. Use a combination of the LEFT function and conditional formatting to shade each cell that meets the desired condition.

▶ To shade product numbers that meet the criteria:

1. In a worksheet, copy the data in cells A4:B15, as shown in Figure 10–30, and select cells A5:B15.

2. From the **Home** tab, go to the **Styles** bar and click on **Conditional Formatting**.

3. Choose **New Rule**.

4. In the **Select a Rule Type** dialog, select **Use a formula to determine which cells to format**.

5. In the **Edit** box, type the following formula: **= LEFT ($A5,3) = LEFT ($A$2,3)**.

6. Click **Format** to select the desired formatting to apply when the cell value meets the condition.

7. Select a color from the **Fill** tab and click **OK**.

8. Click **OK**.

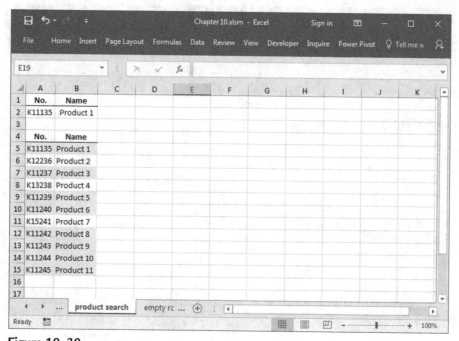

Figure 10–30

Use the AND function to detect empty rows in a range

The last tip in this chapter marks all empty cells in a range. Use a combination of the AND function and conditional formatting to shade each cell that meets the desired condition.

▶ To detect empty rows in a range:

1. In a worksheet, copy the data in cells A1:B12, as shown in Figure 10–31, and select the range A2:B12.

2. From the **Home** tab, go to the **Styles** bar and click on **Conditional Formatting**.

3. Choose **New Rule**.

4. In the **Select a Rule Type** dialog, select **Use a formula to determine which cells to format**.

5. In the **Edit** box, type the following formula: **=AND ($A3> ($A2+1), $B3 > ($B2+1))**.

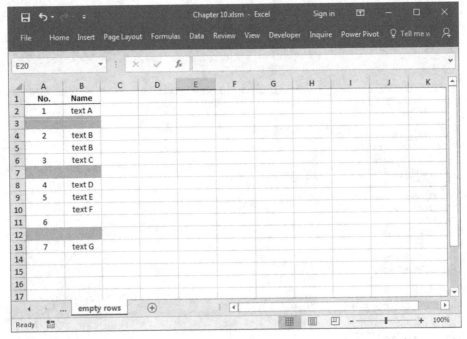

Figure 10–31

6. Click **Format** to select the desired formatting to apply when the cell value meets the condition.

7. Select a color from the **Fill** tab and click **OK**.

8. Click **OK**.

Use the COUNTIFS function to determine value based on multiple filters

The COUNTIFS function is an extension of the COUNTIF function. The COUNTIF function only filters against one value while the COUNTIFS function can use multiple filters to test against. For example, if you wish to determine the number of cats of a certain color instead of just the number of cats, you can use the COUNTIFS function.

1. In a worksheet, copy the data in cells B3:C12, as shown in Figure 10–32.

2. In cell F3, type the formula: = COUNTIFS (B4:B10, "Cat", C4:C10, "Black")

The function brings back a count of only the black cats.

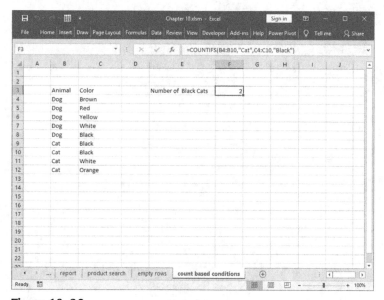

Figure 10–32

Working with Array Formulas 11

Use the ADDRESS, MAX, and ROW functions to determine the last cell used

With this tip, we learn the definition of an array formula. Here, we want to determine the last cell used in a range and shade it. Combine the ADDRESS, MAX, and ROW functions as described below to get the desired result.

▶ To determine the last cell used in a range and shade it:

1. In column A, list any kind of numbers.

2. Select cell B2 and type the following array formula: **=ADDRESS (MAX((A2:A100<>"")*ROW(A2:A100)),1)**.

3. Press **<Ctrl+Shift+Enter>**.

4. Select cells A2:A11.

5. From the **Home** tab, go to the **Styles** bar and click on **Conditional Formatting**.

6. Choose **New Rule**.

7. In the **Select a Rule Type** dialog, select **Use a formula to determine which cells to format**.

8. In the **Edit** box, type the following formula: **=ADDRESS(ROW(),1) =$B$2**.

9. Click **Format,** select a color from the **Fill** tab, and click **OK**.

10. Click **OK**.

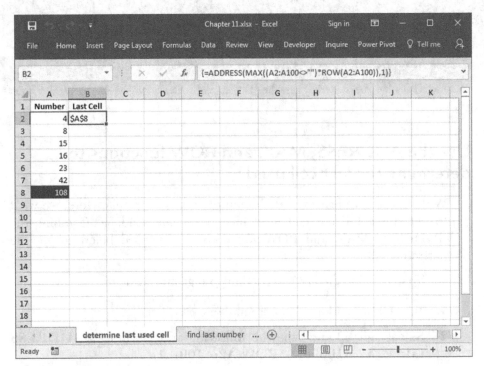

Figure 11–1

NOTE: As shown in Figure 11-1, Excel automatically inserts the combined functions, which are defined as an array formula, between the braces ({ and }). Use an array formula to perform several calculations to generate a single result or multiple results.

Use the INDEX, MAX, ISNUMBER, and ROW functions to find the last number in a column

Use the table from the previous tip and continue with array formulas. Now we want to determine the last value in column A. Use a combination of the INDEX, MAX, ISNUMBER, and ROW functions inside an array formula to have the desired result displayed in cell B2.

Don't forget to enter the array formula by pressing **<Ctrl+Shift+Enter>** to enclose it in braces.

▶ To determine the last number in a column:

1. In column A, list values or use the table from the previous tip.

2. Select cell B2 and type the following array formula:
    =INDEX(A:A,MAX(ISNUMBER(A1:A1000)*ROW(A1:A1000))).

3. Press **<Ctrl+Shift+Enter>**.

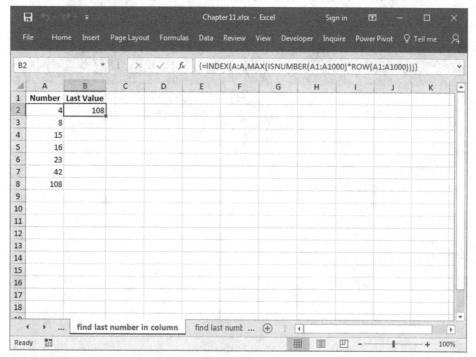

Figure 11–2

Use the INDEX, MAX, ISNUMBER, and COLUMN functions to find the last number in a row

In this example, the last value in each row must be determined and copied to another cell. To do this, combine the INDEX, MAX, ISNUMBER, and COLUMN functions in an array formula.

▶ To determine the last number in a row:

1. Generate a table the one shown in Figure 11–3 using the range A1:F6.

2. In cells A9:A13, enter numbers from 2 to 6.

3. Select cell B9 and type the following array formula:
    =INDEX(2:2,MAX(ISNUMBER(2:2)*COLUMN(2:2))).

4. Press **<Ctrl+Shift+Enter>**.

5. Select cells B9:B13.

6. In the **Home** tab, go to the **Editing** bar and choose the **Fill** button.

7. Select **down** to retrieve the last value in each of the remaining rows.

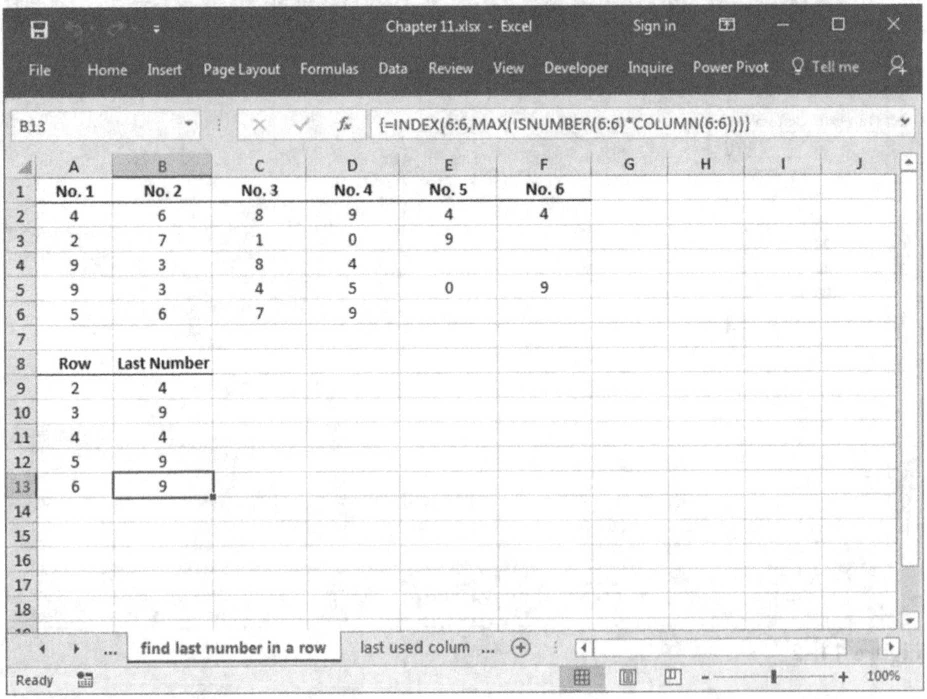

Figure 11–3

Use the MAX, IF, and COLUMN functions to determine the last column used in a range

Now let's determine the last column used in a defined range by using an array formula. All columns in the range A1:X10 need to be checked, and the last column used is then shaded automatically. Here we use the MAX, IF, and COLUMN functions in an array formula and combine them with conditional formatting.

▶ To determine the last used column in a range:

1. Select cells A1:D10 and enter any numbers.

2. Select cell B12 and type the following array formula: **=MAX(IF(A1:X1 0<>"",COLUMN(A1:X10)))**.

3. Press **<Ctrl+Shift+Enter>**.

4. Select cells A1:X10.

5. From the **Home** tab, go to the **Styles** bar and click on **Conditional Formatting**.

6. Choose **New Rule**.

7. In the **Select a Rule Type** dialog, select **Use a formula to determine which cells to format**.

8. In the **Edit** box, type the following formula: **=$B$12=COLUMN(A1)**.

9. Click **Format,** select a color from the **Fill** tab, and click **OK**.

10. Click **OK**.

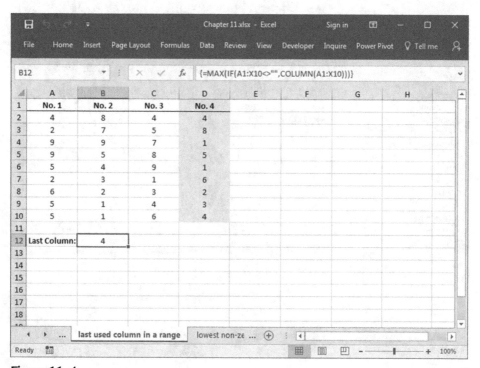

Figure 11–4

Use the MIN and IF functions to find the lowest nonzero value in a range

The sales for a fiscal year are recorded by month. At some point during the year, the month with the lowest sales must be determined. If the list contains all sales from the year, we simply use the MIN function to get the lowest value. However, if we want to find the lowest sales before the year is over and we don't have sales figures available for some of the months, we need to use the IF function to exclude the zero values, so they aren't read as the minimum. Combine the MIN and IF functions in an array formula and use conditional formatting to shade the lowest value.

▶ To detect the lowest nonzero value in a range:

1. In cells A2:A13, list the months January through December.

2. In column B, list some sales values down to row 7.

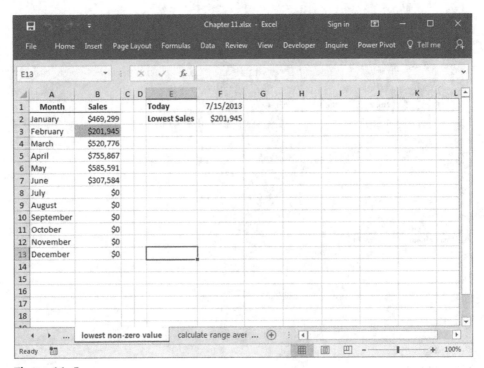

Figure 11–5

3. Select cell F2 and type the following array formula: **=MIN (IF(B1:B13>0,B1:B13))**.

4. Press **<Ctrl+Shift+Enter>**.

5. Select cells B2:B13.

6. From the **Home** tab, go to the **Styles** bar and click on **Conditional Formatting**.

7. Choose **New Rule**.

8. In the **Select a Rule Type** dialog, select **Use a formula to determine which cells to format**.

9. In the **Edit** box, type the following formula: **=$F$2=B2**.

10. Click **Format,** select a color from the **Fill** tab, and click **OK**.

11. Click **OK**.

Use the AVERAGE and IF functions to calculate the average of a range, taking zero values into consideration

Normally, Excel calculates the average of a range without considering empty cells. Use this tip to calculate the correct average when some values in a range are missing. As in the previous example, we use the IF function to exclude the zero values, in this case so they don't reduce the average. Combine the AVERAGE and IF functions in an array formula to obtain the correct average of all listed costs.

▶ To calculate the average of a range, taking zero values into consideration:

1. In cells A2:A13, list the months January through December.

2. In column B, list monthly costs down to row 7.

3. Select cell E1 and type the following array formula:
   =AVERAGE(IF($B$2:$B$13<>0,$B$2:$B$13)).

4. Press **<Ctrl+Shift+Enter>**.

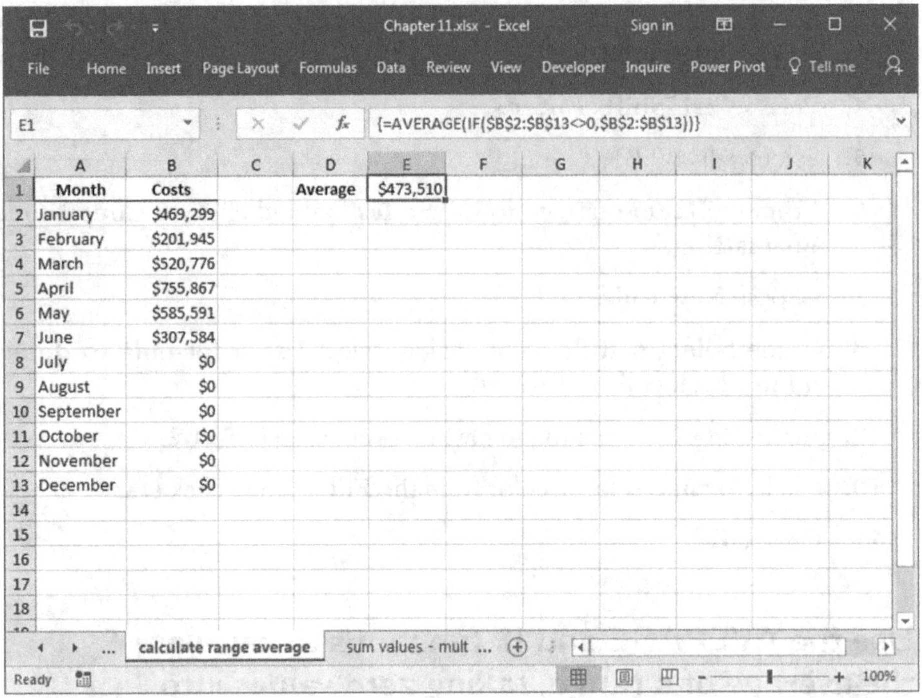

Figure 11–6

NOTE: The result can be checked by selecting cells B2:B7. Right-click in the Excel status bar and select the built-in Average function instead of the usually displayed Sum.

Use the SUM and IF functions to sum values with several criteria

To sum values in a list, the SUMIF function is normally used. Unfortunately, it is not that easy to sum values using different criteria. Using a combination of different functions in an array formula is once again the solution. Use the SUM and IF functions together to take several criteria into consideration. In this example, we want to sum all values in a list that match both the word "wood" in column A and a value larger than 500 in column B. The result is displayed in cell E2.

▶ To sum special values with several criteria:

1. In cells A2:A11, enter materials like wood, earth, and metal.

2. In cells B2:B11, list sizes from 100 to 1,000.

3. In cells C2:C11, enter the corresponding costs.

4. Select cell E2 and type the following array formula:
   =(SUM(IF(A2:A11="wood",IF(B2:B11>500,C2:C11)))).

5. Press **<Ctrl+Shift+Enter>**.

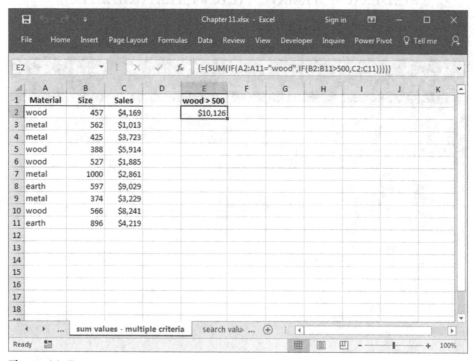

Figure 11–7

Use the INDEX and MATCH functions to search for a value that matches two criteria

To search for a value that takes one or more criteria into consideration, use the INDEX and MATCH functions together. In this example, the search criteria can be entered in cells E1 and F1. Generate a search function using those two search criteria for the range A2:C11 and return the result in cell E2.

▶ To search for a special value considering two criteria:

1. In a worksheet, copy the data in cells A1:C11, as shown in Figure 11–8.

2. Enter **W46** as the first criterion in cell E1 and **1235** as the second criterion in cell F1.

3. Select cell E2 and type the following array formula:
   =INDEX (C1:C11,MATCH (E1&F1,A1:A11&B1:B11,0)).

4. Press **<Ctrl+Shift+Enter>**.

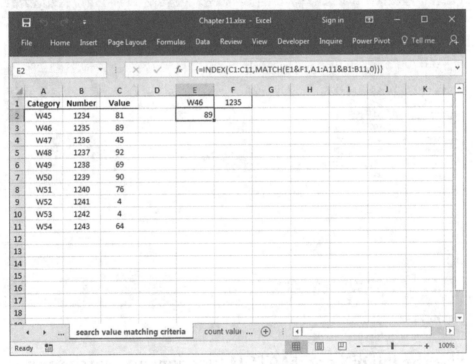

Figure 11–8

Use the SUM function to count values that match two criteria

To count values in a list, normally the COUNTIF function is used. Unfortunately, COUNTIF cannot be used to count when more than one criterion

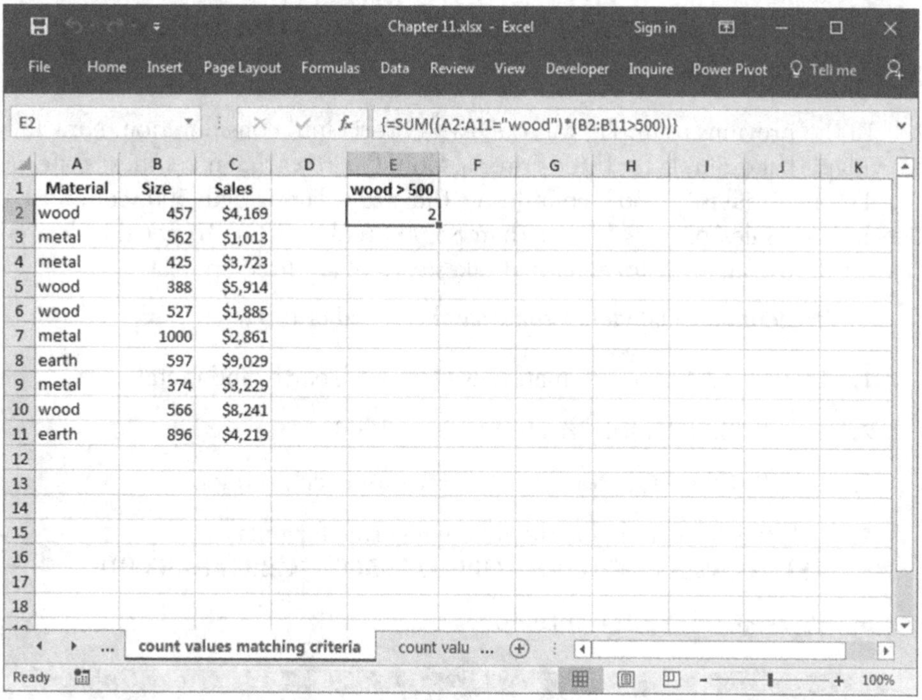

Figure 11–9

must be taken into consideration. However, it is possible to get the desired result using an array formula. Use the SUM function to consider two criteria. In this example, we count the rows that contain the word "wood" in column A and have a size larger than 500 in column B.

▶ To count special values that match two criteria:

1. In cells A2:A11, list materials like wood, earth, and metal.

2. In cells B2:B11, enter sizes from 100 to 1000.

3. In cells C2:C11, list the sales for each product.

4. Select cell E2 and type the following array formula:
   =SUM((A2:A11="wood")*(B2:B11>500)).

5. Press **<Ctrl+Shift+Enter>**.

Use the SUM function to count values that match several criteria

In the previous example, we took two criteria into consideration. Now let's adapt that example for three criteria. Count all rows that meet these criteria: The material is "wood" (column A), the size is larger than 500 (column B), and the sales price is higher than $5,000 (column C). To get the desired result, use an array formula that takes care of all three criteria.

▶ To count special values that match several criteria:

1. In cells A2:A11, enter materials like wood, earth, and metal.

2. In cells B2:B11, list sizes from 100 to 1000.

3. In cells C2:C11, enter the sales price for each product.

4. Select cell E6 and type the following array formula:
   =SUM((A2:A11="wood")*(B2:B11>500)*(C2:C11>5000)).

5. Press **<Ctrl+Shift+Enter>**.

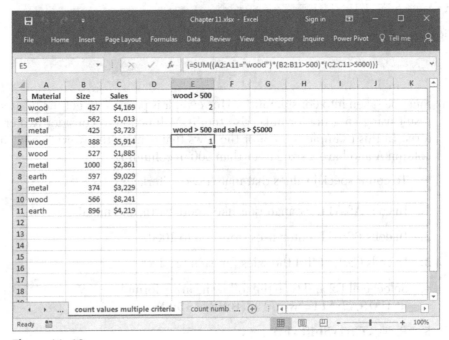

Figure 11–10

Use the SUM function to count numbers from *x* to *y*

For this tip, we want to count all sales from $2,500 to less than $5,000. As previously described, COUNTIF handles only one condition. Use an array formula with the SUM function to get the correct result here.

▶ To count sales from $2,500 to less than $5,000:

1. In cells A2:B11, list the daily sales and dates.

2. Select cell D2 and type the following array formula:
   =SUM((A2:A11>=2500)*(A2:A11<5000)).

3. Press **<Ctrl+Shift+Enter>**.

4. Select cells A2:B11.

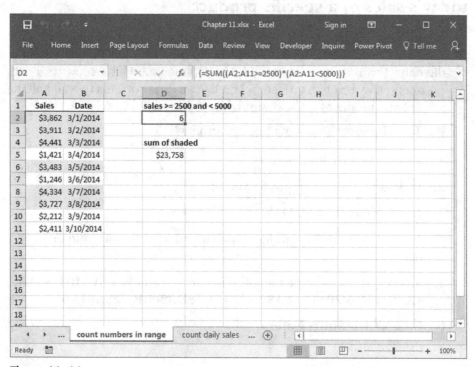

Figure 11–11

NOTE: To sum all shaded sales, use the following array formula: **=(SUM(IF(A2:A11> =2500,IF(A2:A11<5000,A2:A11))))** *and press* **<Ctrl+Shift+Enter>**.

5. From the **Home** tab, go to the **Styles** bar and click on **Conditional Formatting**.

6. Choose **New Rule**.

7. In the **Select a Rule Type** dialog, select **Use a formula to determine which cells to format**.

8. In the **Edit** box, type the following formula:
   =AND($A2>= 2500,$A2<5000).

9. Click **Format,** select a color from the **Fill** tab, and click **OK**.

10. Click **OK**.

Use the SUM and DATEVALUE functions to count today's sales of a specific product

The table in Figure 11–12 contains several products sold on different days. We want to count all sales of one specific product for just one day. To handle dates this way, use the DATEVALUE function, which converts a date represented by text to a serial number. Use an array formula to count all the sales of one product for the desired day.

▶ To count today's sales of a specific product:

1. In cells A2:A15, list dates.

2. In cells B2:B15, enter product numbers.

3. In cell E1, enter **=TODAY()**.

4. In cell D2, enter the product number you want to find (sold on today's date).

5. Select cell E2 and type the following array formula: **=SUM((DATEVALUE("11/25/2017")=$A$2:$A$15)*($D$2=$B$2:$B$15))**.

6. Press **<Ctrl+Shift+Enter>**.

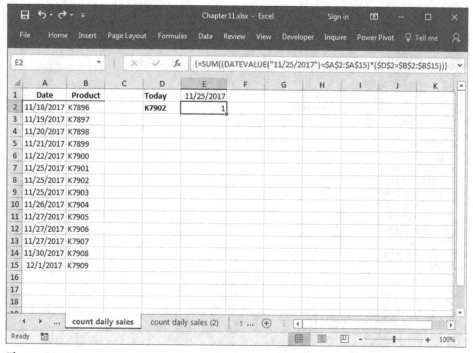

Figure 11-12

Use the SUM function to count today's sales of a specific product

This example is similar to the previous one, except the search criteria are variable. The array formula refers now to cells E1 and E2 and sums up all counted sales for one product on a specified date in cell E4.

▶ To count sales of a specific product for one day:

1. In cells A2:A15, list dates.

2. In cells B2:B15, enter product numbers.

3. Select cell E1 and enter the desired date to be considered for counting.

4. Select cell E2 and select one product number.

5. Select cell E4 and type the following array formula:
   =SUM((E1=$A$2:$A$15)*(E2=$B$2:$B$15)).

6. Press **<Ctrl+Shift+Enter>**.

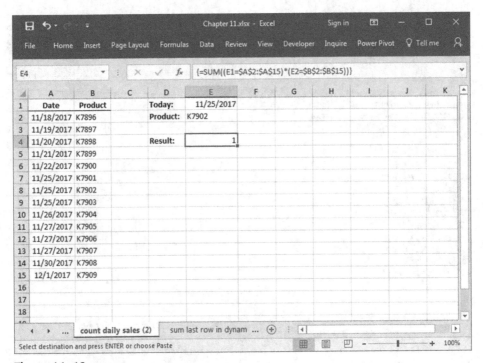

Figure 11–13

Use the SUM, OFFSET, MAX, IF, and ROW functions to sum the last row in a dynamic list

Figure 11–14 shows a list that is updated constantly. The task here is to determine the last row and sum its entries. Use the MAX and ROW functions to detect the last row used, then sum that row with help from the SUM and OFFSET functions. Combine all these functions in one array formula and assign the calculated result to cell H2.

▶ To sum the last row in a dynamic list:

1. In cells A2:A11, enter dates.

2. In cells B2:F11, list numbers for each team.

3. Select cell H2 and type the following array formula: **=SUM(OFFSET (B1:F1,MAX(IF(B1:F100<>"",ROW(1:100)))-1,)).**

4. Press **<Ctrl+Shift+Enter>**.

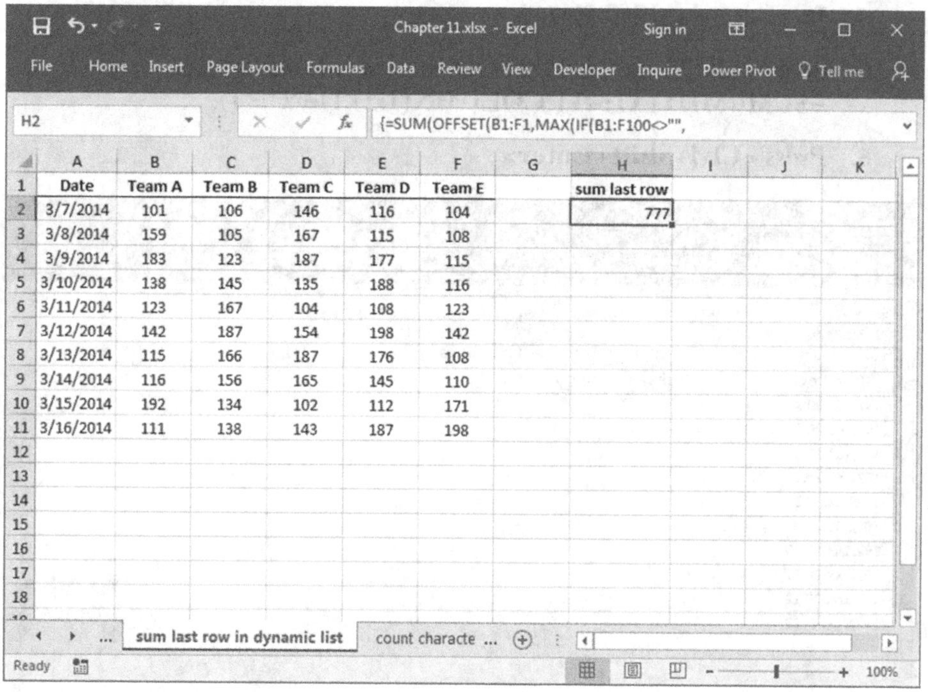

	A	B	C	D	E	F
1	Date	Team A	Team B	Team C	Team D	Team E
2	3/7/2014	101	106	146	116	104
3	3/8/2014	159	105	167	115	108
4	3/9/2014	183	123	187	177	115
5	3/10/2014	138	145	135	188	116
6	3/11/2014	123	167	104	108	123
7	3/12/2014	142	187	154	198	142
8	3/13/2014	115	166	187	176	108
9	3/14/2014	116	156	165	145	110
10	3/15/2014	192	134	102	112	171
11	3/16/2014	111	138	143	187	198

Figure 11-14

NOTE: Check the result by selecting cells B11:F11. With the right mouse button, click on the status bar at the bottom of the Excel window and select the Sum function.

Use the SUM, MID, and COLUMN functions to count specific characters in a range

In this example, we want to count specific characters that appear in a range. Use the MID function to extract each character from the cells, then define the range to be searched using the COLUMN function. The SUM function counts the result. Combine all these functions into one array formula.

▶ To count certain characters in a range:

1. In cells A2:A11, list IP addresses.
2. Insert in any of these cells one or more characters, like x or xxx.
3. Select cell D2 and type the following array formula: **=SUM((MID(A1:A11,COLUMN(1:1),3)="xxx")*1)**.

4. Press **<Ctrl+Shift+Enter>**.

5. Select cell D3 and type the following array formula:
   =SUM((MID (A1:A11,COLUMN(1:1),1)="x")*1).

6. Press **<Ctrl+Shift+Enter>**.

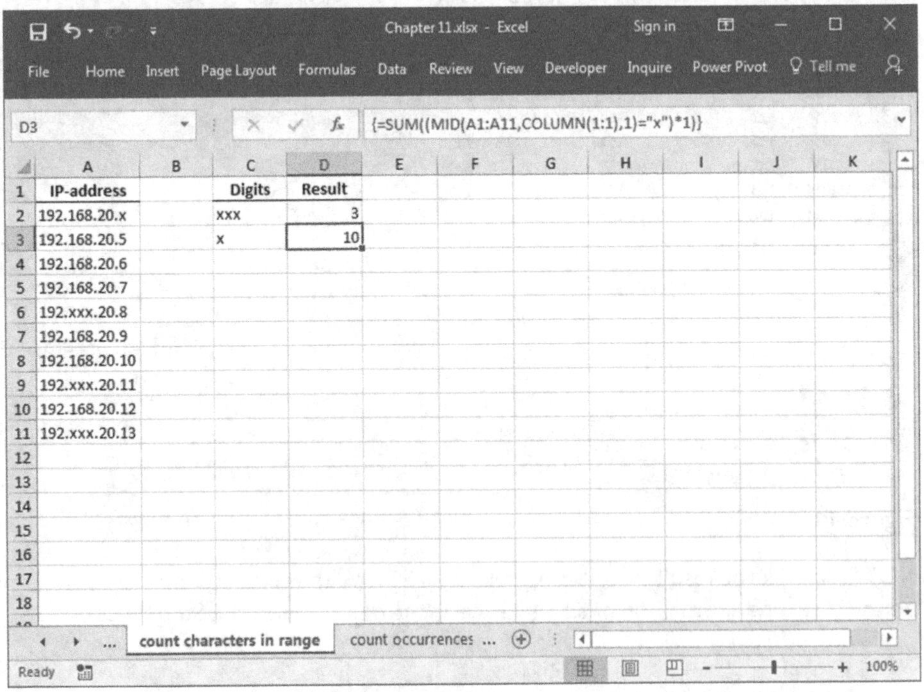

Figure 11–15

Use the SUM, LEN, and SUBSTITUTE functions to count the occurrences of a specific word in a range

In this example, we want to count how many times a specific word appears in a range. Use the SUM, SUBSTITUTE, and LEN functions in one array formula to do this. Enter the criterion in cell C1 and let Excel display the result of the count in cell C2.

▶ To count the occurrences of a specific word in a range:

1. In cells A2:A11, type any text but enter the word **test** at least once.

2. In cell C1, enter the word **test**.

3. Select cell C2 and type the following array formula: **=SUM ((LEN(A1:A10)-LEN(SUBSTITUTE(A1:A10,C1,"")))/LEN(C1))**.

4. Press **<Ctrl+Shift+Enter>**.

5. Select cells A2:A10.

6. From the **Home** tab, go to the **Styles** bar and click on **Conditional Formatting**.

7. Choose **New Rule**.

8. In the **Select a Rule Type** dialog, select **Use a formula to determine which cells to format**.

9. In the **Edit** box, type the following formula: **=$C$1=A1**.

10. Click **Format,** select a color from the **Fill** tab, and click **OK**.

11. Click **OK**.

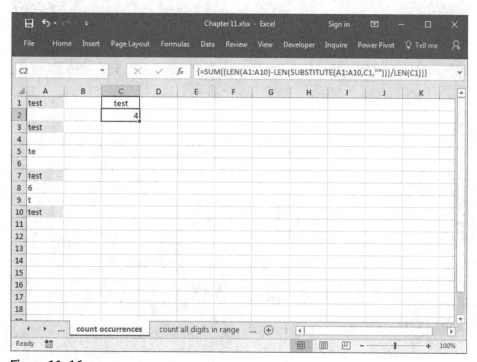

Figure 11–16

Use the SUM and LEN functions to count all digits in a range

With what you have learned so far about array formulas, this task should be easy. Here we will count all digits in the range A1:A10 and display the result in cell C2. As you have probably already guessed, both the SUM and LEN functions can be combined in an array formula.

▶ To count all digits in a range:

1. In cells A2:A10, type any text.

2. Select cell C2 and type the following array formula:
    =SUM(LEN (A1:A10)).

3. Press **<Ctrl+Shift+Enter>**.

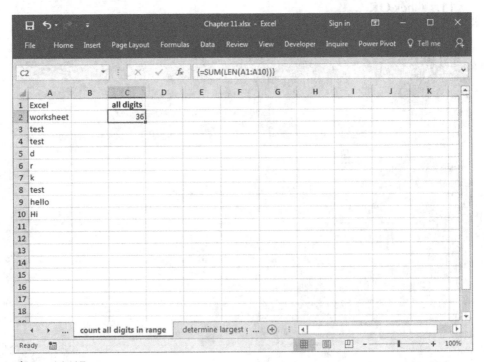

Figure 11–17

Use the MAX, INDIRECT, and COUNT functions to determine the largest gain/loss of shares

Let's say you record the daily share prices of a stock in an Excel worksheet. In this example, you want to monitor your stock to determine the largest gain and loss in dollars.

▶ To determine the largest gain and loss:

1. In cells A2:A11, enter the daily value of a stock.

2. In cells B2:B11, list dates.

3. Select cell D2 and type the array formula **=MAX(A3:INDIRECT ("A"&COUNT(A:A))-A2:INDIRECT("A"&COUNT(A:A)-1))** to find the largest gain.

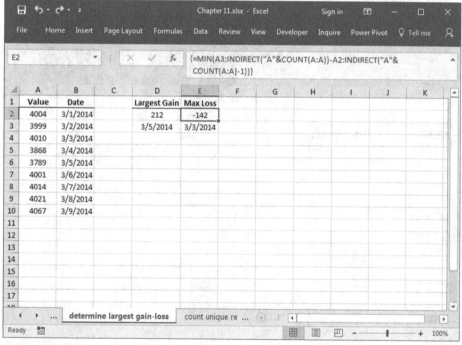

Figure 11–18

NOTE: To determine the dates of the largest gain and loss, use
=INDEX(B:B,MATCH(D2,A$3:A$1002-A$2:A$1001,0)+1) in cell D3 and
=INDEX(B:B,MATCH (E2,A$3:A$1002-A$2:A$1001,0)+1) in cell E3.

4. Press **<Ctrl+Shift+Enter>**.

5. Select cell E2 and type the array formula **=MIN(A3:INDIRECT ("A"&COUNT(A:A))-A2:INDIRECT("A"&COUNT(A:A)-1))** to find the greatest loss.

6. Press **<Ctrl+Shift+Enter>**.

Use the SUM and COUNTIF functions to count unique records in a list

Excel offers a feature to extract unique values from a list. This feature usually is used by filtering the list through the Data menu option Filter | Advanced Filter. But how do you count unique records in a list without filtering them? Use the SUM and COUNTIF functions together in an array formula.

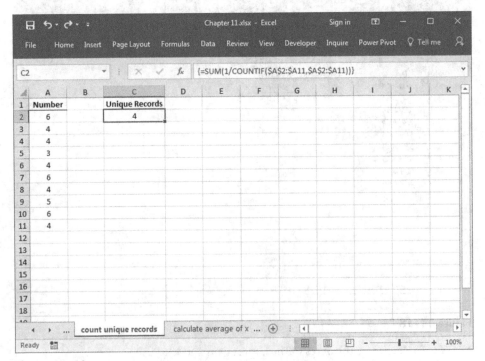

Figure 11–19

▶ To count unique records in a list:

1. . In cells A2:A11, list numbers, repeating some of them.

2. Select cell C2 and type the following array formula: **=SUM(1/COUN-TIF($A$2:$A11,$A$2:$A11))**.

3. Press **<Ctrl+Shift+Enter>**.

Use the AVERAGE and LARGE functions to calculate the average of the *x* largest numbers

In this example, we will calculate the average of the largest five numbers in a list. Combine the AVERAGE and LARGE functions in one array formula.

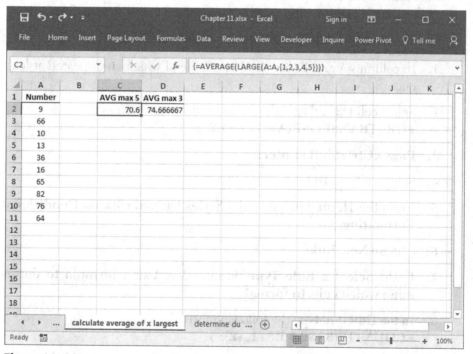

Figure 11–20

NOTE: To calculate the average of the three largest numbers, enter the following formula in cell D2: **=AVERAGE(LARGE(A:A,{1,2,3}))**.

▶ To calculate the average of the five largest numbers:

1. In cells A2:A11, list some numbers.

2. Select cell C2 and type the following array formula:
   =AVERAGE(LARGE(A:A,{1,2,3,4,5})).

3. Press **<Enter>**.

Use the TRANSPOSE and OR functions to determine duplicate numbers in a list

Imagine you have a long list of numbers and your task is to identify all numbers that occur more than once. All of the values need to be checked to see if they appear more than once by using the TRANSPOSE and OR functions. Then all duplicated numbers need to be shaded with the help of the COUNTIF function, which is connected to conditional formatting.

▶ To determine duplicate numbers in a list:

1. In columns A and B, list numbers, some of which are repeated at least once.

2. Select cell D2 and type the following array formula:
   =OR (TRANSPOSE(A2:A11)=B2:B11).

3. Press **<Ctrl+Shift+Enter>**.

4. Select cells A2:B11.

5. From the **Home** tab, go to the **Styles** bar and click on **Conditional Formatting**.

6. Choose **New Rule**.

7. In the **Select a Rule Type** dialog, select **Use a formula to determine which cells to format**.

8. In the **Edit** box, type the following formula:
   =COUNTIF($A$2:$ B$11,A2)>1.

9. Click **Format,** select a color from the **Fill** tab, and click **OK**.

10. Click **OK**.

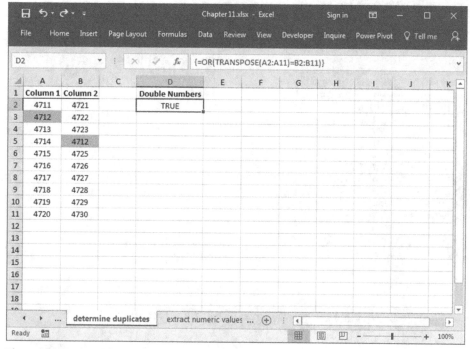

Figure 11-21

Use the MID, MATCH, and ROW functions to extract numeric values from text

This tip can help you extract numeric digits from text. Use the MID, MATCH, and ROW functions and combine them in an array formula.

▶ To extract numeric values from text:

1. In cells A2:A11, enter numbers with leading characters, like YE2004 or FGS456.

2. Select cells B2:B11 and type the following array formula:
   =1*MID(A2,MATCH(FALSE,ISERROR(1*MID(A2,ROW($1:$10),1)),0),255).

3. Press **<Ctrl+Shift+Enter>**.

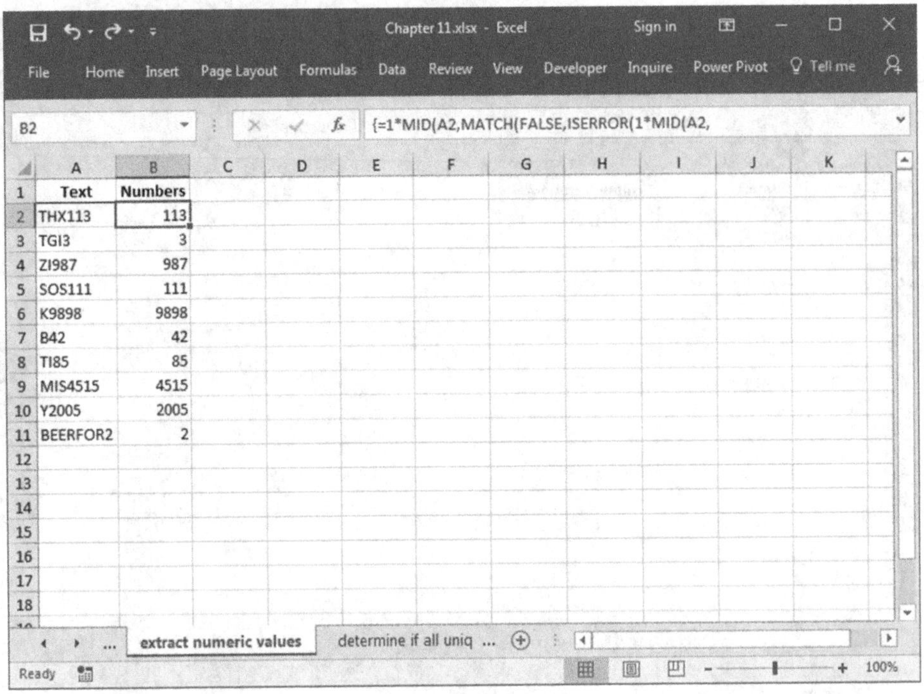

Figure 11–22

Use the MAX and COUNTIF functions to determine whether all numbers are unique

This tip lets you check whether listed numbers are unique. In this example, you use the MAX and COUNTIF functions in combination with an array formula.

▶ To determine whether all listed numbers are unique:

1. In column A, list some numbers.

2. Select cell C2 and type the following array formula:
   =MAX(COUNTIF (A2:A11,A2:A11))=1.

3. Press **<Ctrl+Shift+Enter>**.

4. Select cells A2:A11.

5. From the **Home** tab, go to the **Styles** bar and click on **Conditional Formatting**.

6. Choose **New Rule**.

7. In the **Select a Rule Type** dialog, select **Use a formula to determine which cells to format**.

8. In the **Edit** box, type the following formula:
   =COUNTIF($A$2:$ A$11,A2)>1.

9. Click **Format,** select a color from the **Fill** tab, and click **OK**.

10. Click **OK**.

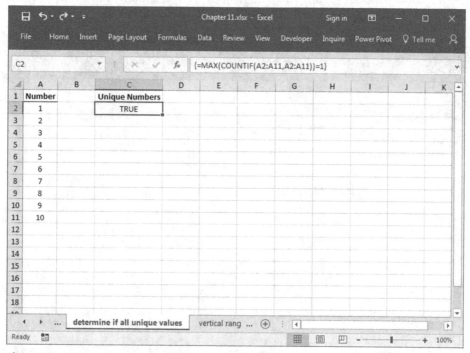

Figure 11–23

NOTE: If any numbers are listed more than once, they will be shaded and cell C2 will display FALSE.

Use the TRANSPOSE function to copy a range from vertical to horizontal or vice versa

Sometimes it is very useful to copy a vertical range of cells to a horizontal range or vice versa. Just copy a range, select a cell outside the range, and click **Paste Special** on the **Edit** menu. **Check** the **Transpose** option and click **OK**. The copied range will be shifted by its vertical or horizontal orientation. To use the same functionality but keep the original references to the copied range, use the TRANSPOSE function in an array formula. Follow this tip to transpose the following table below the range A1:G3.

▶ To transpose a range and keep original cell references:

1. In a worksheet, copy the data in cells A1:G3, as shown in Figure 11–24.

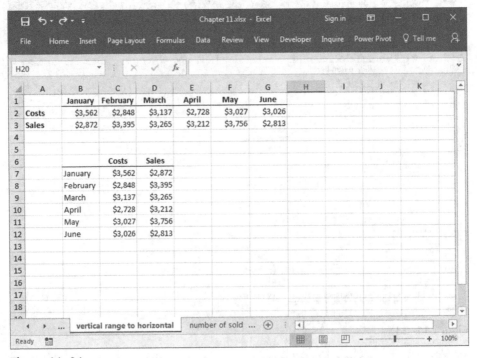

Figure 11–24

NOTE: The order of an array will always be the same; only the vertical or horizontal orientation is shifted.

2. Select cells B7:B12 and type the following array formula:
   =TRANSPOSE (B1:G1).

3. Press **<Ctrl+Shift+Enter>**.

4. Select cells C6:C12 and type the following array formula:
   =TRANSPOSE (A2:G2).

5. Press **<Ctrl+Shift+Enter>**.

6. Select cells D6:D12 and type the following array formula:
   =TRANSPOSE (A3:G3).

7. Press **<Ctrl+Shift+Enter>**.

Use the FREQUENCY function to calculate the number of products sold for each group

The table in Figure 11–25 lists the number of a product sold daily. To do some market analysis and check consumer behavior, group the list and

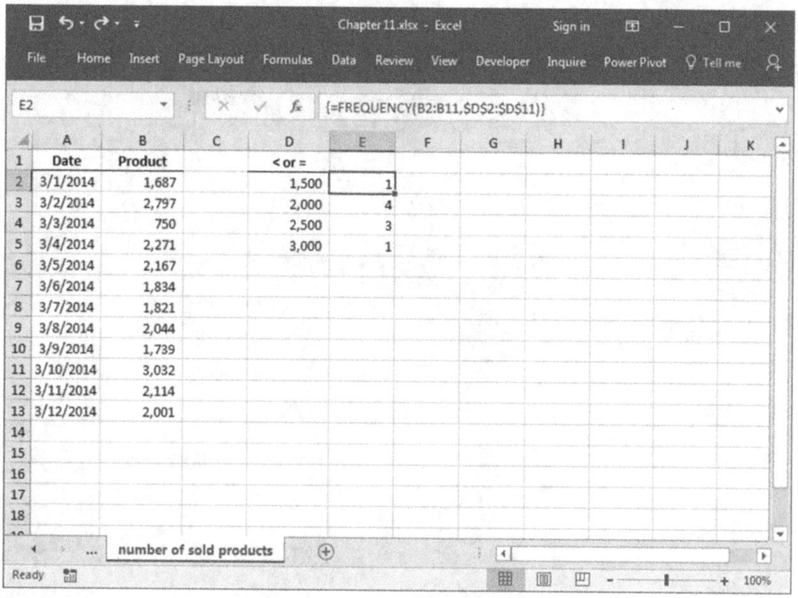

Figure 11–25

NOTE: FREQUENCY ignores blank cells and text.

count the different consumption patterns. Use the FREQUENCY function entered as an array formula to count the frequency by different groups.

▶   To calculate frequency and check purchasing habits:

1. In column A, enter dates in ascending order.

2. In column B, list the number of products sold each day.

3. Define the different groups in cells D2:D5.

4. Select cells E2:E6 and type the following array formula:
    =FREQUENCY (B2:B11,$D$2:$D$11).

5. Press **<Ctrl+Shift+Enter>**.

Special Solutions with Formulas

12

Use the COUNTIF function to prevent duplicate input through validation

This tip shows an easy way to prevent duplicate input in the range A1:A100. Use the **Validation** option and enter a custom formula to get the desired functionality for the specified range in a worksheet.

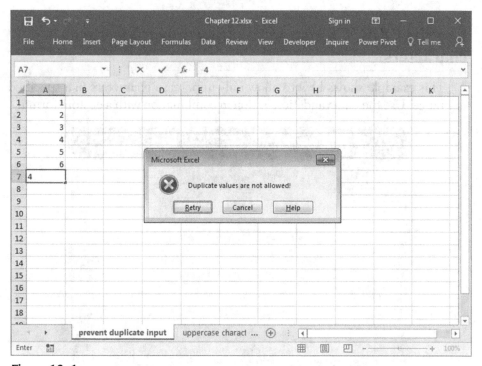

Figure 12–1

NOTE: To remove data validation, select the desired range, click Validation on the Data menu, select the Settings tab, and then click Clear All.

▶ To prevent duplicate input:

1. Select cells A1:A100.

2. On the **Data** tab, in the **Data Tools** group, click **Data Validation**.

3. In the **Data Validation** dialog box, click the **Settings** tab and select **Custom** in the **Allow** drop-down box.

4. In the **Formula** box, type the formula **=COUNTIF($A:$A,A1)=1**.

5. Select the **Error Alert** tab.

6. Enter a custom error message.

7. Click **OK**.

When a user attempts to enter duplicate data, an error message will appear.

Use the EXACT function to allow only uppercase characters

This example shows how to allow only uppercase characters in a specified range. Use the data validation option in combination with a custom formula.

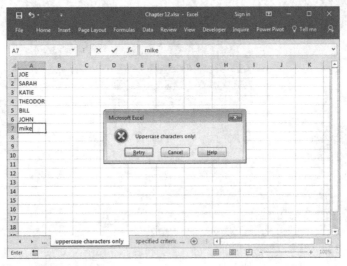

Figure 12–2

NOTE: If you want to allow only lowercase characters, use the formula =EXACT (A1, LOWER (A1)).

▶ To allow only uppercase characters:

1. Select cells A1:A100.

2. On the **Data** tab, in the **Data Tools** group, click **Data Validation**.

3. In the **Data Validation** dialog box, click the **Settings** tab and select **Custom** in the **Allow** drop-down box.

4. In the **Formula** box, type the formula **=EXACT(A1,UPPER(A1))**.

5. Select the **Error Alert** tab.

6. Enter a custom error message.

7. Click **OK**.

Use validation to allow data input by a specific criterion

A range is defined to allow data input as long as it is not locked through a criterion specified in a certain cell. In this example, we allow data input only if the value "Yes" is entered in cell D1. Again, we use data validation in combination with a custom-defined formula to get the solution for this exercise.

▶ To allow data input according to one specified criterion:

1. Enter data in cells A1:A10 as shown in Figure 12–3 and select cells A1:A10.

2. On the **Data** tab, in the **Data Tools** group, click **Data Validation**.

3. In the **Data Validation** dialog box, click the **Settings** tab and select **Custom** in the **Allow** drop-down box.

4. Type the formula **=$D$1="Yes"**.

5. Select the **Error Alert** tab.

6. Enter a custom error message.

7. Click **OK**.

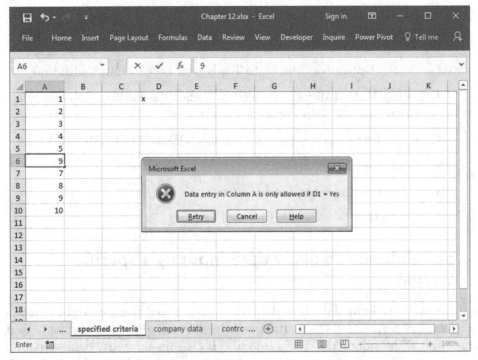

Figure 12–3

NOTE: This formula allows data to be changed only if cell D1 contains the value 1.

Use controls with formulas

The table shown in Figure 12–4 contains an address list with company names and a contact person for each company. Imagine that we can use a drop-down box to select a company, and all corresponding data about the company is automatically displayed in specified cells. Just open a new worksheet and copy the table below to learn more about using drop-down boxes in combination with functions.

▶ To assign a name to a range of data:

1. Select cells A2:D5 as shown in figure 12–4.

2. Click the name box to the left of the formula bar (which shows "A2") and enter **Data**. This name represents all the data inside the range A2:D5.

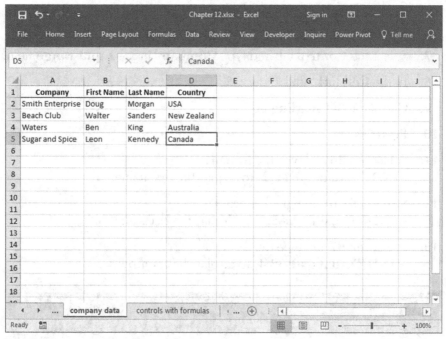

Figure 12–4

3. Press **<Enter>**.

4. Select cells A2:A5.

5. Assign a name to this header row by entering **Company** in the Name box.

6. Press **<Enter>.**

▶ To display addresses by selecting them from a drop-down box:

1. Insert a new worksheet in the same Excel file and display the **Developer** toolbar by selecting the **File** tab. Click **Options** and choose **Customize ribbon**.

2. In the **Main tabs,** tick **Developer.** A new tab will appear in the tabribbon.

3. In this new tab, go to the **Controls** box and click **Insert**.

4. From **Form Controls,** choose **Combo Box**.

5. Move the mouse cursor to the desired location inside the worksheet. Click and drag the combo box to the desired size.

6. Click with the right mouse button on the combo box and select **Format Control**.

7. Select the **Control** tab and type **Company** in the **Input range** field.

8. In the **Cell link** field, enter **E2**.

9. Check the **3D shading** box.

10. Press **OK**.

11. Select cell B6 and type the formula
    =INDEX (data, $E$2,2) to display the first name.

12. Select cell C6 and type the formula
    = INDEX (data, $E$2,3) to display the last name.

13. Select cell B7 and type the formula
    = INDEX (data, $E$2,4) to display the country.

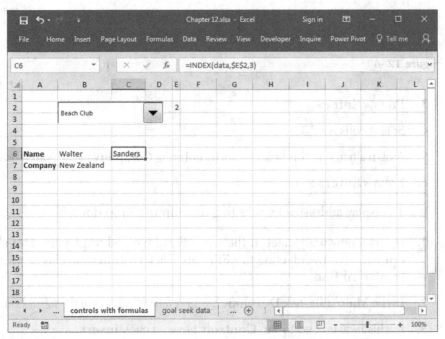

Figure 12–5

NOTE: If the index in cell E2 is not visible, move the combo box so it doesn't cover this cell or change the displayed font style color from Automatic (black) to white.

Use Goal Seek as a powerful analysis tool

Goal Seek is a standard function found on the Tools menu that takes several criteria into consideration and helps find the correct value of a calculation. This example shows the quality control of a production run. The monitoring process sorts out products that don't meet the expected quality standards. The first time we check the quality, we find that 5% of the production does not meet quality standards, and the second time, we find that 2% of the production fails to meet standards. How many more products need to be produced to reach the required number of 1,030 products that meet the quality standards?

▶ Use Goal Seek to determine the total amount of production needed:

1. In cell C2, enter **1030** as the production goal.

2. In cell C3, type the formula **=C2*0.05**.

3. In cell C4, enter the formula **=C2-C3** to calculate how many products are needed to reach the production goal.

4. In cell C5, type the formula **=C4*0.02**.

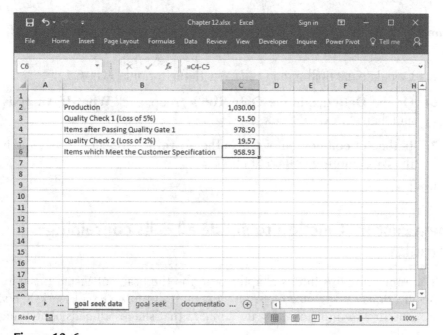

Figure 12–6

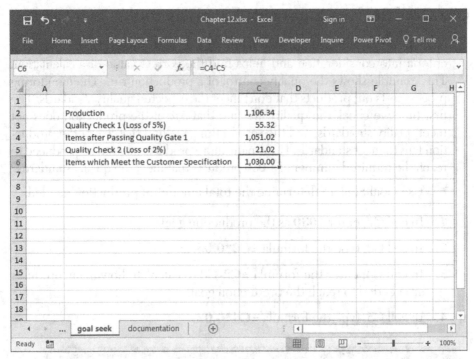

Figure 12–7

5. Calculate the final sum in cell C6 with the formula **=C4-C5**.

6. On the **Data** tab, in the **Data Tools** group, click **What-If Analysis**, and then click **Goal Seek**.

7. In the **Set cell** box, enter **C6**; in the **To value** box, enter **1030**; and in the **By changing cell** box, enter **C2**.

8. Press **OK**.

Use a custom function to shade all cells containing formulas

The remaining tips in this chapter describe the usage of Visual Basic for Applications (VBA) macros to enhance and optimize Excel worksheets. For the first example, we'll write a macro that shades all cells containing formulas.

▶ To shade all cells with formulas:

1. Press **<Alt+F11>** to open the Visual Basic Editor.

2. In the **Insert** menu, click **Module**.

3. Type the following macro:

Sub ColorThem()

  Selection.SpecialCells (xlCellTypeFormulas).Select

  With Selection.Interior

    ColorIndex = 44

    Pattern = xlSolid

  End With

End Sub

4. In the Excel **Tools** menu, select **Macro | Macros**.

5. Select the **ColorThem** macro and click **Run**.

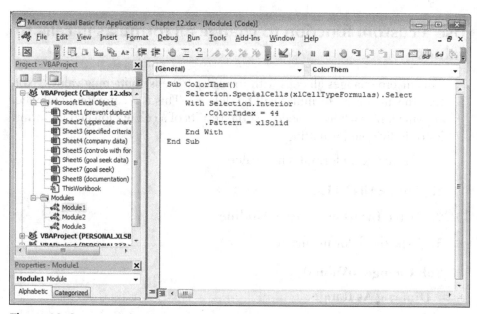

Figure 12–8

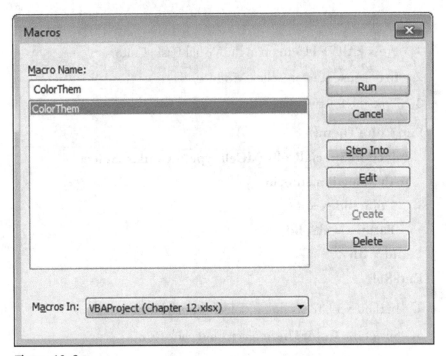

Figure 12-9

Use a custom function to change all formulas in cells to values

This macro changes all cells with formulas to cells containing values. Note that this means all formulas will be deleted. This is a common need when copying tables when we need just the results of a calculation and no formulas or individual formatting.

▶ To change all formulas into values:

1. Press **<Alt+F11>**.

2. In the **Insert** menu, click **Module**.

3. Type the following macro:

Sub ChangeToValue()

    Dim rng As Range

    With ActiveSheet

```
    For Each rng In .UsedRange
        rng.Value = rng.Value
    Next rng
  End With
End Sub
```

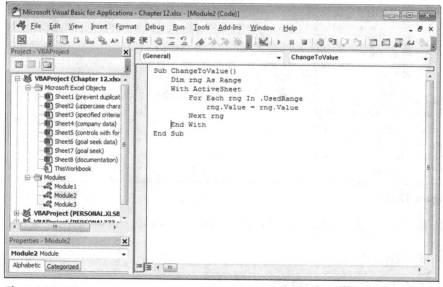

Figure 12-10

NOTE: To start the macro from the Visual Basic Editor, click anywhere within the macro code and press <F5>.

Use a custom function to document and display all cells containing formulas

This powerful macro will document in an **Immediate** window all cells containing formulas. When it is executed, each cell that contains a formula is listed by its cell address, along with the formula and the current value.

▶ To determine and document all formulas in the current worksheet:

1. Press **<Alt+F11>**.

2. In the **Insert** menu, click **Module**.

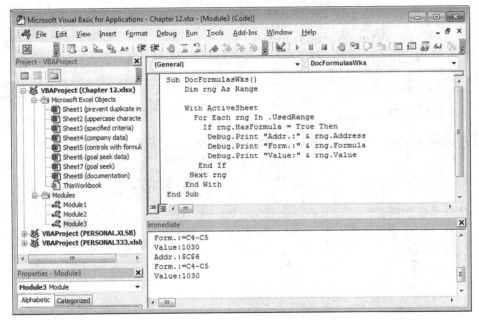

Figure 12–11

NOTE: If you want to document all formulas in the entire workbook, use the following macro:

3. Type the following macro:

Sub DocFormulasWks()
 Dim rng As Range
 With ActiveSheet
  For Each rng In .UsedRange
   If rng.HasFormula = True Then
    Debug.Print "Addr.:" & rng.Address
    Debug.Print "Form.:" & rng.Formula
    Debug.Print "Value:" & rng.Value
   End If
  Next rng
 End With
 End Sub

4. With the cursor in the macro, start it by pressing F5.

5. Click **View** and choose **Immediate window**.

Use a custom function to delete external links in a worksheet

To distinguish between cells containing formulas and cells containing external links, all cells need to be checked. If a cell contains "[" or "]", it is a cell with a hyperlink to another workbook.

▶ To delete all external links in a worksheet:

1. Press **<Alt+F11>**.

2. In the **Insert** menu, click **Module**.

3. Type the following macro:

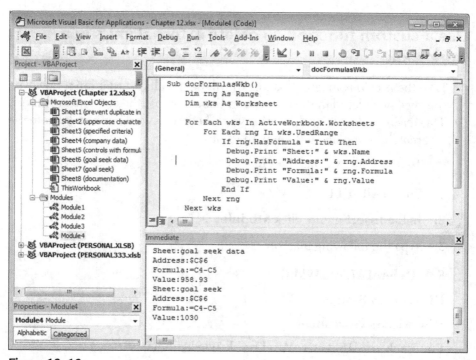

Figure 12–12

```
Sub DeleteExLinks()
Dim rng As Range
With ActiveSheet
 For Each rng In .UsedRange
   If InStr(rng.Formula, "[") > 0 Then
      rng.Value = rng.Value
   End If
 Next rng
End With
End Sub
```

NOTE: Starting this macro will delete all external links, and only values will be displayed.

Use a custom function to delete external links in a workbook

Like the previous macro, this macro will delete all external links; however, they will be deleted in the entire workbook, not just the current worksheet. This macro will look up all existing worksheets of a workbook and delete the external links, replacing them with values.

▶ To delete all external links in a workbook:

1. Press **<Alt+F11>**.

2. In the **Insert** menu, click **Module**.

3. Type the following macro:

```
Sub DeleteExLinksWkb()
Dim rng As Range
Dim wks As Worksheet
For Each wks In ActiveWorkbook.Worksheets
 For Each rng In wks.UsedRange
   If InStr(rng.Formula, "[") > 0  Then
```

```
      rng.Value = rng.Value
   End If
  Next rng
  Next wks
  End Sub
```

Use a custom function to enter all formulas into an additional worksheet

This example utilizes a new worksheet with the name *documentation*. Once started, all formulas inside the active workbook will be documented.

▶ To find all formulas and enter them into a worksheet:

1. Press **<Alt+F11>**.

2. In the **Insert** menu, click **Module**.

3. Type the following macro:

```
Sub NewSheetWithFormulas()
Dim rng As Range
Dim wks As Worksheet
Dim i As Integer

With Sheets("documentation")
i = 1
For Each wks In _
  ActiveWorkbook.Worksheets
 For Each rng In wks.UsedRange
  If rng.HasFormula = True Then
   .Cells(i, 1).Value = wks.Name
   .Cells(i, 2).Value = rng.Address
   .Cells(i, 3).Value = " " & rng.Formula
   .Cells(i, 4).Value = rng.Value
```

```
        i = i+1
      End If
    Next rng
    Next wks
  End With
End Sub
```

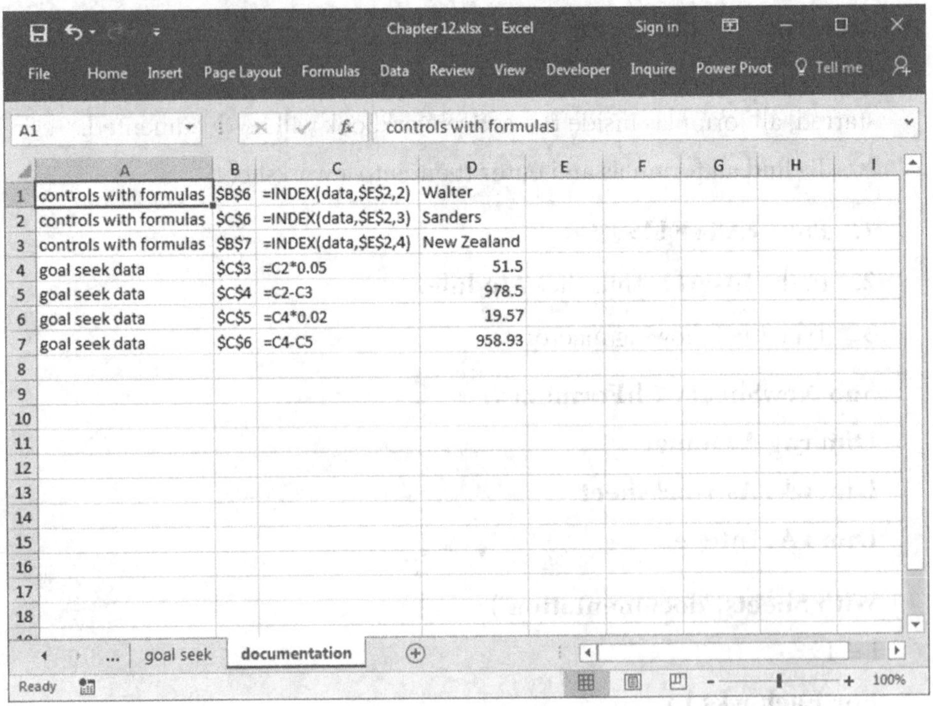

Figure 12–13

User-Defined Functions

13

Use a user-defined function to copy the name of a worksheet into a cell

To copy the name of a worksheet into a cell, you must create a user-defined function.

▶ To copy the name of a worksheet into a cell:

1. Press **<Alt+F11>** to open the Visual Basic Editor.

2. In the **Insert** menu, click **Module**.

3. Type the following function:

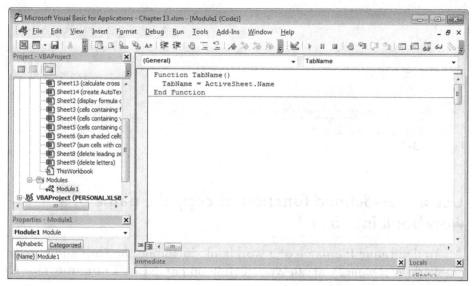

Figure 13–1

Function TabName()

  TabName = ActiveSheet.Name

End Function

4. Close the VBA Editor by pressing **<Alt+Q>**, and type the following function in cell A1: **=TabName()**.

5. Press **<Enter>**.

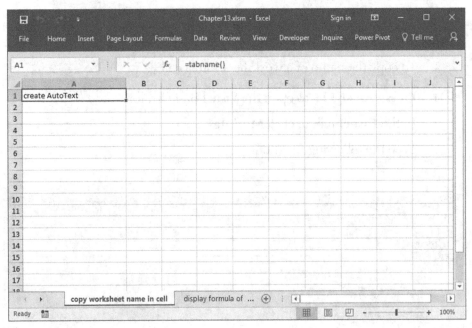

Figure 13–2

Use a user-defined function to copy the name of a workbook into a cell

To determine the name of a workbook, including the path and current worksheet name, you can type the function **=CELL("Filename")** in cell A2.

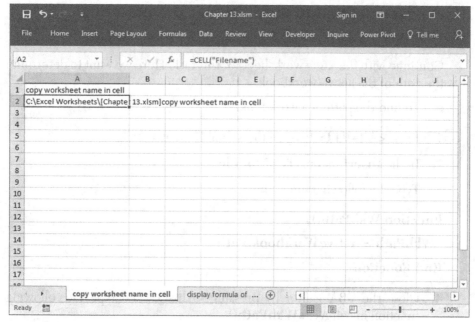

Figure 13–3

Another way to determine the name is to write a user-defined function, as shown here.

▶ To display the workbook name in a cell:

1. Press **<Alt+F11>** to open the Visual Basic Editor.

2. In the **Insert** menu, click **Module**.

3. Type the following function:

Function WkbName()

  WkbName = ActiveWorkbook.Name

End Function

4. Close the VBA Editor by pressing **<Alt+Q>** and type the following function in cell A1: **=WkbName()**.

5. Press **<Enter>**.

Use a user-defined function to get the path of a workbook

Continue with the same worksheet for this task. Here we want to determine the path of the active workbook.

▶ To find the path of a workbook:

1. Press **<Alt+F11>** to open the Visual Basic Editor.

2. In the **Insert** menu, click **Module**.

3. Type the following function:

Function WkbPath()

WkbPath = ActiveWorkbook.Path

End Function

4. Close the VBA Editor by pressing **<Alt+Q>** and type the following function in cell A1: **=WkbPath()**.

5. Press **<Enter>**.

Use a user-defined function to get the full name of a workbook

We have learned how to determine the filename and the path for a workbook. To get both at the same time, we could combine the two text strings. Another, more convenient, way, however, is to use a user-defined function that delivers both the name and path of the active workbook.

▶ To determine the full filename and path of the workbook:

1. Press **<Alt+F11>** to open the Visual Basic Editor.

2. In the **Insert** menu, click **Module**.

3. Type the following function:

Function WkbFull()

WkbFull = ActiveWorkbook.FullName

End Function

4. Close the VBA Editor by pressing **<Alt+Q>** and type the following function in cell A1: **=WkbFull()**.

5. Press **<Enter>**.

Use a user-defined function to determine the current user of Windows or Excel

This tip explains how to determine the current user of Windows and/or Excel. Once again, you will write a user-defined function. In this case, the function will return the name of the current user.

▶ To get the current Windows user:

1. Press **<Alt+F11>** to open the Visual Basic Editor.

2. In the **Insert** menu, click **Module**.

3. Type the following function:

Function User()

  User = Environ("Username")

End Function

4. Close the VBA Editor and type the following formula in any cell: **=User()**.

5. Press **<Enter>**.

▶ To get the current Excel user:

1. Press **<Alt+F11>** to open the Visual Basic Editor.

2. In the **Insert** menu, click **Module**.

3. Type the following function:

Function ExcelUser()

  ExcelUser = Application.UserName

End Function

4. Return to the worksheet and type the following formula in any cell: **=ExcelUser()**.

5. Press **<Enter>**.

NOTE: To get the name of the current Excel user, you can also use Tools | Options | General/username.

Use a user-defined function to display formulas of a specific cell

Using this tip, you can look up the formula text of any cell. It is similar to the keyboard shortcut **<Ctrl+#>**. Generate a worksheet containing data and formulas and then enter the user-defined function shown below.

▶ To make formulas visible:

1. Press **<Alt+F11>** to open the Visual Basic Editor.

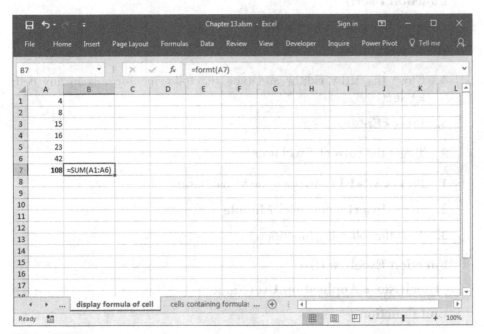

Figure 13–4

2. In the **Insert** menu, click **Module**.

3. Type the following function:

Function FormT(rng As Range)

  FormT = " " & rng.Formula

End Function

4. Return to the worksheet and type the following formula in any cell: **=FormT(A7)**.

5. Press **<Enter>**.

Use a user-defined function to check whether a cell contains a formula

The function described here checks whether a cell contains a formula. Open a new worksheet, list some values in the range A1:A6, and sum them in cell A7. Generate a new user-defined function and use it for the range B1:B7.

▶ To check whether a cell contains a formula:

1. Press **<Alt+F11>** to open the Visual Basic Editor.

2. In the **Insert** menu, click **Module**.

3. Type the following function:

Function FormYes(rng As Range)

  FormYes = rng.HasFormula

End Function

4. Close the VBA Editor by pressing **<Alt+Q>** and type the following function in cell A1: **=FormYes(A1)**.

5. Copy it down to cell B7 by dragging the cell handle in the bottom-right corner of cell B1.

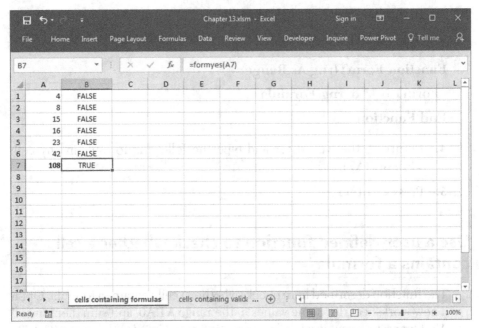

Figure 13–5

Use a user-defined function to check whether a cell contains data validation

When a worksheet contains data validation, sometimes it can be useful to find all cells with data validation. One way to check for this is to create a user-defined function to perform the task. First create a new worksheet and define a date validation for cell A1 that starts with 1/1/2013 and ends with 12/31/2013. Then perform the following steps.

▶ To check whether a cell contains data validation:

1. Press **<Alt+F11>** to open the Visual Basic Editor.

2. In the **Insert** menu, click **Module**.

3. Type the following function:

Function Valid(rng As Range)

Dim intV As Integer

  On Error GoTo errorM

> intV = rng.**Validation.Type**
>
> **Valid = True**
>
> **Exit Function**
>
> **errorM:**
>
> **Valid = False**
>
> **End Function**

4. Return to the worksheet and type the formula **=Valid(A1)** in cell C1.

5. Press **<Enter>**.

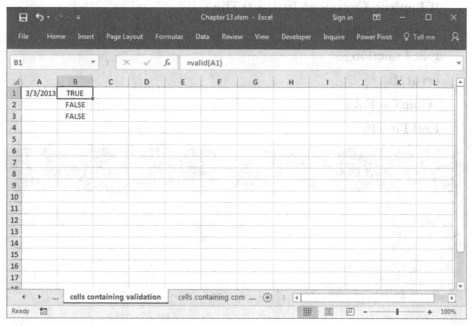

Figure 13–6

Use a user-defined function to find all comments

Cells with comments have red indicator triangles in the upper-right corners. Usually the comments are hidden and appear only if the mouse pointer is rested over that particular cell. It is also possible to hide the red indicator. One way to review all comments is to click Comments in the View menu.

It is also possible to create a user-defined function that returns True if a comment is found.

▶ To check whether a cell contains a comment:

1. Press **<Alt+F11>** to open the Visual Basic Editor.

2. In the **Insert** menu, click **Module**.

3. Type the following function:

Function ComT(rng As Range)

On Error GoTo errorM

If Len(rng.Comment.Text) > 0 Then _

  ComT = True

Exit Function

errorM:

  ComT = False

End Function

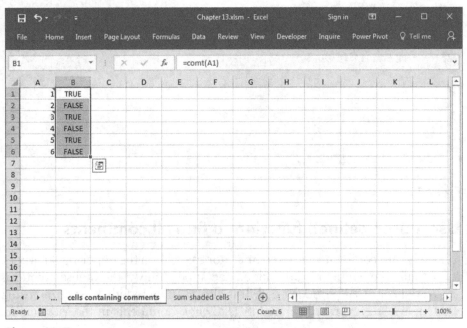

Figure 13–7

4. Close the VBA Editor by pressing **<Alt+Q>**, select cells C1:C5, and type the formula **=ComT(A1)**.

5. Press **<Ctrl+Enter>**.

Use a user-defined function to sum all shaded cells

This tip shows how to sum all shaded cells. Copy the values in range A1:A6 as shown in Figure 13–8 to your worksheet. Format two of the cells with the color red and define a special user-defined function to sum them.

▶ To sum all shaded cells:

1. Press **<Alt+F11>** to open the Visual Basic Editor.

2. In the **Insert** menu, click **Module**.

3. Type the following function:

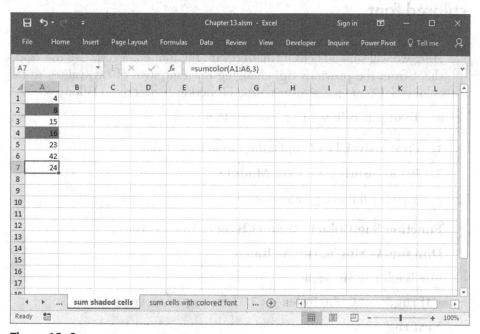

Figure 13–8

NOTE: The integer value Ci is the search criterion for the background color (e.g., 1=black, 2=white, 3=red, 4=green, 5=blue, etc.).

Function SumColor(Area As Range, Ci As Integer)

Dim sng As Single, rng As Range

For Each rng In Area

  If rng.Interior.ColorIndex = Ci Then sng = sng+rng.Value

Next rng

 SumColor = sng

End Function

4. Return to cell A7 of the worksheet and type the formula
   =SumColor (A1:A6,3).

5. Press **<Enter>**.

Use a user-defined function to sum all cells with a colored font

As learned from the previous tip, it is quite easy to sum cells that are shaded. Here we will sum all cells formatted with the font color red. Use the worksheet from the previous tip, changing the font style of two values to the color red. Create a new user-defined function as described below.

▶ To sum all cells with a particular font color:

1. Press **<Alt+F11>** to open the Visual Basic Editor.

2. In the **Insert** menu, click **Module**.

3. Type the following function:

Function SumColorF(Area As Range, Ci As Integer)

Dim sng As Single, rng As Range

For Each rng In Area

  If rng.Font.ColorIndex = Ci Then sng = sng+rng.Value

Next rng

 SumColorF = sng

End Function

4. Return to the worksheet and in cell A7 type the following formula:
   =SumColorF(A1:A6,3).

5. Press **<Enter>**.

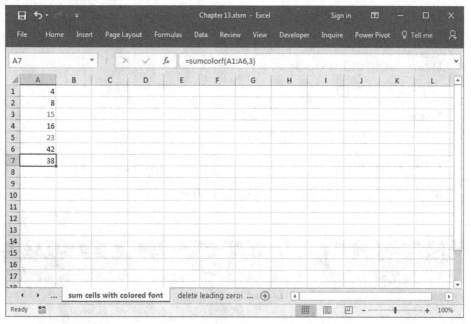

Figure 13–9

NOTE: The integer value Ci is the search criterion for font color (e.g., 1=black, 2=white, 3=red, 4=green, 5=blue).

Use a user-defined function to delete leading zeros for specified cells

In this example, we delete all leading zeros with a user-defined function. Insert a new worksheet and type some numbers with leading zeros. You will must enter an apostrophe before the first digit and continue with zeros. Create a user-defined function as shown below to delete those zeros.

▶ To delete all leading zeros:

1. Press **<Alt+F11>** to open the Visual Basic Editor.

2. In the **Insert** menu, click **Module**.

3. Type the following function:

Function KillZeros(rng As Range)

Dim intS As Integer

intS = rng

While intS-Int(intS) > 0

  intS = intS * 10

Wend

KillZeros = intS

End Function

4. Close the VBA Editor by pressing **<Alt+Q>**.

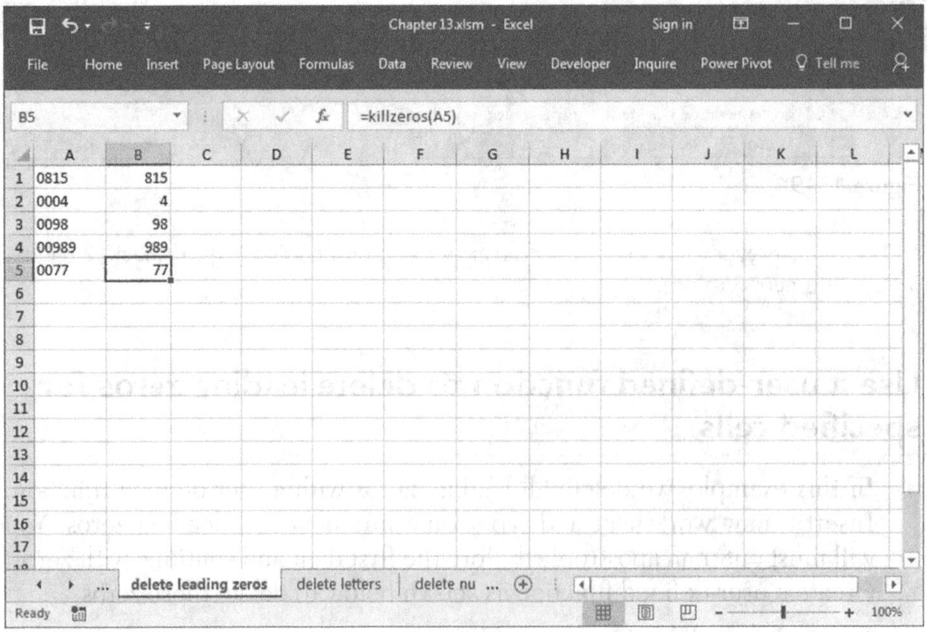

Figure 13–10

5. Select cells B1:B5 and type the formula **=KillZeros(A1)**.

6. Press **<Ctrl+Enter>**.

Use a user-defined function to delete all letters in specified cells

With this tip you can easily delete all letters in specified cells. Doing so manually would take a long time with a large list, but you can automate this process with a user-defined function. Copy the table shown in Figure 13–11 to a new worksheet, create the user-defined function, and test it.

▶ To delete all letters in specified cells:

1. Press **<Alt+F11>** to open the Visual Basic Editor.

2. In the **Insert** menu, click **Module**.

3. Type the following function:

Function LetterOut(rng As Range)

Dim i As Integer

For i = 1 To Len(rng)

  Select Case Asc (Mid(rng.Value, i, 1))

   Case 0 To 64, 123 To 197

    LetterOut = LetterOut & Mid(rng.Value, i, 1)

  End Select

Next i

End Function

4. Return to the worksheet, select cells B1:B5, and type the formula **=LetterOut(A1)**.

5. Press **<Ctrl+Enter>**.

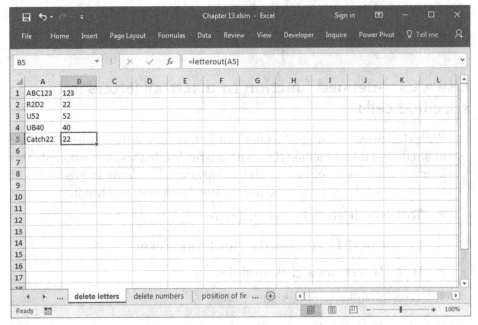

Figure 13–11

Use a user-defined function to delete all numbers in specified cells

Like the previous tip, this task deletes all numbers in specified cells. Again, without the help of a user-defined function or a special macro, this would be a difficult job and take a lot of time. A more convenient way to perform this task is with a user-defined function.

▶ To delete all numbers in specified cells:

1. Press **<Alt+F11>** to open the Visual Basic Editor.

2. In the **Insert** menu, click **Module**.

3. Type the following function:

Function NumberOut(rng As Range)

Dim i As Integer

```
For i = 1 To Len(rng)
   Select Case Asc (Mid(rng.Value, i, 1))
   Case 0 To 64, 123 To 197
   Case Else
   NumberOut = NumberOut & _
   Mid(rng.Value, i, 1)
   End Select
 Next i
 End Function
```

4. Return to the worksheet, select cells **B1:B5**, and type the formula **=NumberOut(A1)**.

5. Press **<Ctrl+Enter>**.

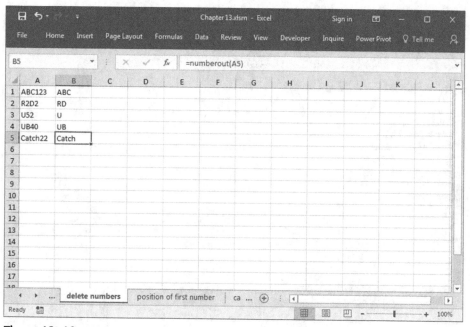

Figure 13–12

Use a user-defined function to determine the position of the first number

The user-defined function described here determines the position of the first number in a text string in a cell.

▶ To determine the position of the first number:

1. Type any data with letters and numbers in cells A1:A5.

2. Press **<Alt+F11>** to open the Visual Basic Editor.

3. In the **Insert** menu, click **Module**.

4. Type the following function:

Function FirstNum(rng As Range)

Dim i As Integer

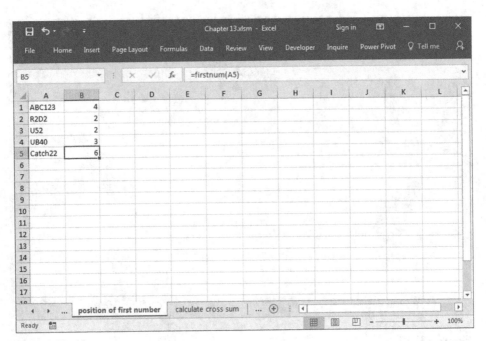

Figure 13–13

```
For i = 1 To Len(rng.Value)
  Select Case Mid(rng.Value, i, 1)
  Case 0 To 9
   FirstNum = i
   Exit Function
  End Select
Next i
End Function
```

5. Close the VBA Editor by pressing **<Alt+Q>**.

6. Select cells B1:B5 and type the formula **=FirstNum(A1)**.

7. Press **<Ctrl+Enter>**.

Use a user-defined function to calculate the cross sum of a cell

With this tip, you can calculate the cross sum of a cell. Create a table like the one in Figure 14 and type any numeric data in cells A1:A5.

▶   To calculate the cross sum of a cell:

1. Press **<Alt+F11>** to open the Visual Basic Editor.

2. In the **Insert** menu, click **Module**.

3. Type the following function:

```
Function Qs(rng As Range)
Dim i As Integer

For i = 1 To Len(rng.Value)
  Qs = Qs+Cint (Mid(rng.Value, i, 1))
Next i
End Function
```

4. Close the VBA Editor by pressing **<Alt+Q>**.

5. Select cells B1:B5 and type the formula **=Qs(A1)**.

6. Press **<Ctrl+Enter>**.

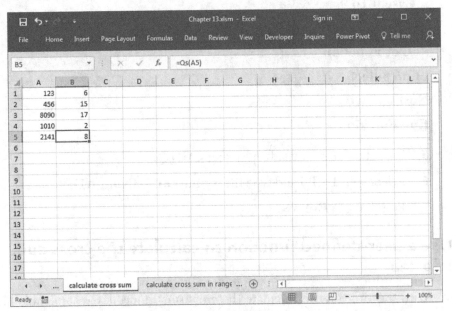

Figure 13–14

Use a user-defined function to sum each cell's cross sum in a range

Continuing from the previous example, now we want to sum each cell's cross sum in a range. Create a table like the one in Figure 13–15 and calculate cross sums in a specified range with a new user-defined function.

▶ To sum each cell's cross sum in a range:

1. Press **<Alt+F11>** to open the Visual Basic Editor.

2. In the **Insert** menu, click **Module**.

3. Type the following function:

Function QsE(Area As Range)

Dim i As Integer

Dim rng As Range

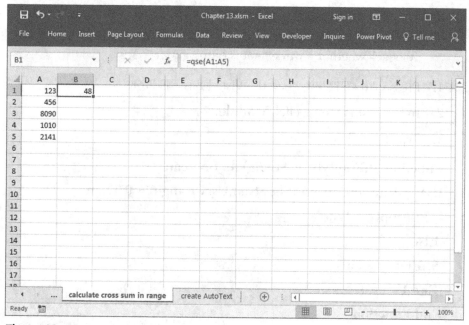

Figure 13–15

> **For Each rng In Area**
>
> **For i = 1 To Len(rng.Value)**
>
> **QsE = QsE+CInt (Mid(rng.Value, i, 1))**
>
> **Next i**
>
> **Next rng**
>
> **End Function**

4. Close the VBA Editor by pressing **<Alt+Q>**.

5. In cell B1, type the following formula: **=QsE(A1:A5)**.

6. Press **<Enter>**.

Use a user-defined function to check whether a worksheet is empty

Sometimes it is necessary to check whether a worksheet is empty or still contains hidden formulas. To do this, choose Worksheet in the Insert menu to add a new worksheet to the current workbook and write a user-defined function in the Visual Basic Editor as described below.

▶ To check whether a worksheet is empty:

1. Press **<Alt+F11>** to open the Visual Basic Editor.

2. In the **Insert** menu, click **Module**.

3. Type the following function:

Function ShEmpty(s As String) As Boolean

If Application.CountA (Sheets(s).UsedRange) = 0 Then

ShEmpty = True

Else

ShEmpty = False

End If

End Function

4. Close the VBA Editor by pressing **<Alt+Q>**.

5. Select any cell in the worksheet and type the formula **=ShEmpty ("Sheet15")**. Be sure to replace "Sheet15" with the name of the sheet you want to check.

6. Press **<Enter>**.

Use a user-defined function to check whether a worksheet is protected

The function described here checks whether a worksheet is protected. First you must create a worksheet and protect it, then you can write a user-defined function to test it.

▶ To check whether a worksheet is protected:

1. Press **<Alt+F11>** to open the Visual Basic Editor.

2. In the **Insert** menu, click **Module**.

3. Type the following function:

```
Function ShProt(s As String) As Boolean
On Error GoTo errorM

If Sheets(s).ProtectContents = True Then
    ShProt = True
End If
Exit Function

errorM:
 ShProt = False
End Function
```

4. Close the VBA Editor by pressing **<Alt+Q>**.

5. Select any cell in the worksheet and type the formula **=shProt ("Sheet15")**. Be sure to replace "Sheet15" with the name of the sheet whose protection you want to check.

6. Press **<Enter>**.

Use a user-defined function to create your own AutoText

The last tip in this chapter provides a way to use AutoText inside your worksheet. This functionality can be useful for many different Excel-based tasks.

▶ To create your own AutoText:

1. Press **<Alt+F11>** to open the Visual Basic Editor.

2. In the **Insert** menu, click **Module**.

3. Type the following function:

```
Function AuTxt(rng As Range) As String
 Select Case rng.Value
 Case 1
  AuTxt = "fire"
```

Case 2

 AuTxt = "water"

Case 3

 AuTxt = "heaven"

Case Else

 AuTxt = "invalid text"

 End Select

End Function

4. Return to the worksheet. Select cells B1:B4 or a much larger range and type the formula **=AuTxt(A1)**.

5. Press **<Ctrl+Enter>**.

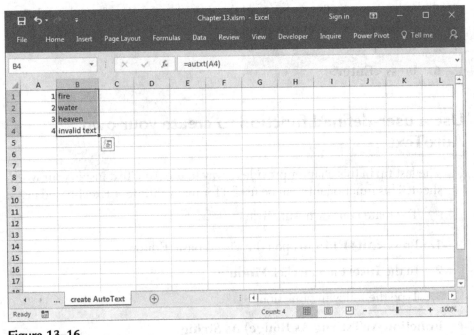

Figure 13–16

Examples

14

This chapter is about how to use the Excel formulas and functions that have been discussed and to gain some more experience with them as well. With these exercises, you need to determine which functions are best to solve the task. Try to solve the tasks, and consult the previous chapters if necessary.

Calculate average fuel consumption

Figure 14–1 lists m iles driven and number of gallons used. What is the average consumption for 100 miles?

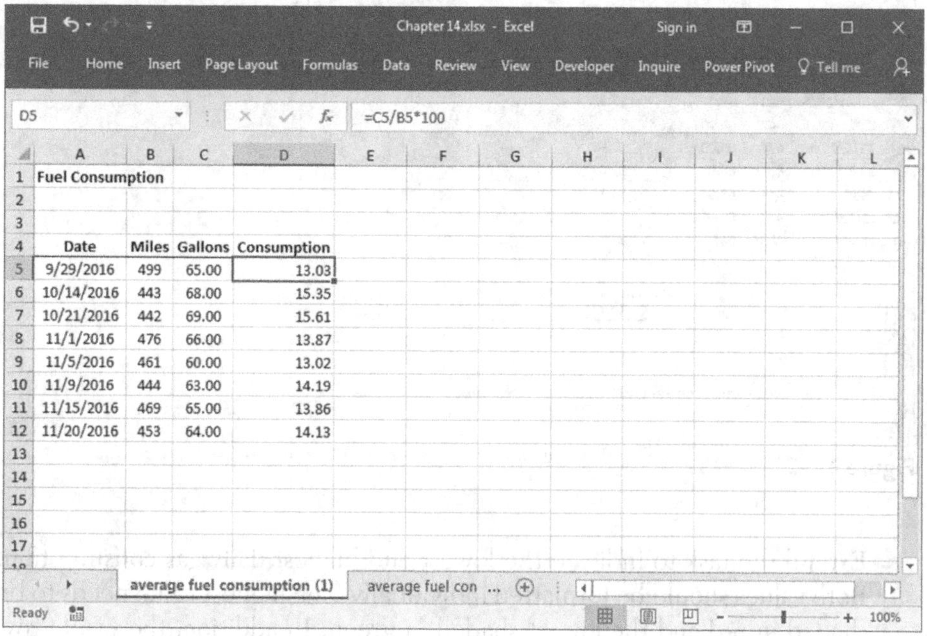

Figure 14–1

▶ To determine average fuel consumption:

1. In a worksheet, copy the data shown in cells A4:D12 in Figure 14–2.

2. Select cells D5:D12.

3. Type the formula **=C5/B5*100**.

4. Press **<Ctrl+Enter>**.

5. Calculate the average consumption by selecting cell D15 and typing the formula **=AVERAGE(D5:D12)**.

6. Press **<Enter>**.

	A	B	C	D	E	F	G	H	I	J	K	L
1	Fuel Consumption											
2												
3												
4	Date	Miles	Gallons	Consumption								
5	9/29/2016	499	65.00	13.03								
6	10/14/2016	443	68.00	15.35								
7	10/21/2016	442	69.00	15.61								
8	11/1/2016	476	66.00	13.87								
9	11/5/2016	461	60.00	13.02								
10	11/9/2016	444	63.00	14.19								
11	11/15/2016	469	65.00	13.86								
12	11/20/2016	453	64.00	14.13								
13												
14												
15				14.13								
16												
17												

D15 fx =AVERAGE(D5:D12)

Figure 14–2

Extend the task to indicate the lowest and highest daily gas consumption. Both values should be formatted individually. The highest value needs to be shaded in red and the lowest shaded in green. In addition, the whole row rather than just the individual cell should be shaded. These requirements can be solved with conditional formatting.

1. Select cells A5:D1

2. From the **Home** tab, go to the **Styles** bar and click on **Conditional Formatting**.

3. Choose **New Rule**.

4. In the **Select a Rule Type** dialog, select **Use a formula to determine which cells to format**.

5. In the **Edit** box, type the following formula:
   =$D5=MAX($D$5:$D$12).

6. Click **Format,** select **R**ed from the **Fill** tab when the cell value meets the condition, and click **OK**.

7. Repeat step 2 and choose **Manage Rule**.

8. Click **New Rule** and insert the following formula:
   =$D5=MIN ($D$5:$D$12).

9. Repeat step 6, but select **Green**.

10. Click **OK**.

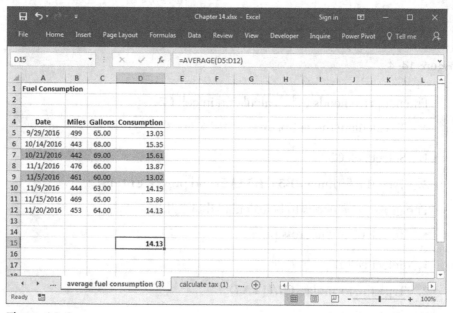

Figure 14–3

Calculate net and corresponding gross prices

Figure 14–4 shows a gross price and a net price. Calculate the corresponding values using a tax rate of 7%.

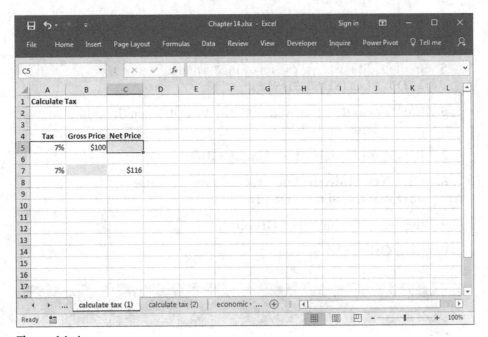

Figure 14–4

The net price needs to be calculated in cell C5.

▶ To calculate the net price:

1. Select cell C5.

2. Type the formula **=B5+(B5*A5)** and press **<Enter>**.

The gross price needs to be calculated in cell B7.

▶ To calculate the gross price:

1. Select cell B7.

2. Type the formula **=C7/(1+A7)**.

3. Press **<Enter>**.

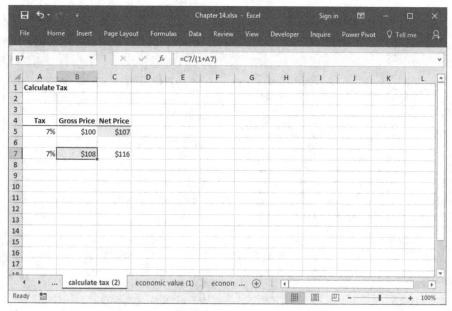

Figure 14–5

Determine the economic value of a product

The table in Figure 14–6 lists the costs, prices, and profit margins of various products. Determine which product is most profitable and use conditional formatting to format it.

▶ To determine the economic value:

1. Using the information in Figure 14–6, select cells E5:E12.

2. Type the formula **=D5/C5**.

3. Press **<Ctrl+Enter>**.

4. Select cells B5:E12.

5. From the **Home** tab, go to the **Styles** bar and click on **Conditional Formatting**.

6. Choose **New Rule**.

7. In the **Select a Rule Type** dialog, select **Use a formula to determine which cells to format**.

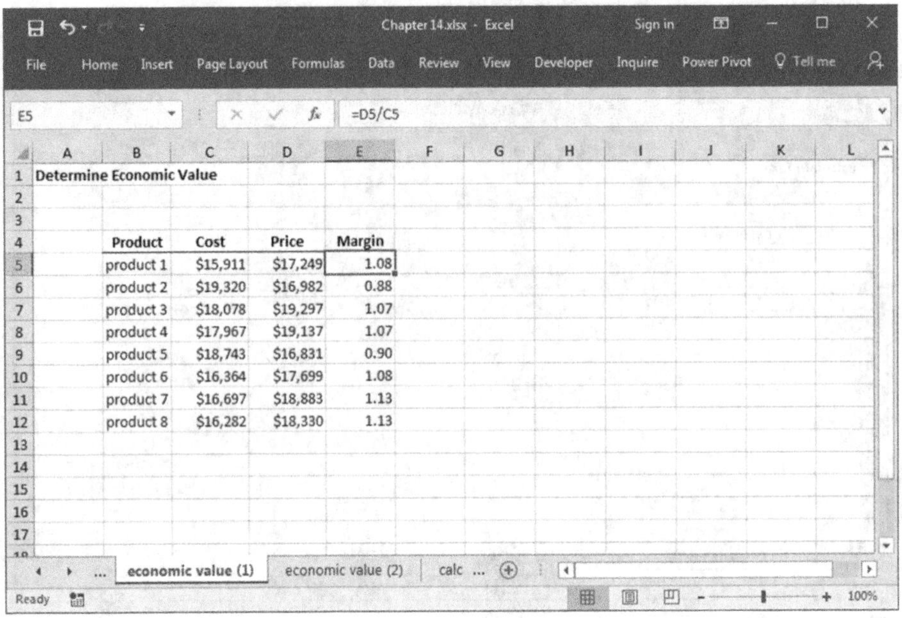

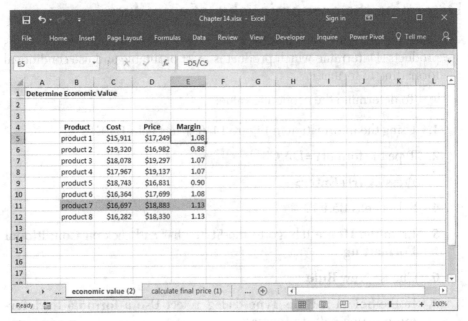

Figure 14-6

Figure 14-7

8. In the **Edit** box, type the following formula: **=$E5=MAX($E$5:$E$12)**.

9. Click **Format,** select a color from the **Fill** tab, and click **OK**.

10. Click **OK**.

Calculate the final price of a product, taking into account rebates and price reductions

Look at the price table in Figure 14–8. The net price of a tractor is listed along with an agreed-upon rebate and a price reduction because of minor defects. To calculate the total price, the reductions need to be considered and then the taxes must be added. Your task is to calculate the final price of the tractor.

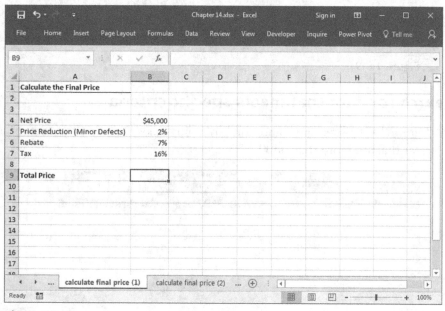

Figure 14–8

▶   To calculate the final price:

1. Select cell B9.

2. Enter the following formula: **= B4*(1-B5)*(1-B6)*(1+B7)**.

3. Press **<Enter>**.

The order of the parameters is not important when multiplying.

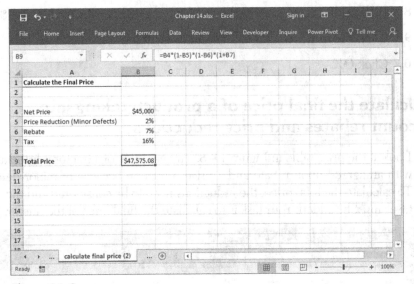

Figure 14–9

Search for data that meets specific criteria

Figure 14–10 lists dates and corresponding sales. Your task is to sum all sales that are more than $500.

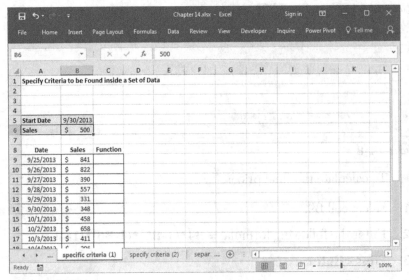

Figure 14–10

There are various ways to solve this task. One solution is to mark the values that fit the given criteria.

1. Select cells C9:C23.

2. Type the formula **=AND(A9>$B$5,B9>$B$6)**.

3. Press **<Ctrl+Enter>**.

4. Select cell C25.

5. Type the formula **=SUMIF(C9:C23,TRUE,B9:B23)**.

6. Press **<Enter>**.

If you'd like to use the built-in data filter, filter column C for the entry TRUE:

1. Select cell C8.

2. Select **Filter | AutoFilter** from the Data menu.

3. In cell C8, select **TRUE** from the drop-down box to filter the list.

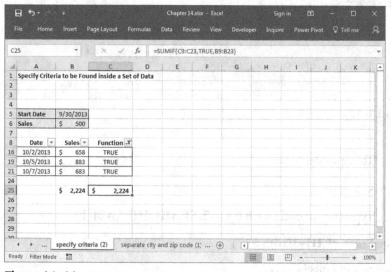

Figure 14–11

NOTE: When you calculate the sum of a filtered list, usually the hidden cells are added as well. Therefore, use the SUBTOTAL function rather than the SUM function. The easiest way to do this is to place the mouse cursor in the target cell and click on the AutoSum symbol in the Standard menu. Excel automatically recognizes the filtered list and uses the correct function, which in this case is SUBTOTAL.

Separate cities from zip codes

The table in Figure 14–12 lists zip codes and their corresponding cities. This information should be separated and shown in two separate columns.

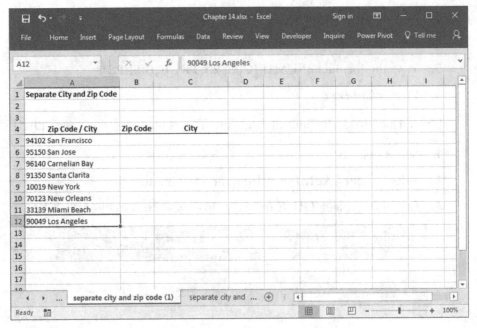

Figure 14–12

▶ To separate data:

1. Select cells B5:B12.

2. Type the formula **=LEFT(A5,SEARCH(" ",A5)-1)**.

3. Press **<Ctrl+Enter>**.

4. Select cells C5:C12.

5. Type the formula **=RIGHT(A5,LEN(A5)-(SEARCH (" ",A5)))**.

6. Press **<Ctrl+Enter>**.

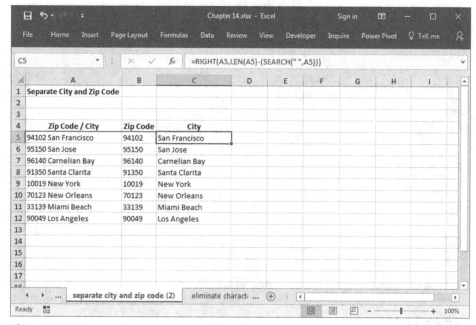

Figure 14–13

Eliminate specific characters

Various telephone numbers are listed in the following table and formatted in a variety of ways. Some contain hyphens or slashes, while others contain spaces.

▶ To eliminate specific characters:

1. Select cells B5:B11.

2. Type the formula **=SUBSTITUTE(SUBSTITUTE(SUBSTITUTE (A5,"-",""),".",""),"/","")**.

3. Press **<Ctrl+Enter>**.

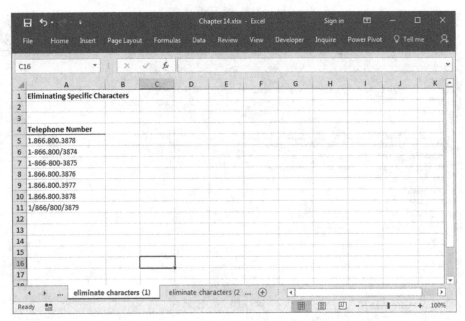

Figure 14–14

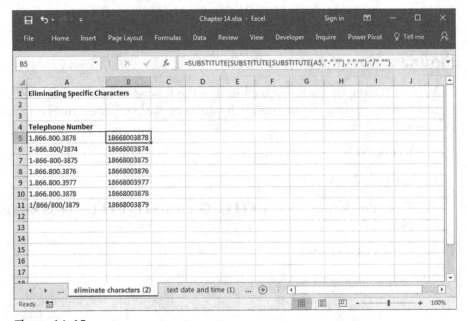

Figure 14–15

Combine text, dates, and timestamps

In this example, there is text that should be combined with dates and times and presented in a single cell. Excel needs to be "tricked" to produce the correct result.

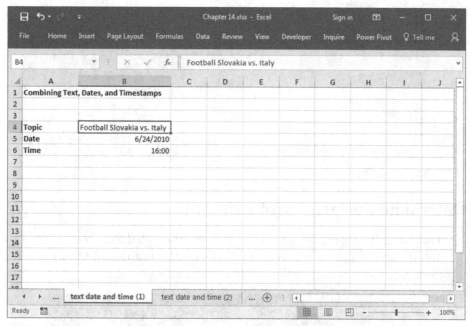

Figure 14–16

▶ To combine dates, times, and text:

1. Select cell A8.

2. Type the formula **="Attention " & B4 & " starts " & TEXT(B5,"DD. MM.YYYY") & " at exactly " & TEXT(B6,"hh:mm") & " !"**.

3. Press **<Enter>**.

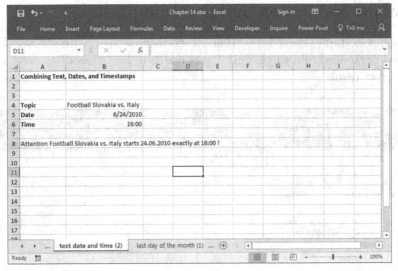

Figure 14–17

Determine the last day of a month

The table in Figure 14–18 contains a number of dates. Your task is to determine the day of the week that falls on the last day of the month for each date, considering the length of each month.

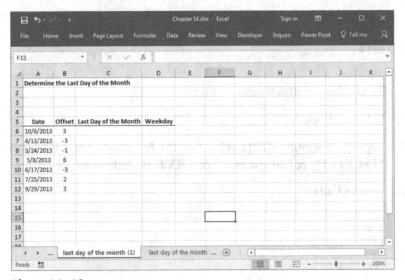

Figure 14–18

To solve this task, you will need to install the Analysis ToolPak add-in for Excel, if it has not already been installed. From the **Tools** menu, select **Add-Ins**. In the dialog that appears, select **Analysis ToolPak** and confirm with **OK**. Now you can proceed as described below:

1. Using the data shown in cells A5:D12 of Figure 14–19, select cells C6:C12.

2. Type the formula **=EOMONTH(A6,B6)**.

3. Press **<Ctrl+Enter>**.

4. Select cells D6:D12.

5. Type the formula **=C6**.

6. Press **<Ctrl+Enter>**.

7. In the **Home** tab, go to the **Cells** bar and click on **Format**.

8. Select **Format Cells** and then the **Custom** option in the **Number** tab.

9. Type **DDDD**.

10. Press **OK**.

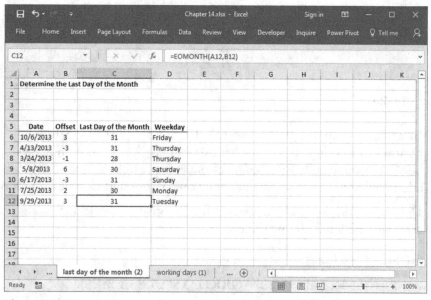

Figure 14–19

Determine the number of available workdays

This task shows the time frame of a project. There are weekends between the start date and the end date, which are usually not workdays. Only the actual workdays need to be determined. Excel supports this task with a specific table function called NETWORKDAYS, which can be found in the Analysis ToolPak add-in.

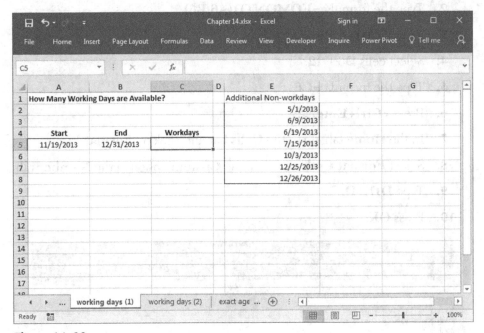

Figure 14–20

In addition to finding the weekends, the NETWORKDAYS function can be used to find holidays. To solve this extended task, some holidays have been entered in cells E2:E8. Of course, it is possible to extend this list for additional non-workdays, such as company parties and various promotions.

Determine the available workdays for the given time frame, taking into account additional non-workdays:

1. Select cell C5.

2. Type the formula **=NETWORKDAYS(A5,B5,E2:E8)**.

3. Press **<Enter>**.

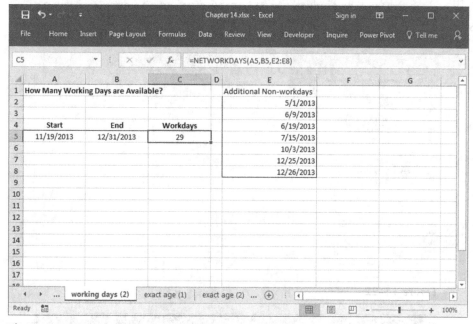

Figure 14–21

NOTE: The WORKDAY function is like the NETWORKDAYS function. WORKDAY needs a start date and the number of workdays and will calculate the end date, considering weekends and holidays.

Determine a person's exact age

Figure 14–22 shows a list of various people and their birth dates. Your task is to determine the exact age of each person in years, months, and days.

▶ To determine the age of a person:

1. Select cells C6:C11.

2. Type the formula **=DATEDIF(B6,$B$3,"Y") & " years and " & DATEDIF(B6,$B$3,"YM") & " months and " & DATEDIF (B6,$B$3,"MD") & " days"**.

3. Press **<Ctrl+Enter>**.

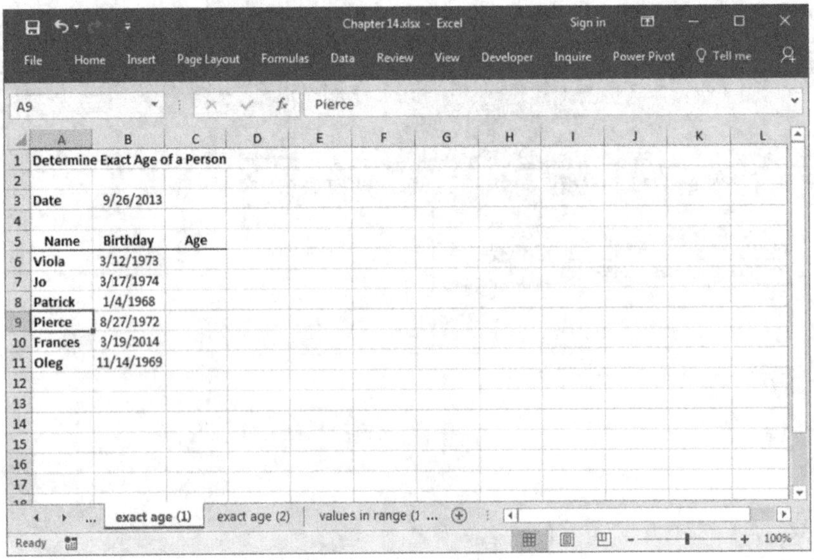

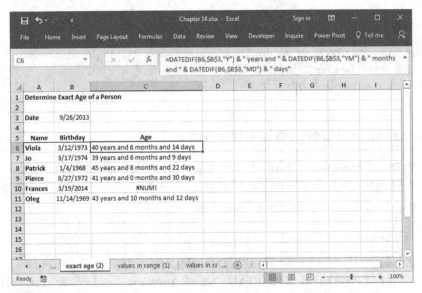

Figure 14–22

Figure 14–23

NOTE: The #NUM! will appear in a cell when the Birthday is after the Date to which it is being compared. The DATEDIF function requires that the first argument passed is less than or equal to the second parameter. Therefore, if you enter a Birthday of 9/26/2013 you will see the Age as being "0 years and 0 months and 0 days."

Determine the number of values in a specific range

Figure 14–24 shows a table containing different values. Your task is to count the number of values that are between 50 and 100. This task can be solved easily with an array formula.

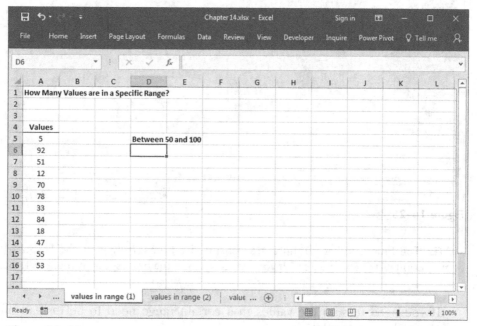

Figure 14–24

▶ To determine the number of values in a specific range:

1. Select cell D6.

2. Type the array formula **=SUM((A5:A16>=50)*(A5:A16<=100))**.

3. With the cursor at the end of the statement while in the formula bar, press **<Ctrl+Shift+Enter>**.

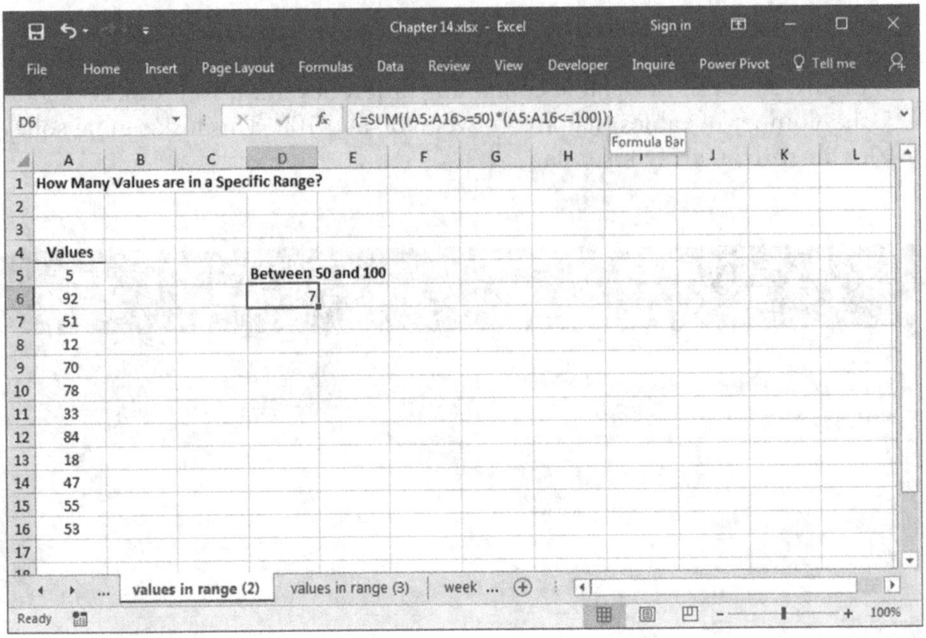

Figure 14–25

NOTE: The braces in the formula are generated automatically with the keyboard combination <Ctrl+Shift+Enter>. If you manually enter the braces, the formula will not work.

If you need to sum the values in a certain range need to be instead of counted, use this solution:

1. Select cell D7.

2. Type the array formula
   =SUM(IF(A5:A16>=50,IF(A5:A16<100, A5:A16))).

3. With the cursor at the end of the statement while in the formula bar, press **<Ctrl+Shift+Enter>**.

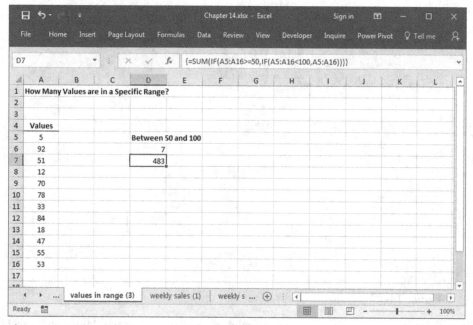

Figure 14–26

Determine the weekly sales for each department

This example involves an unsorted list of sales by individual employees from different departments. Your task is to calculate the weekly sales for each department.

▶ To determine weekly sales:

1. Using the data shown in Figure 14–28, select cells F6:F9.

2. Type the formula **=SUMIF($A$6:$A$16,E6,$C$6:$C$16)**.

3. With the cursor at the end of the statement while in the formula bar, press **<Ctrl+Shift+Enter>**.

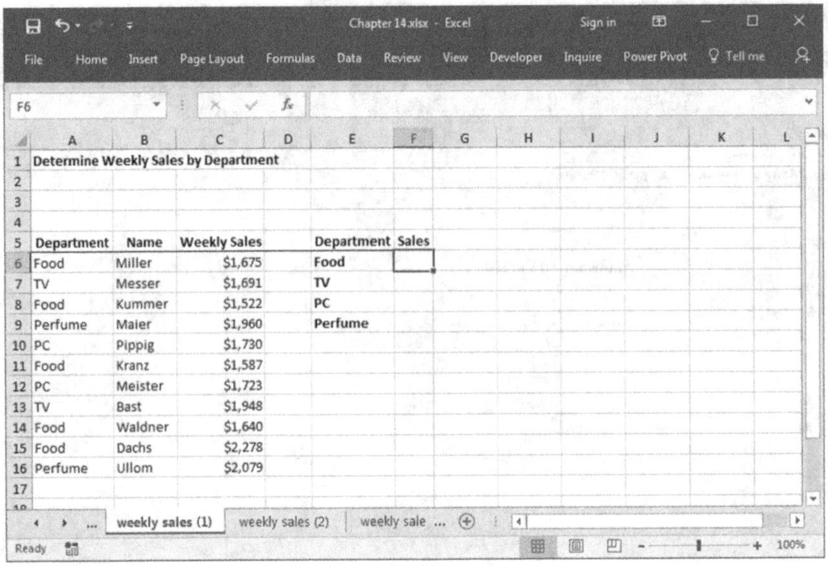

Figure 14–27

Because of the different sizes of each department, the weekly sales figures do not really indicate anything about the performance of each salesperson. As an example, the Food department has more salespeople than the Perfume department. To break down the average sales in each department, you need to consider the number of employees for each department. Now let's determine the average weekly sales per employee for each department and shade the department with the best performance.

1. Select cells G6:G9.

2. Type the formula **=F6/COUNTIF($A$6:$A$16,E6)**.

3. Press **<Ctrl+Enter>**.

4. Select cells E6:G9.

5. From the **Home** tab, go to the **Styles** bar and click on **Conditional Formatting**.

6. Choose **New Rule**.

7. In the **Select a Rule Type** dialog, select **Use a formula to determine which cells to format**.

8. In the **Edit** box, type the following formula: **=$G6=MAX($G$6:$G$9)**.

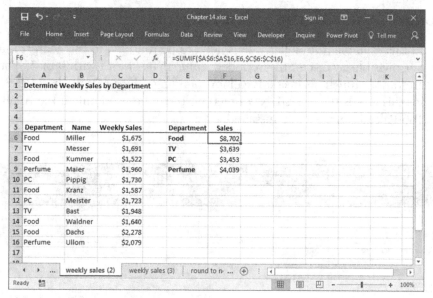

Figure 14–28

9. Click **Format,** select a color from the **Fill** tab, and click **OK**.

10. Click **OK**.

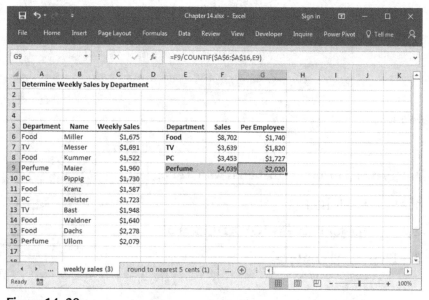

Figure 14–29

Round a value to the nearest 5 cents

In this example, the dollar values need to be rounded to the nearest number divisible by 5; i.e., the rounded number must end with 0 or 5. There are various functions inside Excel for rounding values, but the best function for this task is the MROUND function. It can be used only if the Analysis ToolPak add-in has been installed.

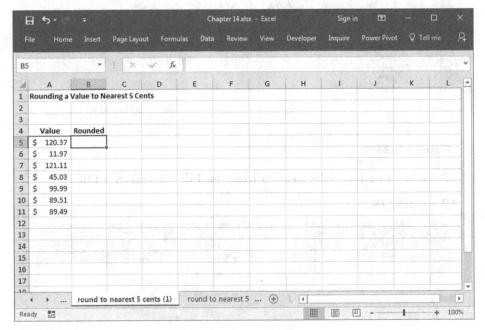

Figure 14–30

▶ To round to a value that ends with 0 or 5:

1. Select cells B5:B11.

2. Type the formula **=MROUND(A5, 0.05)**.

3. Press **<Ctrl+Enter>**.

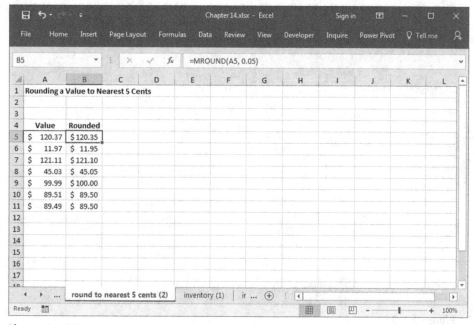

Figure 14–31

Determining inventory value

Figure 14–32 shows a list of items that are in stock, along with their cost and current quantity. Your task is to calculate the total value of the items in inventory.

It is certainly possible to solve this task by adding an additional column to calculate a total for each item and sum those values. But there is a much easier way!

▶ To determine the value of the inventory:

1. Using the data in Figure 14–33, select cell C13.

2. Type the formula **=SUMPRODUCT(B6:B11,C6:C11)**.

3. Press **<Enter>**.

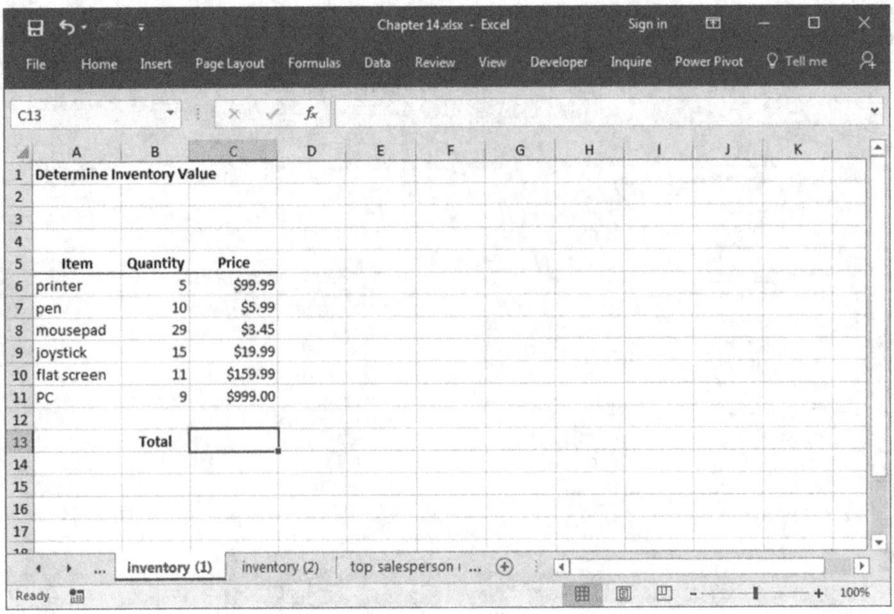

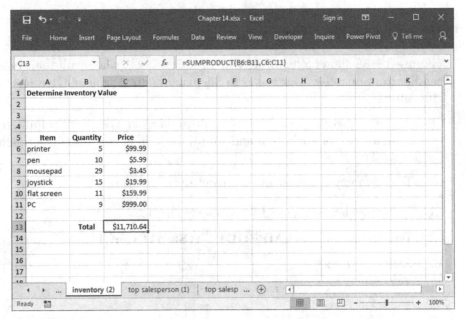

Figure 14–32

Figure 14–33

Determine the top salesperson for a month

Figure 14–34 presents a list of salespeople and their monthly sales volume. Your task is to determine the highest sales total each month and mark it in the list.

▶ To determine the top salesperson:

1. Using the data shown in Figure 14–35, select cells B4:E4.

2. Type the formula **=MAX(B6:B14)**.

3. Press **<Ctrl+Enter>**.

4. Select cells B6:E14.

5. From the **Home** tab, go to the **Styles** bar and click on **Conditional Formatting**.

6. Choose **New Rule**.

7. In the **Select a Rule Type** dialog, select **Use a formula to determine which cells to format**.

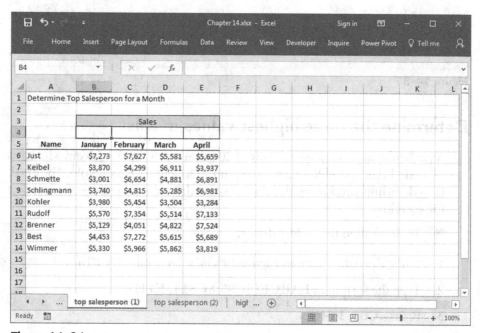

Figure 14–34

8. In the **Edit** box, type the following formula: **=B6=B$4**.

9. Click **Format,** select a color from the **Fill** tab, and click **OK**.

10. Click **OK**.

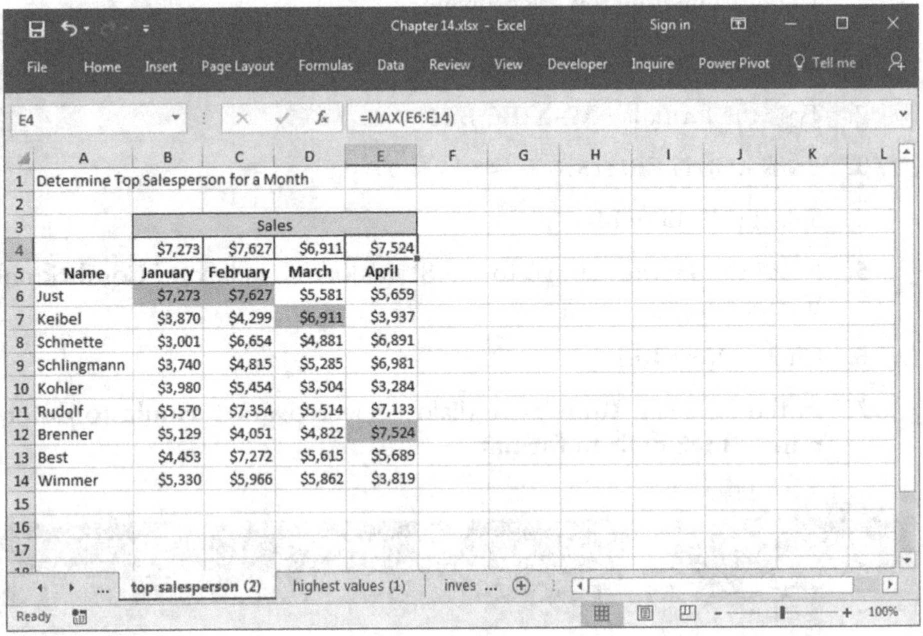

Figure 14–35

Determine the three highest values in a list

A particular area has a speed limit of 20 miles per hour. All drivers who have exceeded that speed limit are listed in the following Excel table. Your task is to determine and mark the three fastest drivers who will receive a ticket for speeding.

▶ To determine the fastest driver:

1. Using the data shown in Figure 14–36, select cells F11:F13.

2. Type the formula **=LARGE($C$5:$C$14, E11)**.

3. Press **<Ctrl+Enter>**.

4. Select cells A5:D14.

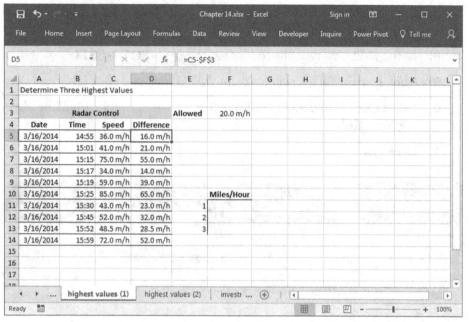

Figure 14–36

5. From the **Home** tab, go to the **Styles** bar and click on **Conditional Formatting**.

6. Choose **New Rule**.

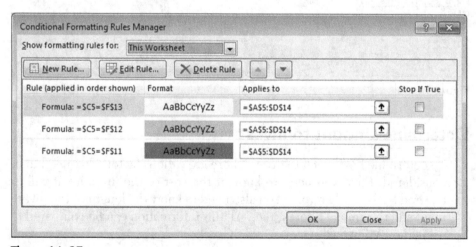

Figure 14–37

7. In the **Select a Rule Type** dialog, select **Use a formula to determine which cells to format**.

8. In the **Edit** box, type the following formula: **=$C5=$F$11**.

9. Click **Format,** select a color from the **Fill** tab, and click **OK**.

10. Insert Condition 2 and Condition 3 as shown in Figure 14–37 by clicking **New Rule**.

11. Click **OK**.

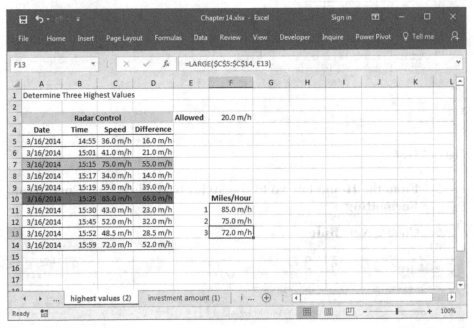

Figure 14–38

Determine amount to invest

To determine how much to invest, there are various factors that need to be considered. First, you need to know if the cost of the investment will be covered by its yearly return. You also need to know the length of the investment and the annual interest rate. All this information can be compared by using the PV formula.

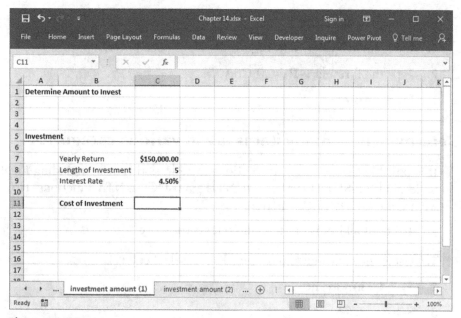

Figure 14–39

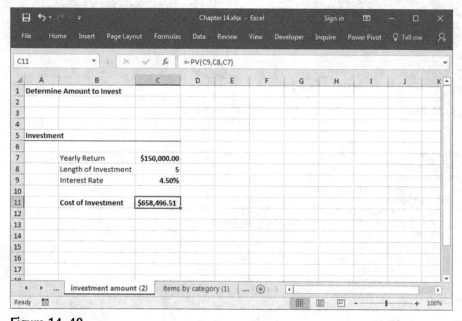

Figure 14–40

▶ To determine the cost of an investment:

1. Using the data shown in Figure 14–39, select cell C11.

2. Type the formula **=-PV(C9,C8,C7)**.

3. Press **<Enter>**.

Determine how many items are in various categories

It is possible to use different solutions to address this task, including Pivot tables and the SUBTOTAL, COUNTIF, and DCOUNTA functions. Here we use the DCOUNTA function.

▶ To count all items in the Components category:

1. Using the data shown in Figure 14–42, select cell C4.

2. Type **Components**.

3. Select cell C5.

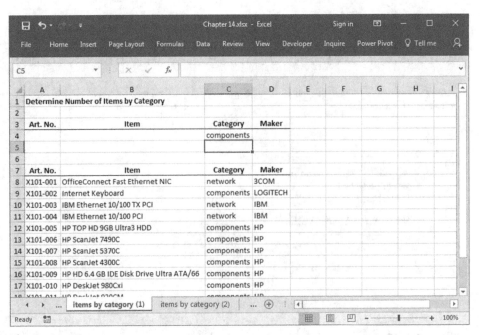

Figure 14–41

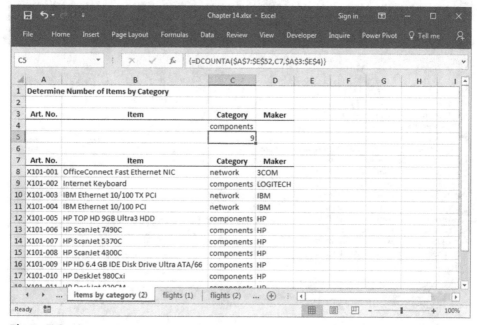

Figure 14–42

4. Type the formula **=DCOUNTA($A$7:$E$52,C7,$A$3:$E$4)**.

5. Press **<Enter>**.

Find a specific value in a complex list

Different flights are listed in the table in Figure 14–43. When a passenger enters a flight number, the corresponding flight information should be shown.

As seen in Figure 14–43, a list of flights starts in row 7. The search field to enter the required flight number is cell B1. Cells B2:B4 display the corresponding flight information if available.

▶ To display specific values from a list:

1. Select cell B2.

2. Type the formula **=VLOOKUP($B$1,$A$6:$E$15,2,FALSE)**.

3. Select cell B3.

4. Type the formula **=VLOOKUP($B$1,$A$6:$E$15,3,FALSE)**.

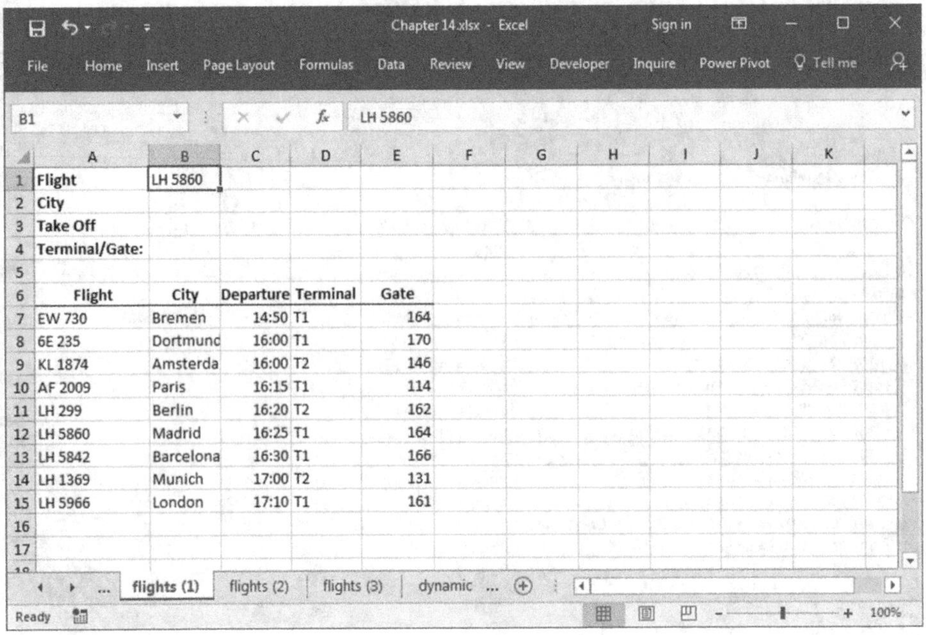

Figure 14–43

5. Select cell B4.

6. Type the formula **=VLOOKUP($B$1,$A$6:$E$15,4,FALSE) & " / " & VLOOKUP($B$1,$A$6:$E$15,5,FALSE)**.

If you need to shade the corresponding row in the range A7:E15, use Excel's conditional formatting feature as described here:

1. Select cells A7:E15.

2. From the **Home** tab, go to the **Styles** bar and click on **Conditional Formatting**.

3. Choose **New Rule**.

4. In the **Select a Rule Type** dialog, select **Use a formula to determine which cells to format**.

5. In the **Edit** box, type the following formula: **=$A7=$B$1**.

6. Click **Format,** select a color from the **Fill** tab, and click **OK**.

7. Click **OK**.

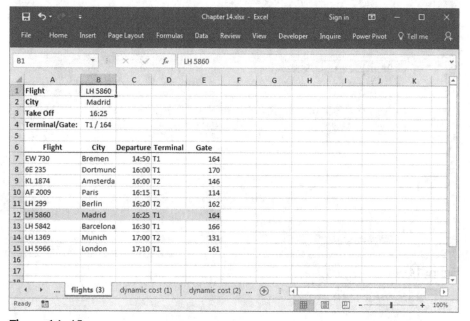

Figure 14–44

Figure 14–45

Dynamically show costs and sales per day

The table in Figure 14–46 contains cost and sales values per day. After the desired date is entered, the corresponding cost and sales values should be found and displayed.

▶ To dynamically show costs and sales per day:

1. Using the data shown in Figure 14–47, select cell C5.

2. Type the formula **=HLOOKUP($B$5,$B$8:$G$10,2,FALSE)**.

3. Press **<Enter>**.

4. Select cell D5.

5. Type the formula **=HLOOKUP($B$5,$B$8:$G$10,3,FALSE)**.

6. Press **<Enter>**.

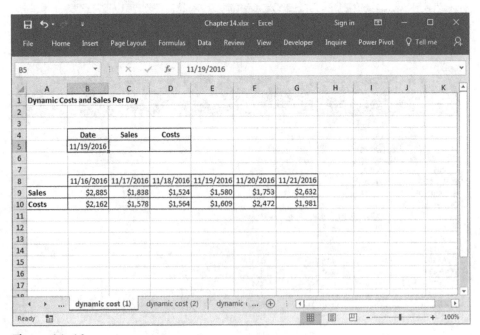

Figure 14–46

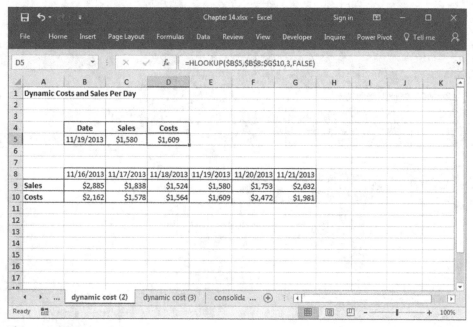

Figure 14–47

For this example, it is also good to use conditional formatting to mark the results in the table, as shown in Figure 14–48:

1. Select cells B8:G10.

2. From the **Home** tab, go to the **Styles** bar and click on **Conditional Formatting**.

3. Choose **New Rule**.

4. In the **Select a Rule Type** dialog, select **Use a formula to determine which cells to format**.

5. In the **Edit** box, type the following formula: **=B$8=$B$5**.

6. Click **Format,** select a color from the **Fill** tab and click **OK**.

7. Click **OK**.

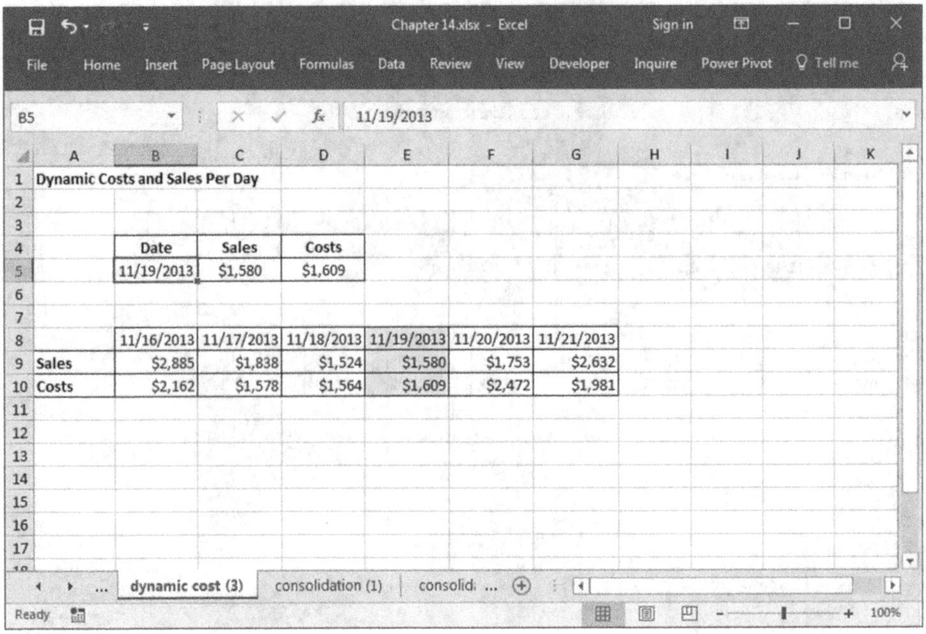

Figure 14–48

Extract every fourth value from a list

A list of measurements taken every two minutes is shown in Figure 14–49. Your task is to extract every fourth value after the first from the list and transfer that value to another list.

▶ To extract every fourth value:

1. Using the data shown in Figure 14–50, select cells D2:D5.

2. Type the formula **=OFFSET($B$2,(ROW()-2)*4,0)**.

3. Press **<Ctrl+Enter>**.

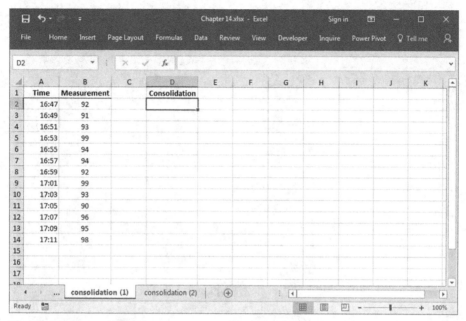

Figure 14–49

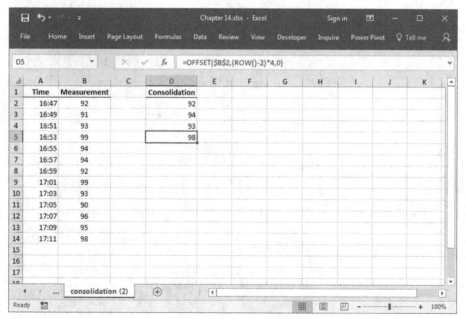

Figure 14–50

Figure 14-49

Figure 14-50

Other Features

15

This chapter explains features within Excel that are beyond formulas. These features enhance the Excel experience and provide shortcuts in accomplishing common business tasks. All these features are available in the Microsoft subscription Office 365 but only a few are available in Excel 2019.

Insert Icons

Table 15-1 displays a list of four food items with corresponding sales. We will create icons for each food item and show you how to link them to a website.

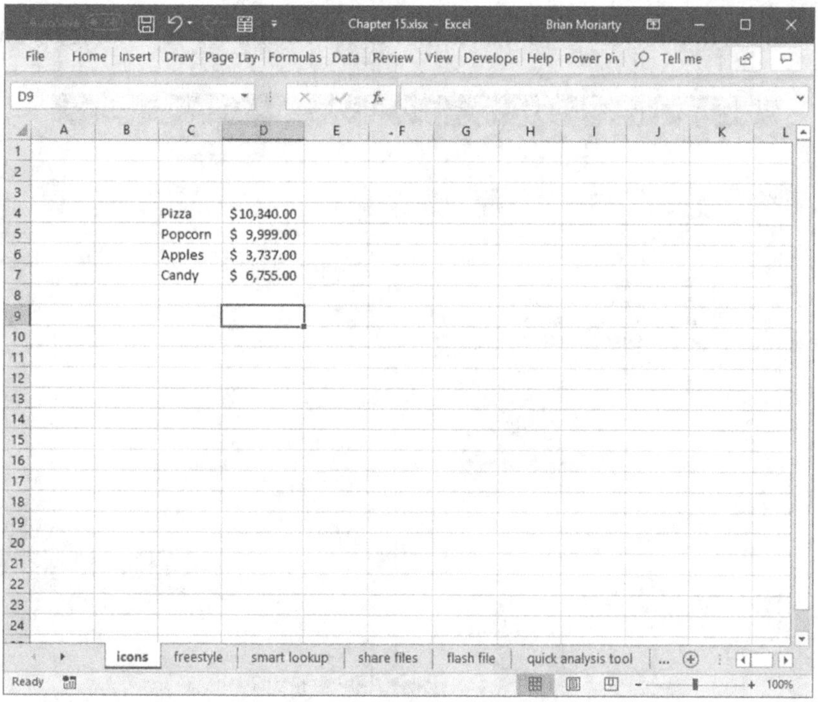

Figure 15–1

▶ To add icons

1. In a worksheet, copy the data shown in cells C4:D7 in Figure 15-1.

2. Click in cell B4.

3. On the menu bar, click Insert, then Illustrations, then Icons. When the Icons dialog box appears, click on Food and Drinks then double-click the pizza icon. At this point the pizza image appears in cell B4. To shrink, click on the image so that the box appears around the pizza image. Place the cursor over the circle in the lower left corner of the image. The cursor should change to a diagonal arrow. Click and hold on the diagonal arrow, then drag the circle up and left until the image is small enough to fit in cell B4.

4. Right-Click on the image and select Link then Insert Link. Type in (or paste in) a website address or reference to another place in the workbook in the Address box.

5. Repeat steps 3 and 4 for Popcorn, Apples, and Candy in cells B5, B6, and B7 respectively.

Below is the worksheet with all icons inserted in the corresponding B column.

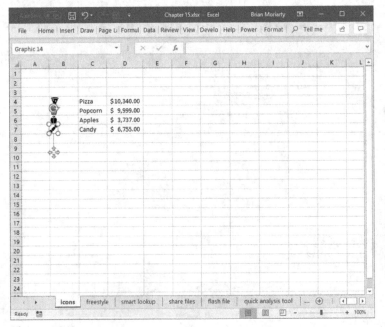

Figure 15–2

Draw Freestyle

In this example, we are going to use the Draw features. Open a worksheet and on the top menu bar, click on Draw. You will see a box of pens and highlighters in different colors. You can change these by click the Add Pen icon to the right of the box. But for now, we will use the defaults.

1. Click on the Red Pen and manually draw the word "Hi" with your mouse over cell B4. You can make it as large or as small as you wish. Once done with your word, press the Esc button on your keyboard to release the pen. The drawing is now an image on the worksheet, and you can move or modify it anyway you wish.

2. Next click on Draw and select the yellow highlighter. Then go to cell B9 and drag the highlighter across a few cells to the right. Then press ESC on your keyboard to release the highlighter.

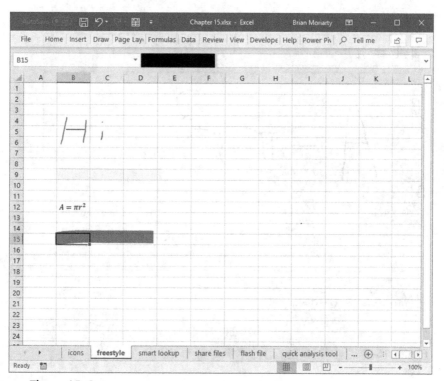

Figure 15-3

3. Now click on Draw again. Find Ink to Math and click on it. A dialog box will appear in which you can write any math equation you wish. In this example, write $A = \pi r^2$ as close as you can get it. It does not have to be perfect. Once you click on Insert, the formula will be cleanly inserted as an image into the cell you originally clicked. The formula $A = \pi r^2$ will appear in the middle of the worksheet. You can now click on it and move it around to wherever you wish and re-size it to your liking.

One final example exhibiting the ability to erase.

1. Click on Draw again, then the red highlighter and trace it across cells B15 to D17 and then again in cells B17 to D17. This will produce two stripes.

2. Then go back to Draw and click on Eraser, then click on the second red high-light. This will erase the second red highlight appear in cells B17 to D17.

The final display will look like Figure 15-4.

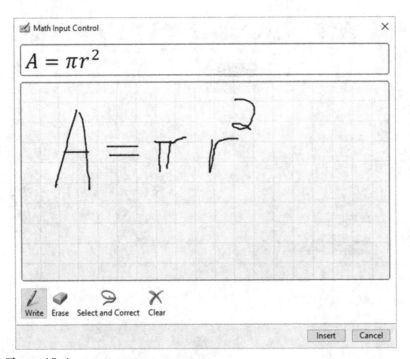

Figure 15–4

As a final example you can replay the steps you created in this example by going into the Draw menu again and clicking on Ink Replay. This will replay the steps you just did on this worksheet.

Smart Lookup

Smart Lookup gather information from a Bing search about a word or phrase that you highlight.

1. Copy the food items and sales you created in the first example in this chapter on the icons worksheet.

2. Paste them in cells C4 to D7. Right-click on cell C4 – Pizza – and select Smart Lookup.

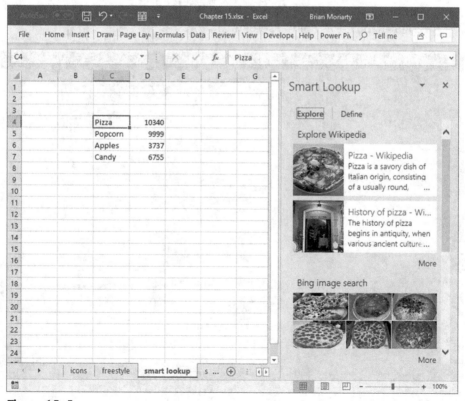

Figure 15–5

A box will appear to the right as though you searched for "Pizza" on the web. You can scroll down the right and discover pages and images for what you looked up. There is also a "Define" option to the right that will display definitions of what you used the Smart Lookup for.

The Lookup and Definitions are based on Microsoft's Bing Search. There are ways to change this through your computers Registry and code, but this is beyond the scope of this book. An Internet search will yield solutions on this matter for you.

Share Files

You also can share the current Excel file you have open with others via a web location or a network folder.

1. To share the Excel file, you are using with others over the web or a network so they can edit and view, click on the Share icon in the upper right-hand corner of the screen.

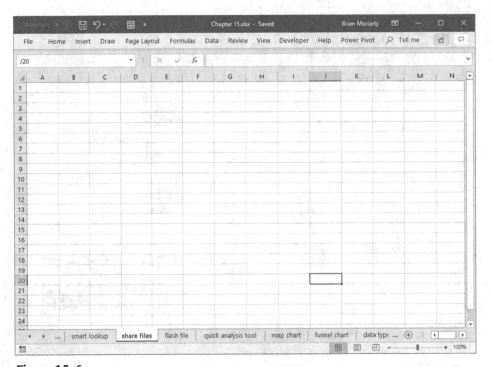

Figure 15–6

2. Then click on the location whether it be a shared folder on a network on a folder in the cloud. You will then see a screen on the right side of Excel in which you can enter emails of those you wish to view and edit your current workbook.

3. Enter email addresses then click Share. You can also click the address box to the right and select names from current email lists you have stored in your Outlook.

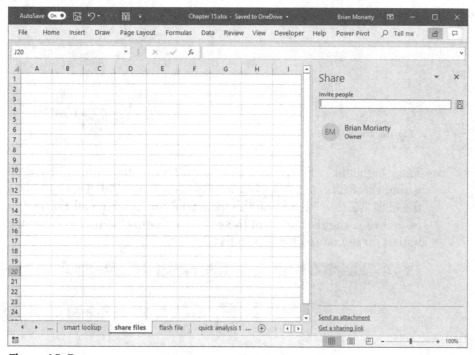

Figure 15–7

Flash Fill

Flash Fill is a feature that will allow you to fill in cells based upon logic you have entered information into another cell. In this instance, Excel is can fill in patterns that you are attempting to enter.

1. Open a new worksheet and enter in the names listed in cells C4 to D7.

2. Then go to cell E4 and type in BR for the initials of the first and last name of the existing name in cells C4 and D4.

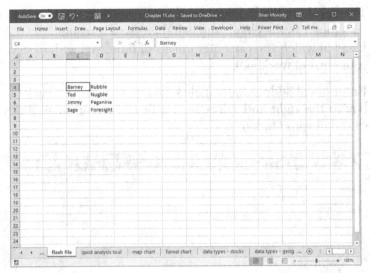

Figure 15–8

3. Then highlight cells E4 to E7, click on Home, then on the far right within the Editing group, click on Fill then Flash Fill. This will fill in the cells E5 to E7 based on the logic you displayed in cell E4. In this case, it took the first letter of the cells in column C and D and created initials for the names listed in cells C5 to D7.

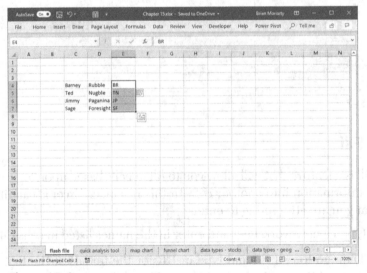

Figure 15–9

Quick Analysis Tool

There is a quick way to highlight data and create charts from data without having to go through the conditional formatting and charts menu.

1. Copy the data in cells C3 to D8 into a blank worksheet.

2. Highlight cells C3 to D8 and a box will appear below the lower right corner. This is the Quick Analysis tool.

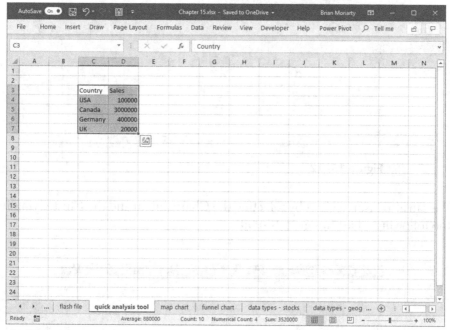

Figure 15–10

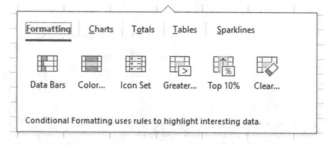

Figure 15–11

3. On this you can hover over each icon to see how the data will appear. In this case, we select the Formatting option and Color to yield the following result in table 15-999

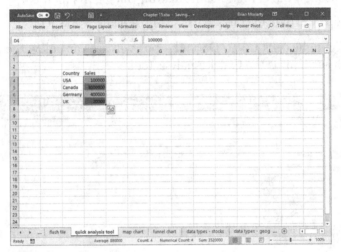

Figure 15–12

We can also insert a chart by selecting the Charts menu and the Cluster yielding the following Chart in figure 15-999

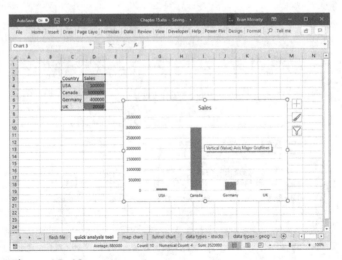

Figure 15–13

Map Chart

In this feature, you can create a map based upon regions such as states, countries, and zip codes.

1. In this example, copy the list of states with the corresponding random gas prices entered in cells B4 to C55.

2. Highlight the cells containing information including the heading. Click on the Insert menu, then within the group Charts, click on Maps, then Filled Map. A map chart will appear to the right with states highlighted based upon the relative weight of the gas price.

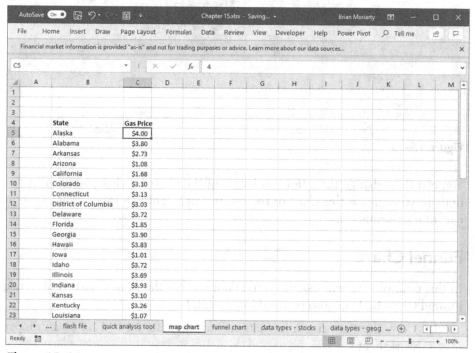

Figure 15–14

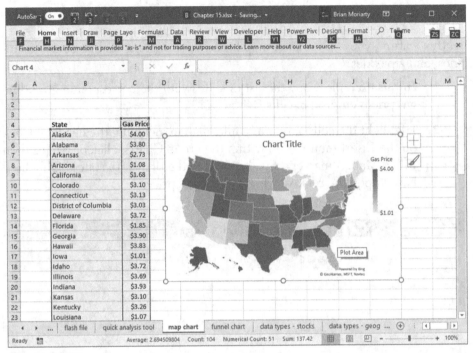

Figure 15–15

You can then change the colors and style of the chart to what you wish. Additionally, you can use this chart or the entire worksheet in a PowerPoint slide as part of a presentation.

Funnel Chart

In this example, we will use the same data used in the Map Chart to display a Funnel Chart that can also be used in presentations.

1. Copy the gas price information into the cells B4 to C55 in an empty worksheet.

2. Then highlight the same cells, go to the Insert menu item, and within the Charts group select the Funnel Chart icon. This will display a funnel chart by state and gas price.

From this you can perform a couple of different actions.

3. Label each bar line with the state to which it applies. Click on the Chart so that it is outlined.

4. Click on the Design menu item.

5. Then within the Chart Styles group select the second Chart from the left on the ribbon.

Figure 15–16

This will yield the following chart with the State labels.

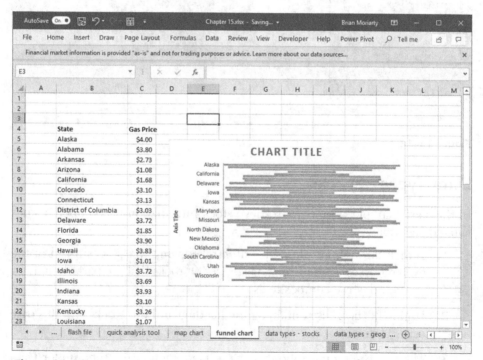

Figure 15–17

You can then sort the data by gas price to show the chart as a funnel. Highlight cells B4 to C55 then select the Data menu item, and within the Sort & Filter group select Filter by gas price. This will yield:

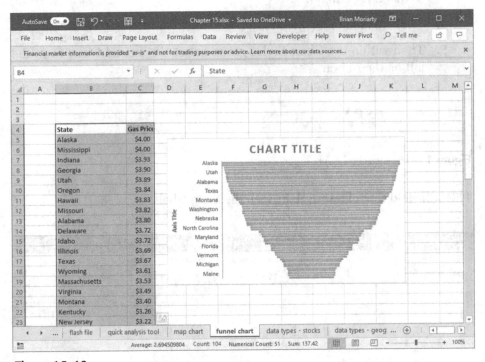

Figure 15–18

Data Types - Stocks

In this next example, Excel can retrieve stock information based upon a stock name or symbol.

1. Either through an internet search or copying the stocks listed in the example Excel spreadsheet, paste the 30 stocks that are part of the Dow Jones Industrial composite list.

2. Highlight the cells containing the heading and the stocks – in this case cells B4 to C34.

3. Then on the menu ribbon, click the Data menu item then under Data Types click the Stocks icon. This will place an icon next to each stock or company that can be linked to Internet information.

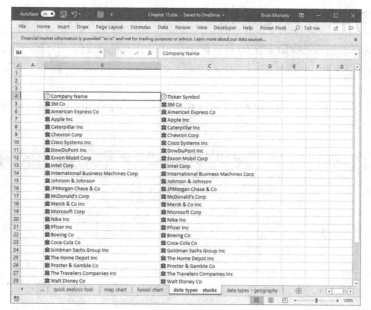

Figure 15-19

4. Then click on the icon of the first one – 3M Co – this will pop up a Card displaying real-time information about 3M stock and the company. You can scroll down to view all the information.

Figure 15-20

Data Types - Geography

The next example is similar to the previous but instead of displaying information about a company, Excel can display information about a country, region, or state.

1. Select a list of countries from the internet or simply type countries into a list as in the following example.

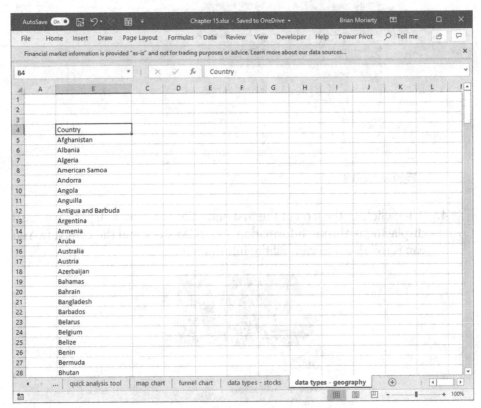

Figure 15–21

2. Then highlight the entire list including the heading.

3. Then click on the Data menu item, then Geography in the Data Types group.

Figure 15–22

This will insert an icon next to each country as such.

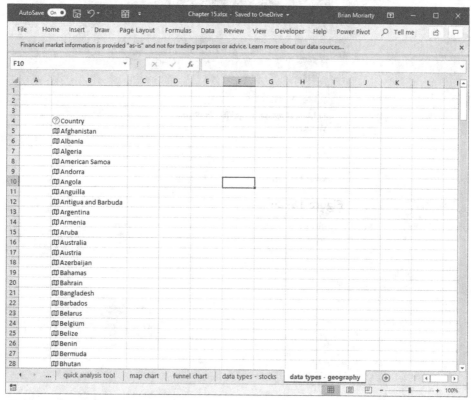

Figure 15–23

4. Click on any icon to display information about the country. Figure 15-24 is the example of clicking on Albania. Scroll through the box to view various characteristics of the country.

Figure 15–24

Excel Interface Guide

Spreadsheet software is used to manage and process large amounts of data. A spreadsheet is organized into a grid of rows (indicated by number) and columns (indicated by letter). The intersection of these rows and columns is called a *cell*; a cell is identified by letter and number, so A1 would be the first cell of the spreadsheet. A spreadsheet document is not delimited by printed pages or slides, as you have previously seen in other software packages. Instead, it is organized as individual spreadsheets or worksheets (identified by the tabs at the bottom of the interface in the common spreadsheet applications); the entire file is called a *workbook*. A worksheet (also called a "tab" or simply a "sheet") can contain many printed pages' worth of material. In fact, a worksheet can contain thousands of rows or columns that would be infeasible to print; the maximum size of a worksheet in Excel contains rows up to row 1048576 and columns up to column XFD.

A *row* in spreadsheet software is the horizontal grouping of data that is divided by columns; rows are signified by numbers.

A *column* in spreadsheet software is the vertical grouping of data that is divided by rows; columns are signified by letters.

A *cell* in spreadsheet software is the intersection of a row and a column, containing a single piece of data, which can be text, a number, a formula, or an object; cells are signified by the letter of the column and the number of the row.

A *range* in spreadsheet software is the combination of one or more contiguous cells. For example, a range can represent an entire column, an entire row, three adjacent cells in a row or a small grid of 9 rows by 11 columns anywhere in a spreadsheet. A range can even be one cell. Ranges are another way to reference information in a spreadsheet when using formulas instead of by cell and/or row (i.e. C5:C22, E10, A:A)

A *formula* in spreadsheet software is a mathematical calculation that results in a data value; the value is displayed in the cell in which the formula is typed.

Cells are not intended for large amounts of text; you should ideally include one piece of data or information per cell. Spreadsheets are best for organizing data and calculating results. If you want the results to accompany text, you should produce your results in a spreadsheet and export the relevant data to a word-processing document. There are an enormous number of applications for spreadsheets across disciplines such as accounting and mathematics. The practical applications of this technology go far beyond the scope of this text. Some general uses that you may find for spreadsheet software are formatting information in large tables, creating charts to display a visualization of data, and performing complex mathematical calculations.

The spreadsheet software application in Microsoft Office is called Excel. The first task you will complete using the spreadsheet software program is the creation of a personal budget. First, open the software and use the *File* menu to save your new open document as *Appendix A*. The native file type in Excel is *Excel Workbook* (*.xlsx*).

Anatomy of Excel

Excel uses the ribbon interface for organizing various tools. Beneath the ribbon interface is the Formula Bar, which is used for naming cells and defining calculations. The main pane of the document window looks very different from those of other Office applications; it displays the rows, columns, and cells of the document. The bottom of the interface contains tabs for you to select the worksheet that is active in the document pane. Depending on the version of Excel you are using, the ribbons and shortcuts available will be slightly different. Below are sections on different versions; you can jump to the section that is relevant to you.

Office 365 vs 2019

Office 365 is a subscription-based service while Excel 2019 is a one-time purchase to be used on a PC or a Mac. Excel 2019 is also referred to as a 'Perpetual' version of Office and can also be considered a subset of Office 365. Office 365 includes most of the Office products such as Excel, Word, PowerPoint and Outlook. With Office 365, you receive the latest features, security updates and bug fixes as they are released. You can always get the latest version by going into File then Account and clicking "Update Options." With Excel 2019, you need to wait until the next release to receive these updates and upgrades. For example, as discussed in Chapter 15, the new data types – stocks and geography – are not available in Excel 2019 but are available with Office 365. There are other functions and features demonstrated throughout this book that may only be available in Office 365.

When opening an Office 365 version, you will see "Office 365" and not a number or a year in the version in the 'About' box that pops up with first starting an Office application. As of this writing, Microsoft does intend to release future perpetual versions.

Microsoft Excel 2019

The interface for Excel 2019 has the same ribbon structure and general layout as the other Office applications. You can see an example of the interface for Excel 2019 in Figure A-1. The Formula Bar, located beneath the ribbon interface, identifies the current cell that you have selected and displays the contents of the cell or the formula used to determine the cell contents. When you begin using functions, the Formula Bar will become much more relevant. It allows you to perform a formula lookup and will help identify any possible errors in your formula construction.

Excel 2019 contains the "Tell me what you want to do" box near the top middle. In this box, you can type in a phrase or sentence you are trying to

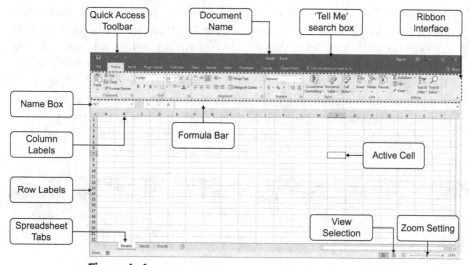

Figure A–1

accomplish, and it will return possible answers it believes can assist you. It also taps into the existing "Smart Lookup" feature that can search the web for other possible answers and solutions.

The document is divided into cells. You can use the arrow keys to navigate from one cell to the next, or you can click on a cell to activate it. The current cell is called the *active cell*, and the row and column in which it resides will also be highlighted for you to identify them quickly. Hold the *Shift* key to select multiple cells. Each cell acts like a text box in which you can type information.

The bottom of the interface has a set of tabs, each of which identifies an individual spreadsheet within the overall workbook (the file itself). You can navigate to these spreadsheets by clicking on the tabs or by using the directional arrows to the left of the tabs. The bottom of the interface also contains the view options, which allow you to see the page breaks in your document in a Page Layout view, a Page Break Preview, or the Normal view; the last of these tends to be the most helpful for document creation. When you have numeric values selected, the bottom of the interface will also display an automatic calculation of the average of the values, the sum of the values, and the number of values you have selected (omitting white space). This is a nice feature for quickly assessing statistics on a list.

The available ribbons and functions are quite different from the interface for Word. The Home ribbon contains the Number panel for formatting numeric values (either as direct text input or as the result of formula calculations), as well as commands for style formatting and for adding, deleting, or formatting cells. Of particular note are the Fill icon, which is used to replicate values or predict entries in a series, and the Sort & Filter icon, both in the Editing panel. The Insert ribbon, shown in Figure A-2, contains several entries of note, particularly the chart creation functionality, single-cell charts called Sparklines, and the icon to create a PivotTable, which is one of the more advanced features of Excel.

Figure A–2

The Page Layout ribbon, shown in Figure A-3, is used to manage the spreadsheet by dividing it into printable areas. You can add a background, insert manual page breaks, and set the printable region size for your spreadsheet. If printing is a concern, it may be helpful to preview the print regions to keep your document confined within the desired page delineations.

Figure A–3

The Formulas ribbon contains categories of formulas from which you can select to insert into your document. This ribbon also contains the functionality to trace dependencies among cells in your spreadsheet and provides manual links to set calculation options for your spreadsheet; by default, all calculations are updated immediately when a value on which they depend is changed. The Formulas ribbon is shown in Figure A-4.

Figure A–4

The Data ribbon, shown in Figure A-5, contains several useful commands, including the Remove Duplicates command to make sure no identical values are repeated in your list and the Text to Columns command to convert continuous text into multiple columns based on a delimiter character. This ribbon also contains commands to manage external sources, perform a What-If Analysis (for goal seeking), validate data, and perform advanced filtering for lists.

Figure A–5

The Review ribbon gives you the ability to add comments to your spreadsheet. Unlike Word, Excel places comments in a triangle icon in the upper-right corner of the cell to which they are attached. The Review ribbon also gives you options for protecting your document from changes or sharing your document on a network location for others to edit. You can also select the Start Inking icon to use your mouse as a pen to mark up your document. The Review ribbon is shown in Figure A-6.

Figure A–6

The View ribbon, shown in Figure A-7, allows you to change the view of the document as usual, but it also allows you to manage your workspace. The views in Excel are primarily the Normal view and views to preview page layouts for printing, such as Page Break Preview. The Page Layout view is not recommended for constructing or working with your document. You can show or hide various document elements from this ribbon as well, such as the gridlines and the Formula Bar. The Freeze Panes functionality allows you to preserve your headings as you scroll through your document. The Split function lets you set up multiple viewing panes of your document, so you can view disjoined elements side by side. You can also use the Save Workspace icon to store the configuration of multiple document windows. The View Side by Side icon allows you to look at two workbooks at the same time. You can set synchronous scrolling for these, so they move in the same direction at the same time.

Figure A–7

Microsoft Excel 2011 for Macintosh

The Macintosh interface for Excel 2011, shown in Figure A-8, is very similar to the other Office applications for Macintosh computers. The interface contains the standard menu and ribbons where most of your functionality is located. In addition, you have a Formula Bar that is used to construct calculations in the spreadsheet and edit information in the cells of the document. The main document is divided into cells, which can be navigated with the arrow keys on the keyboard. The columns are labeled with letters across the top, and the rows are labeled with numbers down the left side. The tabs at the bottom are the individual spreadsheets within the workbook (the overall document).

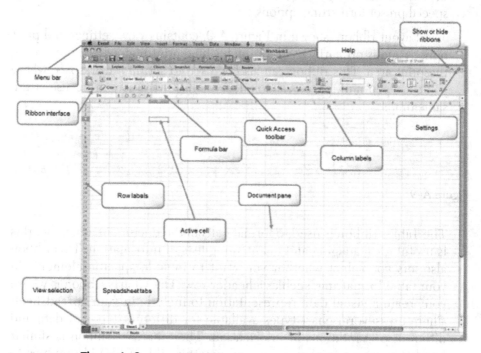

Figure A–8

Clicking with the mouse on a cell in the document makes that cell the active cell; this action outlines the cell in a thick border and highlights the row and column labels for quick reference. The cell reference will also appear in the Name box on the left side of the Formula Bar. Options in the Quick Access toolbar include a toggle that allows you to show or hide the Formula Bar and links to common functions like SUM. The bottom of the interface contains the view selection, where you can alternate between the Normal view and a preview of the page breaks in your document for printing.

The Home ribbon contains the standard text formatting options, along with a panel for formatting numeric values. This is necessary for effectively managing and displaying data in the spreadsheets. The Home ribbon also contains icons for inserting and deleting rows and columns and for using special preset formatting options.

The Layout ribbon, shown in Figure A-9, contains view settings and print options and is primarily used for establishing print regions and previewing the print area. This ribbon can also be used to set up a workspace where you can open multiple workbook documents on the screen for use at the same time.

Figure A–9

The Tables ribbon is used to format cells in the document as a table; this is useful for managing and maintaining lists of information. This ribbon also lets you select whether you want to include specific elements in your table formatting, such as a header row. The Charts ribbon is where you create a visual data representation to include in your spreadsheet. There are several chart types available for different types of data and different presentations of information. The SmartArt ribbon is similar to what is found in Word; you can use this ribbon to add graphics to your document to convey information visually. These three ribbons are shown in Figure A-10.

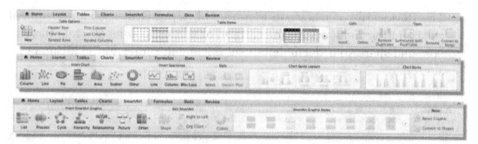

Figure A–10

The Formulas ribbon is where you can access the available formula library in Excel. This ribbon contains an icon for quick access to formulas for summations and averaging, as well as the Formula Builder icon for creating more advanced calculations. You can also control the recalculation options for your formulas from this ribbon (by default, the recalculation is immediate whenever a value is changed) and trace the cells used in your calculations. The Formulas ribbon is shown in Figure A-11.

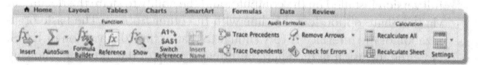

Figure A–11

The Data ribbon, shown in Figure A-12, contains the functionality for managing information in your spreadsheet. You can sort and filter data from this ribbon, manage external data sources, remove duplicate values in a list, and convert the existing text into separate columns. Data validation and grouping is also performed from this ribbon.

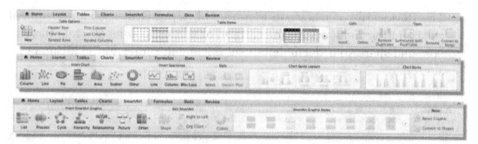

Figure A–12

The Review ribbon, shown in Figure A-13, is primarily used for document collaboration and markup. You can add or address comments from this ribbon, and share your document or set document protection so it cannot be altered.

Figure A–13

Microsoft Excel Web App

From a OneDrive account or Office 365, you can also create a new Excel workbook or edit an existing workbook in your online storage using the Microsoft Excel Web App. You can see the interface of the Excel Web App in Figure A-14. The Excel Web App has a limited subset of the functionality of the Excel program, along with the ability to open the document in the full version installed on the computer and the ability to share the document via the Share option found in line with the other ribbons. The basic organization of the interface is very similar to that in the 2013 version of Excel. Note the inclusion of the Share button at the top of the interface, allowing

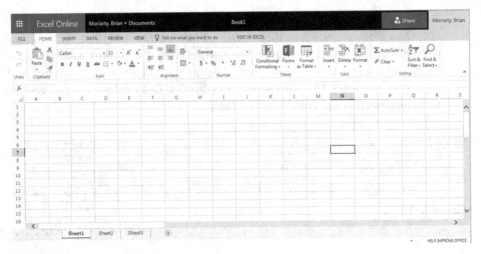

Figure A–14

you to easily collaborate on the same document. There is no Save icon in the Quick Access toolbar, because changes are saved as soon as any action in the document is completed.

The Home ribbon, also shown in Figure A-14, contains formatting commands for text and numerical values. The number formatting options are collapsed in this version into a dropdown list under Number Format; this version also can add or reduce significant digits. Most of the commands on this ribbon should be familiar to you from the use of other Office software.

The Insert ribbon, shown in Figure A-15, provides options for adding charts and formulas (also called functions) to your document. You can also add hyperlinks and tables from this ribbon. The Data ribbon in Figure A-16 contains the Calculate Workbook command to refresh the calculations in the workbook, as well as the options for sorting by column. The View ribbon, shown in Figure A-17, contains only the option to hide the interface in Reading View or show the interface in the standard Editing View. Most of the functions you will need in Excel are limited to the standalone versions installed on the computer, though the Web version can be used for quick edits and computations when you are away from your home or work computer.

Figure A–15

Figure A–16

Figure A–17

Figure A-15.

Figure A-16.

Figure A-17.

INDEX